S0-BGV-607

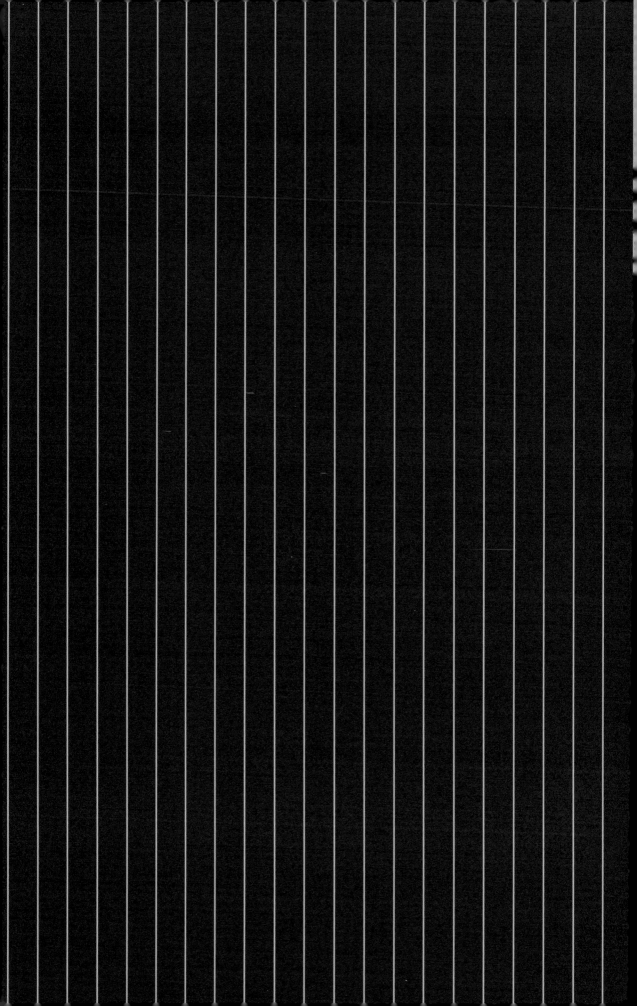

# Biotech 2012:
# INNOVATING
## in the
# New Austerity

BURRILL & COMPANY'S 26TH ANNUAL REPORT
ON THE LIFE SCIENCES INDUSTRY

Biotech 2012: Innovating in the New Austerity
Burrill & Company's 26th Annual Report on the Life Sciences Industry

Printed in the USA
ISBN: 978-0-9743209-1-5
Published by Burrill & Company LLC
One Embarcardero Center, Suite 2700
San Francisco, CA 94111

# Acknowledgements

This year's edition of our annual book on the life sciences, Biotech 2012: Innovating in the New Austerity, represents an intense and collaborative effort. Daniel S. Levine led the charge on this year's edition, along with exhaustive research, writing, and editing contributions from Marie Daghlian, Michael Fitzhugh, and Vinay Singh. Carol Collier designed this year's book and had assistance with graphics and layout from Diana Cao. Lucy Clarke provided additional writing contributions.

Many of Burrill & Company's team lent their expertise to this year's book. This includes Sergey Axenovich, Maurice Enderle, Tania Fernandez, Neal Fischer, Neil Littman, Dirk Lammerts, Darren Streiler, Derek Wong, Roger Wyse, Sarah Thompson, Marissa Craft, Greg Young, and Vincent Xiang.

In addition, we appreciate the generosity of our many friends in the industry, who shared their thoughts and insights with us during the creation of this book. In particular, we would like to acknowledge Jim Lane, editor of Biofuels Digest and Greg Scott, president and founder of ChinaBio.

Thanks to all,

# Biotech 2012: Innovating in the New Austerity
Burrill & Company's 26th Annual Report on the Life Sciences Industry

One thousand years from now, when historians look back to our present day, they will view this time as man's greatest moment, a time when, utilizing our understanding of the molecular basis of life, we harnessed biology to fundamentally transform healthcare, energy and agriculture. Yet, with the distractions of the debt crisis in Europe, the fragile economic recovery in the United States, and the contrasting economic boom of the BRIC nations, it is sometimes difficult to recognize how significant a moment we are living through today.

As we publish this 26th edition of our annual report on the biotech industry, austerity has become the watchword of the day. An aging population, expanding middle class, and the epidemic of chronic diseases are fueling demand

**G. Steven Burrill**
*CEO, Burrill & Company*

for healthcare and driving costs higher. Rising food prices have triggered political unrest in the Middle East and there's concern about the ability of farmers to produce enough food to feed the population by 2050. Growing prosperity in emerging markets is driving consumption of fossil fuels and worsening environmental degradation.

The regulatory, reimbursement, and financing environments continue to create challenges, but now more than ever, companies that produce true innovation will be rewarded. The world that is evolving is one that will not tolerate products that do not deliver value. The market will embrace therapies that address unmet medical need or provide disruptions to the delivery of medical care if they are comparatively effective, both on the basis of cost and utility. Resistance to genetically modified crops will wane as human need trumps unwarranted fear, and the world is ready for developers of biofuels and renewable chemicals who tackle the challenges of scaling up manufacturing in a cost-competitive way.

That doesn't means it will be an easy path to success. In the same way that the marketplace demands innovative products from our industry, so too will the environment demand innovation in business models, financing, and dealmaking. Just because something worked in the past does not mean it will work today. Vision and imagination, once just strong assets to have, will be essential tools of the trade.  Be creative!

G. Steven Burrill
CEO
Burrill & Company
March 2012

# CONTENTS

### Chapter 1

## Innovating in the New Austerity

R&D spending by the industry grew predictably year after year, but that was no longer the case in 2011 as several drug companies sought to cut R&D expenses. In part, such a move was in response to the long anticipated drop in revenues Big Pharma faced with the loss of patent protection on some of the industry's best selling drugs. But it also was an acknowledgement for many that the R&D spending had failed to yield an adequate return on investment.

### Chapter 2

## Gray Matters

Around the world, life spans are increasing and populations are aging. This demographic shift, presents opportunities for drug and device makers, as well as significant challenges for healthcare systems and payers. While policy makers across the globe have taken steps to look for ways to restrict spending, others are turning to innovative approaches that can keep people healthy and allow them to live independently.

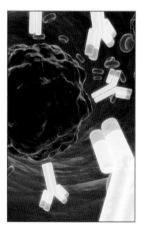

### Chapter 3

## A Watched Pot Begins to Boil

As impatience seemed to grow among scientists and the public over the slow arrival of personalized medicine, the FDA approved a spate of new personalized therapies, studies touted the economic benefits of new predictive tests, the pipeline of powerful new targeted therapies based on the genetics underlying diseases grew, and the cost of sequencing continued its rapid decline moving medical science closer to an ever greater knowledge not only of disease, but also of wellness.

### Chapter 4
## Connected to Health

The convergence of information technology and the life sciences, coupled with ubiquitous connectivity, is revolutionizing the way healthcare is accessed and delivered. Today, a new generation of companies is harnessing information and communication technologies not only to improve care, but also to help people stay well. The phenomena will bend the cost curve of healthcare through improved monitoring of chronic disease, and by enabling people to change their behaviors in ways that keep them healthy.

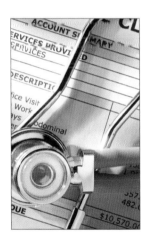

### Chapter 5
## In Search of Disruption

Governments around the world are feeling pressure to control healthcare spending. These pressures have only intensified in the face of the global recession and the push for austerity measures in many countries. Payers increasingly are demanding demonstrations that therapies have value before they will pay for them. Industry and its advocates, however, are concerned that efforts to rein in spending will threaten innovation, which they say is what's needed to address the growing cost of healthcare.

### Chapter 6
## A Balancing Act

There is a growing sense among life sciences innovators that regulatory barriers in the United States have made the process of bringing new drugs and medical devices to market too unpredictable, burdensome, and perilous. Finding new ways to balance risk and benefits will be essential to maintaining the brisk pace of medical innovation on which developed nations have come to rely.

# CONTENTS

BIOTECH 2012

**Chapter 10**

# Exit Strategies

The life sciences continue to attract new ideas and people dedicated to improving lives around the world. But financing life sciences companies is changing as new deal structures evolve to address the problems entrepreneurs and investors face in the risk-averse and often volatile financial climate that now exists.

**Chapter 11**

# Thoughts on Innovation

In the new austerity, innovation is needed not just in the products we produce, but in the way we fund ideas, conduct R&D, regulate our industries, and deliver care. The challenge will be to leverage resources, operate with capital efficiency, and delivery value. What we can't afford today, as we seek to address the health, food, and energy needs of a growing world, is timidity in thought and action.

# About Burrill & Company

A look inside Burrill & Company and its venture capital, merchant banking, international, and media operations.

# LIST OF CHARTS

*Continued on next page*

# List of Charts

Note: USD M = U.S. dollars in millions, USD B = U.S. dollar in billions

# Innovating in the New Austerity

In the past, R&D spending by the industry grew predictably year after year, but that was no longer the case in 2011 as several drug companies sought to cut R&D expenses. In part, such a move was in response to the long anticipated drop in revenues Big Pharma faced with the loss of patent protection on some of the industry's best selling drugs. But it also was an acknowledgement for many that the R&D spending had failed to yield an adequate return on investment. Employees are being fired, research centers shuttered, and budgets slashed. How will pharmaceutical companies create the new products they need to sustain themselves? The industry's answer has been essentially to try to do more with less. To that end companies are jettisoning projects that don't promise adequate returns, entering partnerships that allow them to rely on others to do high-risk discovery and early-stage research, working with each other in pre-competitive alliances to share the cost of pre-development research, and buying innovative assets once they have had a considerable share of the development risk removed. Creativity will also be needed to design new approaches to R&D that can bring new products to market faster and cheaper. Innovation, though, should not be viewed as part of the problem, but part of the solution. In the new austerity, innovation will be measured not only by providing improvements in care, but value as well.

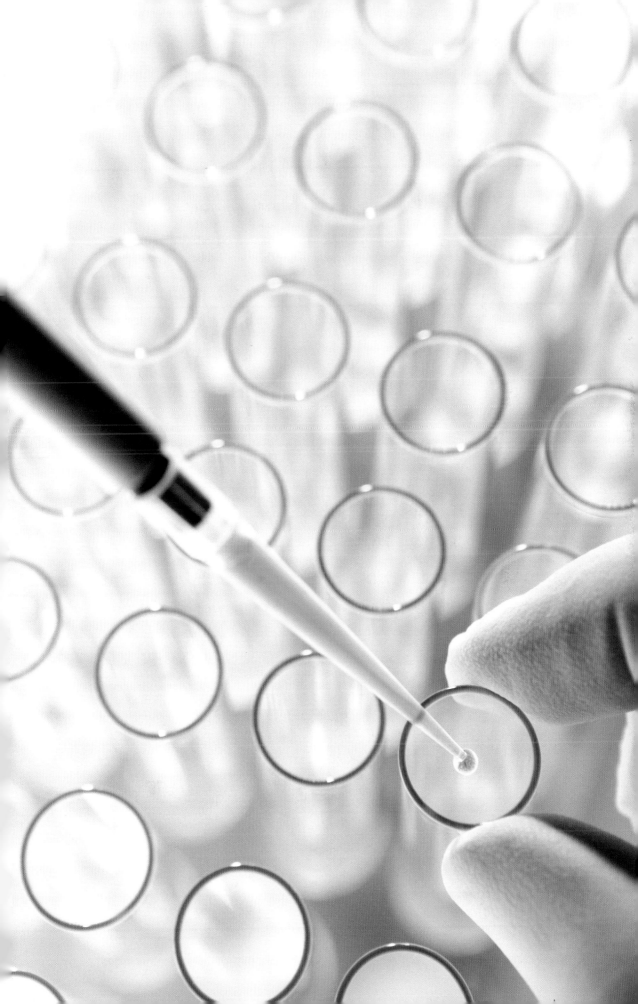

# Chapter 1:

# INNOVATING IN THE NEW AUSTERITY

There are many events that define a moment in time for an industry. In 2011 **Sanofi**, after a somewhat difficult courtship, consummated its acquisition of the biotech **Genzyme**. High-flying **Dendreon** soared on the promise of its breakthrough cancer vaccine Provenge, but came crashing down to earth as investors grew sober to market realities and what it would take to ramp up sales of the product. And then, of course, there was the fight over the debt ceiling in the United States and the sovereign debt crisis in Europe that helped slam the brakes on the momentum that was building in the first half of the 2011, which had been characterized by rising stock prices, growing fundraising, and accelerating dealmaking. But sometimes it's the little things that say the most about a given point in time.

Consider Ken Frazier, CEO of the drug giant **Merck**. It was during a breakfast meeting held by *The Wall Street Journal* that Frazier found himself delivering a defense for his company's large R&D budget. The pharmaceutical industry has long prided itself on its massive investment in R&D. Pharmaceutical companies dominated the lists of top R&D spenders and R&D spending by the industry grew predictably year after year. But that was no longer the case in 2011 as several drug companies sought to cut R&D expenses. In part, such a move was in response to the long anticipated drop in revenues Big Pharma faced with the loss of patent protection on some of the industry's best selling drugs [*SEE FIGURE 1.1*]. But it also was an acknowledgement for many that the massive investment in R&D had failed to yield an adequate return on investment. R&D, once protected from cost-cutting, was no longer immune. The ax fell sharply at many companies including **Pfizer**, where under the leadership of Ian Read, the company prepared for a new era when its statin Lipitor, the best-selling drug of all time, would face competition from generic versions. As Pfizer received encouragement from Wall Street for slashing R&D spending, Merck charged ahead with its $8 billion R&D budget intact. Wall Street applauded Pfizer for its cuts, but chastised Merck. Big spending on R&D was no longer viewed as a sign of strength. It was something that needed defending. "When one runs a company like Merck that has long lead times in terms of development, I think it's important to keep in mind that you're not necessarily running the company for the immediate reaction of the stock market," Frazier told the gathering, according to *Reuters*. "What we're really trying to do is run the company to create sustainable long-term value for our shareholders. The most sustainable strategy is really around innovation."

That's a stark contrast to Pfizer under Read, who took the helm of the world's largest pharmaceutical company at the end of 2010. In announcing the company's financial results in February 2011, Read laid out a plan to cut R&D spending by as much as $3 billion in 2012, dropping its expenditure to between $6.5 billion and $7 billion from $9.4 billion in 2010. The announcement boosted Pfizer's stock by 5.5 percent, its best single day performance in the market in six months. Spending more doesn't mean getting anything out," **Barclays Capital** analyst Tony Butler told *Bloomberg*. "This is all good." How radically has the attitude about pharmaceutical spending on R&D changed on Wall Street? Listen to Sanofi CEO Chris Viehbacher, who said at the *Reuters Health Summit* in May 2011 that

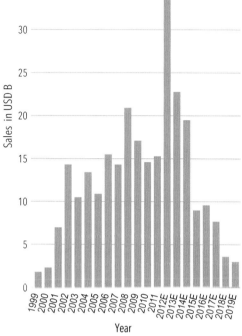

*Figure 1.1* **LOST REVENUE**

**Annual sales of brands with patents expiring**

Source: BAS-ML Research

some investors "believe that what we do in R&D is actually value destroying." In fact, he has said that his goal as CEO is "never to inaugurate a new research and development center."

Pfizer's Read announced that the company would cease funding R&D in certain areas that provided low returns and instead concentrate

**TIMELINE 2011: THE YEAR IN REVIEW**

**January 1**

First BabyBoomers turn 65

**Jan. 9**
Dupont acquires Danisco $6.3 billion

**January 14**

Tunisian President Ben Ali forced to flee country amid protests sparking Arab Spring

**January 19**

**Pfizer** to pay up to $632 million to **Theraclone Sciences** in discovery pact

wikimedia commons

its R&D in more lucrative areas, adjust its R&D footprint to increase its presence in hubs of biomedical innovation, and increase outsourcing for services that don't drive a competitive advantage for Pfizer. The company said it would scrap work in allergy, urology, respiratory, internal medicine and tissue repair, and focus on cancer, neuroscience, inflammation, vaccines, and immunology. The cost-cutting plans under Read have been severe. He slated 19,000 employees, eight plants, and six research centers for elimination. All of that comes on the heels of the elimination of 40,000 jobs from 2004 to 2009, according to *Bloomberg*. "At some point your shareholders and stakeholders demand you have a return on investment in research," Read said. "We're looking at areas where we think it's not a competitive advantage." The company also embarked on an aggressive program of repurchasing shares, buying back $6.5 billion worth of its stock through the first 11 months of 2011 and announcing plans to purchase an additional $5 billion worth in 2012. It is perhaps a more predictable way of boosting earnings per share than investing in R&D, but not a viable strategy for long-term sustained growth.

Pfizer is not alone in its overhaul of its R&D operations. Many other of its Big Pharma brethren have pursued similar strategies of slashing R&D, cutting jobs, and buying back shares [*See Figures 1.2 and 1.3*]. Sanofi at the end of 2010 named former **National Institutes of Health** Director Elias Zerhouni as its new head of R&D. Zerhouni had been serving as a scientific advisor

*Figure 1.2*    **Big Pharma Slashes Jobs**

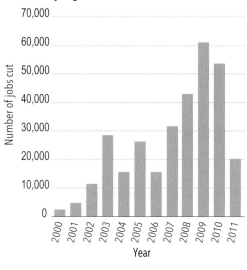

Source: Challenger, Gray & Christmas

to the company looking at ways to reinvigorate its anemic pipeline. But even as the company seeks to reinvent its R&D activities, it has been making cuts as well. *Pharmalot* reported the company has been slashing a targeted $1.1 billion from R&D since 2008 and now, with the completion of its acquisition of Genzyme, the company was preparing to make additional cuts and reorganize its R&D activities. The company in 2011 said it would consolidate its ten cancer research centers worldwide into a single new facility in Massachusetts. That followed its decision in 2010

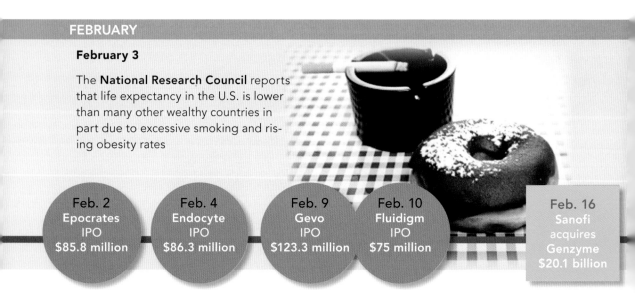

**FEBRUARY**

**February 3**

The **National Research Council** reports that life expectancy in the U.S. is lower than many other wealthy countries in part due to excessive smoking and rising obesity rates

Feb. 2
Epocrates
IPO
$85.8 million

Feb. 4
Endocyte
IPO
$86.3 million

Feb. 9
Gevo
IPO
$123.3 million

Feb. 10
Fluidigm
IPO
$75 million

Feb. 16
Sanofi
acquires
Genzyme
$20.1 billion

to cut about half of the projects in its pipeline to focus on the most commercially promising and clinically viable candidates. It has also reorganized research departments by underlying causes rather than in its traditional manner of organizing them by manifestation of diseases. Gone are therapeutic areas such as cardiovascular disease and in their place have risen groups such as diseases of aging. Under Zerhouni's R&D leadership, the company has touted a strategy of "open innovation" as it looks increasingly beyond internal sources for ideas to academia, biotech, and elsewhere.

**GlaxoSmithKline**, an early mover in efforts to overhaul traditional R&D models, has sought to emulate smaller biotechs and make discovery and development more nimble and lean. The company broke what had been pared back to six research units into so-called Discovery Performance Units. The company has given the units great autonomy and focus, but scientists must now fight for resources based on the progress of their projects. As with fledgling biotechs that must convince investors to fund their work, the discovery units must vie for funding from GSK decisionmakers. Moncef Slaoui, GSK's head of research and development and one of the architects of the overhaul, told *Bloomberg* that talent was "buried in the ocean" under the old system. Now, he says, scientists "live or die with their project."

The pharmaceutical industry is in flux in what to do about research and development. Employees are being fired, research centers shuttered,

*Figure 1.3*

**BIG PHARMA'S CUTS TO R&D SPENDING**

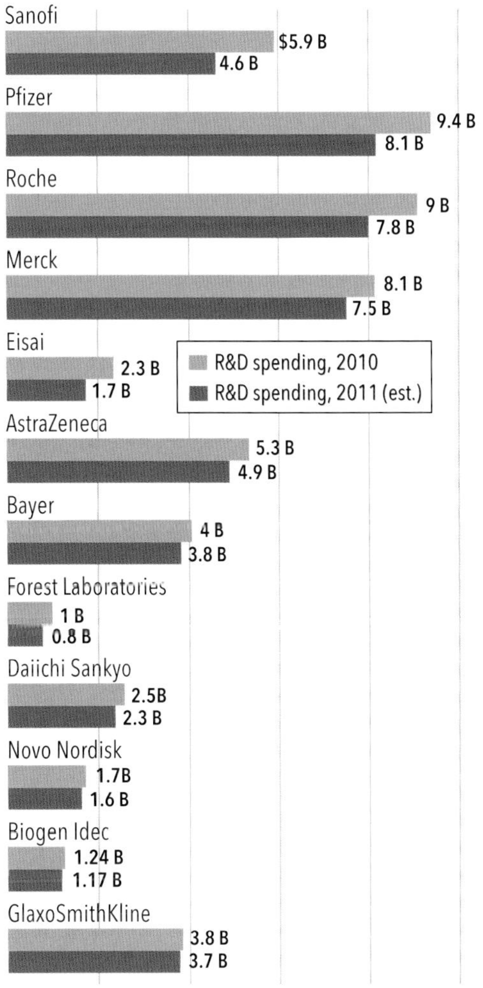

| Company | R&D spending, 2010 | R&D spending, 2011 (est.) |
|---|---|---|
| Sanofi | $5.9 B | 4.6 B |
| Pfizer | 9.4 B | 8.1 B |
| Roche | 9 B | 7.8 B |
| Merck | 8.1 B | 7.5 B |
| Eisai | 2.3 B | 1.7 B |
| AstraZeneca | 5.3 B | 4.9 B |
| Bayer | 4 B | 3.8 B |
| Forest Laboratories | 1 B | 0.8 B |
| Daiichi Sankyo | 2.5 B | 2.3 B |
| Novo Nordisk | 1.7 B | 1.6 B |
| Biogen Idec | 1.24 B | 1.17 B |
| GlaxoSmithKline | 3.8 B | 3.7 B |

*Source: Challenger, Gray & Christmas*

**MARCH**

**March 9**

FDA approves **Human Genome Sciences** and **GlaxoSmithKline's** lupus drug, Benlysta

wikimedia commons

**March 11**

The Tohoku earthquake and tsunami devastate the eastern coast of Japan

**March 1**
Daiichi Sankyo acquires Plexxikon $805 million

and budgets slashed. While some companies such as **Eli Lilly** have seen investment in R&D as their best hope of replacing revenue lost to patent expirations, most of the largest players in the industry have been cutting. Overall, the life sciences industry is expected to cut R&D spending by 5.7 percent in the United States and 2.2 percent globally in 2012, according to the *Battelle-R&D Magazine Annual Global R&D Funding Forecast*. Though the loss of revenue to an onslaught of competition from generic drugs is part of the problem—drugs with sales of $170 billion are slated to lose patent protection through the end of 2016, according to **Bloomberg Industries** research—declining R&D productivity is also a major driver of the changes [*See Figure 1.7*].

A report from **KPMG** found that return on investment for pharmaceutical companies in R&D has been nearly halved between 1990 and 2010 as it's fallen to around 10 percent from 17 percent. A separate report from **Deloitte** and **Thomson Reuters** on R&D productivity at the 12 top global pharmaceutical companies found R&D productivity is declining as development costs rise, revenue forecasts stagnate, and late-stage terminations continue to dog the industry. In fact, the 2011 review by Deloitte and Thomson Reuters found that the industry's internal rate of return from R&D dropped to 8.4 percent in 2011 from 11.8 percent the previous year. Not only is the industry spending more to produce what it does, the value of the drugs it's bringing to market has been declining. The average value of new drugs approved from 2006 to 2010 fell to $7.3

billion. That compares to $10.4 billion for new drugs approved from 2001 to 2005, according to *EvaluatePharma*. Nevertheless, new drugs entering the market in 2010 and 2011 have provided for an encouraging change in the pattern as values have risen [*See Figure 1.4*].

How will pharmaceutical companies create the new products they need to sustain themselves? The industry's answer has been essentially to do more with less, or at least try doing so. To that end companies are jettisoning projects that don't promise adequate returns, entering partnerships that allow them to rely on others to do high-risk discovery and early-stage research, working with each other in pre-competitive alliances to share the cost of pre-development research, and buying innovative assets once they have had a considerable share of the development risk removed. At the same time, the industry is diversifying its product base and moving aggressively into emerging markets, where growth opportunities are enormous and there is huge unmet need.

Consider the non-profit **Asian Cancer Research Group**, or ACRG, a joint effort of Eli Lilly, Merck, and Pfizer aimed at accelerating research on the most prevalent cancers in Asia. The pre-competitive collaboration, announced in 2010, calls for the companies to share resources and expertise and make their data publicly available to inform new approaches to treatment. The group is initially focusing on gastric and lung cancers, among the most common cancers in Asia. As pharmaceutical companies seek to stretch their R&D dollars, they are find-

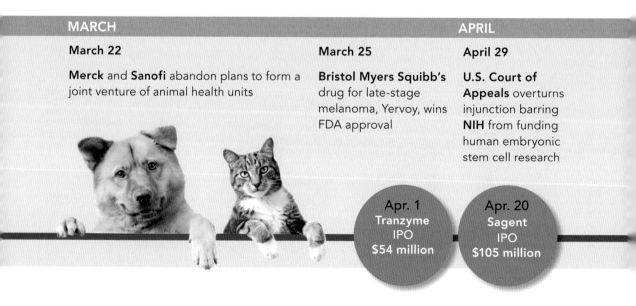

**MARCH**                                                                                                    **APRIL**

**March 22**

**Merck** and **Sanofi** abandon plans to form a joint venture of animal health units

**March 25**

**Bristol Myers Squibb's** drug for late-stage melanoma, Yervoy, wins FDA approval

**April 29**

**U.S. Court of Appeals** overturns injunction barring **NIH** from funding human embryonic stem cell research

Apr. 1
Tranzyme
IPO
$54 million

Apr. 20
Sagent
IPO
$105 million

*Figure 1.4* **VALUE OF NEW DRUG APPROVALS**

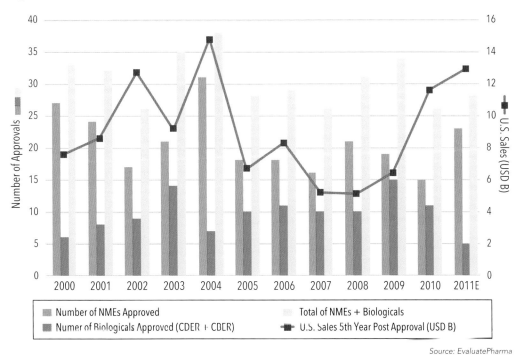

Number of Approvals / U.S. Sales (USD B)

Legend:
- Number of NMEs Approved
- Numer of Biologicals Approved (CDER + CBER)
- Total of NMEs + Biologicals
- U.S. Sales 5th Year Post Approval (USD B)

*Source: EvaluatePharma*

ing strength in numbers. The group is creating an extensive database of information about the influence of genes on drug efficacy and safety based on about 2,000 tissue samples and making that data available to the scientific community in the hopes of accelerating drug discovery. "The ACRG's formation represents a prime example of a growing trend in pre-competitive collaboration in which large pharmaceutical companies combine their resources and expertise to rapidly

increase knowledge of disease and disease processes," the companies said in a joint release. "The goal of the ACRG is to improve the knowledge of cancers prevalent in Asia and to accelerate drug discovery efforts by freely sharing the resulting data with the scientific community." Such joint efforts promise to allow participants to leverage R&D investment, benefit from a greater range of ideas, and eliminate waste in duplicative work.

A separate agreement announced in June

**MAY**

**May 2**

**U.S. Navy SEALs** kill Osama Bin Laden in a covert operation

**May 4**

California's state stem cell agency funds its first clinical trial by giving a $25 million loan to **Geron**

Whitehouse.gov

**April 27**
Johnson & Johnson acquires Synthes $21.3 billion

**May 2**
Teva acquires Cephalon $6.8 billion

# When an Approval Is Not Enough

FDA green light for breakthrough cancer drug sends Dendreon soaring, disappointing sales sends it crashing

**S** reported that doctors' uncertainty about receiving reimbursement for its prostate cancer drug, Provenge, had slowed its adoption and curtailed forecasted sales [*SEE FIGURE 1.5*].

Management reported it would cut expenses and staff following a disappointing second quarter in which "increased sensitivity to the impact of cost density on doctors' practice economics," difficulty in identifying suitable patients, and supply chain issues hampered sales of the drug. But with Provenge sales falling 14 percent short of consensus estimate for the quarter, analysts began to reevaluate the company's prospects, and trading volumes ballooned.

The **U.S. Food and Drug Administration** approved Provenge in April 2010. But, Dendreon, which sells a regular course of the medicine for $93,000, has found that, like many other companies that have recently brought new drugs to market, securing regulatory approval is just the first hurdle to success.

The drug's lackluster performance has drawn fire from analysts, such as **Cowen and Company's** Eric Schmidt, who downgraded Dendreon shares to a "neutral" rating on the news. "By now investors are familiar with a host of reasons to explain a disappointing drug launch. While it could be that Dendreon's explanations ultimately prove true, and that Provenge's ramp is simply delayed, we are tired of making excuses for what has been a disappointing commercial trajectory since day one of launch," Schmidt wrote in a note to investors. "In our view, the simplest explanation for the drug's poor commercial performance is that demand is lower than we had predicted."

With that, Schmidt lowered Cowen's worldwide Provenge sales estimate to $1.6 billion from roughly $3 billion. The company lowered its estimates too. It withdrew its previous guidance of $350 million to $400 million in 2011 revenue and now expects "modest quarter over quarter revenue growth," it said in its second quarter earnings statement.

Dendreon says that reimbursement issues will begin to clear as more doctors become aware of Medicare's decision to reimburse them for the vaccine and other administrative barriers to timely reimbursement alleviate concern over the long time it can take to obtain reimbursement under the current way in which reimbursement claims are handled.

"However, we believe this will take time," said Mitchell Gold, Dendreon's president and CEO during a conference call with investors, "and for the remainder of 2011, the launch trajectory will reflect a more gradual adoption of Provenge as physicians gain confidence in this positive reim-

**MAY**

**May 5**
Greece protests begin, sparked by austerity measures put in place to secure a bail-out to solve its debt crisis

**May 11**
**NIH** director Francis Collins announces that NIH grant application success rate is heading for historic lows in 2011

**May 13**
The **FDA** approves **Merck's** hepatitis C drug Victrelis

Victrelis™
(boceprevir) Capsules
200 mg
Rx only    12 Capsules

**May 16**
Shanghai Pharmaceuticals IPO $2 billion

*Figure 1.5*     **DENDREON'S RISE AND FALL**

**Provenge approval not enough for success**

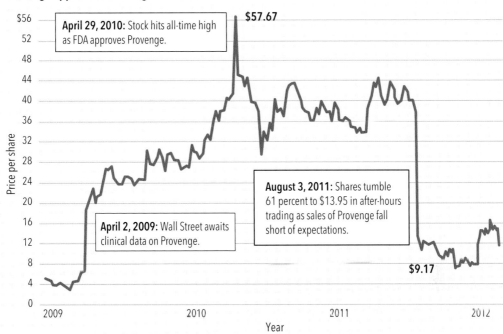

> **April 29, 2010:** Stock hits all-time high as FDA approves Provenge.

**$57.67**

> **April 2, 2009:** Wall Street awaits clinical data on Provenge.

> **August 3, 2011:** Shares tumble 61 percent to $13.95 in after-hours trading as sales of Provenge fall short of expectations.

**$9.17**

*Price per share*

2009     2010     2011     2012

Year

*Source: Yahoo! Finance, Burrill & Company*

bursement landscape."

In September 2011, Dendreon announced plans to eliminate 500 positions or roughly 25 percent of its workforce as part of its restructuring plan in response to disappointing sales of Provenge. The cost of the job cuts is expected to be approximately $21 million, about $5 million of which are non-cash charges related to stock-based compensation. At the time, Dendreon said it expected to have sufficient cash to enable the company to achieve a cash flow break-even position in the United States at an annual run rate of approximately $500 million in revenue. ■

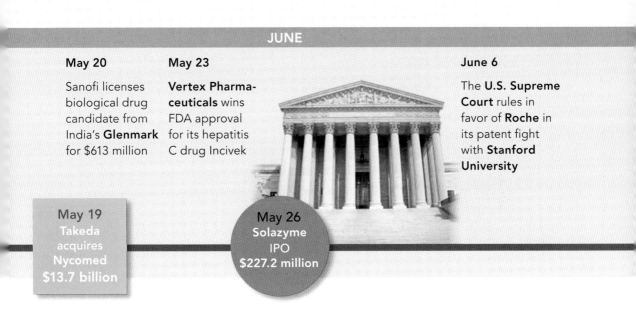

**JUNE**

**May 20**

Sanofi licenses biological drug candidate from India's **Glenmark** for $613 million

**May 23**

**Vertex Pharmaceuticals** wins FDA approval for its hepatitis C drug Incivek

**June 6**

The **U.S. Supreme Court** rules in favor of **Roche** in its patent fight with **Stanford University**

**May 19**
Takeda acquires Nycomed
**$13.7 billion**

**May 26**
Solazyme
IPO
**$227.2 million**

## Figure 1.6    BIG PHARMA PAIRS WITH ACADEMIA

### Selected discovery alliances with academic institutions

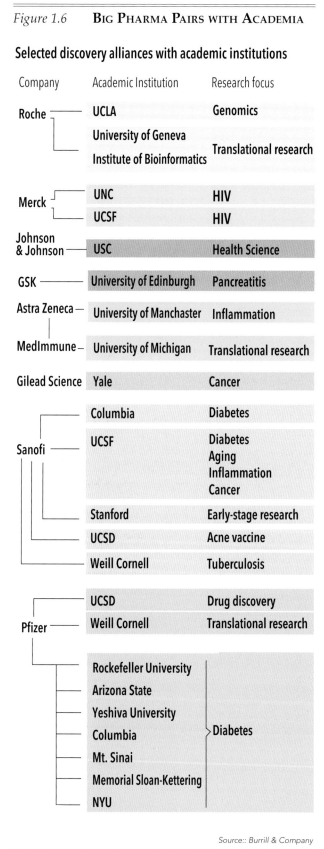

| Company | Academic Institution | Research focus |
|---|---|---|
| Roche | UCLA | Genomics |
| | University of Geneva Institute of Bioinformatics | Translational research |
| Merck | UNC | HIV |
| | UCSF | HIV |
| Johnson & Johnson | USC | Health Science |
| GSK | University of Edinburgh | Pancreatitis |
| Astra Zeneca | University of Manchaster | Inflammation |
| MedImmune | University of Michigan | Translational research |
| Gilead Science | Yale | Cancer |
| Sanofi | Columbia | Diabetes |
| | UCSF | Diabetes Aging Inflammation Cancer |
| | Stanford | Early-stage research |
| | UCSD | Acne vaccine |
| | Weill Cornell | Tuberculosis |
| Pfizer | UCSD | Drug discovery |
| | Weill Cornell | Translational research |
| | Rockefeller University | |
| | Arizona State | |
| | Yeshiva University | |
| | Columbia | Diabetes |
| | Mt. Sinai | |
| | Memorial Sloan-Kettering | |
| | NYU | |

*Source:: Burrill & Company*

2009 between Merck and **AstraZeneca** provided another view of the growing willingness among Big Pharma companies to work cooperatively. It was described by the two companies as the first time that large pharmaceutical companies established a collaboration to evaluate the potential for a combination therapy based on two product candidates that were so early in the development process. The two drugs work on different proteins abnormally activated in cancer. Both AstraZeneca's drug, a MEK inhibitor, and Merck's drug, which acts on the AKT pathway, had undergone early-stage clinical trials. The joint effort reflects the reality that cancer cells are adaptive and that single therapies by themselves can lead to resistance. The agreement calls for the two companies to jointly share development costs. The hope is that the collaboration will accelerate the development of the combined therapies, something that in the past would have happened when both of the drugs were either in late-stage development or already approved for sale.

A string of similar collaborations have sprung up in the wake of the AstraZeneca and Merck agreement. They include agreements between **Bristol-Myers Squibb** and **Roche** to develop a combination therapy of two experimental skin cancer drugs, a Sanofi and **Merck KGaA** agreement to jointly develop Sanofi's experimental drug targeting PI3K and Merck KGaA's experimental MEK inhibitor, and GSK's agreement with **Novartis** to develop a combination therapy for solid tumors. **Millennium Pharmaceuticals** CEO Deborah Dunsire, who was seeking a similar collaboration, says that such collaboration was not something the industry has typically had to do. "Now we have to collaborate on drugs that are new, proprietary, and not yet approved, which makes us all nervous," she told *Bloomberg* in June 2011. "But we can't continue throwing out potentially good drugs because they don't have enough activity as a single agent."

As pharmaceutical companies have looked at ways of boosting their R&D productivity, they have moved away from discovery and instead turned to relationships with external sources for new ideas, including universities. Such relationships were once the source of great controversies as critics complained about the effects agreements would have on academic freedom and that corporations would profit from tax-payer funded labs. But increasingly the approach is seen as a way to leverage both public and private investment in research and see that such work has a better chance of being developed into products that actually deliver benefits to the public. In 2011, this was seen in the form of a sharp increase in alliances between academic centers and large pharmaceutical companies [*See Figure 1.6*]. For the academic partner, these relationships provide a predictable source of funding during a time of uncertainty about federal funding of research. The success rate of NIH grant applications is hovering near an all-time low and despite a small boost in funding in the 2012 budget, it reflects a decrease in real

"This is a tangible effort to bridge the gap in life sciences innovation by enabling greater interaction between industry and academia."

**Anthony Coyle**
*Vice president,*
*Pfizer's Centers for*
*Therapeutic Innovation*

terms and leaves in place across-the-board cuts that could be automatically triggered as part of deficit reduction plans, which could make matters worse.

Pfizer, among the most aggressive in this area, has signed a long list of agreements with universities starting in November 2010 when it announced a five-year agreement worth up to $85 million with the **University of California, San Francisco**. The collaboration seeks to significantly reduce the cost and time to develop new drugs. The agreement, which created an open network of researchers dubbed the **Centers for Therapeutic Innovation**, calls for broad collaboration between UCSF and Pfizer scientists to identify and advance promising experimental drugs to proof-of-concept studies. The agreement, among other things, gives UCSF researchers access to Pfizer's compound libraries and antibody technologies. That is expected to accelerate the time it takes to translate research from preclinical and animal testing to human clinical trials. "This is a tangible effort to bridge the gap in life sciences innovation by enabling greater interaction between industry and academia in a truly meaningful way," says Anthony Coyle, vice president of Pfizer's Centers for Therapeutic Innovation.

## JULY

### July 8

Atlantis begins the final mission for the Space Shuttle program

### July 14

The FDA issues guidance on in-vitro companion diagnostic devices

### July 19

The FDA issues guidance on mobile medical applications

**June 24**
**KiOR**
**IPO**
**$150 million**

**July 21**
**Express Scripts**
acquires
**Medco Health**
**Solutions**
**$29.1 billion**

# Geron Dumps Stem Cells for Cancer Focus

## Trailblazer seeks economic shelter, faster payoff for shareholders

Pioneering stem cell company **Geron** made a stunning announcement in November 2011 when it said it would discontinue its stem cell therapeutics programs to focus on the relatively near-term promise of cancer drugs.

The Menlo Park, California-based company is seeking partners to take on GRNOPC1, an early-stage human embryonic stem cell-based therapy for acute spinal cord injuries, as well as four other programs with indications including heart disease, and diabetes.

"Stem cells continue to hold great medical promise," said Geron's CEO, John Scarlett. But a scarcity of capital and economic uncertainties has convinced the company to focus on its two mid-stage cancer candidates, Imetelstat and GRN1005. Geron anticipates having $150 million left at the end of 2011, enough to fund it through important clinical development milestones for both candidates during the next 20 months.

Unwinding its stem cell program will cost about $8 million and eliminate about 66 full-time jobs, 38 percent of its workforce, the company estimates. Geron planned to close its GRNOPC1 trial for spinal cord injury to further enrollment, but will continue to follow patients enrolled in the study, accrue data, and update the FDA and the medical community on their progress, the company said.

Finding a partner willing to bet on a potentially promising but risky portfolio of stem cell therapies may be difficult for Geron. In the United States, potential partners may be put off by public concerns over the morality of destroying embryos and the ongoing battle over federally funded human embryonic stem cell research remains. Potential European partners are also likely to be discouraged, given the recent ruling by the **Court of Justice of the European Union**, which determined that E.U. researchers couldn't patent inventions relying on the destruction of human embryos.

Moving forward, Geron will focus on several mid-stage trials. Imetelstat is now being tested in non-small cell lung cancer, breast cancer, essential thrombocythemia, and multiple myeloma. Two trials of GRN1005 will also begin this year, one in brain metastases arising from non-small cell lung cancer and the other for brain metastases from breast cancer.

By narrowing its focus to oncology therapeutics, Geron said it will have sufficient financial resources to reach important near-term value inflection points for shareholders without the necessity of raising additional capital. That, it said, would not be possible if it continues to fund the stem cell programs at the current levels.

"Every company has to make decisions about what they can do, not just what they aspire, or like, to do," Geron's Scarlett told attendees at the JPMorgan Healthcare Conference in January 2012. "Today, more than ever, the resources of every biotechnology company at this conference are very finite." ■

---

## JULY

**July 27**

**U.S. District Court** reverses initial ruling and dismisses lawsuit that charged federal funding of research for embryonic stem cells was in violation of the *Dickey-Wicker Amendment*

**July 27**
**Horizon Pharmaceuticals IPO $50 million**

**July 27**

**The Robert Koch Institute** declares Germany's E. Coli epidemic over. The deadliest E. Coli outbreak ever, it struck over 4,000 people and killed 52 people

**July 29**

**U.S. Federal Appeals Court** affirms the right of **Myriad Genetics** to patent the BRCA genes, stating that isolated DNA molecules are not products of nature and are therefore eligible for patent protection.

13

Pfizer followed the announcement of the UCSF collaboration in January 2011 with news that seven leading research-based medical centers in New York City including **Rockefeller University**, **NYU Langone Medical Center**, **Memorial Sloan-Kettering Cancer Center**, **The Mount Sinai Medical Center**, **Columbia University Medical Center**, **Albert Einstein College of Medicine of Yeshiva University**, and **Weill Cornell Medical College**, had joined Pfizer's Centers. It later added biomedical research centers in Massachusetts and California to the effort. The **University of California, San Diego** joined the growing roster of universities involved with Pfizer's Centers in August 2011 with an agreement worth up to $50 million over five years. "Public-private partnerships are increasingly important in scientific research, especially in an era of decreasing federal grant support when resources are needed to commercialize innovations related to healthcare," says Gary Firestein, director of the **Clinical and Translational Research Institute** at the **University of California San Diego School of Medicine**.

But it's not just academia that the pharmaceutical industry has been seeking to work with in new ways. As the industry overhauls its playbook and tries to address the obstacles along the path from the lab to the marketplace, companies have started to reach out and work with payers early in the drug development process. They are doing this to ensure the studies they perform and the therapies they bring to market will satisfy the demands of payers, who are not only concerned

> Companies have started to work with payers early in the drug development process to ensure the studies they perform and the therapies they bring to market will satisfy the demands of payers.

about the safety and efficacy of the products they pay for, but also the value those products deliver. A December 2011 report from *Reuters* found that some companies are meeting with payers as much as five years before regulators review a product. "If you're going to go out there with a drug that you don't know whether it's better than what's out there, what are you trying to do?" **Shire** CEO Angus Russell said to *Reuters*. "Who are we all trying to kid?" Shire has doubled its pharmaco-economic staff in recent years and other companies, such as Sanofi, are meeting with payers such as **Medco Health Solutions** when experimental drugs are still in early-stage testing to discuss the structure of their clinical trials to make sure that they answer the types of questions that will show their new drugs provide better outcomes and better value than what is already on the market.

## AUGUST

### August 4

The **Dow Jones Industrial Average** drops 512 points— the biggest one day drop since December 6, 2008

### August 4

Biotechnology company **Dendreon** reports lower-than-expected earnings for its Provenge vaccine sending its shares into a tailspin, along with those of some other biotechnology companies

### August 5

**Standard & Poor's** downgrades U.S. Credit Rating for the first time ever, dropping the nation's rating from AAA to AA+

# Merck Outlines $1.5 Billion Commitment To Expand R&D in China

## Pharma profiles blueprint for new R&D facility in Beijing

**M**erck said it will establish an Asia research and development headquarters for innovative drug discovery in Beijing, China. The new facility is part of a $1.5 billion commitment the company is making to invest in R&D in China over the next five years.

Merck's move is not unprecedented. Every major multinational pharmaceutical player is establishing relationships and presences in China to take advantage of its growing healthcare market and increasing scientific capabilities. As they cut employees and close R&D centers in Europe and the United States, they are increasing their workforce and presence in China and other emerging markets.

Merck has not only the BRIC countries, but Mexico, South Korea, and Turkey as important emerging markets to target. It plans to bring existing drugs to treat unmet needs in these markets and to access their growing innovation to develop drugs for the global market.

"By strategically locating in China, we are able to complement our existing R&D capabilities, and facilitate new collaborations with scientists in the region and across emerging markets," says Peter Kim, president, **Merck Research Laboratories.**

Merck expects the first phase of construction of its Asian headquarters to be completed by 2014. It will have space for 600 researchers to work in the areas of drug discovery, translational research, clinical development, regulatory affairs, and external scientific research.

Merck, known as MSD outside the United States and Canada, has already established commercial headquarters in China in Shanghai and has manufacturing capabilities throughout the country. Recently MSD formalized a collaborative partnership with China's genomics powerhouse **BGI** to identify and characterize biomarkers with an emphasis on drug discovery and development across many therapeutic areas.

The drugmaker also said it was setting up a joint venture with Chinese pharmaceutical **Simcere** to increase access to its drugs in important therapeutic areas such as cardiovascular and metabolic diseases. The incidence of non-communicable chronic conditions such as diabetes and the precursors of heart disease, linked to China's growing middle class and its inherent lifestyle changes, are growing rapidly in the country.

"The establishment of the MSD Asia R&D headquarters," says Kim, "represents an important milestone as we implement our strategy of building capabilities, and relationships to succeed in fast growing geographic regions." ■

## AUGUST

**August 5**

The **U.S. Patent and Trademark Office** approves its first patent for technology used to make induced pluripotent stem cells

**August 17**

Roche and Daiichi Sankyo get FDA approval for their drug Zelboraf as a treatment for melanoma

**August 19**

Seattle Genetics wins FDA approval for its antibody-drug conjugate Adcetris

**August 26**

The FDA approves Pfizer's lung cancer drug, Xalkori

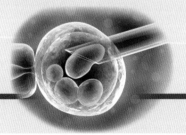

In other cases, such as an alliance between AstraZeneca and **HealthCore**, pharmaceutical companies are working with payers to study ways to treat disease more cost-effectively. These alliances are helping drugmakers better understand how their products are used, how their competitors' products compare to their own, and what they need to set as endpoints in clinical trials. "We want to make sure," German Pasteris, who oversees the development of Alzheimer's drugs for GSK told *Reuters*, "that the endpoints, the trial design, the clinical development plan, the medicine development strategy—it's all aligned, and it's all trying to meet the payer needs."

All of this is taking place in a world of new austerity. Shareholders are pressuring life sciences companies to cut spending. Bondholders and taxpayers are pressuring governments to cut deficits, which in turn puts pressure on governments to rein in spending on healthcare and cut back on their investment in R&D. As healthcare costs around the world continue to rise, one way governments have sought to control spending has been by instituting new price controls or tying pricing for drugs to the value they demonstrate. These efforts have ranged from countries such as China, which cut prices an average of 19 percent on more than 150 drugs at the end of 2010, to efforts such as Germany's 2011 law that instituted a value-based pricing scheme that is expected to save the country $2.7 billion a year. In debt-laden European countries, the situation is likely to grow worse. In Spain, which is struggling with the region's third-largest budget defi-

> "It's impossible for drugmakers to recover in such a tough environment and many may have to relocate. The effects are devastating."
>
> **Huberto Arnes**
> *Director general for the Spanish industry group Farmaindustria, speaking of the financial crisis in Spain*

cit, the government is cutting healthcare spending and requiring doctors to prescribe generic drugs rather than brand names. As a result, drugmakers are facing as much as a 10 percent drop in sales in 2011 and as much as a 15 percent decline in 2012. "The entire industry is in danger," Huberto Arnes, director general for the industry group **Farmaindustria** told *Bloomberg*. "It's impossible for drugmakers to recover in such a tough environment and many may have to relocate. The effects are devastating."

At the same time as pressure is increasing from payers and governments to use generic drugs and pay only for drugs that demonstrate value, the biotech industry is increasingly viewed as an important source of innovative, high-value products with demonstrable benefits. The good

## SEPTEMBER

**September 8**

The **U.S. Senate** passes The America Invents Act. The patent reform act moves the United States to a first-to-file system, where patents are granted first filers

**September 17**

Occupy Wall Street movement begins

**September 22**

**Advanced Cell Technology** is given the OK to conduct a trial that makes use of human embryonic stem cells in the United Kingdom—the first such approval outside the United States

## Figure 1.7 R&D PRODUCTIVITY DECLINE 1996 TO 2010

Cost based on average of 12 different estimates.

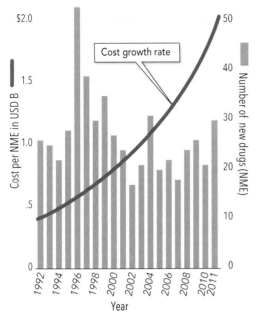

Source: Bernard Munos, Burrill & Company

maceuticals for its preclinical pipeline in a second licensing deal with the company, **Alexion**'s $1 billion acquisition of privately-held, rare disease drug developer **Enobia**, and **Gilead**'s acquisition of hepatitis C drug developer **Pharmasset** for $11 billion, an 89 percent premium over the closing price before the deal was announced [*SEE FIGURE 1.8*].

The question for the biotech industry is how does it fund innovation today? In 2011, the industry seemed to raise significant capital, but the raw numbers don't tell the story. Public market financing mostly funded large and established companies. Smaller companies relied on venture investors and other sources of private financing to fund their R&D. While the global life sciences industry raised $93.2 billion in 2011, the largest portion—some $55.5 billion—represented debt offerings from large public companies. By contrast, U.S. therapeutics companies at seed- and series A financing rounds raised just $669 million in 2011. Of that amount, nearly two-thirds or $428 million went to fund just 13 companies while the 49 remaining companies raised a combined total of $241 million.

news for biotech is that it can reap the rewards of the pharmaceutical industry's difficult position. In 2011, there were a number of big dollar acquisitions of biotech companies at significant premiums and big dollar partnership agreements, even when the biotechnology company's lead product was in either an early- or mid-stage development. This included transactions such **Abbott**'s $400 million upfront payment to **Reata Phar-**

One concern within the industry is that some venture investors have backed away from the sector. In November 2011, **Scale Venture Partners** said it was exiting the life sciences and the life science practices at the venture firms **Morgenthaler** and **Advanced Technology Ventures** announced they were breaking off from their information technology counterparts to form a new firm. That followed news in October 2011 that **Prospect**

## SEPTEMBER

### September 20

**Pacific Biosciences** lays off 130 employees in the wake of poor sales numbers, signaling that gene sequencing equipment might not be as big a boon as originally thought

### September 28

Obama administration officially petitions the **U.S. Supreme Court** to review the **11th Circuit Court of Appeals** decision striking down the *Patient Protection and Affordable Care Act's* individual mandate as unconstitutional

## OCTOBER

### October 3

**The Carlyle Group** and **Hellman & Friedman** pay $3.9 billion to take the contract researcher Pharmaceutical Product Development private

*Figure 1.8*    TOP DRUG SALES IN 2016: BIG PHARMA DOMINATES WITH BIOLOGICS

| | PRODUCT | COMPANY | PHARMACOLOGICAL CLASS | WORLD PRODUCT SALES 2010 (USD M) | WORLD PRODUCT SALES 2016 (USD M) |
|---|---|---|---|---|---|
| 1 | Humira | Abbott + Eisai | Anti-TNFa MAb | 6,742 | 9,696 |
| 2 | Avastin | Roche | Anti-VEGF MAb | 6,214 | 7,831 |
| 3 | Rituxan | Roche + Biogen Idec | Anti-CD20 MAb | 6,113 | 7,684 |
| 4 | Crestor | AstraZeneca + Shionogi + Chiesi | Statin/ HMG CoA reductase inhibitor | 6,106 | 7,518 |
| 5 | Enbrel | Amgen + Pfizer + Takeda | TNFa inhibitor | 7,257 | 7,190 |
| 6 | Seretide/ Advair | GSK + Almirall + Faes | Beta 2 adrenoreceptor agonist & corticosteroid | 8,067 | 6,953 |
| 7 | Januvia/ Janumet | Merck + Ono + Almirall | DPP-IV inhibitor | 3,503 | 6,800 |
| 8 | Herceptin | Roche | Anti-HER2 (ErbB-2) MAb | 5,221 | 6,466 |
| 9 | Remicade | J&J + Merck + Mitsubishi | Anti-TNFa MAb | 6,520 | 6,107 |
| 10 | Prevnar 13 | Pfizer | Pneumococcal vaccine | 2,416 | 5,805 |
| 11 | Lantus | Sanofi | Insulin | 4,658 | 5,585 |
| 12 | Revlimid | Celgene | Immunomodulator | 2,469 | 5,550 |
| 13 | Incivek | J&J + Vertex + Mitsubishi | Hepatitis C protease inhibitor | 0 | 4,226 |
| 14 | Lyrica | Pfizer + Eisai | Alpha 2 delta ligand | 3,077 | 3,998 |
| 15 | Xarelto | Bayer + J&J | Factor Xa inhibitor | 100 | 3,991 |
| 16 | Atripla | Gilead Sciences | NNRTI & NRTI | 2,927 | 3,687 |
| 17 | NovoRapid | Novo Nordisk | Insulin | 2,120 | 3,672 |
| 18 | Neulasta | Amgen + Kyowa Hakko | Colony stimulating factor | 3,558 | 3,442 |
| 19 | Xgeva/Prolia | Amgen + GSK + Daiichi Sankyo | Anti-RANKL MAb | 41 | 3,361 |
| 20 | Truvada | Gilead + Torii | NRTI | 2,746 | 3,345 |
| | TOTAL BIOLOGICS | | | 70,575 | |
| | TOTAL SMALL MOLECULE | | | 42,332 | |
| | TOTAL | | | 112,907 | |

*Source: EvaluatePharma*

**October 5**

**Apple** co-founder and CEO and technology visionary Steve Jobs dies at the age of 56

**October 18**

The **European Court of Justice** rules that procedures using stem cells derived from human embryos cannot be patented

**October 19**

**Abbott Laboratories** says it will split into two companies

# A Bloody Revolution

## Markets deal next-generation sequencing companies a drubbing

A promising development in the area of personalized medicine has been the rapid drop in the cost of sequencing driven by new technologies that have been collectively referred to as "next-generation" sequencing. A reflection of the excitement around next-generation sequencing and the potential growth of demand for sequencing as a result of the falling costs were the completion of initial public offerings from both **Pacific Biosciences** in October 2010 and **Complete Genomics** in November 2010, two of the emerging players. But for these two upstarts, as well as their well heeled competitors such as **Life Technologies** and **Illumina**, 2011 proved to be a difficult year.

> Economic constraints and the turbulent stock market took their toll on these companies in the second half of 2011.

Despite technical advances, significant agreements, and new understandings of the genetics underlying disease made by researchers using their technology, economic constraints and the turbulent stock market took their toll on these companies in the second half of 2011 as they tempered their forecast, missed targets and cut staff.

**Jay Flatley**
*President and CEO, Illumina*

One concern has been the economic pressures in the United States and Europe to curtail government spending on research. In a conference call in July 2011, Life Technologies CEO Greg Lucier said the company would accelerate its plans to cut spending by $20 million a year. Not only was the company feeling sluggish demand, but also suffered from damage to an assembly plant in Japan as a result of the March 2011 earthquake there and difficulties in China as the company moved to establish an internal sales team to reduce reliance on outside sales organizations.

Pacific Biosciences announced in September 2011 that it would cut staff. The Menlo Park, California-based company said it was laying off 130 staff, or 28 percent, of its workforce because of economic uncertainties and because adoption of its sequencing products was slower than expected. Although the cuts occurred across the board, they were deeper in its operations and research and development areas.

In October 2011, Illumina generated sales of $235.5 million, about $40 million below Wall

## OCTOBER

**October 23**

**Ely Lilly** loses patent protection of its biggest worldwide seller, its schizophrenia drug Zyprexa

**Oct. 24**
Cigna acquires HealthSpring $3.8 billion

**October 27**

Eurozone leaders agree on a package of measures to help prevent the collapse of member economies due to spiraling debt

**October 30**

World population reaches 7 billion

## Figure 1.9 PACIFIC BIOSCIENCES STOCK PRICE 2010-2012

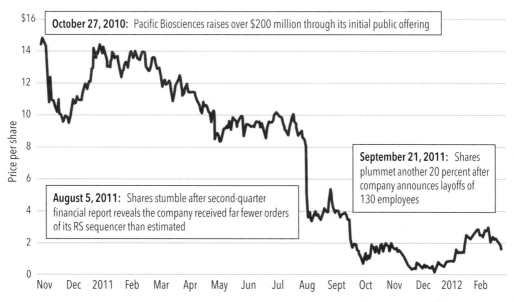

**October 27, 2010:** Pacific Biosciences raises over $200 million through its initial public offering

**September 21, 2011:** Shares plummet another 20 percent after company announces layoffs of 130 employees

**August 5, 2011:** Shares stumble after second-quarter financial report reveals the company received far fewer orders of its RS sequencer than estimated

Price per share axis: $16, 14, 12, 10, 8, 6, 4, 2, 0

X-axis: Nov, Dec, 2011, Feb, Mar, Apr, May, Jun, Jul, Aug, Sept, Oct, Nov, Dec, 2012, Feb

Source: Yahoo! Finance and Burrill & Company

Street's expectations and withdrew its sales forecast for 2011. Profits for the quarter fell by 43 percent from the same period a year ago to $20.2 million. That was followed by news that the company would embark on a restructuring that would shed 200 employees or about 8 percent of its workforce.

"Clearly, we are highly disappointed with our revenue for the third quarter. In the quarter, we saw what we believe to be an unprecedented slowdown in purchasing due to uncertainties in research funding and overall economic conditions, as well as a temporary excess of sequencing capacity in the market. We expect these conditions to continue through at least the fourth quarter, while the 2012 - 2013 U.S. budgets for NIH and other related agencies are determined," said Jay Flatley, president & CEO of Illumina in its earnings release.

Some have seen this as a buying opportunity. In January 2012, **Roche** launched a hostile $5.7 billion bid to buy Illumina. The $44.50 a share bid from Roche, however, is well below the $79.40 high Illumina reached in July 2011 before the market turned sharply lower. ■

## OCTOBER

### October 31

After the *Preserving Access to Life-Saving Medications Act* sat idly in Congress for nine months, President Barack Obama signs an executive order to address critical shortages of life-saving prescription drugs

## NOVEMBER

### November 1

**Alnylam** announces positive preliminary results from its early-stage clinical trial that shows that its experimental RNAi therapy might be the first to be able to silence a disease-causing gene in humans

### November 8

Voters in Mississippi reject a state constitutional amendment to redefine "person" as "every human being from the moment of fertilization, cloning, or the equivalent thereof"

> "The political brinksmanship of recent months highlights what we see as America's governance and policymaking becoming less stable, less effective, and less predictable than what we previously believed."
>
> *Statement from Standard and Poor's on downgrading the credit rating of the United States*

**Ventures** would not raise a fourth healthcare fund and would return committed capital to limited partners. A survey from the **National Venture Capital Association** has found that nearly 40 percent of life sciences venture capitalist firms plan to invest less in the sector during the next three years. That reflects both frustration with regulatory barriers and the weak market for initial public offerings that have made it difficult for venture investors to cash out of their investments in recent years.

In 2011, a total of 16 life sciences companies went public in the United States, but by year-end their shares were down an average of 27 percent. These companies ended up selling 28 percent more shares than they had planned to sell and wound up raising an average 13 percent less than they had hoped to raise. In fact, a total of ten companies went public below their target range. In the first half of the year, though, momentum was building for IPOs, and, as a class, these shares were trading up from their offering prices. But the willingness of investors to buy IPO shares

from life sciences companies changed dramatically at the end of July 2011 when the debt ceiling fight in the United States triggered a turn in markets. Partisan fighting reached a boiling point in the United States Congress over a vote to raise the debt limit. Facing the threat of a default by the United States government, lawmakers reached an accord to raise the debt ceiling by as much as $2.1 trillion, but only by tying that to spending cuts of up to $2.4 trillion over ten years. The political gamesmanship that delayed action until lawmakers struck a last minute deal led to **Standard and Poor's** downgrading the credit rating of the United States. It was the first time ever that the United States lost its AAA rating. What's more, S&P warned that the agreement didn't go far enough to address debt concerns and said that the fight over a resolution revealed severe dysfunction that threatened future economic health. "The political brinksmanship of recent months," S&P said, "highlights what we see as America's governance and policymaking becoming less stable, less effective, and less pre-

## NOVEMBER

| November 14 | November 14 | November 18 | November 21 |
|---|---|---|---|
| The U.S. Supreme Court agrees to review the constitutionality the *Patient Protection and Affordable Care Act of 2010* | Geron announces that it will shut down its stem cell program | The FDA withdraws its accelerated approval of **Genentech's** Avastin for use as a breast cancer treatment | The Congressional Super Committee formed to cut the deficit says it will fail to meet its deadline to have a reduction plan in place |

Nov. 11
New Link
Genetics
IPO
$43 million

Nov. 15
Clovis
Oncology
IPO
$130 million

Nov. 21
Gilead
acquires
Pharmasset
$11 billion

dictable than what we previously believed."

Part of the agreement established a so-called Congressional Super Committee, a bipartisan group charged with finding at least $1.5 trillion in spending cuts through 2021. The committee, however, ended its work in a stalemate, leaving in place $1.2 trillion in automatic defense and domestic spending cuts that will be triggered in 2013 if no action is taken.

While the fight over the debt ceiling weighed heavily on financial markets, it was amplified by new pressures from the unfolding debt crisis across the Atlantic as the European Union raced to put new measures in place to address a growing problem with members' sovereign debt and to prevent problems in nations such as Greece, Italy, and Spain from spreading throughout the eurozone and triggering credit downgrades, problems for the banking system, and threats to breakup or reduce the size of the eurozone [SEE FIGURE 1.10].

These burdens came as governments around the world struggle to get control of rising healthcare costs as an aging population and growing incidence of chronic disease threaten to push their healthcare systems to a breaking point. In the United States, healthcare reform legislation is significantly expanding care, but is also raising costs. Solutions to these problems will not be easy, but it's a false choice to say our only choice is to either drive ourselves to bankruptcy or ration care.

As a result of the economic and political situation in Europe and the United States, capital markets behaved quite differently in the second

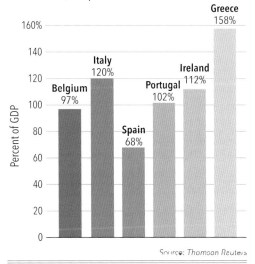

*Figure 1.10* **EUROPEAN GOVERNMENTS' DEBT BURDEN**

**Government Debt as Percent of GDP**
2012 forecast, European Commission

Source: Thomson Reuters

half of 2011 than they did during the first half and it made an already challenging environment for emerging biotechs to raise capital even more so. Nevertheless, capital remains available for innovative ideas, if not from traditional venture investors, then from others that are stepping in to fill the void. This includes corporate venture investors, angel investors forming syndicates to leverage their investment, and private equity. Traditional venture investors are moving away from building companies to investing in the development of products that can be licensed

## NOVEMBER

**November 30**

Patent protection runs out on **Pfizer's** cholesterol-lowering drug Lipitor, the world's top-selling prescription medicine

## DECEMBER

**December 6**

**Samsung** and **Biogen Idec** form $300 million joint venture focused on biosimilars

**December 9**

U.S. HHS Secretary Kathleen Sebelius orders the FDA to disregard its scientific findings and reject Plan B emergency contraceptive for over-the-counter sale to adolescents 17 and younger

> Capital remains available for innovative ideas, if not from traditional venture investors, then from others that are stepping in to fill the void.

or sold to pharmaceutical companies. In some cases, venture investors have decided to bypass funding companies and instead are backing molecules by employing a virtual business model and outsourcing all aspects of the process of discovery and development with the hope of eventually licensing a drug to a pharmaceutical or biotech partner. Under such an arrangement, the virtual company would take a candidate to proof-of-concept and then license or sell it to a pharmaceutical company that would complete development, handle regulatory filings, and manufacture and market the product. In other cases, venture investors are partnering with pharmaceutical companies to fund companies, and building in an exit strategy by structuring the agreements so that the pharmaceutical partner becomes an acquirer if agreed upon milestones are met.

And then there's the issue of regulation in the United States, which industry executives have complained has grown too costly and unpredictable. Increasingly drug and device companies are looking overseas as a faster route to market because of lower regulatory barriers. But there's also an effort to address the growing cost and time of drug development by crafting new clinical development pathways that can avoid a situation that has too often happened in recent years where a company funds a large, late-stage trial at great expense only to find its experimental drug fails. One step toward that is the **U.S. Food and Drug Administration**'s issuance of draft guidance for biomarkers. Other efforts include the growing use of adaptive clinical trials that allow researchers to alter the design of a trial in progress to adjust for what the trial data is telling them. The trade group the **Biotechnology Industry Organization**, has also proposed alternatives, such as progressive approvals for certain innovative therapies that address unmet medical needs.

Given a financing environment where investors are reticent to invest in high-risk ventures that require large amounts of capital and the patience to achieve returns, the challenge for life sciences companies are many. Can biotech in 2012 make a compelling case for generating attractive returns? The traditional venture capital to IPO model may not work for most companies today. But as the industry has in the past, it will once again need to look to creative new financing mechanisms and business models to attract the capital necessary to fund innovation. Creativity will also be needed to design new approaches to R&D that can bring new products to market faster and cheaper.

One solution has been to turn to disease

## DECEMBER

### December 15

The **Human Variome Project**, aiming to log all genetic variations that cause human disease, adds China to its roster of countries

### December 19

**Amgen** and **Watson Pharmaceuticals** forge $400 million cancer biosimilars collaboration

### December 20

New York City signs off on **Cornell University's** bid to build a $2 billion graduate science and engineering school on Roosevelt Island

> The type of innovation that will be most highly valued is disruptive innovation that provides new ways of accessing and delivering healthcare, provides treatments for unmet medical conditions, and bends the cost curve of healthcare.

advocacy groups, which have stepped in to close a gap in funding for early-stage development and advance promising experimental therapies to proof-of-concept. For instance, **Amylin Pharmaceuticals** in May 2011 entered into a research collaboration with the **Juvenile Diabetes Research Foundation**, which will fund a series of early-stage clinical studies in type 1 diabetes. To date, the JDRF effort has funded 39 partnerships with 32 companies and committed approximately $73 million as part of its Industry Discovery & Development Partnership program.

Some might argue that innovation has been part of the problem we face with the rising cost of healthcare. There is a case that can be made about how innovation has driven, rather than cut costs, calling into question the cost-effectiveness of technologies ranging from expensive imaging technology to robotic surgery. The problem is not only that new technology tends to be more expensive, but also that once hospitals and doctors have invested in it, they have a financial incentive to maximize its use whether or not the applications of the technology deliver a commensurate improvement in the quality of care and outcomes.

Innovation though should not be viewed as part of the problem, but part of the solution. In the new austerity, innovation will need to not only provide improvements in care, but value as well. As such, the type of innovation that will be most highly valued and able to attract funding and the support of payers is not incremental innovation that raises costs without delivering commensurate improvements in quality, but disruptive innovation that provides new ways of accessing and delivering healthcare, provides treatments for unmet medical conditions, and bends the cost curve of healthcare. In some instances, the results may be technology that is inferior to what is available today in terms of its power, but is nevertheless transformational because of its cost, speed, or portability. This is something we are seeing over and over in the digital health arena as complex multimillion dollar machines operated by highly trained technicians and physicians are giving way to patient-operated devices linked to smartphones.

Can we innovate ourselves out of the mess we are in today? We're doing it already. ■

## DECEMBER

**December 22**

**Baxter** and **Momenta** team up to form a $452 million biosimilars venture

**December 28**

Iran threatens that it will close off the Strait of Hormuz, a vital oil route

**December 31**

The **Dow Jones Industrial Average** closes at 12,217.56, up 5.53 percent for the year. The **Burrill Biotech Select Index** closes at 432.49, up 18.45 percent for the year

# 2 Gray Matters

Around the world, life spans are increasing and populations are aging. This demographic shift presents opportunities for drug and device makers, as well as significant challenges for healthcare systems and payers. Diseases of aging are among the costliest and most intractable diseases faced. These include heart disease, stroke, cancer, neurological disease, pulmonary disease, and diabetes. While policymakers across the globe have taken steps to look for ways to restrict spending, others are turning to innovative approaches that can keep people healthy and allow them to live independently. New approaches to care are both improving the quality of life and helping control the demands the elderly put on healthcare systems. There's also the hope that scientific breakthroughs in treatments can address the ravages caused by diseases of aging and, if not reverse the aging process, at least slow and halt the damage that we've come to view as part of it. Simple cost-control is not a viable solution to the challenges posed by aging populations. Instead, society will require innovative solutions that can both improve outcomes and contain costs.

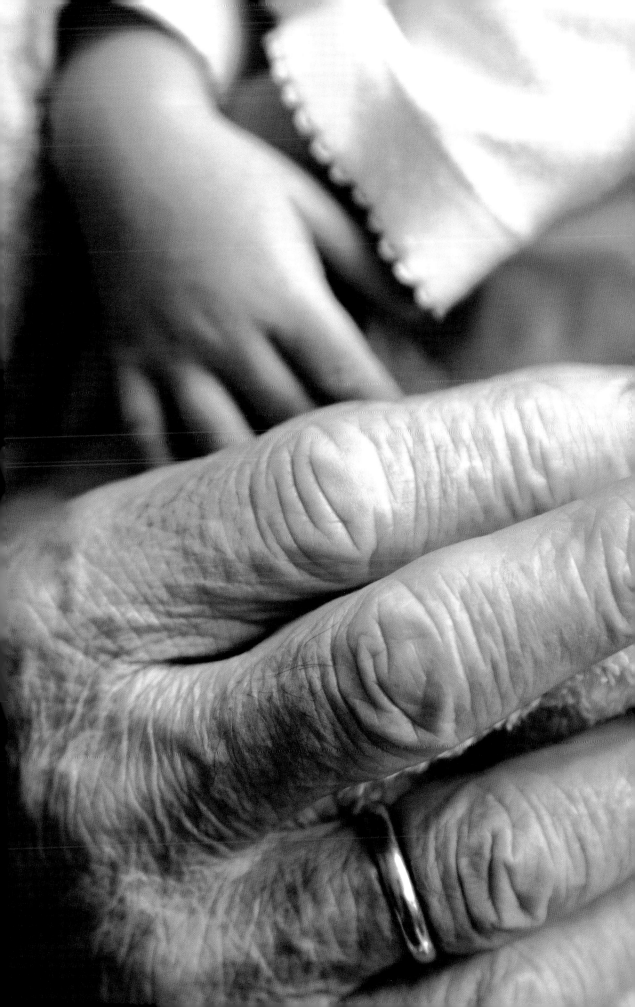

# Chapter 2: GRAY MATTERS

When retired school teacher Kathleen Casey-Kirschling turned 65 at midnight on January 1, 2011 the event garnered media attention. Though by itself, her birthday might not appear extraordinary, it was newsworthy because Casey-Kirschling, born in 1946 at one minute after midnight, has long been considered the first of the Baby Boom generation.

Her personal milestone of crossing the threshold into what has traditionally been thought of as old age will be repeated by some 78 million Baby Boomers in the United States who will turn 65 at a rate of about 10,000 people per day through 2030. That's expected to increase the elderly as a percent of the total population to about 19 percent of the total population from around 13 percent today. Around the world, life spans are increasing, adding to the senior population. With that demographic shift comes opportunities for drug and device makers, as well as significant challenges for healthcare systems and payers.

Diseases of aging are among the costliest and most intractable diseases faced. These include heart disease, stroke, cancer, neurological disease, pulmonary disease, and diabetes. Though estimates vary, the cost of chronic diseases is associated with about 75 percent of total healthcare spending in the United States.

In the United States, healthcare spending

*Figure 2.1* **PERCENT OF HEALTHCARE SPENDING BY AGE GROUP**

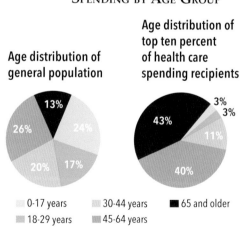

**Age distribution of general population**

**Age distribution of top ten percent of health care spending recipients**

- 0-17 years
- 18-29 years
- 30-44 years
- 45-64 years
- 65 and older

*Source: Center for Financing, Access, and Cost Trends, AHRQ, Household Component of the Medical Expenditure Panel Survey*

is concentrated. In 2009, just 1 percent of the population accounted for about 20 percent of healthcare expenditures with an annual mean cost of a little more than $90,000, according to **The Agency for Healthcare Quality** [*SEE FIGURE 2.2*]. A total of 5 percent of the population accounted for nearly half of all healthcare expenditures that year. Not surprisingly, the elderly make up a disproportionate share of that concentration of healthcare spending. While elderly people, defined as those 65 and over, represent a little more than 13 percent of the population, they account for nearly 43 percent of the top decile of healthcare spenders. [*SEE FIGURE 2.1*].

Aging populations and the diseases they face are a growing source of pressure on healthcare systems around the world. While policymakers across the globe have sought ways to restrict spending, others are turning to innovative approaches that can keep people healthy and allow them to live independently. Changing approaches to care can improve the quality of life while helping control the demands the elderly put on the healthcare system. There's also hope that scientific breakthroughs in treatments can address the ravages caused by diseases of aging and if not reverse the aging process, at least slow and halt the damage that we've come to view as part of it.

"With all the discussion in Washington and other parts of the country in terms of the healthcare problems we face, we think it's important to recognize you can't simply cost-control your way out of that," says Gil Van Bokkelen, chairman of the **Alliance for Regenerative Medicine**. "You've got to innovate your way out of those types of challenges by developing these types of technologies that can improve outcomes and also improve the overall economic efficiency."

### Rising sun and graying heads

In Japan, where the graying of the population is most dramatic, the issues surrounding an aging population are perhaps being felt most acutely [*SEE FIGURE 2.3*]. Per capita medical costs for Japan's elderly are nearly five times higher than for its younger population. More than half of all medical spending in Japan goes to pay for the care of people over 65. The problems have been exacerbated by the country's low birth rate and increasing longevity. The transformation in Japan has happened rapidly. In just 24 years

*Figure 2.2* **HEALTHCARE SPENDING BY PERCENTILE RANK**

**Top spending percentages in the United States***

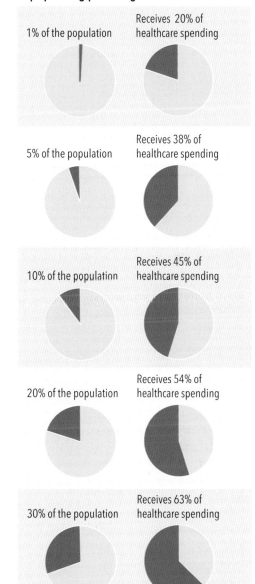

1% of the population — Receives 20% of healthcare spending

5% of the population — Receives 38% of healthcare spending

10% of the population — Receives 45% of healthcare spending

20% of the population — Receives 54% of healthcare spending

30% of the population — Receives 63% of healthcare spending

50% of the population — Receives 75% of healthcare spending

* U.S. noninstitutionalized civilian population, 2008 to 2009

*Source: Center for Financing, Access, and Cost Trends, AHRQ*

*Figure 2.3* **THE GRAYING OF JAPAN**

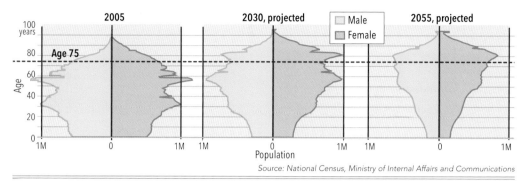

Source: National Census, Ministry of Internal Affairs and Communications

the country has moved from an aging to an aged society with the percent of people over 65 doubling during that period.

Japan's answer has been to try to turn a potential economic and health crisis into a strength. The *New Growth Strategy*, a document issued in June 2010 by the cabinet of then-Japanese Prime Minister Naoto Kan seeks "to achieve economic growth by turning the problems faced by the economy and society into opportunity for creating new demand and employment." The plan focuses on seven strategic areas, one of which is identified as "life innovation." It calls for Japan to turn itself into a healthcare superpower. It views its position as the oldest population as a chance to develop new manufacturing and service growth industries by promoting innovation in the medical and nursing sectors. In the healthcare sector, the government expects its plan to lead to more than $650 billion annually in new markets and create 2.8 million jobs by 2020.

The plan not only calls for the development of innovative drugs and medical technologies within Japan, but also calls for cooperation between government, industry, and academia to promote research and development in areas such as regenerative medicine, remote medical technologies, information and communication technologies that can be used to improve mobility for the elderly, and medical and nursing care robots. With those priorities comes a frank acknowledgment from the Japanese government that it will need to make urgent fixes to address problems in its regulatory review process to eliminate the lag in new drugs and devices coming to market, improve the clinical testing environment, and expedite drug approval decisions.

Japan's *New Growth Strategy* calls for pro-moting independent living among the elderly by eliminating physical barriers in housing, such as interior stairs and installing handrails. It also calls for increasing the number of trained doctors and nurses and centralizing sophisticated specialized medicine while expanding nursing care and home-based care services. "We will work to build a society in which the elderly can live out their lives while maintaining ties to their families and society," the plan said. "We will also transmit Japan's new social system to other parts of Asia and the world as a leading elderly society model."

## A Worldwide Phenomena

Of course, while the problem may be acute in Japan, it is echoed throughout the rest of the world [*SEE FIGURE 2.4*]. A **United Nations** report on aging populations that looked at the period from 1950 to 2050 said population aging trends now underway are "unprecedented" and "without parallel in the history of humanity." The United Nations forecast that the percent of the world population that is over the age of 60 will grow to 21 percent by 2050, up from 10 percent in 2000. The trend is happening in concert with a decline in the percent of people under the age of 15. By 2050, the United Nations said for the first time in human history, the number of older people in the world will exceed the number of younger people. In fact, this turn of events, it said, is already being seen in many developed countries today.

In countries known for their government funded healthcare, such as Canada, the growing share healthcare spending represents is forcing difficult actions. Healthcare spending accounted for about 40 percent of provincial budgets in

*Figure 2.4* **As Global Population Grows, an Increasing Proportion is Over 65**

## Comparison of population factors 1950 to 2050

*Projected based on current rate

**Old-Age Dependency Ratio: Ratio of population 65 and older vs. employment-age population (15-64)

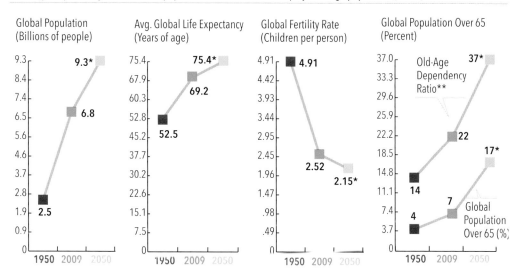

Sources: earthtrends.wri.org, UN World Population Project (2008), Google Public Data Explorer, Science Vol. 296, pg 1029

2009. Seniors are expected to make up a quarter of the population by 2036. The pressure from the country's aging population and budget deficits have forced authorities to find places to make cuts. *Reuters* reported that the province of Ontario in 2010 told drug companies and pharmacies it would cut the prices for generic drugs in half and eliminate incentive fees to generic drugmakers. British Columbia replaced block grants with fee-for-service payments, and Quebec imposed a flat health tax. Other provinces are considering means testing and pay-for-performance models in order to address the funding problems. "There's got to be some change to the status quo whether it happens in three years or 10 years," Derek Burleton, a senior economist at **TD Bank**, told *Reuters*. "We can't continually see health spending growing above and beyond the growth rate in the economy because, at some point, it means crowding out of all the other government services."

The problem in many countries is not an aging population, but the concurrent imbalance in the ratio between young and old. Gone are the classic population age pyramids. Increasingly longevity coupled with declining birth rates in many countries means that as greater demands are put on healthcare systems, a smaller population of wage earners will be supporting those systems. This change is expressed in a calculation known as the old-age dependency ratio—a reflection of an increasing number of health and pension beneficiaries supported by a shrinking relative group of working people (age 15 to 64) paying into health and pension systems [*See Figure 2.5*]. Governments with high old-age dependency ratios will find it harder to address the rising costs of healthcare because they face not only rising demand, but a shrinking base of taxpayers to support those costs. The problem is acute in countries such as Japan and China, but being felt throughout the world. In the United States, the old-age dependency ratio is expected to rise 75 percent by 2050 from its current level today.

The challenge for global healthcare systems will be how to control costs while addressing increasing demand [*See Figure 2.6*]. That issue will be looked at in greater depth in the chapter on healthcare, but in the context of aging populations, there are several approaches being used that could address the challenges. This includes applying technologies to shift the way care is delivered, changing the approach to end-of-life care, and developing regenerative therapies that can change the cost equation of some of the diseases that are the costliest to treat.

## Europe Looks to Digital Health

In Europe, keeping the aging population active and healthy has been made a central focus of the first **European Innovation Partnership**. The partnership is part of the **Innovation Union**, one of seven flagship initiatives that make up the *Europe 2020 Strategy* aimed at promoting sustainable growth. The Innovation Union is designed to advance Europe's scientific standing by both removing obstacles to innovation and fostering cooperation between the public and private sectors through innovation partnerships between European institutions, national and regional authorities, and businesses.

In May 2011, a steering group for the pilot **European Innovation Partnership on Active and Healthy Aging** was established. The partnership consists of more than 30 stakeholders with a track record of innovation in the areas of health and aging, including nurses, caregivers, doctors, hospital representatives, academics, industry, and venture capital organizations in **European Union** member states. The group published a strategic plan in November highlighting priority initiatives with the objective of ensuring that the average European citizen has two more active and healthy years to live by 2020.

The number of people in Europe aged 65 and older will almost double over the next 50 years to 151 million in 2060 from 85 million in 2008. As in Japan, the partnership approaches aging as a positive opportunity rather than a burden, by focusing on the contribution older people make to society and user-centered innovation and service delivery to empower them. Above all, says the partnership, Europe must move from reactive care for the elderly, who are often provided acute or chronic care and hospital-based care, to proactive care, based in the home and integrated with social care. In tandem with these changes, living and working environments need to be adapted so that they do not intimidate the elderly but empower them to remain functional and active longer.

In 2012, E.U. member states implementing plans advanced by the partnership will seek

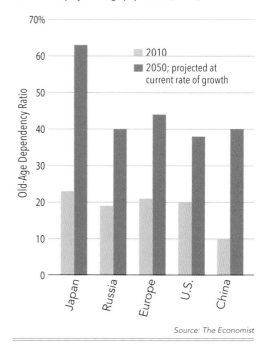

*Figure 2.5* **A Rising Old-Age Dependency Ratio**

Old-Age Dependency Ratio: Ratio of population 65 and older vs. employment-age population (15-64)

*Source: The Economist*

to achieve five goals. They inlcude developing innovative ways to ensure patients follow their prescriptions—a concerted action in at least 30 European regions; innovative solutions to prevent falls and support early diagnosis for older people; cooperation to help prevent functional decline and frailty, with a particular focus on malnutrition; promotion of successful innovative integrated care models for chronic diseases among older patients, such as remote monitoring; and increasing the uptake of technology-based independent living solutions to help older people stay independent, mobile, and active for longer.

In addition, the plan calls for networking and knowledge sharing on ways to create buildings, cities, and environments that are friendlier to the elderly, based on the **World Health Organization's** age-friendly cities initiative. "We want to make a real difference to the lives of older Europeans and this plan seeks to do exactly that," says Neelie Kroes, European Commission vice president for the *Digital Agenda*. The European Commission has been invited to respond to the plan in early 2012, and to present it for discussion and endorsement to the **Euro-**

## *Figure 2.6* COMPARISON OF EU SPENDING ON SOCIAL PROGRAMS

Projected growth through 2060

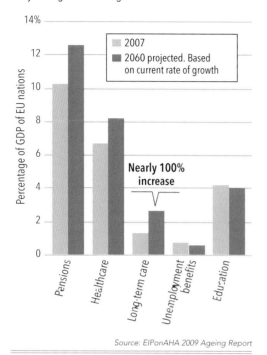

Source: EIPonAHA 2009 Ageing Report

**pean Parliament** and **the Council**.

"It is only through their innovative approaches that we can turn the challenge of demographic aging into a great opportunity for people, careers, and businesses," the partnership says. "We will play our part, for example, through regulation and funding, and will talk to government leaders in partnership with stakeholders, to make this plan a reality."

## Tech giants see opportunity

Not surprisingly the private sector has come to recognize the opportunities before it to develop new products and services to keep an aging population healthy and out of the hospital. As with the European Innovation Partnership on Active and Healthy Aging, much of the emphasis has been on enlisting ubiquitous technologies to help allow elderly people to live independently longer, better manage chronic diseases, and avoid injuries and other health problems that might lead to costly hospitalizations. Consider **Care Innovations**, a venture formed out of a combination of **Intel's Digital Health Group** and **GE Healthcare's Home Health Division**. GE and Intel, when they

announced their initial partnership that would lead to the formation of the new company, committed to spending $250 million over five years on research and development in the area of home health monitoring. Care Innovations threw open its doors at the start of 2011 to stake a claim in the rapidly emerging telehealth and home healthcare monitoring market, an opportunity the company estimates will reach $7.7 billion in 2012. It is an example of how a world of devices is beginning to change how care is accessed and delivered and how widely available technology is being applied in new ways to address health issues.

Kate Marcus describes the Care Innovations Guide as looking a bit like a George Foreman grill, but open it up and it reveals a simple to use touch screen that checks in daily with chronically ill patients to make sure they are taking their medication, monitors information such as blood pressure and weight, and asks a series of questions that change depending on the answers it gets. The device provides the information it gathers daily to a healthcare professional and allows a patient to communicate through a video screen directly with a caregiver.

Marcus, process manager for **Humana's** chronic disease management and services division **Humana Cares**, is overseeing an 18 month, 2,000 patient study of the Care Innovations Guide to see if it can improve the care and prevent rehospitalization of congestive heart failure patients. Though the study won't be completed until mid-2012, she says there's already anecdotal evidence for how the device may have allowed for interventions that prevented costly hospitalizations.

For instance, in one case, a nurse contacted a congestive heart failure patient when data collected by the device showed a patient experiencing a slight weight gain and no longer taking her medication. Weight gain can be a sign of an accumulation of fluid in the heart and indicate a worsening condition that could lead to a hospitalization. It turned out the patient had run out of the diuretic she was prescribed and when the drug store refused to refill it, she simply discontinued its use. The nurse immediately saw to it that the woman's prescription was refilled. Her weight dropped once she began her drug therapy again. "Through the years, as people become more comfortable with technology, I anticipate

*Figure 2.7* **HEALTHCARE AND LOST PRODUCTIVITY COSTS OF MAJOR DISEASES**

Costs of five diseases with potential regenerative medicine treatments

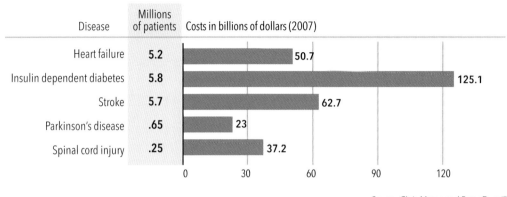

| Disease | Millions of patients | Costs in billions of dollars (2007) |
|---|---|---|
| Heart failure | 5.2 | 50.7 |
| Insulin dependent diabetes | 5.8 | 125.1 |
| Stroke | 5.7 | 62.7 |
| Parkinson's disease | .65 | 23 |
| Spinal cord injury | .25 | 37.2 |

*Source: Chris Mason and Peter Dunnill*

that this will grow exponentially to be a really important piece of healthcare and how it's delivered and managed," says Marcus, who talked about how the device has not only improved patient compliance, but also their understanding of why it's important to do the things their doctor has told them to do. "To really hear people to be able to verbalize and understand how everything fits together to me is the ah-ha moment. It really is different than giving someone a scale and saying weigh yourself and write it down every day and call me if your weight goes up three pounds. Most people don't check."

Care Innovations' products fall into three categories. The Guide represents the company's disease management product line. These products are targeted to hospitals that seek to avoid costly readmissions as well as self-insured employers and governments. A separate set of products are focused on enabling elderly people to live independently. These products include the QuietCare Monitor, a motion sensor technology that learns the daily living patterns of senior community residents and alerts staff when certain out-of-the-ordinary events occur. The system provides information that facilitates the delivery of personalized care to help improve response times and identify potential problems before they become emergencies. QuietCare could alert staff in an independent living facility to a fall or that a patient got up an abnormal number of times during the night to use the bathroom, a possible sign of a developing bladder infection. Or, as it did in

one case, it could alert staff to intervene when someone had failed to emerge from their bathroom after a prolonged period. In that case, staff discovered the resident had suffered a breathing problem and had turned blue, unable to emerge from the bathroom. They were able to intervene and save his life. The final product in the offering is the Intel Reader, designed to help both elderly patients with vision problems as well as students with learning disabilities that may hinder their ability to read. The mobile device takes printed text and converts it to speech. This product is

**Kate Marcus of Humana Cares demonstrates the company's at-home monitoring device**

sold directly to end users as well as large school districts.

Joe Smith, chief medical and science officer for the **West Wireless Health Institute**, says seeing big players such as GE and Intel in the arena reflects the arrival of business models in healthcare that will propel adoption of digital health technologies as financial incentives for care providers shift. "With bundled payments, accountable care organizations, the notion that there are going to be medical homes, organizations are going to be at risk based on how patients do in terms of their outcomes, not just in terms of how many procedures they get or how many bed days they are in a hospital," he says. "They now have an appetite and a reason to start using these technologies to keep people well and at home."

### Delivering what patients want

But even if we can prolong life and allow people to live healthier and more independent lives, one area where we can attack the high cost of spending is in end-of life care. A lasting addition to the lexicon of health policy that emerged from the divisive debate over healthcare reform in the United States came from Republican vice presidential candidate Sarah Palin when she derided a provision in the proposed legislation as creating "death panels." Echoing the idea, Ohio Congressman John Boehner, then minority leader, warned we were heading "down a treacherous path toward government-encouraged euthanasia."

The provision in question would have allowed **Medicare** to pay doctors to have discussions about end-of-life care with patients and obtain advanced directives to instruct physicians to follow a patient's wishes about how aggressive they would want care to be if they were dying. The provision, which was in the original version of

the **Patient Protection and Affordable Care Act** passed by **the U.S. House of Representatives**, did not make it into the final version of the legislation. The **Obama Administration** managed to get a similar provision into Medicare payment guidelines in November of 2010, but at the start of 2011 the administration removed it saying the public should have been allowed to comment on it when they published a draft version of the guidelines in July, but failed to include it.

The failure to address the need for open discussions between physicians and patients about end-of-life care comes at a substantial cost. About one quarter of Medicare spending goes to cover care for people in their last year of life and the treatment of chronic disease has driven much of the growth in Medicare spending in recent decades, according to the **Atlas Project**. In fact, nine out of 10 deaths of Medicare patients are associated with one of nine chronic diseases. The good news, according to the Dartmouth Atlas Project's most recent report on end-of-life care of Medicare patients is that between 2003 and 2007, patients spent fewer days in the hospital and received more hospice care in 2007 than they did in 2003. The bad news is that there's been an increase in the intensity of care for patients who were hospitalized. Unnecessarily aggressive care, the authors say, not only carries a high financial cost, but also has effects on a patient's quality of life [*SEE FIGURE 2.8*].

When the researchers compared end-of-life care in different regions they found that in regions with more hospitals and more specialists, patients tend to be admitted to the hospital more often and tend to see more specialists. The researchers have dubbed this phenomenon "supply-sensitive care." Physicians uncertain how to treat patients with chronic diseases, the researchers say, have a tendency to use the resources available to them. David Goodman, director of

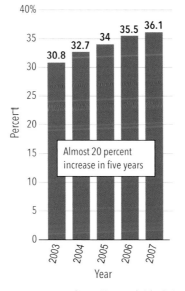

*Figure 2.8* **DOCTORS SEEN AT END OF LIFE**

Change in the U.S. average percentage of chronically ill Medicare patients seeing ten or more doctors during the last six months of life.

Almost 20 percent increase in five years

*Source: Dartmouth Atlas Project*

# An Audacious Plan to Combat Alzheimer's

## U.S. expert panel targets treatment or prevention by 2025

A draft plan from an expert panel convened by the **U.S. Department of Health and Human Services** sets an audacious goal of having a means to effectively treat or prevent Alzheimer's disease by 2025. The development of such a plan is mandated by the *National Alzheimer's Project Act,* which was signed into law at the start of 2011. Though the act called for the creation of a coordinated national plan to address the rising toll of Alzheimer's disease and an evaluation of national research efforts, the law did not provide any new funding for such research.

What makes the goal so audacious is not only the long development times needed to bring drugs to market, but the lack of understanding about the underlying causes of the neurodegenerative disease, which afflicts as many as 5.4 million Americans. Efforts to bring a drug to market have been stymied by spectacular late-stage failures including the failure of two high profile late-stage drug candidates in the past two years.

**Eli Lilly** quit developing Semagacestat when it found the drug not only failed to slow the disease's progression, but also worsened the cognitive function of trial patients and heightened their risk of skin cancer. **Pfizer** and **Medivation** watched Dimebon prove no better than a placebo, much to their surprise after the drug showed promise in early testing. The partners said on January 18 they would cease development of Dimebon after it failed to meet two primary endpoints in a late-stage trial.

The issue is urgent. The **Alzheimer's Association** estimates the economic toll from the disease will rise to more than $1 trillion by 2050 from nearly $200 billion today. It is already the sixth leading cause of death and the only one for which there is no way to cure, prevent, or slow its progression, the group says.

"Developing an urgent, achievable and accountable strategy for Alzheimer's is about hope for millions of people today and tomorrow," says Harry Johns, president and CEO of the Alzheimer's Association

"This process is about changing the course of Alzheimer's disease," says Harry Johns, president and CEO of the Alzheimer's Association and member of the advisory council that produced the draft report. "It is about setting the path for that change right away with an aggressive timeline. Developing an urgent, achievable and accountable strategy for Alzheimer's is about hope for millions of people today and tomorrow. What we need now is a meaningful plan with appropriate resources that, when fully implemented, will bring us from possibility to reality."

The draft plan calls for the setting of research priorities, enhanced research, coordination of efforts with international public and private entities to leverage resources, and facilitating the translation of discoveries into treatments.

The plan also calls for enhancement of early diagnostics, expanded support for caregivers, better care and education for patients, and improvements to early diagnosis.

Some have criticized the draft plan for creating a deadline and setting up a perception of failure should the goals of the plan go unmet. But disease advocates, long critical of the relatively small investment being made in Alzheimer's research, see this as an important step forward. The **National Institutes of Health** in fiscal 2011 was expected to spend just $480 million for Alzheimer's research. That compares to $2.1 billion for heart disease research and $6 billion for cancer research.

"There's no doubt that we have no time to waste, but it will be vital to engage Congress and sustain their commitment in order to achieve a national plan to defeat Alzheimer's disease and help countless families now and in the future," says Eric Hall, president and CEO of the **Alzheimer's Foundation of America** and a member of the Advisory Council. "Much work lies ahead, but I am confident that we are on the right path toward the resolution of this crisis." ∎

the **Center for Health Policy Research** at the **Dartmouth Institute for Health Policy and Clinical Practice** and lead author of the study, says there's been a pretty dramatic expansion in terms of intensive care units and intensive care beds. "A built bed is a filled bed," he says. "It may be very well meaning, but on the ground, you don't have the perspective in the way that tends to bias care and decisions."

The problem is that there's a mismatch between what patients want and what hospitals are delivering. A large-scale study funded by the **Robert Wood Johnson Foundation** found that patients with serious illness said they would prefer to die at home, but most patients died in the hospitals, and care was rarely aligned with their reported preferences. The evidence, the researchers say, suggests that patients often prefer a more conservative approach to end-of-life care than they actually receive. They also say it suggests that a patient's wishes can be less influential than the practice patterns at the hospital where care is delivered.

Part of the problem, says Goodman, is training. Doctors often don't take the time to discuss with a dying patient what is important to them and what kind of care they want to receive. While there are patients who want very aggressive care, others are more concerned about being out of pain, or being ambulatory or alert enough to interact with family. "We make a lot of well meaning assumptions about patients," says Goodman. "We're making recommendations, but we're not very good at listening." That's exacerbated by financial incentives that reward doctors for procedures and aggressive care, but pay relatively poorly for care that involves time, such as helping manage patients' symptoms and spending time to understand what their goals are at the end of their lives.

What perhaps is surprising is that palliative care—care focused on quality of life and minimizing symptoms, and designed to address patients' goal and values—has been shown to not only save money, but also improve the quality of care and, in the case of three randomized clinical trials of late-stage cancer patients, extend life. "It may be possible to reduce spending," says Goodman, "while also improving the quality of care by ensuring that patient preferences are more closely followed."

# Types of Regenerative Medicine

## Tissue engineering

The creation of new organs or tissues to replace or repair existing organ function.

*Example:* Organ regeneration of bladders for patients with organ loss or impairment due to bladder cancer or other maladies.

## Cell therapy

Cells used therapeutically to restore or repair function to bodily tissue or organs.

*Example:* Restoring insulin production in pancreas via a transplant of the patient's own stem cells.

## Medical devices

Cell-based products used for medical purposes in patients for diagnosis, therapy or surgery.

*Example:* Creation of skin-like biomaterials for plastic surgery to limit visible malformations in children.

## Drug discovery

Regenerative medicine science used to develop highly accurate biological models for understanding states of disease and health.

*Example:* Use of regenerative medicine-based bioassays to screen small molecules for the treatment of liver disease.

## Cell modulation

Development of new small molecule and biologic drugs that can selectively modulate the body's own naturally occurring stem cells for therapeutic purpose or to create and differentiate iPS cells for use in personalized cell therapy treatments or drug development.

*Example:* Development of conventional small molecule and biologic therapeutics that would activate specific stem cells in the body to repair tissues or repress stem cells to treat diseases such as cancer.

*Source: Alliance for Regenerative Medicine*

*Figure 2.9*     BIG PHARMA INVESTING IN REGENERATIVE MEDICINE

| BIG PHARMA | PARTNER(S)/ ACQUISTIONS | PURPOSE |
|---|---|---|
| Johnson & Johnson | Tengion and Novocell | Johnson & Johnson's venture capital arm took an equity stake in Tengion, which is making bladders and other organ in the lab, and led a $25 million round of funding for Novocell. |
| Pfizer | Athersys, Wisconsin Alumni Research Foundation | Pfizer inked a $111 million deal to license the rights to develop Athersys' cell therapy for inflammatory bowel disease. In February 2011, the company scrapped programs in RNAi and regenerative medicine as part of a strategic realignment. |
| Roche | UCLA Broad Stem Cell Research Center | Discoveries made by UCLA scientists will help provide Roche scientists with insight on academic research and can be used to refine Roche opeartions or develop new applications. |
| GlaxoSmithKline | Harvard University | GSK and the Harvard Stem Cell Institute announced that they entered into a five-year, $25 million-plus collaborative build a unique alliance in regenerative and stem cell science. |
| Novartis | Harvard University | The Novartis Institutes for Biomedical Research initiated a multi-year project with a group at Harvard Stem Cell Institute in the stem cell and regenerative medicine area. |
| AstraZeneca | UCL | AstraZeneca and scientists at the UCL Institute of Opthalmology will collaborate to identify new thereapeutic tools that can modulate the regenerative capacity of stem cells. |
| Astellas | Cytori | Entered into a strategic agreement to evaluate the potential of adipose (fat) derived regenerative cells for the treatment of serious illnesses for which no treatments exists. |
| Teva | Cephalon (Mesoblast) | Teva Pharmaceuticals paid $6.2 billion for Cephalon soon after the latter's partnership with regenerative medicine company Mesoblast. Teva cited Cephalon's deal with Mesoblast as being one of the elements that inspired the takeover. |
| Shire | Advanced BioHealing | Shire established a new regenerative medicine business unit through the acquisition of Advanced BioHealing. The creation of the new strategic tissue regeneration platform works to complement Shire's existing specialty focus and biologics manufacturing capability. |
| Sanofi | Genzyme | As part of Sanofi's $20.1 billion deal for Genzyme, Sanofi gets access to Genzyme's regenerative medicine assets, including the two cell therapy products Genzyme has on the market, Carticel and Epicel. |

*Source: Company Websites, Bloomberg, the Wall Street Journal*

## Replacement parts

The question is can emerging medical technologies not only help people live longer, enhance patient care and quality of life, and improve clinical outcomes, but also be used to actually shift the cost curve on heart disease, stroke, and neurological disease to improve the economic efficiency of clinical care? That's the hope behind regenerative medicine, which not only seeks to treat disease, but reverse its effects and cure what previously could not be cured [SEE FIGURE 2.7].

Though regenerative medicine is often thought simply as stem cell therapies, it actually refers to a much broader range of technologies [SEE BREAK-OUT—REGENERATIVE MEDICINE BY TYPE]. The emerging area of medicine uses living tissue or cells to repair or replace tissues or organ function that has been lost, damaged or destroyed. Proponents envision a time when custom, lab-grown organs can replace ones that have ceased to function adequately. "If human cell-based technology is to become the third arm of medicine along with small molecules and macromolecules, such as recombinant proteins, it will need to address some of the big remaining health issues that are currently poorly served, and do so affordably," wrote Chris Mason and Peter Dunhill of the **Advanced Centre for Biochemical Engineering** at the **University College London** in a 2008 analysis that argues that in the United States alone, in just five indications

# Government Wins Stem Cell Victory

### Federal judge rules Dickey-Wicker does not prohibit federal funding of human embryonic stem cell research

The federal judge who stunned researchers in 2010 when he placed an injunction on federal funding of human embryonic stem cell research in a suit that said such funding violates federal law, issued a summary judgment in 2011 in the case that allows such funding to continue.

The case *Sherley v. Sebelius*, brought by two researchers focused on adult stem cells, charged that federal funding of human embryonic stem cell research violates the *Dickey-Wicker Amendment*. The amendment, a rider to an appropriations bill, prohibits the **U.S. Department of Health and Human Services** from funding research that involves the destruction of human embryos.

*"…Such research is not 'research in which a human embryo or embryos are destroyed.' "*

**U.S. District Judge Royce Lamberth**

*Writing in a 2011 summary judgment*

In August 2010, **U.S. District Court** Judge Royce Lamberth imposed a temporary injunction on federal funding of human embryonic stem cell research saying all human embryonic research is research in which a human embryo is destroyed and is therefore prohibited by the Dickey-Wicker amendment. The decision overturned guidelines crafted by the **Obama administration** that lifted the restrictions put into place by President George W. Bush. The Obama administration argued its guidelines don't violate the Dickey-Wicker amendment because they do not allow for federal funding to derive new stem cell lines.

An appeals court issued a stay on the injunction the following month and then in April 2011, it ruled that the **National Institutes of Health's** implicit interpretation of Dickey-Wicker was reasonable and vacated the injunction in a 2-1 decision that returned the case to Lamberth.

Lamberth, in issuing summary judgment for the government, expressed his reluctance in reaching his ruling, but said he was bound to the appeals court's interpretation that the Dickey-Wicker amendment was ambiguous as to what constitutes research and that the NIH's interpretation was reasonable. "This court, following the D.C. Circuit's reasoning and conclusions, must find that defendants reasonably interpreted the Dickey-Wicker Amendment to permit funding for human embryonic stem cell research because such research is not 'research in which a human embryo or embryos are destroyed…'," wrote Lamberth.

Stem cell groups and researchers hailed the ruling saying it cleared away legal uncertainty and will restore needed stability to the field. "Young scientists uncertain about future funding might opt to work in areas other than stem cell science, which could slow progress toward new cures," said **California Institute for Regenerative Medicine** chair Jonathan Thomas. "This ruling is a positive step, but with the possibility that the case might be appealed, a predictable source of state and private funding continues to be essential."

Hank Greely, director of the **Center for Law and the Biosciences** at **Stanford University** in a blog post following the summary judgment called Lamberth's opinion "graceful, gracious, and fully professional." He said even though Lamberth disagreed with the appeals court "he did what a judge is supposed to do in applying the law in light of his position in the judiciary hierarchy." Greely expects the latest ruling to be appealed, but expects the plaintiffs will not be successful.

Not everyone was happy about the ruling. The conservative policy group the **Family Research Council** called it "disappointing" that Lamberth had to reverse his earlier decision, but said he was "constrained by the previous Appellate Court split decision."

"This is unfortunate," said David Prentice, the Family Research Council's Senior Fellow for Life Sciences, "as this allows the flow of taxpayer funds to continue for this unethical, scientifically unworthy embryonic stem cell research." ∎

# HIV Gene Therapy Trial Awaiting FDA Green Light

## Calimmune backed with $20 million from California's stem cell agency

**David Baltimore**
*Nobel Laureate;*
*Co-founder,*
*Calimmune*

**C**alimmune, a young biotech that has garnered $20 million in grant money from the **California Institute for Regenerative Medicine**, said it is in discussions with regulators to begin a phase 1/2 trial of its experimental gene therapy that aims to alter key immune cells in patients to render them immune to HIV.

The four-year-old company, founded by several top scientists, including Nobel Laureate David Baltimore, seeks to alter a patient's T-cells so they are without the protein CCR5, a co-receptor exploited by HIV to enter and hijack the immune cells. Baltimore more than ten years ago proposed gene therapy as a potential approach to treating the virus through the use of genetically modified blood stem cells.

Though Calimmune's approach is unique, it is not alone in trying to alter a patient's T-cells to mimic the naturally occurring mutation, found in about 1 percent of Europeans and rendering them impervious to the virus. Among others seeking to apply gene therapy to this end is **Sangamo Biosciences**, which initiated an early-stage trial of its zinc finger protein technology in 2009.

The case of an HIV-positive leukemia patient in Berlin who needed a bone marrow transplant to treat his cancer has validated the potential of such approaches. In 2007, the man was given a transplant from a matching bone marrow donor who naturally had the mutation that leaves him unable to produce the CCR5 protein, the gateway used by the virus to enter the T-cell.

However, such bone marrow transplants are viewed as too costly and risky to be a practical treatment. Nevertheless, it showed that a patient could be rid of the virus by giving rise to a population of T-cells that could not be invaded by the virus.

> The treatment would alter a patient's T-cells so they are without the protein CCR5, a co-receptor exploited by HIV to enter and hijack the immune cells.

Calimmune's approach involves taking the stem cells contained in the bone marrow—the hematopoietic stem cells that give rise to the blood and immune system—and using RNA interference in the lab to alter the cells so they don't encode for the CCR5 protein. Those cells are then put back into the patient. The hope is that a single administration of the cells could provide lifetime protection to an HIV patient.

Though the company says it is too early to speculate on how such a therapy would be priced, it could provide not only a life-saving therapy, but one with a substantial economic impact. The company estimates the cost of antiretroviral therapy for an HIV patient costs $25,000 a year and close to $750,000 over the lifetime of the average patient.

"CIRM has substantively increased the funding trajectory of the state's biotech industry in the past two years," say Ellen Feigal, vice president of research and development for CIRM. "The pairing of business and regulatory acumen with the scientific research is a key component of CIRM's strategy to advance our translational programs into clinical trials in the next few years."

"Our mission is to eradicate the ravages of HIV," says Louis Breton, CEO of Calimmune. "We are focused on helping people gain greater freedom from medication, from high cost burdens, and from the longer-term toll of this formidable disease." ∎

including heart failure, insulin-dependent diabetes, stroke, Parkinson's disease, and spinal cord injury, regenerative medicine could save $250 billion a year. Other diseases, such as Alzheimer's disease and end-stage renal failure were not included because at the time of the study the authors said there was not enough early-stage evidence to suggest that regenerative medicine therapies would be addressing those diseases. "One of the strongest arguments for regenerative medicine is that human cell-based therapies have the potential," the authors write, "which most molecular medicines for chronic conditions do not, of returning the patient to health with respect to that condition without further intervention."

Consider Cleveland-based **Athersys**, a development-stage biotechnology company developing a product called MultiStem for inflammatory, neurological, cardiovascular, and autoimmune disorders. MultiStem is derived from progenitor cells harvested from the bone marrow of young, healthy donors. Like stem cells, progenitor cells have the ability to differentiate. The company says it can make hundreds of thousands of doses from a single donor.

The cells have potent healing properties. They naturally home to areas of damage within the body and limit tissue damage and inflammation from injury, promote healing and repair, promote formation of new blood vessels, protect and preserve tissue after ischemic injury, and interact with other cell types to promote healing and repair. The company has a number of ongoing clinical trials underway including in heart attack, stroke, and inflammatory bowel disease.

And while many people may think of small, young companies like Athersys leading the charge in the field, the reality is that major pharmaceutical companies, through partnerships and acquisitions, have established a significant foothold in the area of regenerative medicine. Pfizer is a partner of Athersys for its MultiStem product in inflammatory bowel disease. Other major pharmaceutical companies with programs in regenerative medicine include **Johnson & Johnson**, **Roche**, **GlaxoSmithKline**, **Baxter**, and **Astellas**. In 2011, several other major pharmaceutical companies entered the fray through acquisitions. **Sanofi** took a leading position in cell therapies through its 2011 purchase of **Genzyme** for $20.1 billion. Similarly **Teva Pharmaceutical Indus-**

> In June 2011, doctors in Stockholm successfully implanted a lab-grown human trachea in a patient for the first time. The trachea was created from an artificial scaffold soaked in stem cells from the recipient's bone marrow.

tries' $6.8 billion purchase of **Cephalon** puts it in partnership with **Mesoblast**, which is developing regenerative therapies based on adult stem cells. **Shire** also added itself to the list when it acquired **Advanced BioHealing** for $750 million just hours before the tissue regeneration company was set to go public [*SEE FIGURE 2.9*]. Advanced BioHealing is the maker of Dermagraft, a bioengineered skin substitute used to treat diabetic foot ulcers. Eventually, proponents of regenerative medicine expect not just cells and tissues to be replaced, but organs with replacement organs grown in the lab [*SEE GRAPHIC SPARE PARTS*].

If that sounds too futuristic, think again. In June 2011, more than a decade after the first human bladder was grown from scratch, doctors at the **Karolinska University Hospital** in Stockholm successfully implanted a lab-grown human trachea in a patient for the first time. The trachea, grown for a man whose own trachea became blocked with an inoperable tumor, was created from an artificial scaffold soaked in stem cells from the man's own bone marrow. It was prepared at the Karolinska Institute with help from University College London and implanted at Karolinska University Hospital in Sweden and, as of November 2011, the man was reportedly doing well. A second stem cell-seeded bioartificial tracheal transplant has already been done and a third is in the works.

Many of the biggest challenges to the creation of viable lab-grown organs have been addressed. The design and selection of bio-materials for manufactured organs that will do well in the human body

# EU High Court Bans Embryonic Stem Cell Patents

## Critics of the decision say it will dull Europe's competitive edge

Europe's highest court in October 2011 ruled that scientific researchers in the European Union cannot patent inventions relying on the destruction of human embryos. The ruling by the **Court of Justice of the European Union** won't prevent the use of human embryos in research. But it does make the funding of such research significantly less attractive for commercial entities, since the results will not be able to secure intellectual property protection.

"With this unfortunate decision, the fruits of years of translational research by European scientists will be wiped away and left to the non-European countries," said Oliver Brüstle, Director of the **Institute for Reconstructive Neurology** at the **University of Bonn**, in a comment to **EuroStemCell**, an association of European stem cell and regenerative medicine research labs.

The decision arose out of a dispute in which **Greenpeace** sought to invalidate a 1997 patent awarded to Brüstle for the isolation and purification of neural precursor cells produced from human embryonic stem cells used to treat neurological diseases, such as Parkinson's disease. Greenpeace argued that the use of precursor cells derived from human embryos violates elements of both European Union and international laws that forbid the patenting of inventions for which commercial use could be considered contrary to public order or morality.

The court reviewed the question of whether legal concepts forbidding the granting of patents on uses of human embryos for industrial or commercial purposes also cover the use of human embryos for purposes of scientific research. It decided "the grant of a patent for an invention implies, in principle, its industrial or commercial application." The use of human embryos for therapeutic or diagnostic purposes applied to the human embryo, such as to correct a malformation and improve the chances of life will remain patentable. ∎

over time is mostly solved. So too is the challenge of getting enough of at least certain kinds of a patient's own cells to grow outside of their body. "Nature has designed you to regenerate," says Anthony Atala, director of the **Wake Forest Institute for Regenerative Medicine**. "So in a way we're unlocking some of the mechanisms that nature does well."

But, despite the tremendous number of advances, major scientific and funding challenges are still ahead, Atala says. On the biological front, not all cells grow well in the lab, outside the human body. These include liver, nerve, and pancreatic cells. Also, it is difficult for certain organs to achieve the proper vascularity—the supply of blood to get those organs to survive. Researchers at Atala's lab are trying a number of different approaches to overcome the challenge of vascularization in solid organs. In one approach, the team is creating organs using sophisticated printers that can lay down vasculature and tissues one layer at a time. In another approach, it is trying to coat structures piecemeal with cells. There are even experiments

being run using de-cellularized organs. "We take mild detergents, leaving just the natural scaffold of the human organ," he says. "No Ajax."

Two other approaches are also being tried. One uses a combination of growth factors and cytokines to induce cell regeneration of an organ itself while a different approach simply employs cellular therapy to repair a damaged organ without the aim of regenerating a new one. "You're dealing with these challenges every day. There are really very minute improvements day after day, month after month," says Atala. "You have to look at these organs from a 360 perspective—you can't just hook it up and make it work. You have to look at all these areas, because that's what the body does."

The biggest biological challenge that remains is solid organs, says Atala. About 90 percent of patients on transplant lists are waiting for a kidney. But while printed kidney structures are being prototyped and studied in Atala's lab today, they remain years away from functional and clinical use and a solid organ has yet to be implanted into a patient for a clinical trial. Furthermore, moving regenerative technologies closer to commercial viability is a costly and difficult process.

**Tengion,** a clinical-stage regenerative medicine company, knows the challenges well. The East Norriton, Pennsylvania-based firm, formerly advised by Atala, is focused on developing a Neo-Urinary Conduit. The conduit, for use in bladder cancer patients in need of urinary diversion following removal of the bladder, is grown from a patient's own cells in order to avoid rejection. But despite interest from **Medtronic,** which holds a right of first refusal on Tengion's pre-clinical kidney regeneration program, it has found investors to be wary of the risks associated with regenerative medicine. In May 2011, its share price was nearly halved following news that an initial clinical trial of the conduit would require changes in the associated surgical procedure and post-surgical care, extending the time to obtain interim trial data. Now, with a new CEO appointed in December 2011, the company is seeking to reinvigorate interest in the potential of its organ regeneration platform in hopes of wooing a new partner or financing. "Nobody wants to accept the fact that it's ten years and millions of dollars before that will happen," said Mark Stejbach, then-vice president and chief commercial officer of Tengion. "We're involved in doing that hard work. The challenge for us is that we feel like we're working on the important innovations that the industry needs, yet you [need to] have a lot of cash on the sidelines."

Critical to spurring investment in the sector, says the **Alliance for Regenerative Medicine**'s Van Bokkelen, is making the economic case for the payoff regenerative therapies stand to deliver. It's a case companies need to make not only to investors, but also to payers, who will ultimately decide whether or not these technologies deliver enough benefit to justify their costs. "We all recognize that there are enormous pressures on the healthcare system and that we need to do something to address that," says Van Bokkelen. "I think the most powerful thing that companies can do is to take this challenge head-on, and when they are running clinical studies, incorporate into their clinical trials analyses of pharmacoeconomic effectiveness. [We must] not just to look at whether or not we are improving clinical outcomes, but whether we are doing that in a cost effective way."

Biogerontologists believe we can reduce the human and economic toll of the sharp rise in the number of elderly people through public health policies together with medical and scientific advancements.

## The Plasticity of Aging

A group of biogerentologists writing in *Science Translational Medicine* in June 2010 lay out a case for investing in research to "preempt a global aging crisis." They call for a three-pronged approach to retard, arrest, and reverse aging damage. They argue that what the past two decades of research has shown is that aging is plastic. Through dietary manipulation or genetic manipulation, scientists have been able to reduce the cellular damage of aging, enhance repair, and increase the tolerance of the molecular damage caused by aging in certain species. They argue that through public health and medical advancements, the modulation of the metabolic determinants of aging damage, and regenerative therapies, we can prevent the human and economic toll being brought about by the sharp rise in the number of elderly people.

That, however, will require new policy priorities. "What we can be certain of today is that a policy of aging as usual will lead to enormous humanitarian, social, and financial costs," the authors write. "Efforts to avert that scenario are unequivocally merited, even if those efforts are costly and their success and full consequences uncertain. To realize any chance of success, the drive to tackle biological aging head-on must begin now." ■

# Regenerative Medicine: Spare Parts

Biotech companies and medical universities are developing technology for regenerating and replacing damaged and worn out body parts. Here are some of the projects and their developers:

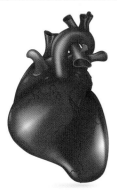

## Heart Valves, Arteries, and Veins

Genetically engineered proteins have already been successfully used to re-grow blood vessels. And researchers have successfully implanted manipulated fibroblast cells into mice that transformed into functional, beating muscle within weeks.

**Companies:**
- Athersys
- Tengion
- Organogenesis

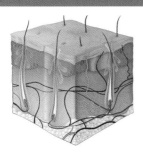

## Skin

Shire bought Advanced BioHealing for $750 million in 2011, an indication of more interest in regenerative medicine. Companies like Advanced BioHealing and Organogenesis are pursuing bioengineered skin grafts for chronic conditions like venous leg ulcers and diabetic foot ulcers.

**Companies:**
- CytoMedix
- Advanced BioHealing
- LifeCell
- Integra LifeSciences
- Advanced Tissue
- Organogenesis
- Stratatech
- ACell
- Theregen
- McGowan Institute for Regenerative Medicine at the University of Pittsburgh

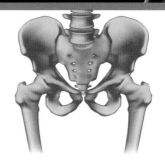

## Bone

Bone-growth factors or stem cells are inserted into a porous material cut to a specific shape, creating new limbs. Mesoblast is developing a new technology that can generate both new bone and new blood vessels, enabling better bone regeneration in leg fractures.

**Companies:**
- BioMimetic Therapeutics
- Citagenix
- Osiris Therapeutics
- Mesoblast

## Trachea

Surgeons in Sweden removed a malignant tumor from a man's trachea and replaced it with a tissue-engineered trachea created from the man's own stem cells.

**Companies:**
• McGowan Institute for Regenerative Medicine at the University of Pittsburgh
• Advanced Center for Translational Regenerative Medicine

## Spinal Cord/ Nerve Regeneration:

Rather than treating spinal cord injuries with embryonic stem-cell based approaches, Axonia Medical is exploring ways to use a novel technology to grow axons outside the body and then implant them in injured limbs.

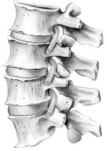

**Companies:**
• Regeneron
• StemCells Inc.
• ReNeuron
• AxoGen
• Axonia Medical

## Bladder

After successfully growing bladders from skin cells and implanting them in sheep, Children's Hospital in Boston is planning on trying the same process in babies born without a bladder.

**Companies:**
• Tengion
• McGowan Institute for Regenerative Medicine at the University of Pittsburgh
• ACell
• Children's Hospital in Boston
• Regeneron
• StemCells Inc.
• ReNeuron
• AxoGen
• Axonia Medical

## Cartilage

Genzyme's Carticel is the first and only FDA-approved cell therapy product used to repair cartilage damage in knees using a patient's own cells.

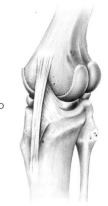

**Companies:**
• Genzyme
• Histogenics
• Osiris Therapeutics
• TiGenix
• CellSeed
• Mesoblast
• BioMimetic
• StemCells Inc.
• ReNeuron
• AxoGen
• Axonia Medical

SOURCE: Burrill & Company, Business Week, Company Websites

# A Watched Pot
# Begins to Boil

As impatience seemed to grow among scientists and the public over the slow arrival of personalized medicine during 2011, the U.S. Food and Drug Administration approved a spate of new personalized therapies, studies touted the economic benefits of new predictive tests, the pipeline of powerful new targeted therapies based on the genetics underlying diseases grew, and the cost of sequencing continued its rapid decline, moving medical science closer to an ever greater understanding of not only disease, but also wellness. Complexity has indeed been a barrier to the development of personalized medicine, but scientific challenges have not been the sole barrier to realizing its promise. Although the environment is evolving, product developers must still contend with a system where regulators have yet to put into place clear guidelines for addressing issues of personalized medicine, reimbursement processes still make it difficult for molecular diagnostics companies to get paid for the value they provide, and healthcare systems and doctors continue to operate in a world of perverse financial incentives. With the approval of new personalized medicine drugs and incentives for the various players within the healthcare ecosystem, work to remove the barriers that exist has begun. The question is not whether personalized medicine will become a reality, but how quickly and how broadly it will become integrated into medical practice.

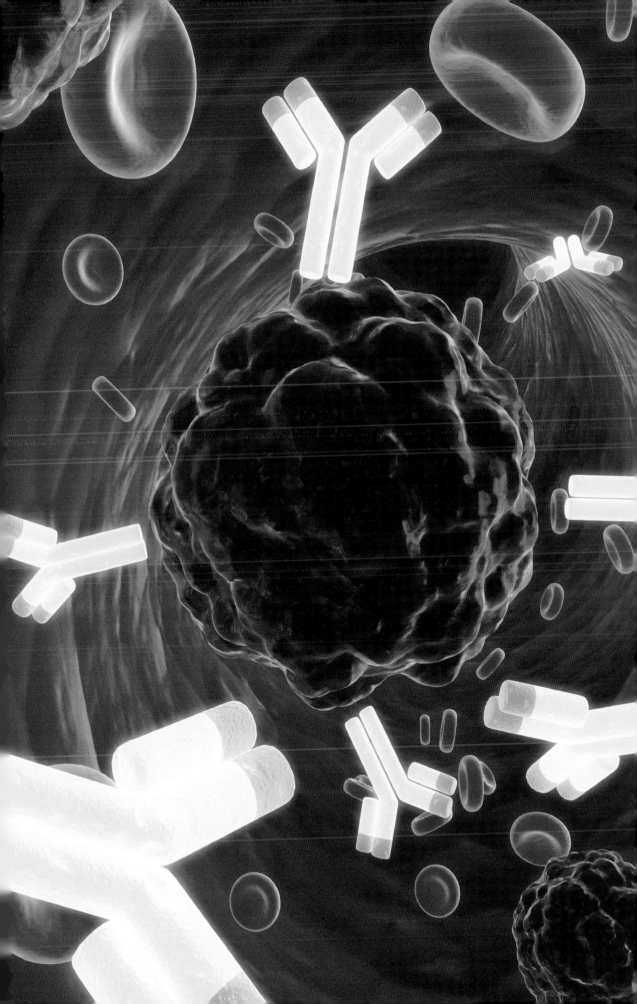

# Chapter 3:

# A WATCHED POT BEGINS TO BOIL

In August 2006, researchers at **Duke University** published an article in the *New England Journal of Medicine* saying they had developed a model that could predict which lung cancer patients were likely to experience a recurrence of a tumor and therefore would benefit from chemotherapy. In November of that year, the same researchers published a separate study in *Nature Medicine* that said they had found genetic markers to predict a patient's response to a specific type of chemotherapy.

The studies suggested a groundbreaking discovery that could advance cancer therapy and make personalized medicine a reality for a growing number of patients. Reflecting their enthusiasm for their findings, the researchers formed the company **Oncogenomics**, later renamed **CancerGuide Diagnostics**, to commercialize the discoveries.

But rather than providing a breakthrough in cancer treatments, the work would upend careers, create institutional embarrassment, and end in litigation. Eventually publications retracted four scientific papers relating to the work, Duke halted three clinical trials, and the **American Cancer Society** withdrew a grant. Anil Potti, the researcher at the center of the evolving controversy, would resign and another would lose his prominent post. Duke, the **National Cancer Institute**, and the **Institute of Medicine** all launched investigations. What was left has been a

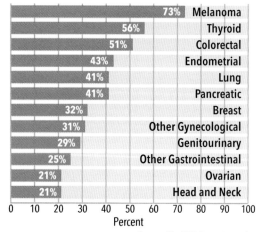

*Figure 3.1* **PERCENT OF CANCERS DRIVEN BY MUTATIONS**

Percentage of patients whose tumors were driven by certain genetic mutations that could be targets for specific drugs, by type of cancer.

| Percent | Cancer type |
| --- | --- |
| 73% | Melanoma |
| 56% | Thyroid |
| 51% | Colorectal |
| 43% | Endometrial |
| 41% | Lung |
| 41% | Pancreatic |
| 32% | Breast |
| 31% | Other Gynecological |
| 29% | Genitourinary |
| 25% | Other Gastrointestinal |
| 21% | Ovarian |
| 21% | Head and Neck |

*Source: The Wall Street Journal*

> Studies touted the economic benefits of new predictive tests; the pipeline of powerful new targeted therapies based on the genetics underlying diseases grew; and the cost of sequencing continued its rapid decline, moving medical science closer to an ever-greater understanding of not only disease, but also wellness.

rather public hand wringing about the failure of genomics research to deliver on a promised era of personalized medicine.

The Duke case unfolded at a propitious time for personalized medicine. As scientists and the public seemed to be growing impatient over the unfulfilled promises of an era of personalized medicine ushered in with the mapping of the human genome, the **U.S. Food and Drug Administration** approved a spate of new personalized therapies; studies touted the economic benefits of new predictive tests; the pipeline of powerful new targeted therapies based on the genetics underlying diseases grew; and the cost of sequencing continued its rapid decline, moving medical science closer to an ever-greater understanding of not only disease, but also wellness.

## A sordid tale

A lawsuit filed in September 2011 against **Duke University**, **Duke University Health System**, the researchers, and others weaves a troubling tale of unethical research practices, sloppy errors, and flawed science, alleging the original study used data improperly obtained from the National Cancer Institute and that the researcher who had generated the NCI data had warned both Duke and the *New England Journal of Medicine* that the Duke researchers' analysis was "highly suspect." The study also came to the attention of two researchers at **The University of Texas MD Anderson Cancer Center**, who set out to replicate the results of the research and found they were unable to do so. MD Anderson's Keith Baggerly and Kevin Coombes contacted the Duke researchers and eventually published studies saying that the Duke research was faulty and that any trials based on the research exposed

patients to potentially ineffective or dangerous treatments. Throughout the challenges, the researchers denied significant problems existed with their data.

By May of 2007, the first clinical trial of the diagnostic Duke developed to guide cancer treatments for patients with late-stage, non-small cell lung cancer was under way. Potti, along with Joseph Nevins, then director of the **Center for Applied Genomics & Technology** at Duke, eventually published two corrections to their *Nature Medicine* article, but continued to deny their results were flawed or unreliable. In October of 2007, they initiated a second clinical trial that sought to use their test in early non-small cell lung cancer. MD Anderson's Baggerly and Coombes published a study of the Duke research in the *Annals of Applied Statistics* in September 2009 and, a month later, *The Cancer Letter* picked up on the study outlining errors in labeling of the gene signatures for one of the chemotherapeutics. Following publication in *The Cancer Letter*, the National Cancer Institute contacted Duke to express concerns. Duke halted enrollment in three clinical trials and both Duke and NCI initiated investigations. According to a letter published online by **Duke University School of Medicine** in January 2010, a panel of experts was able to validate Nevins' and Potti's research. That month, Duke restarted the trials. But a **Freedom of Information Act** request from *The Cancer Letter* to NCI for the Duke report found that despite the university's public pronouncements, the panel had in fact not reproduced the work of the two researchers. When *The Cancer Letter* later reported that Potti was not, as he had claimed in grant applications, a Rhodes Scholar, the American Cancer Society withdrew its funding for the trials and Duke suspended the trials once again in July 2010. Potti resigned from Duke in November 2010. Nevins no longer heads the university's Center for Applied Genomics & Technology. The Institute of Medicine is investigating what went wrong at Duke and is expected to issue its report in mid-2012.

Months before the filing of the lawsuit by clinical trials participants and their families, the unfolding scandal provided fodder for a front-page story in *The New York Times*. The story appeared in July 2011, using the Duke scandal to call attention to the failings of the emerging field of personalized medicine. It pointed to two other cases where enthusiasm for the business prospects for diagnostics to guide cancer treatment led companies to race to market products not yet ready for prime time.

"While researchers agree there is great promise in this science, it has yet to yield many reliable methods for diagnosing cancer or identifying the best treatment," wrote *The Times'* Gina Kolata. "Instead, as patients and their doctors try to make critical decisions about serious illnesses, they may be getting worthless information that is based on bad science."

## A familiar ring

As *The New York Times* noted, the Duke case is not an isolated incident. Other molecular diagnostics have faced controversies over their accuracy and have been questioned as a result of analyses that raised concerns about a rush to commercialize them before showing that they indeed provided sound scientific guidance upon which doctors could base treatment decisions.

A March 2011 article in *Nature* that examined the problems surrounding the development of reliable tests for early detection of cancer pointed to the case of **Laboratory Corporation of America's** ovarian cancer test OvaSure, which had been pulled from the market after four months when it came under the scrutiny of the FDA.

The test was based on a panel of biomarkers developed by a **Yale University** researcher. A study underlying the test had come under criticism by other researchers who found fault in the statistical model used to determine the predictive value of the test. Statisticians at NCI's **Early Detection Research Network** discovered a significant flaw in the statistical model used by the

Yale researcher. In calculating the positive predictive value of the test—a measure of the test's ability to accurately identify patients with the disease, the Yale researcher determined the test had a positive predictive value of 99.3 percent. But the NCI researchers found the positive predictive value of the test was actually 6.5 percent. Such a number would indicate that the test was not reliable enough to use. The difference between the calculations lay in the fact that the Yale researcher relied on the study population to determine the

> The Duke case is not
> an isolated incident.

prevalence of ovarian cancer, but the NCI statisticians said the correct way to calculate the reliability of the test required the use of the prevalence of ovarian cancer in post-menopausal women overall.

The controversy over the test grew. In June 2008, LabCorp began marketing the test to women with a high risk of ovarian cancer. Critics complained it was premature to market the test and expressed concern that false positives could subject women to unnecessary surgeries. The FDA notified the company in August 2008 that the data seemed insufficient to support claims it made for the test. A month later it charged the company didn't have the necessary clearance to market the test. LabCorp disagreed with the agency, but removed the test from the market nevertheless.

During a December 2010 meeting of a committee assembled by the Institute of Medicine to discuss lessons learned on developing molecular diagnostics and bringing them into the clinic, Dan Hayes, a breast cancer researcher at the **University of Michigan** offered a perspective on the difficulties faced in bringing worthwhile diagnostics into the clinic. "Why don't we have assays out there with this enormous promise?" *Nature* quoted him as saying. "It's either because these things just don't work, or because we've used sloppy science to test them." [See Sidebar DTC]

## Sloppy science and useless information

There is a case to be made that sloppy science has become an issue of concern. In an August 2011

# DTC Genetic Companies Evolve

## Business models diverge as companies seek path to profits

**B**usiness models in the direct-to-consumer genetics field are diverging as companies face regulatory uncertainty, consumer resistance, and difficult capital markets. Though some continue to provide information to individuals about the substance and meaning of their DNA, they are betting that their best opportunity for success lies elsewhere.

**DNA Direct** is one example of how these companies have evolved. It was acquired in 2010 by **Medco Health Solutions** and now operates as a subsidiary of the pharmacy benefits manager. In 2005, DNA Direct's tailored messages on the home page of its web site primarily to consumers. Today, the company provides a list of services to help patients, physicians, hospitals, and payers understand and navigate the world of genetic testing.

Industry watchers say while most companies haven't given up on their consumer focus, it has shifted. Some companies are focusing more on working with physicians and employer groups. Others are emphasizing supporting researchers. And still others are looking to additional models to leverage their customer base to conduct research.

"They've definitely morphed. If you go back to the beginning of what most people generally think of as the DTC era, there was this thought that people were going to be interested and going to pay to access their genomes directly," says Dan Vorhaus, editor of *Genomics Law Report* and an attorney with **Robinson, Bradshaw & Hinson**. "It's changed a lot since then. I'm not sure people have given up on the consumer focus, it's just shifted."

The pivotal shift for another DTC company, **Navigenics**, came more than two years ago, when it began to focus on the use of genomics to motivate behavior change, such as diet, exercise and compliance. "If you look at who those sorts of behavior changes are most important to, it is health plans, employers, and physicians," says Vance Vanier, CEO of Navigenics. "For the last couple of years, we've focused our efforts on partnering with those organizations where our genomic service is part of a broader prevention package."

In April 2012, Navigenics announced a partnership with **Highmark**, one of the nation's largest **Blue Cross** and **Blue Shield** plans. Under the partnership, Highmark offers a personalized wellness and prevention program to the employers it covers that starts with Navigenics identifying genetic risk factors of a covered employee through DNA analysis using a saliva sample. Navigenics selects only health conditions where it says genetic insight can guide an individual to an informed plan of action.

Results are coupled with access to a board-certified genetic counselor, the ability to coordinate with personal physicians, and the tools and resources to understand steps to address the identified health risks in conjunction with an individual's overall health profile. Highmark then offers its personalized wellness program through its group customer relationships.

For **23andMe**, its consumer business remains an important focus, but it is seeking to build out a community of customers. It has dropped the price of its service to $99, but at that price also requires customers to subscribe for one year to a $9 a month service that provides interpretative tools and information on an ongoing basis. It is also entering into partnerships with institutions conducting research using customers who volunteer to participate.

To that end, the critical task is to build a broad base of participants willing to share not only their genetic information, but information about their health and behavior. Akin to the kind of social network research model of **PatientsLikeMe**, the inducement is not only to participate in research that could improve understanding of diseases, but also to get access to greater levels of information about themselves as it becomes available. ∎

*Figure 3.2* **SPURIOUS SCIENCE**

**Retractions are rising across most fields...**

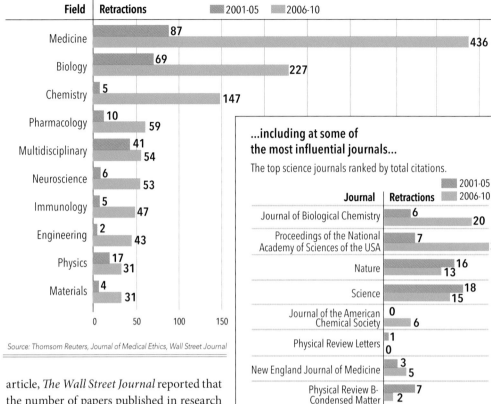

| Field | Retractions | 2001-05 | 2006-10 |
|---|---|---|---|
| Medicine | | 87 | 436 |
| Biology | | 69 | 227 |
| Chemistry | | 5 | 147 |
| Pharmacology | | 10 | 59 |
| Multidisciplinary | | 41 | 54 |
| Neuroscience | | 6 | 53 |
| Immunology | | 5 | 47 |
| Engineering | | 2 | 43 |
| Physics | | 17 | 31 |
| Materials | | 4 | 31 |

**...including at some of the most influential journals...**

The top science journals ranked by total citations.

| Journal | Retractions | 2001-05 | 2006-10 |
|---|---|---|---|
| Journal of Biological Chemistry | | 6 | 20 |
| Proceedings of the National Academy of Sciences of the USA | | 7 | 24 |
| Nature | | 16 | 13 |
| Science | | 18 | 15 |
| Journal of the American Chemical Society | | 0 | 6 |
| Physical Review Letters | | 1 | 0 |
| New England Journal of Medicine | | 3 | 5 |
| Physical Review B-Condensed Matter | | 7 | 2 |
| Astrophysical Journal | | 0 | 0 |
| Applied Physics Letters | | 4 | 5 |

**...while lag time grows between publication and retraction.**

Average time in medicine and biology. Based on an analysis of 742 medicine and biology papers retracted from the PubMed database

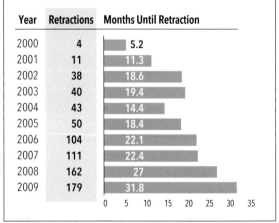

| Year | Retractions | Months Until Retraction |
|---|---|---|
| 2000 | 4 | 5.2 |
| 2001 | 11 | 11.3 |
| 2002 | 38 | 18.6 |
| 2003 | 40 | 19.4 |
| 2004 | 43 | 14.4 |
| 2005 | 50 | 18.4 |
| 2006 | 104 | 22.1 |
| 2007 | 111 | 22.4 |
| 2008 | 162 | 27 |
| 2009 | 179 | 31.8 |

article, *The Wall Street Journal* reported that the number of papers published in research journals has increased 44 percent since 2001, while the number of retractions have grown 15-fold. The article, based on data compiled by *Thomson Reuters Web of Sciences*, draws on an index of 11,600 peer-reviewed journals. The service found that the number of retractions in 2010 reached 339, up from just 22 in 2001. A separate analysis of 742 medicine and biology studies retracted between 2000 and 2010 published in the *Journal of Medical Ethics* found retractions related to fraud increased seven-fold between 2004 and 2009. That compares to a doubling of retractions related to error during the same period. [*SEE FIGURE 3.2*]

Among the examples cited by the newspaper is the infamous case of Andrew Wakefield, who produced a study published in *The Lancet* that drew a link between the vaccine administered to children to prevent measles, mumps, and rubella and development of autism. The study caused some parents to opt out of vaccinating their children and a subsequent spike in measles cases in the United Kingdom is blamed on it. British authorities determined Wakefield engaged in serious professional misconduct and took away his medical license. Though *The Lancet* eventually withdrew the paper, it took 12 years after publication to do so.

The frustration expressed about a lack of progress in personalized medicine in the wake of the Duke scandal continues an outpouring of criticism that began with the tenth anniversary of the draft of the human genome.

"For biologists, the genome has yielded one insightful surprise after another," wrote Nicholas Wade in a June 2010 article in *The New York Times*. "But the primary goal of the $3 billion **Human Genome Project**—to ferret out the genetic roots of common diseases like cancer and Alzheimer's and then generate treatments— remains largely elusive. Indeed after 10 years of effort, geneticists are almost back to square one in knowing where to look for the roots of common disease."

J. Craig Venter, whose **Celera Genomics** had entered into a race with the Human Genome Project to map the first human genome, ten years after he stood at a White House press conference alongside his rival, Human Genome Project Director Francis Collins, President Bill Clinton, and U.K. Prime Minster Tony Blair announcing the completion of the draft genome, reflected on the occasion in an interview with the German magazine *Der Speigel*. When asked why it was taking so long for the results of genome research to be applied in medicine, Venter was blunt in his assessment. "Because we have, in truth, learned nothing from the genome other than probabili-

ties," he said. "How does a one or three percent increased risk for something translate into the clinic? It is useless information."

## A return on investment

In the wake of the criticism, others have sought to highlight all that has been accomplished and how much progress has been made. A May 2011 **Battelle Technology Partnership Practice** report that examined the economic impact of the Human Genome Project, called that work "arguably the single most influential investment to have been made in modern science." It found that in the ten years since the U.S. government made its $3.8 billion investment, it is paying dividends, not only in the genomic revolution's influence in healthcare, but in fields including renewable energy development, industrial biotechnology, agricultural biosciences, and other fields. [*SEE FIGURE 3.3*]. The report, funded by the **Life Technologies Foundation**, found that between 1988 and 2010, the project and associated research and industry activity directly and indirectly generated $796 billion in economic output in the United States, produced $244 billion in personal income for Americans, and created 3.8 million job years of employment. In fact, in 2010 alone, Battelle found the genomics-enabled industry generated $3.7 billion in federal taxes and $2.3 billion in U.S. state and local taxes, essentially returning in one year nearly the entire investment made by the government over 14 years.

"Some of these impacts are really only just getting started because the genome project revealed a genomic complexity that perhaps most people didn't think was there. What we found with the

*Figure 3.3* **FINANCIAL IMPACT OF THE GENOMIC REVOLUTION (USD B)**

| IMPACT | EMPLOYMENT (JOB/YEARS) | PERSONAL INCOME | OUTPUT | STATE/LOCAL TAX REVENUE | FEDERAL TAX REVENUE |
|---|---|---|---|---|---|
| Direct Effect | 710,819 | 71.4 | 264.8 | 3.5 | 13.0 |
| Indirect Impacts | 1,298,216 | 89.2 | 265.8 | 10.8 | 18.0 |
| Induced Impacts | 1,818,459 | 83.3 | 265.7 | 15.2 | 17.9 |
| Total Impact | 3,827,495 | 243.9 | 796.3 | 29.5 | 48.9 |
| Impact Multiplier | 5.38 | 3.42 | 3.01 | 8.37 | 3.75 |

*Source: Economic Impact of the Human Genome Project, Battelle Technology Partnership Practice*

# BGI Builds Its Global Footprint

Ambitious Chinese sequencing powerhouse emerges

Despite the tough time sequencing companies in the United States have had as governments around the world cut spending, ambitious research projects continued to be announced. More and more, with the announcement of a new genome being sequenced, or a new research partnership announced, it was done so in conjunction with the Chinese sequencing powerhouse **BGI**, formerly the **Beijing Genomics Institute**.

The Chinese government has made BGI's success a high priority, granting the Beijing-based company a $1.5 billion long-term loan in January 2010 to support its development. The institute purchased 128 sequencers from **Illumina**, at the time the largest single purchase of next-generation sequencing systems, helping establish BGI's center in Shenzen, China as the largest sequencing center in the world. It set up an office in Boston in 2010 and has established partnerships and collaborations with leading academic and government research institutions, as well as global biotechnology and pharmaceutical companies. In May 2011, BGI announced it entered into an agreement with **Australian National University** to establish joint research programs and create a genomics sequencing facility at the **John Curtin School of Medical Research** to conduct research. Already work is underway in obesity, clinical depression, personalized therapeutics, and the mouse genome. BGI also has signed an agreement with **Sydney University** to conduct joint research projects.

In 2010, BGI committed $10 million in investment to establish **BGI Europe** in Copenhagen and then in June 2011 it entered into an agreement with the **University of California, Davis** to establish a state-of the-art sequencing facility in Sacramento. That was followed in November 2011 with an announcement that it had formed a partnership with T**he Children's Hospital of Philadelphia** to conduct large-scale human genome sequencing and bioinformatics analysis at the newly established **Joint Genome Center at Children's Hospital**. The partnership will focus on the discovery of genes underpinning rare and common pediatric diseases and capitalize on the pediatric biobank, the largest of its kind, built by CHOP. "Because many of these samples have been linked to clinical data using an electronic medical record we can now follow disease processes into adulthood," says Hakon Hakonarson, director of the **Center for Applied Genomics** at Children's Hospital. "Through our partnership with BGI, we now have a clear path forward into the genomics-based personalized medicine arena."

BGI's sequencing ambitions are multidimensional. It is positioning itself to become a major force in bioinformatics with the launch of an analysis service that uses cloud computing to crunch through the massive amounts of data generated from sequencing genomes. Research labs often don't have the computing power to store and make sense of the flood of data from sequenced genomes. BGI has recently updated its bioinformatics tools to enable a more thorough analysis and exploration of biological data. Cloud computing will be especially useful as the rapid development of genomics looks to identify and annotate single nucleotide polymorphisms, or SNPs, in the context of structure, function, and disease. Several studies have shown that there are a large number of structural variations that have been discovered in the human genome that may have equal or greater functional impacts than SNPs. Already boasting a sequencing output equivalent of 15,000 human genomes, BGI's move to cloud computing will enable it to also assemble and analyze the data. The founders of BGI are also launching a new open-access, peer-reviewed journal called *GigaScience*, which will be based in China and focused on large-scale data. ∎

genome is that human biology, and in fact most organisms' biology, is much more complex and that what was thought to be junk DNA was not junk DNA at all, but involved in regulatory processes," said Simon Tripp, senior director of Battelle's technology partnership practice. "Because it showed the genome was much more complex than previously thought, it is proving harder in some areas, such as the growth of personalized medicine, to bring economic activity to fruition" [*SEE SIDEBAR BGI*].

### Barriers to development and adoption

Complexity has indeed been a barrier to the development of personalized medicine as scientists are finding the need to not only understand the role individual genes play in the onset of disease, but also to understand how a network of genes may be at play in a given disease, as well as the interplay between genes and the environment. With the emergence of low-cost sequencing, researchers are getting good at generating exponentially increasing amounts of data that promise to help piece together parts of the puzzle. The cost of sequencing has shattered Moore's law as it has fallen to around $10,000 in 2011 from roughly $10 million in 2006, according to the **National Human Genome Research Institute** [*SEE FIGURE 3.4*]. The challenge, though, remains to translate that data into new drugs and diagnostics that will prevent, treat, and cure disease. The volume of data, particularly as it has become less expensive to generate, has created a challenge for scientists to manage, store, and analyze [*SEE SIDEBAR BIOINFORMATICS*]. "Data handling is now the bottleneck," David Haussler, director of the **Center for Biomolecular Science & Engineering** at the **University of California, Santa Cruz** told *The New York Times* in November 2011. "It costs more to analyze a genome than to sequence a genome."

Scientific challenges have not been the sole barrier to realizing the promise of personalized medicine. Though the environment is evolving, product developers must still contend with a system where regulators have yet to put into place clear guidelines for addressing the issues of personalized medicine. Reimbursement processes still make it difficult for molecular diagnostics companies to get paid for the value they provide, and the healthcare system and doctors continue

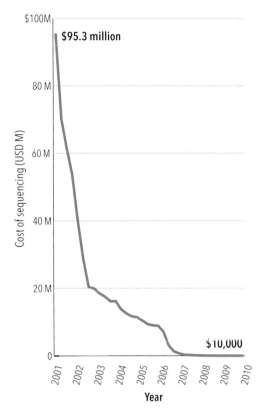

*Figure 3.4* **FALLING COST PER GENOME**

Source: National Human Genome Research Institute

to operate in a world of perverse financial incentives where invasive biopsies are simply more profitable than blood draws that may lead to earlier interventions at considerably lower costs.

Today, because reimbursement codes don't generally exist for the new generation of molecular diagnostics, diagnostics makers have had to use an approach known as "code-stacking" to get paid for their tests. Rather than be paid for the test as a single entity, steps used in performing the test are billed individually. Payers don't particularly like the current system because the codes stack linearly. A test with 100 steps pays 100 times more than a single step. And when a payer is billed for steps, it's not always clear what exactly they are paying for when a claim form moves through the system, only that a test for a gene was performed a certain numbers of times. For diagnostics makers, such a payment system doesn't take into account the benefit a test provides.

"It's blind to value," says Bruce Quinn, senior health policy analyst at the law firm **Foley Hoag**.

# After the Deluge

## Bioinformatics companies seize on the opportunities created by the flood of genomic data

The large quantities of investments and research going into genomics and diagnostics is driving the evolution of healthcare to a more predictive, preventive, and personalized state. But the deluge of genomic information has also spurred the need to store, organize, and analyze the new data.

Bioinformatics is the field of science in which biology, computer science, and information all converge to form a single discipline. Early in the genomics revolution, bioinformatics companies attempted to create and maintain databases to store biological information. Now, however, the ultimate goal is to analyze and interpret the vast array of information (including nucleotide and amino acid sequences, protein domains, and protein structures) and provide a comprehensive picture of the genomics world.

The influx of biological data, as well as a more aggressive effort by the life sciences industry to invest more in personalized medicine, has lead to sharp growth within the global bioinformatics industry.

The bioinformatics market, still nascent, is expected to grow at a compound annual growth rate of nearly 26 percent through 2013 and reach a market capitalization of $6.2 billion, according to **RNCOS Industry Research Solutions**.

As the landscape sits today, the bioinformatics industry is highly fragmented, with several companies offering only specific services. The need for comprehensive deliverables will push the industry towards more multi-faceted companies that can provide more than just specialized services. Some of the major players pushing this trend are **3rd Millennium**, **Accelrys**, **Agilent Technologies**, **IBM Life Sciences**, **Life Technologies**, and **Rosetta Inpharmatics**, according to a report from **BizAcumen**.

As the increased demand for breakthrough personalized therapies continues to spew enormous amounts of genetic and biological information, creating value out of the information flood becomes a priority. The bioinformatics industry has the potential to help companies meet those demands by shortening discovery times and costs as they push towards making personalized medicine a greater reality. ■

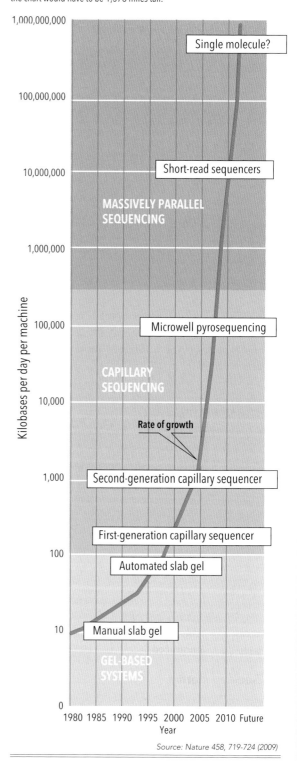

*Figure 3.5* **TECHNOLOGY IS ACCELERATING DATA GENERATION**

**Development of new systems in bioinformatics has led to exponential growth in the amount of biodata.**

This graph is exponential rather than numerical in proportion, with each increment showing a tenfold increase over the previous measure. To be numerically proportionate, with the quantity ten represented as one inch, the chart would have to be 1,578 miles tall.

*Source: Nature 458, 719-724 (2009)*

> "(We) support the development of innovative new targeted
> medicines and their corresponding diagnostic tests."
>
> **Jeffrey Shuren,** *Director, FDA Center for Devices and Radiological Health*

"Especially if you have got a test where say you look at 20 genes in a panel and you spent $30 million to $40 million to generate that test, but the 20 genes, if blindly code-stacked, would pay about $400. You would never recoup your cost."

That is changing, but so too are the demands payers will make for proof that tests perform and deliver the insight they claim to provide. New rules introduced by the **Centers for Medicare and Medicaid Services'** West Coast administrator in October 2011 will raise the bar on what molecular diagnostics companies will need to do to get paid for their tests. Among other things, the guidelines call for only paying for tests that companies have proved to be both valid and useful in the clinic. Under the guidelines from **Palmetto GBA**, the administrator for Medicare, claims will be required to name each gene tested and Palmetto said it will reserve the right to make the decision about what to pay for and what not to pay for rather than using code stacking. The draft guidance also says it will only pay for tests that have analytic validity, clinical validity, and clinical utility. The policies, if implemented, will only affect Western states including California, but would likely spread to other jurisdictions.

Palmetto's efforts came weeks ahead of news that the **American Medical Association's** coding group has been working to overhaul the codes used for diagnostic billing and in November 2011 issued proposed codes, a step toward introducing hundreds of new codes for molecular diagnostic tests and eliminating the need for code stacking by the end of 2012. "This specificity in the coding system, from the old world to a new world that is more specific, is coming one way or another," says Quinn. "Palmetto thinks it can accelerate that by a year or so through the policy it's announced."

## Seeking clarity

The FDA took steps to bring new clarity to the regulation of personalized medicine and signaled its interest in having the type of evidence companion diagnostics could provide for the appropriate use of a drug. The FDA has been forging new policies intended to ease the way for more approvals of targeted therapies and to help ensure the safety of patients as the field develops further. In July 2011, it issued draft guidance for the development of companion diagnostics aimed at facilitating the development of personalized medicines and diagnostics. "Because an IVD companion diagnostic device with inadequate 'performance characteristics' or other issues related to safety and effectiveness could expose a patient to preventable treatment risks, FDA will assess the safety and effectiveness of the IVD companion diagnostic device as used with the therapeutic when a therapeutic product depends on the IVD companion diagnostic device for its safe and effective use," the draft guidance said. The guidance does contemplate circumstances where the agency may choose to approve a therapeutic product even if a companion diagnostic for which it is labeled is not being approved at the same time. Such instances could include new therapies to treat serious or life-threatening conditions or cases where an already approved therapy needs safety changes to its label.

"These proposed guidelines support the development of innovative new targeted medicines and their corresponding diagnostic tests and are intended to provide manufacturers with greater predictability," says Jeffrey Shuren, director of the **FDA's Center for Devices and Radiological Health**. "It is the agency's goal to help stimulate early collaborations between drug and device makers so they can develop the best medical products for treating patients." The agency offered additional guidance in August to help clarify the process companies will need to follow to show that the biomarkers they pick to guide more personalized therapeutic use and dosing reflect the biological process, response, or event, that the drugmakers claim. That guidance should also help support the agency's goal

56

# Medco Drives Personalized Medicine Adoption

With 2010 acquisition of DNA Direct, the pharmacy benefits manager is an important force behind putting new approaches into practice

The integration of personalized medicine into medical practice faces a number of challenges, including physicians' lack of understanding of genetic tests, the difficulties payers have separating molecular diagnostics that are valuable and ones that are not, and insurers' and hospitals' need to know when a test is appropriate to use. It is this last gap that the pharmacy benefits manager **Medco Health Solutions** is seeking to fill.

In February 2010, Medco reached an agreement to acquire San Francisco-based **DNA Direct**, one of the pioneers of consumer genetics. Already the company had been expanding its business model to work with physicians and payers. But its integration into Medco has been transformative as Medco has leveraged its Fortune 50 muscle to turn its DNA Direct subsidiary into a significant force advancing personalized medicine into everyday clinical practice.

Ryan Phelan, president and founder of DNA Direct, says she saw the deal as a way to not just help people provide these services, but to really get them into mainstream healthcare systems. "Before Medco, it was really challenging having anyone with real clout at the table," she says. "As a start-up company, whether it was providers, big medical centers, or healthcare payers, I think they would look at a company like DNA Direct as a small, entrepreneurial, venture-backed company and say, 'This is great, but before we could run this kind of program out to our millions of members we need to know it could scale.'"

Today Medco, has integrated all of its personalized medicine programs under the umbrella of its DNA Direct subsidiary. Through DNA Direct, Medco provides a list of offerings that is helping bring personalized medicine into the here and now.

Through more than 300 mid- and large-sized employers who have enrolled their employee bases into Medco's clinical testing programs, more than 10 million members can have the choice of pharmacogenetic testing where they are prescribed any of a growing list of drugs with a known safety or efficacy related to a patient's genetics.

The company also provides members an extensive electronic database with information on 800 genetic tests. In addition, its genetic counseling call center provides information to physicians on more than 2,000 genetic tests and provides pre-authorization services for the use of these tests to clients such as the health insurance giant **Humana**. Through DNA Direct, Humana's coverage management system targets high cost tests that are at risk of misuse. They found that about 25 percent of tests were ordered inappropriately. At the same time, about 35 percent of tests were being done at labs outside their networks and could instead be steered to labs within their network.

DNA Direct is also building out a Genomic Medicine Network to work with hospitals to help their physicians develop insight into new diagnostics and provide continuing medical education and webinars to improve their understanding of genomic medicine. These same network members can become clinical sites for testing related to diagnostics, speed the translation of those tests into accepted clinical use, and share best practices.

Ultimately, with 40 million members who have expressed a willingness to participate in research, Medco is in a unique position to work with research institutes and diagnostic companies to both help identify genes at play in specific disease and speed the translation of research findings into clinical benefits. **Express Scripts** in July 2011 reached an agreement to purchase Medco for $29.1 billion. As of this writing, that deal had not yet passed muster with the **Federal Trade Commission**, but should it go through, it could greatly expand the reach of Medco's personalized medicine efforts. ■

of establishing the reliability of diagnostic tests to support major medical decisions.

## Physicians and personalized medicine

There's also the problem of doctors themselves, most of whom feel ill-prepared to address the day-to-day challenges of this rapidly emerging area of personalized medicine even though they expect it to become part of everyday clinical practice. The healthcare communications firm **CAHG** queried 800 U.S. physicians about their attitudes towards personalized medicine. They found only about 20 percent of doctors received personalized medicine education in medical school. Among those who graduated within the past five years, less than half received such training. The study found that doctors are also concerned about having the time to counsel patients in a personalized medicine world through a standard office visit and their ability to talk to patients about the results of genetic testing in a way that patients will understand. Jerry Coamey, senior vice president and practice leader for personalized healthcare at CAHG, likens personalized medicine's adoption to what was seen with the Internet and smartphones.

"You wake up one day and all of a sudden it's part of your life. You don't realize it's slowly been creeping into your life over time," he says. Coamey argues that new physician training needs to integrate personalized medicine into the curriculum, but that practicing physicians, with the right amount of education, some support from experts, and innovative tests and targeted therapies, will find it becomes much more a part of their practice.

"The biggest issue, honestly, is going to be the ability to access those tests and therapies and the ability to reimburse for them," he says. "Those are going to be bigger issues to work through. Will the system pay for the tests and will the system pay for these targeted therapies? I don't think doctors will be the barrier at that point [*See Sidebar Medco*].

Figure 3.6 **PERSONALIZED MEDICINE PARTNERING**

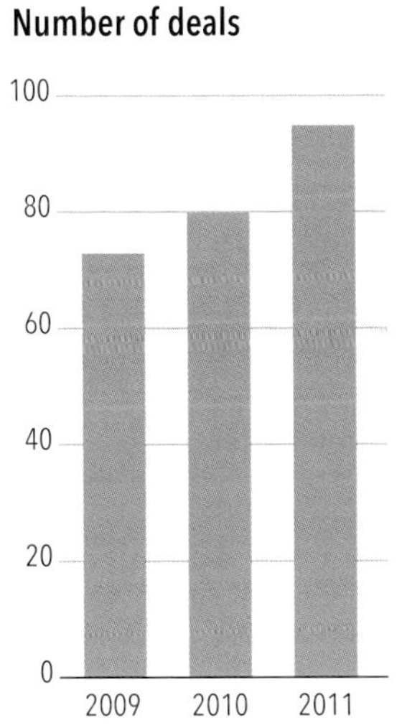

**Number of deals**

Source: Burrill & Company

## A fair shake

Then there's the issue of whether pharmaceutical companies and diagnostic makers will be able to work together as companion diagnostics become more common.

Traditionally, diagnostics have accounted for less than 2 percent of healthcare spending but influenced more than 60 percent of critical healthcare decisions, according to a 2011 report from **PwC**. As regulatory pressure increases on pharmaceutical companies to incorporate diagnostic development at earlier stages of drug development for potential companion therapeutics, they may need to find terms that diagnostics companies will view as more equitable. Diagnostics makers want a greater share in the value of companion diagnostic therapies. They may have to wait years for a drug to get approved, and, if it is approved, may have a very limited market for a test even though the companion drug generates significant revenues. They argue that in the absence of their tests, a targeted therapy may never get to market and could not succeed. Pharmaceutical companies, though, feel that they must bear the high cost and risk of drug development and should therefore also enjoy the rewards.

"At best, the implications of not addressing these issues could be that diagnostics innovation is handed over too cheaply to pharma," says PwC in its *Diagnostics 2011* report. "At worst, these issues could eventually discourage continued investment into diagnostics ventures and delay patient access to important new health technology."

## Driving Deals

The need of pharmaceutical companies to have reliable development of diagnostics will drive deals in the sector and could make in vitro diagnostic makers attractive acquisition targets as regulators, payers, and drugmakers embrace personalized medicine.

In 2011, there was a sharp rise in the value of

M&A transactions involving personalized medicine companies. Companies completed a total of 43 M&A transactions valued at $14.7 billion in the personalized medicine sector in 2011 [SEE FIGURES 3.7 AND 3.8]. Although there was an equal number of deals in 2010, the M&A activity in 2011 represented a more than a threefold increase in the dollar volume of the $4.1 billion in M&A transactions in 2010. Two large transactions drove the big increase in dollar volume in 2011.

In February, **Danaher** announced plans to acquire **Beckman Coulter** for $6.8 billion, a deal that would add the biomedical testing company to a growing portfolio of life sciences and diagnostic toolmakers. Including cash and debt, Danaher's $83.50 per share offer represented about a 45 percent premium to Beckman's closing price on December 9, 2010, the date on which market speculation began regarding a potential sale of the company. The medical testing equipment and supply market is competitive and is becoming tougher as industry consolidation and intense pricing pressures from group purchasers take their toll. Danaher has a reputation for achieving cost reductions and productivity gains in its portfolio companies and is betting it will boost the margins in Beckman's diagnostic supplies line-up, which accounts for the biggest part of its revenue. Beckman was expected to become

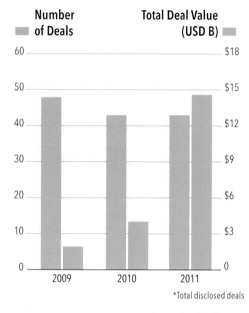

*Figure 3.7* **PERSONALIZED MEDICINE M&A DEALS AND VALUE***

*Total disclosed deals

*Source: Burrill & Company*

part of Danaher's life sciences and diagnostics unit, which already includes **Leica Microsystems, AB Sciex, Radiometer,** and **Molecular Devices.** Danaher is believed to have beat out several private equity firms that were also seeking to buy Beckman.

*Figure 3.8* **PERSONALIZED MEDICINE M&A: NUMBER OF DEALS AND DEAL VALUE**

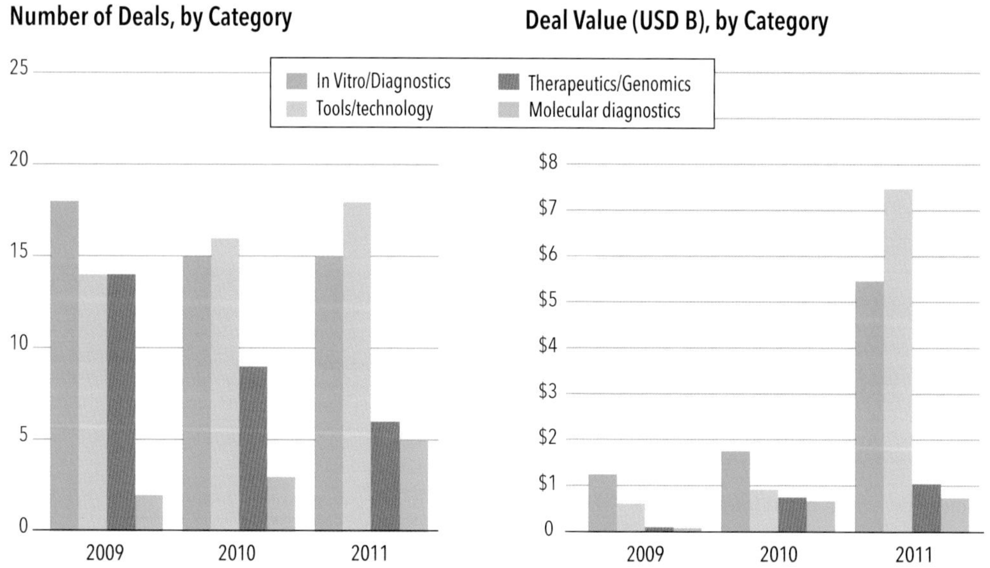

**Number of Deals, by Category**

In Vitro/Diagnostics
Tools/technology
Therapeutics/Genomics
Molecular diagnostics

**Deal Value (USD B), by Category**

*Source: Burrill & Company*

*Figure 3.9* **PERSONALIZED MEDICINE FINANCINGS**

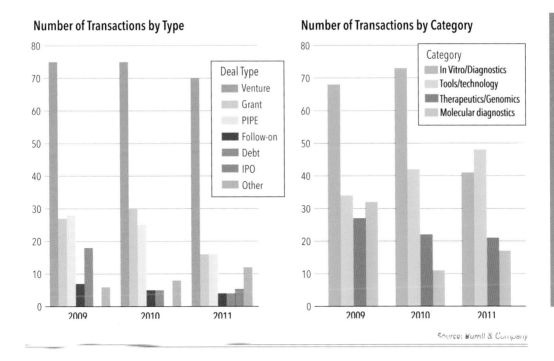

**Number of Transactions by Type**

Deal Type
- Venture
- Grant
- PIPE
- Follow-on
- Debt
- IPO
- Other

**Number of Transactions by Category**

Category
- In Vitro/Diagnostics
- Tools/technology
- Therapeutics/Genomics
- Molecular diagnostics

*Source: Burrill & Company*

The acquisition was followed in May with a second multibillion deal in the sector when **Thermo Fisher Scientific**, the world's largest maker of laboratory instruments, announced it would acquire Swedish specialty diagnostics firm **Phadia** for $3.5 billion (€2.47 billion) in cash from European private equity firm **Cinven**. Phadia develops, manufactures, and markets complete blood test systems used to identify allergies and autoimmune diseases. Phadia has been a pioneer in bringing new allergy diagnostic tests to market and a European leader in autoimmunity diagnostics. The deal was part of broader efforts by Thermo Fisher to expand its presence within specialty diagnostics. It followed the company's failed attempts in 2010 to by lab equipment maker **Millipore**, which **Merck KGaA** snapped up for $7.2 billion in cash and assumed debt.

Expect more in 2012. At the start of the year **Roche** made a $5.7 billion hostile bid for the tools and sequencing systems company **Illumina**. The wrangling between Roche and Illumina was expected to drag on for months. It reflects Roche's efforts to build itself into a personalized medicine powerhouse and its belief that sequencing technology will eventually migrate from the lab to the doctor's office.

*Figure 3.10* **PERSONALIZED MEDICINE NUMBER OF FINANCINGS AND TOTAL VALUE**

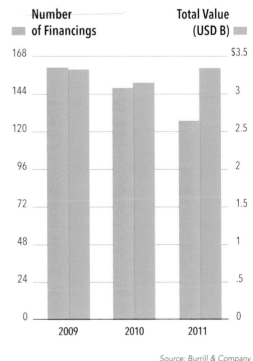

**Number of Financings**

**Total Value (USD B)**

*Source: Burrill & Company*

60

PERSONALIZED MEDICINE

3

On the financing front, the personalized medicine sector raised a total of $3.3 billion in 127 transactions in 2011 [SEE FIGURES 3.9 AND 3.10]. That included two large debt offerings in March 2011 — a $1.3 billion financing by **Quest Diagnostics** and an $800 million financing by Illumina—that together represented more than half of the total raised in the sector during the year. These two financings also account for why the tools and technology sector, among personalized medicine companies, outstripped fundraising in other areas. For the year, investment in in vitro diagnostic companies fell to $362.2 million compared to $897.3 million in 2010, and investment in genomics companies fell to $207.9 million, from $269.4 million the previous year. Molecular diagnostics companies saw an increase in investment to $161.4 million from $46.8 million in 2010.

Worldwide, a total of five personalized medicine companies went public during 2011, after no personalized medicine companies completed IPOs in the three previous years [SEE FIG. 3.11]. This included offerings by **Endocyte** and **BG Medicine** in the United States, **Glycominds** in Israel, **Median Technologies** in France, and **Sphere Medical Holdings** in the United Kingdom. These companies raised a total $171.7 million. Overall, these IPOs posted a 16.5 percent decline from their inital offering prices at the end of 2011. That compared to a 27 percent drop for U.S. life sciences IPOs as a whole by the end of the year.

## A need for approval

If critics of the industry complain about rate of progress toward the integration of personalized medicine into the practical world of healthcare today, boosters could point to concrete progress in the sector in 2011, particularly in the development of new targeted therapies. In fact, during a two-week period in August, the FDA approved three cancer drugs that benefitted from personalized medicine advances, a development that makes an argument that despite the criticism, personalized medicine is a reality of the here and now, even if its progress is slower than most would like.

Zelboraf (vemurafenib), a personalized therapy, was approved by the FDA in August 2011, with a first-of-its-kind companion diagnostic, for patients with tumors that have a spe-

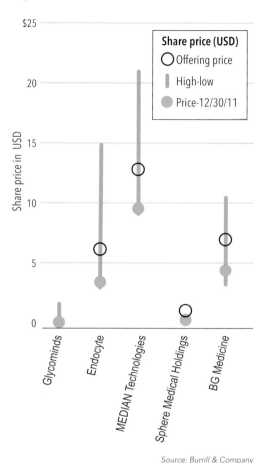

*Figure 3.11* PERSONALIZED MEDICINE IPOS

Share price (USD)
○ Offering price
❘ High-low
● Price-12/30/11

Share price in USD

*Source: Burrill & Company*

cific mutation in the BRAF gene. In announcing the approval, Alberto Gutierrez, director of the **Office of In Vitro Diagnostic Device Evaluation and Safety** in the FDA's Center for Devices and Radiological Health, said it was "a great example of how companion diagnostics can be developed and used to ensure patients are exposed to highly effective, more personalized therapies in a safe manner." Though such targeted therapies limit their markets by definition, drugmakers have come to realize that the opportunities can still nonetheless be significant [SEE FIG 3.13]. Zelboraf, developed in partnership with **Daiichi Sankyo's Plexxikon**, is expected to reach peak sales of $1.2 billion to $1.5 billion a year. The mutation it targets is found in about half of patients with melanoma.

Less than two weeks later, the FDA approved **Pfizer's** Xalkori (crizotinib) to treat certain patients with late-stage, non-small-cell lung can-

*Figure 3.12* **ANTIBODY-DRUG CONJUGATES: HOW THEY WORK**

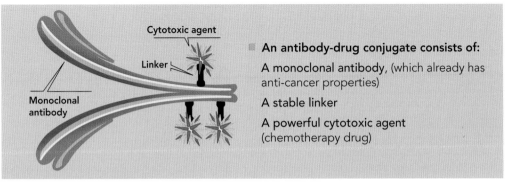

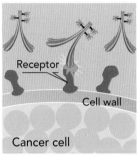

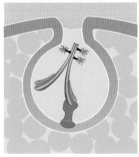

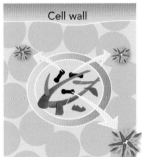

■ An antibody-drug conjugate consists of:

A monoclonal antibody, (which already has anti-cancer properties)

A stable linker

A powerful cytotoxic agent (chemotherapy drug)

■ The cytotoxin remains inert as the conjugated antibody circulates through the body, looking for cancer cells. Because the monoclonal antibody seeks out only the cancer cell, other cells in the body are not affected. This makes it possible to attach a cytotoxin up to 1,000 times more potent than those used in conventional chemotherapy.

■ The antibody locates the target receptor ion the surface of the cancer cell and is accepted.

■ The receptor draws the antibody through the cell wall, a process known as receptor-mediated endocytosis.

■ The cancer cell attacks the monoclonal antibody, breaking it down and releasing the cytochemicals from their linkers.

■ The chemotherapy drugs begin to interact with cellular machinery, which leads to the death of the cancer cell.

Source: pharmastrategyblog.com, Genentech, Spirogen

cers that express the abnormal anaplastic lymphoma kinase (ALK) gene, in combination with a first-of-a-kind diagnostic test to determine if a patient has the ALK gene mutation that causes cancer to develop and grow. A total of 1 to 7 percent of patients with non-small cell lung cancer have the ALK gene mutation.

In between those two approvals, the FDA granted accelerated approval to **Seattle Genetics'** Adcetris (brentuximab vedotin) to treat Hodgkin lymphoma and a rare lymphoma known as systemic anaplastic large cell lymphoma. The therapy, an antibody-drug conjugate, is the first new treatment for the disease since 1977 and the first specifically indicated to treat systemic anaplastic large cell lymphoma. Antibody-drug

conjugates are antibodies that are married to a small molecular drug with a linker that releases the drug once it is delivered directly to cancer cells [*SEE ILLUSTRATION ANTIBODY*]. In the case of Adcetris, the monoclonal antibody carries the drug to the CD30 receptor found on lymphoma cells. The technology is particularly promising because it could allow the use of cancer drugs otherwise deemed too toxic to deliver systemically to be paired with antibodies and can turn them into targeted therapies that can then be dosed at safe levels.

Adcetris, at the time of this writing, was the only antibody-drug conjugate on the market in the United States. Pfizer's acute myeloid leukemia drug Mylotarg (gemtuzumab ozogamicin),

# Bringing the Benefits

NIH spearheads initiatives to make personalized medicine a reality

**N**ational Institutes of Health Director Francis Collins is a believer in personalized medicine. As head of the **National Human Genome Research Institute**, he led the groundbreaking work to map the human genome. Now, as head of the National Institutes of Health, he is pushing to bring the benefits of personalized medicine to patients.

NIH-supported tissue banks holding thousands of tumor samples alongside information linking them to clinical outcomes represent one prong of the NIH strategy for personalized medicine. Such data will be essential in supporting broad assessments of

**Francis Collins**

*Director, National*

*Institutes of Health*

the clinical importance of genetic variation across a range of conditions, yielding the sort of insights that can only come from large and long-term studies. Already it is amassing what Collins anticipates will be 73,000 genomes by the end of 2013, as well as their exomes, the part of the genome that contains the coding portions of genes. "The amount of information that is going to be pouring out of this is pretty phenomenal and will certainly extend what is already a pretty amazing database of information on genetic risk factors to an even longer list," says Collins.

In particular, he said **The Cancer Genome Atlas** is now making it possible to derive information about recurring themes about what causes a good cell to go bad and cause a malignancy. Collins expects this to accelerate with the rapid decline in the cost of sequencing. The NIH has also built out the **Therapeutics for Rare and Neglected Diseases** program, or TRND, a program created to accelerate the development of new drugs for rare and neglected disease, many of which are single-gene disorders. Under the program, researchers are able to take promising compounds through preclinical development and ultimately to a stage where a drug could be licensed to biopharmaceutical companies for later stages of clinical development.

While that program is still in its early days, it has already advanced five projects to a pilot stage, including a project initiated in May to focus on further development of an existing small molecule drug used to treat arthritis called auranofin as a treatment for the rare disease relapsed chronic lymphocytic leukemia. TRND's mission is to get such projects through "the valley of death" between idea and clinical testing. But it is also designed to address other barriers that continue to stymie the creation of new personalized medicines. TRND is really an experimental lab for drug development, says its founder, Chris Austin, a scientific director for the NIH **Center for Translational Therapeutics.**

The **Genetic Testing Registry**, another key part of NIH's plans for advancing personalized medicine, will aggregate information about the availability, validity, and usefulness of the more than 2,000 genetic tests currently available through clinical laboratories. It launched in early 2012. The registry will provide access to information about genetic tests for inherited and somatic genetic variations, including newer types of tests, such as arrays and multiplex panels. That information primarily comes from voluntary data submissions by test developers and manufacturers.

NIH won a victory just before year-end when Congress approved a budget of $575 million to establish the **National Center for Advancing Translational Sciences**. The center seeks to reengineer the process of developing diagnostics, devices, and therapeutics. ■

won accelerated approval from the FDA in 2000 as the first such drug, but Pfizer voluntarily withdrew it from the market at the request of the agency in 2010 because of safety concerns after additional studies showed the drug provided no clinical benefit to patients with the bone marrow cancer. But the pipeline is growing with at least 20 antibody drug conjugates currently in clinical development at companies including Pfizer, **Genentech, Sanofi, Biogen Idec, Bristol-Myers Squibb** and **Bayer** among others. Though their utility should not be limited to cancer, early molecules in development in this area are focused on oncology. The limited success to date has some wondering how broad their utility will be and questions remain about under what conditions such drugs can be effective.

"We are on the cusp of learning a tremendous amount about what it takes to make an antibody-drug conjugate," said Jonathan Drachman, senior vice president of research and translational medicine for Seattle Genetics, during a panel discussion at the **BIO Investor Forum** in October 2011 in San Francisco. "But by no means do we know the rules at this point. There have been many, many attempts at making targeted drug therapy, targeted toxin delivery that have not been successful. We don't know the limits and parameters yet, so a wide variety of targets are being looked at."

In addition to antibody-drug conjugates,

> "We are on the cusp of learning a tremendous amount about what it takes to make an antibody-drug conjugate... We don't know the limits and parameters yet, so a wide variety of targets are being looked at."
>
> Jonathan Drachman
> *Senior vice president of research and translational medicine, Seattle Genetics*

there are other targeting mechanisms that are being employed to deliver toxic payloads. **Endocyte** is working on small molecule drug conjugates for the treatment of cancer and inflammatory disease. One benefit of Endocyte's approach is that it is able to link imaging agents to its small molecules and is developing companion imaging diagnostics alongside its small molecule drug conjugates. Its lead compound, EC145 targets the folate receptor, which is over-expressed in a number of common cancers, such as certain ovarian, non-small cell lung, breast, colorectal, kidney, and endometrial cancers. Folate is required for cell division and rapidly dividing cancer cells often over-express folate receptors in order to capture enough folate to support cell division. By attaching a chemotherapy drug to the vitamin folate through the use of proprietary chemistry, EC145 targets cancer cells while avoiding most normal cells. In the same way that the cancer cells bind to the vitamin and its chemotherapeutic payload, Endocyte is also able to link imaging agents to diagnose patients and identify whether they would likely benefit from the drug. **Burrill & Company**, publisher of this book, is an investor in Endocyte.

In June 2011, at the **American Society of Clinical Oncology** annual meeting, the company reported encouraging results from a mid-stage trial of its lead experimental small molecule drug conjugate in combination with pegylated liposomal doxorubicin in patients with plati-

*Figure 3.13* **ZELBORAF – A TARGETED MELANOMA THERAPY**

**70,000 new cases of melanoma are diagnosed each year in the United States:**

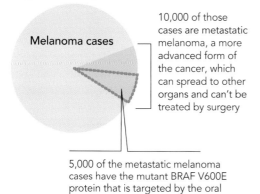

Melanoma cases

10,000 of those cases are metastatic melanoma, a more advanced form of the cancer, which can spread to other organs and can't be treated by surgery

5,000 of the metastatic melanoma cases have the mutant BRAF V600E protein that is targeted by the oral medicine Zelboraf

*Source: The Wall Street Journal*

*Figure 3.14* UNDERSTANDING OF LYMPHOMA – 100 YEARS AGO AND TODAY

**How Leukemia was seen...**

| 100 YEARS AGO |
|---|
| Disease of the blood |

| 80 YEARS AGO |
|---|
| Leukemia or lymphoma |

### 60 YEARS AGO

| | |
|---|---|
| Chronic leukemia | Indolent lymphoma |
| Acute leukemia | Aggressive lymphoma |
| Preleukemia | |

### TODAY

**ABOUT 38 LEUKEMIA TYPES IDENTIFIED:**
- acute myeloid leukemia (~12 types)
- acute lymphoblastic leukemia (2 types)
- acute promyelocytic leukemia (2 types)
- acute monocytic leukemia (2 types)
- acute erythroid leukemia (2 types)
- acute megakaryoblastic leukemia
- acute myelomonocytic leukemia
- chronic myeloid leukemia
- chronic myeloproliferative disorders (5 types)
- myelodysplastic syndromes (6 type)
- mixed myeloproliferative/myelodysplastics syndromes (3 types)

**51 LYMPHOMAS IDENTIFIED:**
- mature B-cell lymphomas (~14 types)
- mature T-cell lymphomas (15 types)
- plasma cell neoplasm (3 types)
- immature (precursor) lymphomas (2 types)
- Hodgkin's lymphoma (5 types)
- immunodeficiency-associated lymphomas (~5 types)
- Other hermatolymphoid neoplasms (~7 types)

*Source: Genzyme*

num-resistant ovarian cancer. The drug met its primary endpoint by showing an 85 percent, 2.3 month, improvement in median progression-free survival in the intent-to-treat population and a 260 percent, 4.0 month, improvement in a subset of folate receptor-positive patients. Historical data show that for these patients on standard therapy, progression-free survival is approximately three months and overall survival is approximately 12 months.

Though the company was unable to win accelerated approval from the FDA, it is planning on filing for approval with the **European Medicines Agency** in the first quarter of 2012, based on the strength of the results. Endocyte's shares tumbled more than 60 percent in December 2011 when the company reported clinical trial results showed patients using the drug did not survive as long, but the company notes that the study was not powered for overall survival and that the results were not statistically significant. The company is planning a larger late-stage trial.

### Emerging therapies show promise

Beyond antibodies and drug conjugates, there are other emerging personalized therapies that are driven by a genetic understanding of a disease and that work by altering, shutting off, or replacing defective genes. This includes developing areas, such as stem cell therapeutics, gene therapy, and RNAi therapies. After generating great excitement over their possibilities, these new therapies have gone through practical challenges that have diminished interest in them just as they are showing promise in human clinical trials.

In November 2011, **Alnylam Pharmaceuti-**

cals reported preliminary positive results in an early-stage trial of its experimental RNAi therapy to treat the rare genetic disorder known as TTR-mediated amyloidosis, a disorder caused by mutations in the TTR gene that lead to serious tissue and organ damage. The trial results are significant because they are believed to represent the first time that RNAi has been shown to silence a disease-causing gene in humans. RNA interference, or RNAi, is a natural biological process in which the body silences specific genes. It has been seen as a basis for a promising new class of drugs that could potentially treat everything from cancers to infectious disease by enlisting a biological process to silence genes that produce disease-causing proteins.

Pharmaceutical companies had embraced RNAi and have entered into big-dollar deals to gain access to the technology, which can open a world of new therapeutic targets, but significant barriers remain to being able to develop RNAi products that can act like drugs. Among the challenges that have hampered development of these therapies have been difficulties in targeting the desired genes with systemic dosing, and getting these drugs to stay active in the body long enough to have a therapeutic effect.

Big Pharma, once enamored with the technology, has been backing away. In 2006, Merck paid an eye-popping $1.1 billion to purchase **Sirna Therapeutics**, but is no longer developing any of the drugs that had been in Sirna's pipeline. Roche, which had been four years into an RNAi partnership with **Alnylam**, abruptly ended a potential $1 billion deal at the end of 2010 saying it had "higher priorities." **Novartis** didn't extend its RNAi partnership with Alnylam when it expired, and **Abbott** and Pfizer have both shut down their RNAi programs. In the face of this, Alnylam cut staff and in January announced it was transforming itself to a product maker, rather than a platform company. With that, it announced an ambitious plan to have five RNAi therapeutics to address genetically-defined diseases with high unmet medical need in advanced clinical development by 2015 [*See Sidebar NIH*].

## A new world of opportunity

**Severin Schwan**, CEO of Roche, reflected on the dramatic turn in attitude among Big Pharma

> "The vast majority of drugs—more than 90 percent—only work in 30 or 50 percent of the people. I wouldn't say that most drugs don't work. I would say that most drugs work in 30 to 50 percent of people."
>
> **Allen Roses**
> *Worldwide vice president for genetics at GlaxoSmithKline, quoted at a 2003 scientific conference*

toward personalized medicine. The subject of an August 2011 article in *The Wall Street Journal* following the approval of his company's Zelboraf, Schwan made the case to the paper that new understanding of genetics and molecular biology is opening a new world of opportunity to the pharmaceutical industry despite some industry naysayers who argue that "all the low-hanging fruits have been harvested and that the pharmaceutical industry is at an end."

"We have a huge potential with our targeted therapies and believe that this strategy is working," Schwan told *The Journal*. "And more is expected to come when we consider that all of today's existing medicines address only some 150 different targets, whereas there are more than two million proteins in the human body, of which many potentially can cause diseases. We are only scratching the surface."

## Blockbusters give way to targeted drugs

In November 2011, the patent on Pfizer's blockbuster statin Lipitor expired. Lipitor, the best-selling drug of all time, reached sales of $13.4 billion at its peak. In many ways, Lipitor, the biggest of the blockbusters, also represents the end of an era, as several pressures are pushing the pharmaceutical industry away from traditional, one-size-fits-all blockbusters to focus increasingly on targeted therapies. That's not to say targeted therapies will not be able to reach the billion-dollar sales mark—several already have—but in an age of molecular biology, where diseases are increasingly defined by their underlying mechanisms rather than their overt symptoms, precision is being increasingly demanded from everyone in the healthcare continuum, including drugmakers themselves, which are seeking ways to cut their development time and cost and increase their success rate at bringing new drugs to market [SEE CHART LYMPHOMA].

For the public, personalized medicine represents safer, more effective drugs. For payers, it represents a greater likelihood that their money isn't being wasted on a therapy that generates no medical benefit for a given patient. And for regulators, it can provide better scientific evidence that a drug that is being approved will work in the patients who get it.

In 2003, Allen Roses, worldwide vice president for genetics at **GlaxoSmithKline** raised eyebrows when quoted by the newspaper *The Independent,* saying at a scientific conference, "The vast majority of drugs—more than 90 percent—only work in 30 or 50 percent of the people. I wouldn't say that most drugs don't work. I would say that most drugs work in 30 to 50 percent of people."

Though the newspaper characterized this as an "open secret within the drug industry," it said that the declaration was the first time a senior executive within the industry had stated so publicly. Given individual genetic variance and the differing molecular mechanisms underlying diseases, as much as $350 billion a year, by some estimates, are wasted on ineffective medications [SEE FIGURE 3.15].

Consider Pfizer's Lipitor, which the drugmaker's ads had boasted reduced the risk of heart attack

# A Trial Size of One

## Cancer Commons seeks to capture data from off-label use of cancer drugs to customize treatments

Personalized medicine approaches offer the promise of the right dose to the right patient at the right time. But its corollary, personalized healthcare, is more broadly transforming the role of patients in taking charge of their own healthcare. This is in part being driven by an emerging array of digital technology devices and apps, that are changing the relationship between doctor and patient and empowering patients to take a greater role in maintaining wellness and practicing preventive measures. But technology is also empowering patients to play an unprecedented role in research and helping find treatments for themselves that are best tailored to their needs.

**Marty Tenenbaum**

*Founder,*

*Cancer Commons*

Marty Tenenbaum's own experience with cancer taught him much about the need patients and doctors have for information about the treatment of the disease that is both personalized and actionable. As an executive at the Internet company **CommerceOne**, doctors diagnosed Tenenbaum with melanoma and delivered a dire prognosis. One frustration was that no doctor could tell him what the right treatment was for him. He made a gut call and became a patient in an experimental cancer vaccine. The trial failed, but he was one of the patients for whom the therapy appeared to have worked. "No one can say for sure whether it helped me or not, but it did raise the specter that there are many trials that go through phase 3 and fail. They wouldn't have gotten to phase 3 if they weren't helping some patients, so what disease did these patients have that perhaps has been cured and how many other patients have that disease?"

One lesson from molecular biology is that cancer is not a heterogeneous disease. Tenenbaum is hoping to capture data from patients who have failed available therapies and instead are being treated with off-label use of cancer drugs. To that end, he created the nonprofit **Cancer Commons**. The effort seeks to capture data that can allow researchers, doctors, and patients to learn

in patients with multiple heart-disease risk factors by 36 percent. As a 2008 *Businessweek* story noted, according to the fine print in Pfizer's ad, a large clinical study found that three percent of patients using a placebo suffered a heart attack compared to two percent of patients taking Lipitor. Stated another way, out of 100 people using the drug, Lipitor would prevent one percent of users from suffering a heart attack.

But what if a test could determine precisely which patients stood to benefit from such a drug? **Celera** has developed a KIF6 Genotyping Assay, a test the company says identifies a gene that is a marker for coronary heart disease independent of traditional risk factors and could aid in determining in the clinic whether statin therapy would provide benefit to a patient. The company at the start of 2011 announced it had filed for regulatory approval to market the test in the United States. Abbott, its partner for Europe, has since applied for regulatory approval in the European Union.

### Reducing the cost of drug development

The benefits to drugmakers of pursuing targeted therapies may on its face seem counterintuitive—why would someone sink massive investment into research and development of a drug and typically exclude 50, 80, or even 95 percent of patients with a given condition? But the reality is that the industry has come to recognize that defining a subpopulation for which a given drug can be effective is one way to attack the time and cost of drug development that has ballooned to an estimated $1.3 billion. Peter Hirth, CEO of Plexxikon, which co-developed the melanoma drug Zelboraf, noted when it was approved that one benefit of such a personalized medicine has been the ability to accelerate its development. Plexxikon and its collaborators brought the drug to market in less than six years from the discovery of the molecule in 2005.

A November 2010 study from **The Tufts Center for the Study of Drug Development** found

> Based on the responses of patients to different therapies, Tenenbaum hopes to capture individual experiences to learn as much as possible from each patient to understand the biology driving the tumor and the mechanism of action of the drug to benefit the next patient.

as much as possible from individual patient experiences and help them match a growing arsenal of targeted therapeutics to the needs of individual cancer patients based on their subtype of the disease. Tenenbaum said in this industry if a trial fails, people walk away from it as fast as possible. In other fields, if something fails, they try to figure out how to make it better and better.

With genomics, there is a rational basis for matching patients to therapies that are most appropriate for them. Based on the responses of patients to different therapies, Tenenbaum hopes to capture individual experiences to learn as much as possible from each patient to understand the biology driving the tumor and the mechanism of action of the drug to benefit the next patient. As such, he envisions Cancer Commons as a rapid learning community of doctors, patients, and researchers designed to get each patient the best possible outcome and learn as much as possible.

Cancer Commons aggregates the information and combines it with expert knowledge to determine actionable subtypes, the tests needed to determine if a patient is in or out of the subtype, and what potential treatments or trials are available that might rationally help them. "We want to transform the knowledge that's in this model into information that's personalized and actionable so that patients and their physicians can take action on that knowledge," he says. To that end **CollabRx**, Tenenbaum's for profit app developer, harnesses the information in Cancer Commons to inform treatment decisions in an actionable way and to implement the decision by ordering tests, enrolling patients in trials, or applying for compassionate use of a drug. ∎

that 94 percent of the companies it surveyed were investing in personalized medicine and that 100 percent were employing personalized medicine approaches, such as using biomarkers, to identify compounds to pursue. While the report identified cancer as the greatest area of personalized medicine research, it also noted that it is by no means the only therapeutic area where drug developers are applying personalized medicine. Other therapeutic areas include cardiovascular diseases, central nervous system conditions, and immunology. It also noted that personalized medicine is expanding into other areas, such as metabolic disease, respiratory conditions, and virology. Often, the application of personalized medicine is not to develop a companion diagnostic, but to better understand the way in which a drug candidate works.

## Saving more than lives

For some drug developers, finding a companion diagnostic for a given drug has been the difference between writing off years of research and development and winning approval for a lucrative therapy that might otherwise never have been able to reach the market and benefit patients.

**Genentech's** breast cancer drug Herceptin helped define the new era of personalized medicine when it was first approved in 1998 with a companion diagnostic for women with HER2-positive breast cancer, an aggressive cancer that affects about 20 percent of breast cancer patients and is characterized by an overexpression of the HER2 gene. Genentech has said that if the drug's late-stage clinical trial had used a general breast cancer population rather than HER2-positive patients, it would have had to enroll 2,000 patients over 10 years to show a statistically significant benefit. By narrowing the focus to a smaller population more likely to benefit, the trial included just 400 patients over 18 months. Despite the limited population for the drug, it has worldwide sales in excess of $5 billion. It is also now being developed by Genentech and **ImmunoGen** as part of an antibody-drug conjugate known as TDM-1 that is in late-stage development.

In the absence of a diagnostic, it's likely that Herceptin would never have reached the market. In the same way, by using diagnostics to iden-

tify subgroups of patients for which a specific drug would be effective, drugmakers have been able to bring products to market that otherwise might have failed to withstand regulatory rigor. European regulators rejected **Amgen's** colorectal drug Vectibix in 2007, but Amgen was soon able to win conditional approval for it based on a biomarker used to identify patients with a gene mutation that rendered some people resistant to the drug. By eliminating patients with the mutation, the company was able to use the clinical data it had to demonstrate a high enough response rate to win European approval.

Personalized medicine is becoming critical, not just for winning approval for drugs, but also sometimes for retaining approval and expanding markets, too. Genentech's Avastin, which won accelerated approval in 2008 for use in breast cancer patients, had its approval in that indication revoked in November 2011.

**Margaret Hamburg**
*Commissioner, Food and Drug Administration*

"After reviewing the available studies it is clear that women who take Avastin for metastatic breast cancer risk potentially life-threatening side effects without proof that the use of Avastin will provide a benefit, in terms of delay in tumor growth, that would justify those risks," FDA Commissioner Margaret Hamburg said in issuing her decision. "Nor is there evidence that use of Avastin will either help them live longer or improve their quality of life." The decision, outlined in a 69-page opinion from Hamburg, involves Avastin's use in combination with the cancer drug paclitaxel for patients who have not been treated with chemotherapy for HER2-negative breast cancer that has spread. The decision does not affect Avastin's approved use as a treatment for certain types of colon, lung, kidney, and brain cancer.

The controversy surrounding the use of Avastin in breast cancer had been at times heated, emotional, and politically charged. Oncologists and the breast cancer community are divided over its use. The expense of the drug—$88,000 a year for a breast cancer treatment—has led some to suggest the FDA was taking the steps for financial, rather than scientific, reasons and pointed to it as a form of rationing that would become more common under healthcare reform efforts. The FDA, though, has insisted its decision has been driven by science. For Roche, which acquired Genentech in 2009, the stakes are high. Analysts have previously estimated the company stood to lose $1 billion a year in sales were Avastin to lose the indication of breast cancer. The controversy curtailed its use. Avastin sales have fallen and some insurers have already said they would not pay for use of the drug in breast cancer patients.

Though the company expressed disappointment in the FDA's decision, Genentech isn't abandoning hopes of restoring Avastin as an approved breast cancer drug. Instead, it's banking on finding a personalized medicine solution. Hal Barron, chief medical officer and head of global product development for Genentech, said the company will move forward with studies to identify possible subpopulations of breast cancer patients that will benefit from Avastin. The company also said it will start a new late-stage study of Avastin in combination with paclitaxel in previously untreated metastatic breast cancer and will evaluate a potential biomarker that may help identify which people might derive a more substantial benefit from Avastin.

## Integration will happen

The question is not whether personalized medicine will become a reality, but how quickly and how broadly it will become integrated into medical practice. Barriers still remain, but there are incentives for the various players within the healthcare ecosystem to work to remove them. Payers want more cost effective solutions and paying for therapies that don't benefit a patient makes no sense for anyone. Regulators want clearer proof that a drug is safe and effective for a patient. Drug

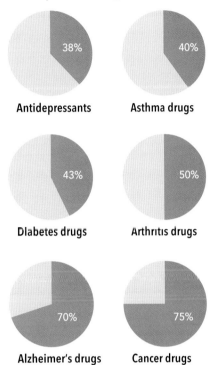

*Figure 3.15* **INEFFECTIVE THERAPIES – ONE SIZE DOES NOT FIT ALL**

Average percent of patient population for whom a particular drug in a class is ineffective.

38% Antidepressants

40% Asthma drugs

43% Diabetes drugs

50% Arthritis drugs

70% Alzheimer's drugs

75% Cancer drugs

*Source: Personalized Medicine Coalition*

companies want to bring drugs to market faster and more cost-effectively. And patients want to take a more active role in their own healthcare and have access to therapies that work. New technology is enabling patients to take an unprecedented role in their own healthcare from research to disease management [*SEE SIDEBAR COMMONS*]. As digital health technology evolves, individuals will be able to not only have tools for better prediction and prevention of disease, but the ability to act upon that information. ∎

# Europe: Customized Care for the Masses

Government, industry, and research institutes band together
to advance personalized medicine in the European Union

Europe has lagged the United States in the development of personalized medicine, but a careful look at the individual countries shows that there are an increasing number of programs underway that are harnessing the potential of tailored drugs.

A United Kingdom program that aims at creating personalized cancer care was set up in 2012 and led by **Cancer Research UK** with backing from the government's **Technology Strategy Board**, **AstraZeneca**, **Pfizer**, and **PA Consulting**, which will provide managerial and IT expertise. The collaboration began collecting up to 9,000 tumor samples, which will undergo molecular diagnosis to identify gene faults specifically linked to cancer. Molecular diagnosis of tumors is not yet available for all patients from the **National Health Service** and is currently only possible using a single test for each mutation. The new program aims to develop a multi-gene panel that can test for genetic markers for drugs already used in the clinic as well as those for new drugs in late-stage trials. Customized cancer care, it is hoped, will both improve patient outcomes and help the cash-strapped health service save money.

While the new combined-diagnostic project has the highest profile of any personalized medicine program backed by the Technology Strategy Board to date, it is not the board's first. Earlier in 2012, it announced that it was backing two other programs in the fields of inflammation. In one program, the board is working with the **Medical Research Council** and the **Association of the British Pharmaceutical Industry** on chronic obstructive pulmonary disease and arthritis. In another project the board is working to address the mismatch between the work being carried out by the pharmaceutical and diagnostics industries, with the goal of making their work complementary and allowing for more drug stratification.

The Technology Strategy Board's work in what the United Kingdom now refers to as stratified medicines began in October 2010 and aims to invest $79.7 million (£50 million) over five years to push forward the concept of tailor-made drugs and healthcare. Programs are selected through a competitive process and funding from the board is generally matched by partners.

In the rest of Europe, the picture is fragmented, but several programs are underway which could help pave the way for a wider rollout of personalized medicine. In France, the **National Cancer Institute** set up a network of 28 regional centers in 2006, linked with both public and private hospitals, where cancer patients' tumors can be rapidly analyzed to establish their suitability for drug treatment. Between 2004 and 2010, 31 cancer drugs were approved in France for use in 49 indications, of which almost half are targeted therapies. Furthermore, the institute estimates that targeted cancer therapies now account for around 57 percent of cancer treatments used in France's public hospitals sector.

Once a new cancer drug is approved in France, the National Cancer Institute moves quickly to allocate funding to the testing centers and to put the appropriate molecular diagnostics in place. For example, in 2008, when Erbitux and Vectibix were approved for patients with wild type KRAS tumors, the institute allocated $3.9 million (€2.8 million) to the 28 centers. In 2009, following the approval of Iressa for patients with active mutations of EGFR in their tumors, the institute allocated $2.4 million (€1.7 million). To improve the time-to-access for new drugs, the institute is now planning to anticipate new drug

> Customized cancer care, it is hoped, will both improve patient outcomes and help the cash-strapped health service save money.

launches and this year has earmarked $4.9 million (€3.5 million) to detect biomarkers in lung and colorectal cancers and melanoma. The National Cancer Institute concludes that "targeted cancer treatment in France shows that innovation can be successfully integrated into the healthcare system, that molecular stratification is cost effective, and that this organization could be easily expanded in other European settings."

In the Netherlands, Rene Bernards is at the helm of many of the current initiatives in personalized medicines. He is head of the division of molecular carcinogenesis of the **Netherlands Cancer Institute**, professor of molecular carcinogenesis at Utrecht University, as well as co-founder and chief scientific officer of the molecular cancer diagnosis company **Agendia**. Agendia's work has been attracting a lot of attention from the EU and industry, as well as at the public level in the Netherlands. In July 2012 the company announced that it was in line to receive $1.8 million (€1.3 million) in funding from the EU under the **7th Framework Program** over a five-year term for the development of new molecular diagnostics to help guide individualized treatment of cancer patients. Agendia has also teamed up with collaborators in clinical centers and translational research groups, launching the RATHER (Rational Therapy for Breast Cancer) and COLTHERES (Colon Cancer and Therapeutics) consortia. The partnerships will also receive funding under the 7th Framework Program, which will be in excess of $14 million (€10 million).

Agendia has signed collaborations with AstraZeneca and the Netherlands Cancer Institute to develop targeted therapies for colorectal cancer patients, and the company is also working with the **MD Anderson Cancer Center** in the same area.

**EuropaBio**, the pan-European biotechnology association, has been raising the profile of personalized medicine since 2008, when it set up a 20-company, expert task force. Several workshops have been held to give the **European Commission** a comprehensive overview of the impact of personalized medicine across the biotech industry as well as the future challenges and potential solutions. In parallel with the workshops, EuropaBio is in dialogue with the Commission's **Directorate General for Enterprises and Industry**. Together they are considering the implications of a shift towards a personalized medicine paradigm on current health technology assessment practices and pricing and reimbursement to ensure that the value of personalized medicine is recognized and that it effectively delivers on its promises to patients, healthcare systems, and society as a whole.

Europe is fast getting on board with personalized medicine as it realizes that it helps address two of the major problems facing society: the increasing incidence of chronic diseases and the need to spend scarce resources effectively. But the challenges are many—research, regulatory and implementation—and will need to be agreed to across the board at European, national, regional, and local levels. ■

# 4
# CONNECTED TO HEALTH

The convergence of information technology, the life sciences, and ubiquitous wireless connectivity is revolutionizing the way healthcare is accessed and delivered. Today, a new breed of healthcare companies is harnessing information and communication technologies not only to improve care, but also to help people stay well. The phenomena will bend the cost curve of healthcare to save money for both patients and payers by providing opportunities for earlier medical intervention through improved monitoring of chronic disease, and enabling people to change their behaviors in ways that keep them healthy. The evolution of mobile computing power, online social networks, and the growing ecosystem of wireless technologies are supporting the deployment of convenient and connected tools to promote health more cheaply than ever before. Technology alone will not adequately address the rising costs facing healthcare systems internationally, but it is already helping eliminate costly errors, improve diagnoses, and shifting power away from doctors to a new breed of patient-consumers taking control of their health and wellbeing.

# Chapter 4:

# CONNECTED TO HEALTH

The contagious enthusiasm of Todd Park reverberates at many gatherings of America's entrepreneurial digital health entrepreneurs. Chopping the air, Park punctuates every phrase with sharp gestures. Rather than being a government bureaucrat, the chief technology officer of the U.S. Department of Health & Human Services is a passionate advocate for what he frames as a historic shift in healthcare—the dramatic changes to the incentives driving healthcare decision-making and the liberation of massive amounts of health data. They are joining together to create what Park calls "rocket fuel" for innovation.

They also offer an opportunity to retool a $2.5 trillion healthcare industry to optimize it for outcomes rather than number of procedures performed. "I think it's the greatest entrepreneurial opportunity since the Internet," Park told an audience at **Stanford University's** 2011 **Graduate School of Business Healthcare Summit**, "and one that will actually change the course of American healthcare and create huge economic value at the same time." The low-cost technologies propelling the changes that Park and a growing contingent of healthcare technology innovators embrace take aim at some of the biggest drivers of healthcare costs. These new technologies are rapidly changing the ways healthcare is accessed and delivered, improving the communication between patients and doctors, closing the gaps in medical expertise and resource worldwide, and unearthing valuable health insights that might otherwise be buried in the mountain of medical

records stored on paper.

Digital health technologies, from mobile apps and telehealth, will be crucial to bringing about this change. Using ubiquitous technology such as smartphones that people already carry, multinational corporations and startup entrepreneurs are creating new opportunities for patients to take charge of their healthcare in cheaper, easier ways to allow for early interventions before medical problems grow costly. With healthcare costs approaching an average 10 percent of GDP in most member countries of the **Organization for Economic Cooperation and Development** and 17 percent of GDP in the United States, there is growing pressure to find new ways to bend the cost curve.

At its heart, this digital health revolution is about giving both healthcare providers and the people they care for the tools to take action to cut costs while simultaneously improving the qual-

Using ubiquitous technology such as smartphones that people already carry, multinational corporations and startup entrepreneurs are creating new opportunities for patients to take charge of their healthcare in cheaper, easier ways.

ity of care. In areas of big opportunity, such as chronic disease management and care for the elderly, digital health technologies are already taking hold.

In 2011, some of the world's biggest companies, both inside the healthcare arena and outside of it, stepped up their commitments to the space. **Intel's** Digital Health Group and **GE Healthcare's** Home Health Division in January 2011 launched their digital health joint venture **Care Innovations**, which has already introduced a portable touch-screen computer designed to help elderly people to live independently longer and better manage chronic conditions.

**Qualcomm** formalized its own new unit,

**Qualcomm Life**, with the launch of its 2net Platform and Hub, a system designed to bridge wireless medical devices in a way that makes biometric information more secure and easily accessible to device users, their healthcare providers, and caregivers. It's already being put to use in MyGlucoHealth, a bluetooth-enabled blood glucose meter created by **Entra Health Systems**.

Even the automaker **Ford** began to form partnerships in 2011 with healthcare companies interested in creating voice-controlled connections between its in-car computing system, Sync, and digital health aids, from glucose monitoring devices and diabetes management services to web-based allergen alerts. "Ford's approach to

*Figure 4.1* **GLOBAL MOBILE SUBSCRIPTIONS**

Cellular subscriptions, total and per 100 inhabitants, 2001-2011*

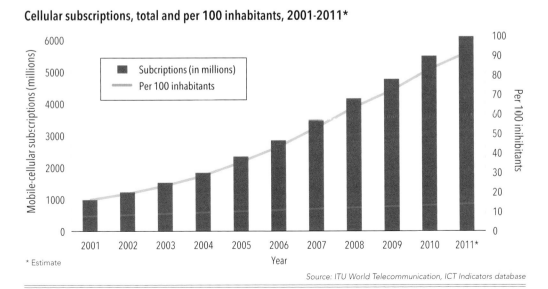

* Estimate

Source: ITU World Telecommunication, ICT Indicators database

*Figure 4.2* **GLOBAL SMARTPHONE PENETRATION**

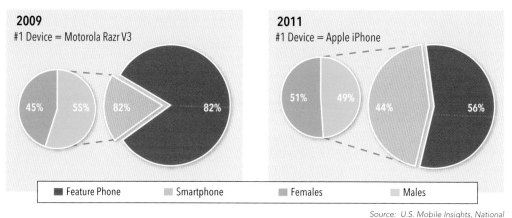

Source: U.S. Mobile Insights, National

health and wellness in the vehicle is not about trying to take on the role of a healthcare or medical provider. We're a car company," says Ford's Gary Strumolo. "Our goal is not to interpret the data offered by the experts, but to work with them to develop intelligent ways for Ford vehicles using the power of Sync, in essence, creating a secondary alert system and alternate outlet for real-time patient coaching services if you will."

Another place digital health technology is being deployed to address health issues is in improving compliance with drug regimens through the use of simple, inexpensive and connected technology. As many as half of all patients in the United States fail to take their medications as prescribed, compromising the effectiveness of therapies and adding $290 billion in drug-related morbidity costs—about 13 percent of total healthcare expenditures, according to **NEHI**, a nonprofit, independent health policy institute. **Vitality**, the maker of GlowCaps, is providing one solution to this problem with Internet-connected pill bottles that prod patients into adhering to their prescription drug regimens. The caps can illuminate, play a melody, and even send a text message or ring a home phone to prompt people to take their medications when they forget. Patients can also elect to have Glow-Caps share their pill-taking history with family members or a physician. This is particularly important for people with dementia or other problems that may inhibit their ability to take their medication as prescribed. GlowCaps also have an embedded push-to-refill button that can initiate a call to a pharmacy to request a refill.

The device fits standard pill bottles and costs as little as $10 per month, the company says. The surgeon and entrepreneur, Patrick Soon-Shiong was so convinced by the effectiveness of the caps that he bought Vitality in February 2011 for an undisclosed amount. At the time, Vitality said the price represented a tenfold return on investment to its shareholders.

## Health in our hands

Despite the great sophistication of the systems described above, the promise of such technologies are likely to be overshadowed by what is rapidly becoming one of the most important

*Figure 4.3* **GLOBAL MOBILE BROADBAND SUBSCRIPTIONS**

**Active mobile-broadband subscriptions per 100 inhabitants, 2007-2011\***

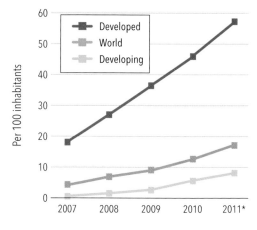

Source: ITU World Telecommunication, ICT Indicators database

digital health tools in the world, the mobile phone. More than three-quarters of the world's population already has access to mobile phones. Total global mobile connections were set to surpass 6 billion by the end of 2011, driven in large part by the Asia-Pacific market, according to **Wireless Intelligence** [*SEE FIGURE 4.1*]. Around the world, a growing number of mobile subscribers are using smart phones capable of running applications that often mirror those of much larger, costlier, and less portable computers [*SEE FIGURE 4.2*]. That growth in computing power is resulting in an increasing number of mobile phones tied to mobile broadband subscriptions and creating new opportunities to extend the reach of telemedicine initiatives employing high-bandwidth video and imaging [*SEE FIGURE 4.3*].

In the United States, at least, growing smartphone adoption has been shadowed by rising interest in accessing health information using mobile devices. **ComScore**, a U.S.-based digital analytics company, estimates that 16.9 million mobile users in the U.S. accessed health information on their device during the three-month period ending November 2011, up 125 percent from the previous year. Among those that accessed health information, nearly 3 in 5 were under the age of 35, the company found.

Physicians too are rapidly adopting smartphones and tablets. As many as 75 percent of U.S. physicians owned some form of **Apple** device, such as an iPhone, iPad or iPod, according to a study conducted of 2,041 doctors by **Manhattan Research** in May 2011. This budding love affair between physicians and Apple was given voice by John Halamka, chief information officer of **Beth Israel Deaconess Medical Center**, who appeared in a video shown at Apple's iPad 2 launch event in March 2011. "What we try to do on the iPad is give doctors, at the point of care, the exact tools they need at the exact moment the doctor can make the difference," says Halamka. "What we're finding with the iPad is that doctors are spending more time with patients. In fact, doctors are engaging patients by showing them images, showing them data on the screen. So it has empowered doctors to be more productive."

That enthusiasm though has not bubbled over into U.S. hospitals, where fewer than 1 per-

"What we're finding with the iPad is that doctors are spending more time with patients. In fact, doctors are engaging patients by showing them images, showing them data on the screen. So it has empowered doctors to be more productive."

**John Halamka**
*Chief information officer,*
*Beth Israel Deaconess Medical Center*

cent had developed functional tablet systems at the end of 2011, according to Jonathan Mack, director of clinical research and development at the **West Wireless Health Institute**. Many hospitals that have tried using tablets as a mobile interface to existing electronic health record systems have found them to be inadequate as an interface to complex records systems, offering limited screen-space and read-only access to records.

### The Rise of Apps

That lack of adoption has not stopped developers from trying to find a home in the space. [*SEE FIGURE 4.5 AND 4.6*]. In fact, despite growing government scrutiny of mobile healthcare apps [*SEE SIDEBAR FDA*], there has been an explosion of interest in medical apps designed for both smartphones and tablets. By the end of 2011,

*Figure 4.4*  **DIGITAL HEALTH TECHNOLOGY PROVIDING DISRUPTIVE INNOVATION**

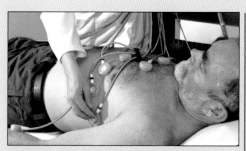

| Traditionally, electrocardiography has required a visit to a medical facility and a technician's assistance. | The EKG app, which works through a sensor attached to the back of a phone, transforms the procedure. |

### Electrocardiography

- Expensive
- Requires an expert to use
- Limited to institutions
- Not useful for monitoring or screening
- No ongoing feedback

### AliveCor iPhone EKG app

- Inexpensive ($99 range)
- Consumer and expert use
- Available where needed
- Ideal for monitoring and screening
- Ideal for ongoing feedback

*Source: Burrill & Company*

there were more than 13,000 healthcare and fitness apps and more than 10,000 medical apps in Apple's iTunes App Store. Meanwhile, **Google**'s Android Market offered more than 7,000 health and fitness apps and more than 3,000 medical apps.

Mobile health app revenue rose to $718 million in 2011 as smartphone sales and developers doubled the number of health-related apps in the market, according to **research2guidance**. "In 2011 we saw the quality of the solutions has increased quite dramatically," says Ralf-Gordon Jahns, the company's research director. The rise of sensor-based applications capable of monitoring things like blood pressure, temperature, and blood glucose levels has raised the level of sophistication in the market, he says. One popular application, iTriage, helps both patients and doctors find health information. By the end of 2011, more than three million people had used iTriage to view information on symptoms, diseases, procedures, medications, and to access a nationwide directory of medical providers. The app became so popular that in December 2011, **Aetna** acquired iTriage for an undisclosed sum. Apps like iTriage could prove important tools with the rise of accountable care organizations—groups of doctors, hospitals, and other healthcare

providers who coordinate care to capture incentives for lowering costs. By helping guide patients to specialists within its network with suggestions made through the iTriage app, Aetna hopes to lower the expenses incurred when people it insures seek out-of-network help or need high-cost emergency care instead.

Another interesting app, **Illumina's** MiGenome for iPad, arrived at Boston's **Consumer**

*Figure 4.5* **HEALTHCARE APPS BY SEGMENT**

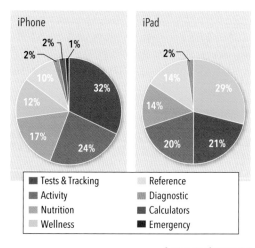

iPhone

iPad

| Tests & Tracking | Reference |
| Activity | Diagnostic |
| Nutrition | Calculators |
| Wellness | Emergency |

*Source: appshopper.com*

**Genetics Show** in June 2011. Illumina created the app to put "genomic information at the individual's fingertips." Customers of Illumina's individual genome sequencing service can use MiGenome to visualize their genome and "interrogate it for mendelian disorders, disease risk and pharmacogenomic drug response," according to the company.

Other apps, such as **EyeNetra**, are leveraging smartphones to get "free" computing, display, storage, mobile connectivity, and power simply by pairing them with low-cost accessories capable of standing in place of much more complex, bulky, and expensive medical equipment. EyeNetra pairs its app with a small attachment

*Figure 4.6* **MEDICAL APPS BY SEGMENT**

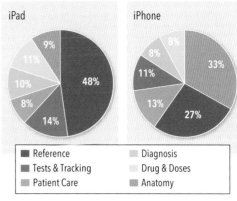

Source: appshopper.com

# FDA takes an interest in Mobile Medical Apps

## Oversight applies to a narrow range of surging market's offerings

The regulation of mobile medical apps came into clear focus in 2011 In the United States when the **U.S. Food and Drug Administration** issued its first draft guidance on the subject. Mobile apps for the diagnosis, prevention, and treatment of disease should be regulated as medical devices, according to draft guidance issued by the FDA in July 2011.

"Consumers are utilizing these tools almost as quickly as they can be developed," says Bakul Patel, a policy advisor in the FDA's **Center for Devices and Radiological Health**. "The agency plans to work closely with application developers and manufactures so they can clearly navigate the best path to market for their technologies."

The market for mobile medical apps is growing quickly, with as many as 500 million smartphone users worldwide expected to use healthcare apps by 2015, according to the consulting firm **research2guidance**.

Mobile medical apps on smartphones and tablets will revolutionize healthcare delivery, says Jeffrey Shuren, director of the FDA's Center for Devices and Radiological Health. "Our draft approach calls for oversight of only those mobile medical apps that present the greatest risk to patients when they don't work as intended," he says.

The developers of countless tracking apps for dieters, joggers, and expectant moms need not worry. Mobile apps used only to log, record, track, evaluate, or make suggestions related to general health and wellness are not targeted by the draft guidance, nor are medical textbooks and other reference works. The guidance is concerned with apps that could pose medical risks. That includes apps used as an accessory to a regulated medical device or to transform a mobile platform into a regulated medical device.

However, an app used to interpret radiological images on a mobile device would be subject to review the guidance suggests because readings could be hampered by the devices' smaller screen sizes, lower contrast ratios, and uncontrolled ambient lighting during use.

The FDA first issued a draft software policy in 1989, but abandoned the guidelines in that document when it became clear that an overarching software policy to address all the issues related to the regulation of all medical devices containing software was impractical.

With the draft guidance on mobile apps now published, the agency is readying for what it clearly anticipates will be a new wave of applications for the approval of apps to come. ∎

*Figure 4.7* NUMBER OF TEXTS SENT/RECEIVED PER DAY BY AGE GROUP

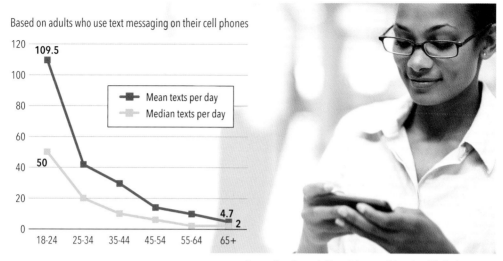

Based on adults who use text messaging on their cell phones

Legend:
- Mean texts per day
- Median texts per day

Source: Pew Research Center's Internet & American Life Project surveys

to allow anyone to test for nearsightedness, far-sightedness, and astigmatism anywhere. It can even connect users to optometrists.

**AliveCor**, a credit card-sized wireless device that turns smartphones and tablets into clinical-quality low-cost heart monitors, is another example of mobile diagnostics. Both patients and doctors can use it with an iPhone or Android phone, negating the need to order an expensive electrocardiogram. While AliveCor hasn't yet set pricing, it is expected to cost $100 or less. That means a patient can be followed for six months and provide that information to a doctor without worrying about reimbursement [*SEE FIGURE 4.4*].

Though text messaging may seem mundane by comparison to such innovative applications of smartphones, it is far more widely used—especially among people aged 18 to 24 [*SEE FIGURE 4.7*]. Clever programs such as text4baby, a free mobile information service designed to promote maternal and child health, are taking advantage of the technology to reach new and underserved patient populations. The first in-depth-study of the program, which in November 2011 had enrolled more than 2,200 participants in California's San Diego County, found mothers highly satisfied with what it offered. About 63 percent of women reported that text messages sent by the program helped them remember an appointment or immunization that they or their child needed. Just over three quarters of the women reported that text4-baby messages informed them of medical warn-

ing signs they did not know. And more than 70 percent reported talking to their doctors about a topic brought to their attention by a text4baby text message.

## Enabling global health

Mobile technologies are opening new frontiers for healthcare delivery across the globe. Already, 53 percent of low- to middle-income **World Health Organization** member nations offer mobile telemedicine programs. The initia-

*Figure 4.8* THE GROWTH OF SOCIAL NETWORKS

### Social networking site used by online adults.

The percentage of all adult internet users who use social networking sites since 2005.

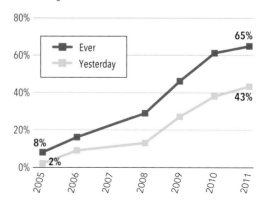

Legend:
- Ever
- Yesterday

Source: Pew Research Center's Internet & American Life Project surveys

> The 2009 study, "The Social Life of Health Information," found that 59 percent of all adults and 80 percent of those who use the Internet have looked online for information regarding a specific disease or treatment.

tives include programs supporting consultations between healthcare providers and transmission of a patient's health data using mobile devices and are increasingly targeting diseases linked with poverty, including HIV/AIDS, malaria, and tuberculosis.

Health professionals in developing African nations are informally reaching out to each other through both calls and text messages for second opinions, supported in cases such as Ghana's free mobile phone service provided by a network operator there. Meanwhile, initiatives such as **FrontlineSMS'** Mobile Medic are showing just how powerful telehealth programs can be. During a pilot program at a hospital in Malawi designed to eliminate many long trips to visit patients in favor of communication via text messages, healthcare workers were taught to use text messages to support patient adherence reporting, issue appointment reminders, and direct physician queries. At the end of the pilot, the hospital saved approximately 2,048 hours of worker time, about $2,750, and doubled the capacity of its tuberculosis treatment program.

### U.S. encourages texting for health

In much the same way smartphone applications have caught the interest of regulators, so too has texting. The **U.S. Department of Health and Human Services** has established a **Text4Health Task Force** which has already developed recommendations for HHS' role in encouraging and developing health text messaging initiatives that would deliver health information and resources to individuals via their mobile phones. Its recommendations for health text messaging and mobile health programs were announced in September 2011.

Finding new ways to reach people where they are and convince them to actively participate in their own healthcare will take on increasing importance especially in the United

States, where millions of new people could potentially be added to health insurance rolls under the *Patient Protection and Affordable Care Act.* As many as 90 million Americans lack basic health literacy skills, according to an **Institute of Medicine** study. Technologies that reach these people in the course of their daily lives, such as text messaging, have the potential to make significant inroads in encouraging preventive health practices.

### Turning to Each Other

"The internet has changed people's relationships with information," says Susannah Fox, Associate Director of the **Pew Research Center's Internet & American Life Project**, a researcher at the forefront of assessing the new ways in which people are accessing and using health information.

**Susannah Fox**
*Associate Director, Pew Research Center's Internet & American Life Project*

During a keynote presentation to the **Medicine 2.0 Congress** at **Stanford University** in September 2011, she described the growing social impact of the Internet on healthcare in this way: "Peer-to-peer healthcare acknowledges that patients and caregivers know things — about themselves, about each other, about treatments — and they want to share what they know to help other people. Technology helps to surface and organize that knowledge to make it useful for as many people as possible."

In a 2009 study, "The Social Life of Health Information," Fox found that 59 percent of all adults and 80 percent of those who use the Internet have looked online for information regarding a specific disease or treatment. What started as a loose collection of individuals opening their lives to friends and strangers through the pages of early blogging sites has morphed into a movement of social media. The technical barriers that once kept people with minimal technical skill from sharing their lives online have slipped away with sites such as **Facebook, Twitter,** and health related social networks, such as **PatientsLikeMe** [*SEE FIGURE 4.8*].

As these sites have drawn broader and more diverse audiences, technical barriers to sharing health information have begun to melt away. People of varied ages and genders are well-represented among what media critic Jay Rosen calls "the people formerly known as the audi-

# Pfizer's Electronically Tracked Clinical Trial

## Overactive bladder study allows patients to report in by phone, web

In June 2011 **Pfizer** launched its first-ever effort to use mobile phones and the web to track about 600 patients in ten states as they participated in a randomized clinical trial.

The pilot project, dubbed REMOTE, for Research on Electronic Monitoring of Overactive Bladder Treatment Experience, is part of a growing list of web- and mobile-enabled trials sure to be watched closely by the **U.S. Food and Drug Administration**, which has its own initiatives to improve the quality and efficiency of clinical trials. The study assessed the safety and efficacy of Detrol LA, a treatment for overactive bladder. Pfizer hopes the results of the virtual trial will mirror results of a previously completed late-stage trial of the drug, thereby validating what the company sees as a "patient-centered" approach to clinical research.

"Studies like REMOTE could make biomedical science much more accessible to people who have long been excluded from or under-represented in clinical trials.

**Freda Lewis-Hall**
*Executive vice president and chief medical officer, Pfizer.*

"Studies like REMOTE could make biomedical science much more accessible to people who have long been excluded from or under-represented in clinical trials. Putting research within reach of more diverse populations has the potential to advance medical progress and lead to better outcomes for more patients," says Freda Lewis-Hall, an executive vice president and chief medical officer for Pfizer.

Clinical study patients typically have to register in person with researchers and often make doctor visits to receive trial medications and report on treatment effects. In the REMOTE trial, investigators instead shipped study medication to participant's homes. Researchers also were able to remotely manage the study and share clinical trial data and results with patients. Such flexibility offers not just efficiency, but the possibility of reaching a broader patient population, says Steven Cummings, Emeritus Professor of Medicine at the **University of California San Francisco**.

The digital infrastructure enabling Pfizer's novel study was provided by San Francisco-based **Mytrus**, a small startup that will help patients find trials that interest them, screen for patients meeting study criteria, and handle additional logistics. Upcoming trials listed on the company's web site include studies of treatments for osteoarthritis, binge eating, chronic obstructive pulmonary disease, diabetes, and sleep disorders.

"This approach, if proven successful, holds considerable promise in speeding up clinical trials while improving their quality," says Briggs Morrison, Pfizer's senior vice president of worldwide medical excellence. "This program and similar programs that may follow could lead to an entirely new way for patients to participate in trials and contribute to biomedical research." ■

*Figure 4.9* DIGITAL HEALTH FINANCINGS BY TECHNOLOGY IN 2010 VS. 2011

**Amount of financings raised and number of deals**

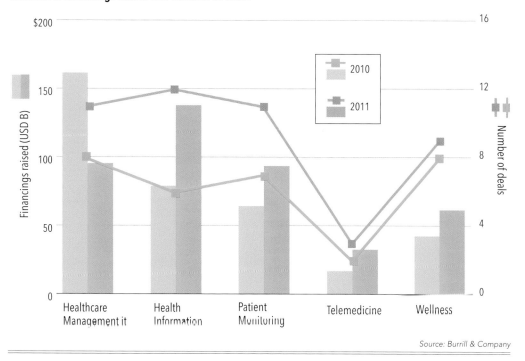

Source: Burrill & Company

DIGITAL HEALTH

4

ence." The one-time sole consumers of information have now become creators too. They share news and information about developments for dealing with rare and chronic disease, swap insights on the latest clinical trials and their own medical histories and experiences [*SEE SIDEBAR PFIZER*].

The pharmaceutical industry, slow to engage because of regulatory concerns and legacy mass media approaches to communication, are trying to figure out how best to capitalize on social media as both a rich source of information about their customers as well as a means of engaging with them directly. Pew's Internet & American Life Project found that, "doctors, nurses, and other health professionals continue to be the first choice for most people with health concerns, but online resources, including advice from peers, are a significant source of health information in the U.S." So far, just 11 percent of social network site users, or 5 percent of adults, have posted comments, queries, or information about health or medical matters online, the study found. But online conversation is growing, it concluded, propelled by the growing availability of social networking tools

and "the motivation, especially among people living with chronic conditions, to connect with each other."

Already, Facebook, the U.S. king of social networking sites, has moved to capitalize on this trend by adding to the once-simple status-sharing box a "Health and Wellness" category,

*Figure 4.10* **DIGITAL HEALTH FINANCINGS IN 2011**

Total Amount Raised: $421 million

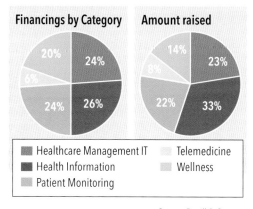

Source: Burrill & Company

# Europe Embraces eHealth

## Programs for seniors harness potential of communication technologies

Europe is embracing digital health as a major tool to manage healthcare challenges. **The European Council** first endorsed the concept of eHealth in 2004, when in the report "eHealth— making healthcare better for European citizens," it called for the first formal commitments from EU member states to collaborate in the field. Refining the concept in 2009, EU officials defined eHealth as meaning "better, safer and more efficient healthcare systems."

From the start, electronic health record systems were identified as a priority in EU member states. But many countries are still in the planning stage. Having a patient's entire healthcare history easily available is expected to improve treatment. Policymakers also hope to reduce strain on healthcare systems and boost patient autonomy.

England is striving to create summary care records (SCR) for at least half its population by mid-2013. So far, about 33.5 million patients have been contacted in the course of creating such records, and just 1.24 percent of the population has opted out of the program. SCRs are viewed in 20 to 30 percent of clinical encounters where they are available. A survey of after-hours doctors found 43 percent felt that having access to an SCR made them feel more confident and 70 percent felt that the SCR increased safety in treating patients.

> From the start, electronic health record systems were identified as a priority in EU member states. But many countries are still in the planning stage.

Germany too has ambitious plans. By 2013, it expects to roll out 60 million encrypted electronic health cards capable of carrying patient information including emergency, medication, and drug allergy data. About 6 million of the cards, created by **Infineon Technologies**, were slated for distribution by the end of 2011.

At a EU-wide level, a pilot scheme known as Smart Open Services for European Patients has engaged 23 countries in a limited cross-border data sharing initiative. The program aims to help set guidelines and standards for "a seamless exchange of health information across Europe."

Programs for seniors are increasingly harnessing information and communication technologies to allow seniors to maintain independent lives, with a particular emphasis on managing dementia, maintaining mobility, and minimizing social isolation.

The Ambient Assisted Living Joint Programme, set up in 2008, is working with 23 European countries and the **European Commission** to develop technology and know-how to help foster senior health. The program has a total budget of $829 million (€600 million) over six years, half public, half private.

A January 2011 **eHealth Strategies** report on Europe's progress concluded that European countries are making significant progress in eHealth and highlighted the potential of digital patient data to strengthen public health, clinical trials, and patient safety.

To improve the outlook for eHealth in Europe, the report recommends increased cooperation, training and education, and standardization. It also highlights the need to broaden eHealth to become an "integrated well-being and caring approach which includes social care providers, ambient assisted living initiatives, prevention, and wellbeing services."

The recommendations represent a challenge for the wide variety of European countries, but to harness fully the potential of eHealth, the member states need to continue building on the significant progress so far and work towards a coherent, Europe-wide practice. ■

*Figure 4.11*     **S**ELECTED **D**IGITAL **H**EALTH **D**EALS **2010** TO **2011**

| LICENSER | LICENSEE | DEAL TYPE | DETAILS |
|---|---|---|---|
| Proteus Biomedical | Novartis | License | Exclusive worldwide license and collaboration to develop and commercialize drugs that incorporate Proteus' sensor-based technologies in organ transplantation, Proteus gets $24 million upfront in cash and equity investments, royalties on sales |
| Keas | Pfizer | Alliance | Collaboration in personalized online care plans using Keas interactive service |
| Epocrates | Pfizer | Partnership | Collaboration to give healthcare providers mobile access to Pfizer Medical Information through Epocrates drug reference app for iPhone |
| Medical Platform Asia | Qualcomm | Agreement | Provide remote patient monitoring in rural Japan as part of Qualcomm's wireless Reach Initiative |
| Intel | GE | Joint Venture | 50/50 joint venture to create new company focused on telehealth and independent living that combines assets of GE Healthcare's Home Health division and Intel's Digital Health Group |
| eCardio Diagnostics | AT&T | Collaboration | AT&T will provide wireless data and connectivity for remote monitoring of cardiac patients with eCardio's devices |
| AirStrip Technologies | Physio-Control | Partnership | Partnership to deliver mobile solutions integrating AirStrip's remote patient monitoring applications with Physio Control's patient data transmission network |
| Siemens | PositiveID | License | Siemens grants PositiveID rights to use key IP to expand its next generation patient monitoring systems including wireless body communication |
| Vitality | Patrick Soon-Shiong | Acquisition | Vitality is developing Glo-Caps, the first wireless Internet-connected smart pill bottle that improves medication adherence |
| PositiveID | Connected Development | Partnership | Complete final stage of development of its iglucose wireless communication device that automatically transmits blood glucose readings from any data-capable glucometer to the iglucose database |
| Proteus Biomedical | Avery Dennison Medical Solutions | Partnership | Development of patch-based wearable sensors for consumer, home health care and remote medical applications |

*Source: Burrill & Company*

offering custom forms for sharing with friends everything from new eating habits to the triumph over an illness.

## Federal Support

Money for digital health initiatives is flowing from many different stakeholders, primarily from either private investors or governments, with each pursuing their own take on the opportunities at hand. Governments are making the biggest investments now, spending billions of dollars today to lay the infrastructure for the healthcare networks of tomorrow. Private investors are betting on the hottest startups, hoping they might find ones that gain traction and scale

to make money by delivering disruptive change.

In the United States, the biggest investment in digital health comes from the *Health Information Technology for Economic and Clinical Health Act*, or HITECH for short. HITECH was enacted as part of the *American Recovery and Reinvestment Act* of 2009 and sets aside $27 billion in federal stimulus money for health information technology. The biggest part of that funding is targeted at sparking meaningful use of electronic health records by healthcare providers.

Essentially, HITECH authorizes Medicare and Medicaid to pay bonuses to doctors and hospitals for the adoption and meaningful use of electronic health records. What's important

Patients will be an important source of change, through consumer preference for certain mobile applications and their willingness to log and monitor their own health with digital tools.

about the financial incentives, which can amount to as much as $63,750 per doctor and $2 million per hospital, is that they're attached not simply to the implementation of electronic health records, but to their use in ways to improve care. Adoption is picking up. In 2011, the U.S. government spent $2.5 billion on awards to physicians and hospitals that met the guidelines for procuring and putting into meaningful use electronic medical record systems [*See Sidebar VA*].

There is also a tremendous amount of support for digital health efforts building within the **National Institutes of Health**, the largest supporter of biomedical and behavioral research in the world. The enthusiasm for innovative tools to help address the threat of noncommunicable diseases, such as coronary heart disease, diabetes and cancer, was expressed by Robert Kaplan, the director of NIH's **Office of Behavioral and Social Sciences Research**.

"We believe that mHealth and wireless technologies are an essential part of our future,"

Kaplan said at the mHealth summit in Washington D.C. in December 2011. "The NIH Office of Behavioral and Social Sciences Research, and several of the 27 NIH institutes and centers have been exploring how advances in sensors, monitors, and mobile phones will create portable and affordable diagnostics, will help manage chronic disease, and allow us to monitor the health of populations living in remote locations."

### Digital Health Financings

Governments are not alone in their belief that digital health technologies will play a critical role in shaping the future of healthcare. Investors are also betting on the sector to deliver disruptive innovation. Despite the turbulent year for capital markets in 2011, venture financings of digital health companies rose nearly 16 percent in 2011 in terms of total capital raised. As a group, digital health companies raised $421 million in 46 deals during 2011, as compared to $364 million in 31 deals during 2010. Health information compa-

*Figure 4.12* **In It To Win It - Selected Health Challenges**

| SPONSOR | PRIZE MONEY (USD) | GOAL |
| --- | --- | --- |
| Robert Wood Johnson Foundation and Aligning Forces for Quality | $130,000 | Help patients access better health care using publicly available measures of health care quality |
| Office of the National Coordinator for Health Information Technology | $100,000 | Help providers improve patient safety, better engage with patients, and identify populations at risk |
| Qualcomm | $10,000,000 | Creation of a mobile platform to accurately diagnose disease. |
| General Electric | $100,000,000 | Identify and accelerate ideas that advance breast cancer early detection and diagnostics |

*Sources: Health 2.0, Qualcomm, GE*

# VA Awards $1.4 Billion in Telehealth Contracts

## Six companies will deploy technology to improve care to vets

**B**etting on telehealth as a way to improve access to care for America's 22 million veterans, the **Department of Veterans Affairs** in April 2011 awarded contracts totaling almost $1.4 billion to six information technology companies to run its growing program, already one of the largest in the world. Telehealth systems allow patients remote access to healthcare professionals from their homes or rural clinics.

Individual contracts run from $150 million to $372 million over five years, starting with a one-year base period, and four optional one-year renewal periods.

**Authentidate, American Telecare, Cardiocom, HealthHero** network, **Visual Telecommunication Network/ViTelCare**, and **Viterion TeleHealthcare** all received contracts.

New Jersey-based Authentidate and Minneapolis-based Cardiocom will supply the VA with web-based systems to monitor patients and manage the in-home care of patients. Clinicians will use the systems to remotely monitor their patients' vital signs and gather other pertinent information about their patients' health to supplement in-person visits. They can also remotely manage or adjust their patients' care plans, medication reminders and related information, and provide disease-specific education to their patients in real-time.

The VA's goal is to use telehealth capabilities to "ensure veteran patients get the right care in the right place at the right time and aims to make the home into the preferred place of care, whenever possible," according to its website.

Services include traditional clinical video telehealth that connects rural clinics to doctors and specialty services available only at medical centers; remote patient monitoring with digital devices that patients and physicians can use to monitor their vital signs; and technologies that can acquire and store clinical information, such as data, image, sound, and video, that is then retrieved at another site for evaluation. ∎

---

nies led the way, accounting for 33 percent of the total, while healthcare management IT companies captured 23 percent of financing dollars, closely followed by patient monitoring ventures, which attracted 22 percent. Wellness-focused companies received 14 percent of financing dollars, while telemedicine businesses captured just 8 percent [*See Figure 4.9 and 4.10*].

**ZocDoc**, a medical appointment booking service, led the pack, attracting $75 million in 2011, including $50 million from **Digital Sky Technologies**, the multi-billion dollar Russian investment firm that has backed Facebook, Twitter, and **Zynga**. **Goldman Sachs** supplied the remaining $25 million. Much like the restaurant reservation service **OpenTable**, ZocDoc has taken aim at a fragmented and inefficient system—the availability of medical appointments—and found a way to streamline it, offering patients free web and mobile access to the real-time schedules of doctors, dentists, and various medical specialists who pay

ZocDoc a monthly fee. The service taps into the 10 to 20 percent of medical appointments it says are cancelled or rescheduled at the last-minute to offer millions of available appointments with doctors and medical practitioners. By the end of 2011, it was serving nearly 800,000 patients each month in thirteen major metropolitan areas.

The asset and personnel-tracking firm **Awarepoint** scored one of the most notable healthcare IT financings of the year, landing $27 million. Meanwhile, **NovaSom**, a cloud-based diagnostics provider focused on obstructive sleep apnea, raised $35 million and **Lumos Labs**, the creator of a suite of online games for cognitive enhancement, raised $32.5 million, putting the growing company with 14 million users, on track for a potential IPO in 2013.

In the medical device realm, AliveCor, secured $3 million in series A financing led by **Burrill & Company**, the publisher of this book, along with **Qualcomm Ventures** and the **Okla-**

> As social media sites have drawn more diverse audiences, technical barriers to sharing health information have begun to melt away.

homa **Life Science Fund**.

**Epocrates**, an enormously popular mobile drug reference app used by more than half of U.S. doctors and the only digital health company to IPO in 2011, had a strong showing when it debuted on the **Nasdaq** in February. It raised $62.2 million in proceeds from the IPO, net of underwriters' discounts and commissions and other offering costs. Despite raising 14 percent more than planned, the company's shares ended the year at $7.80, down 51.3 percent from their $16 initial offering price. The shares fell dramatically in August 2011 after the company lowered its guidance for the year.

In addition to these traditional types of financing, some companies are also chasing after a different type of funding: prize money. One of the most famous purses sought by healthcare startups is the $10 million **Qualcomm Tricorder X PRIZE**. The "Star Trek"-inspired award is designed to spur innovations in areas such as artificial intelligence and wireless sensing on the way to the creation of the mobile platform that most accurately diagnoses a set of 15 diseases across 30 consumers in three days. In addition, new challenges sponsored by governments, non-profits, and corporations have sought to direct the development of new digital health tools [*SEE FIGURE 4.12*].

What's at stake in such contests and the rise of digital health technologies in general is not only the vast sums of money to be made in selling the software, services, and devices that take hold, but the power to influence healthcare decisions that will accrue to those who ultimately manage and integrate the digital healthcare systems that achieve the most widespread adoption.

Patients will be one important source of change, through the exercise of consumer preference for certain mobile applications and their willingness to log and monitor their own health with digital tools. But any true progress will also turn on the willingness of healthcare providers to solicit and embrace patient-generated data, adopt electronic health records, and act on the data and trends recorded in each.

## Big Pharma's Role

Far from sitting on the sidelines of the digital health movement, Big Pharma is increasingly looking for new ways to participate [*SEE FIGURE 4.11*]. **Janssen Healthcare Innovation**, an upstart unit within **Johnson & Johnson's** pharmaceutical arm, Janssen Pharmaceuticals, offers one example of how this is happening.

"There are many different ways in which we could be significantly enhancing human health, beyond the traditional way in which we do it by prescribing drugs," says Diego Miralles, head of the West Coast research center for **Janssen Research and Development**. Coming to that realization wasn't necessarily easy. Big corporations spend a lot of time focused internally, with executives talking most often to each other, he says. But Janssen has increasingly looked outside its walls, visiting hospitals and other settings in which care is delivered to find new ideas about how to create business models that can improve the quality of care. Initially, the company is working to apply technology to improve its existing businesses by better managing aspects of clinical trials—from patient recruiting to the retention of trial participants. It is also creating more reliable communications channels to aid with problems like adherence to prescription regimens.

However, as Janssen becomes increasingly focused on emerging opportunities within healthcare, it is looking at three market changes that will reshape its business—and truly the whole healthcare sector—over time: the expansion of "the place of care," from the doctor's office to nearly anyplace new mobile phones and other mobile technologies can reach; wellness, with a focus on the prevention of disease; and a realignment of incentives for all the stakeholders in healthcare through new models of payment for services.

## Bending the cost curve

Rich opportunities to increase the scale and reach of digital health initiatives lie ahead. The rising use of mobile phones, tablets, and other wireless devices are expected to create a $7 billion mobile health market opportunity in the Asia Pacific region by 2017, suggests the **GSMA**, an international association of mobile phone operators. Meanwhile, technology's potential to help create closer ties between patients and healthcare providers is likely to become increasingly apparent to healthcare payers, who will be eager to harness the power of improved information to enable better coordination of care, reduce medical errors and, hopefully, bring about longer and more independent lives for everyone. ■

"There are many different ways in which we could be significantly enhancing human health, beyond the traditional way in which we do it by prescribing drugs"

**Diego Miralles**
*Head of the West Coast research center for Janssen Research and Development*

DIGITAL HEALTH

4

# IN SEARCH OF DISRUPTION

Governments around the world are feeling pressure to control health-care spending. These pressures have only intensified in the face of the global recession of recent years and the push for austerity measures in many countries. Some countries have implemented new price controls and increasingly are demanding demonstrations that therapies have value before they will pay for them. Industry and its advocates, however, are concerned that efforts to rein in spending will threaten innovation, which they say is what's needed to address the growing cost of healthcare. As governments seek to cut healthcare spending, they are also looking at new ways healthcare can be more efficiently accessed and delivered and new models for payment that better align payer, provider, and patient interest by shifting away from compensating for the number of proce-dures performed and instead paying for the quality and results of the care that's delivered. In the United States, the landmark healthcare reform legislation passed in 2010 will come before the Supreme Court in 2012. Regardless of the outcome of the case, patients, payers, and providers will continue driving changes to healthcare with or without the legislation. At the heart of these changes will be the emergence of empowered con-sumers who no longer play a passive role in their own healthcare, but are actively engaged in decision-making with an eye toward both their long-term health and the cost of care. In the absence of innovation-driven solutions, the rationing of care will be inevitable.

# Chapter 5:

# In Search of Disruption

**Eli Lilly** CEO John Lechleiter stood before the *Federation of German Industries Conference* in Berlin in July 2011 speaking about competing interests in the healthcare arena, such as the growing needs of aging populations and the limited funds in government and private-sector budgets. While he said competition can be good, such as when it is between pharmaceutical companies seeking to develop innovative drugs, he was critical of competition between the public and private sectors. "We're on the same side in the fight to advance public health," he said. "We have a common enemy—disease, disability, and premature death.  And we have a common interest in the only means by which our healthcare systems can help more people 'live longer healthier' within constrained budgets – and that's innovation."

Lechleiter had a target that day. It was Germany's pharmaceutical market reorganization act *AMNOG* that sat in his crosshairs. The act, which took effect at the start of 2011, requires pharmaceutical companies introducing new drugs into the German market to demonstrate their value by comparing them to existing drugs on the market against which they will compete. The law is expected to save the German government at least $2.7 billion a year on drugs.

While Lechleiter said it would be hard to argue that prices should reflect the added benefit new products provide, his problem is with the law's approach to determining the value of pharmaceutical innovations. His concern is that it places too much emphasis on cost and that not enough

effort is being made to understand innovation. He argues that there's a need to move away from

**John Lechleiter**
*CEO, Eli Lilly*
═══════════

population-based measures of quality to instead focus on individual needs and outcomes. "No other country in the world has a set of requirements quite like those imposed by AMNOG," said Lechleiter. "The potential effects are serious: launches of new medicines that can benefit patients delayed or withdrawn, erosion of Germany's strength in pharmaceutical innovation, and the loss of high-paying jobs in research and development."

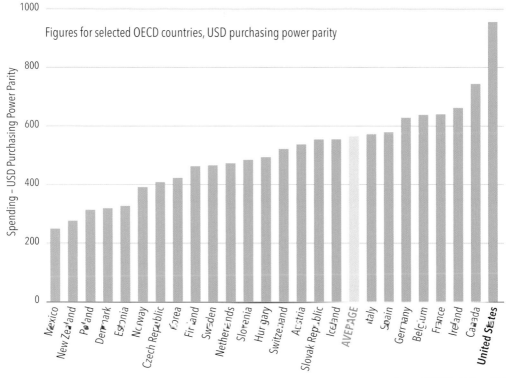

*Figure 5.1* PER CAPITA EXPENDITURE ON PHARMACEUTICALS AND OTHER MEDICAL NON-DURABLES BY COUNTRY

Figures for selected OECD countries, USD purchasing power parity

Spending – USD Purchasing Power Parity

Mexico, New Zealand, Poland, Denmark, Estonia, Norway, Czech Republic, Korea, Finland, Sweden, Netherlands, Slovenia, Hungary, Switzerland, Austria, Slovak Republic, Iceland, AVERAGE, Italy, Spain, Germany, Belgium, France, Ireland, Canada, United States

*Source: OECD Health Data 2011*

The discussion was not a policy abstraction for Lechleiter, but an issue of very real consequences. Not only is Germany the third largest market in the world for Eli Lilly, but one in which the company had hoped to begin marketing its new diabetes drug Tradjenta in partnership with **Boehringer Ingelheim**. The two companies had launched the once-daily diabetes pill in the United States in June 2011 and won **European Medicines Agency** approval in August for people who are unable to control their blood sugar levels through diet and exercise alone. Though the drug offers convenience as the only once-a-day treatment that does not require dose adjustments for people suffering from loss of kidney function, its benefits are comparable to other drugs already available in Germany. In September 2011, Lilly and Boehringer said they would not launch the drug in Germany because of concerns they would be unable to get an adequate price for the drug. About 6.8 million people in Germany suffer from type 2 diabetes. Of those, about two-thirds suffer from kidney problems.

Lilly is not alone in turning away from the German market. The Swiss pharmaceutical giant

**Novartis** in September 2011 decided to discontinue sales of its high blood pressure medication Rasilamlo, a combination of the two drugs aliskiren and amlodipine. Novartis won European approval for the combination therapy in April 2011 in patients who could not control their high blood pressure with either aliskiren or amlodipine alone. Novartis pulled the drug after it determined it could not provide the data necessary for the benefit assessment of the drug under AMNOG [*SEE SIDEBAR: ROCHE*].

**Pressure to control spending**

The moves in Germany reflect efforts across the world as governments take steps to rein in spending on healthcare, particularly in the United States, Europe, and Japan where concerns about debt burdens are forcing new austerity measures. As Novartis noted in a January 2012 regulatory filing, governments throughout the world are imposing industry-wide price cuts, mandatory pricing systems, and reference pricing initiatives while also increasing imports of drugs from lower-cost countries to higher-cost countries, shifting payment burdens to patients through higher copayments, limiting physicians' ability to choose among competing medicines, and requiring substitution of generic drugs for patented equivalents.

"The growth of overall healthcare costs as a percentage of gross domestic product in many countries means that governments and payers are under intense pressure to control spending even more tightly," Novartis said in the filing with the **U.S. Securities and Exchange Commission**. "These pressures are particularly strong given the lingering effects of the recent global economic and financial crisis, including the ongoing debt crisis in certain countries in Europe, and the risk of a similar crisis in the U.S. As a result, our businesses and the healthcare industry in general are operating in an ever more challenging environment with very significant pricing pressures."

In April 2011, Italy introduced temporary price cuts with the aim of saving $834 million by the end of year. Germany, in addition to implementing AMNOG, increased the mandatory rebates imposed on pharmaceutical companies to 10 percent from 6 percent. China cut prices an average of 19 percent on more than 150 drugs

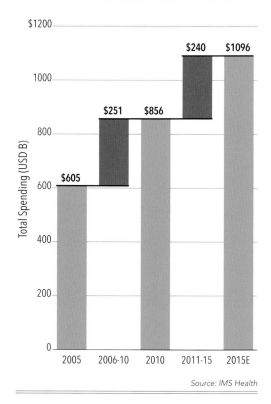

*Figure 5.2* **GLOBAL SPENDING ON MEDICINES 2005 TO 2015**

*Source: IMS Health*

# Roche Offers Germans a Money-Back Guarantee

Pay-for-performance plan addresses concerns about cost of Avastin

**R**oche's cancer drug, Avastin, costs about $4,584 (€3,300) in Germany per patient each month, making public expenditures on the drug an easy target for criticism in a country where a value-based drug-pricing scheme has been implemented. The country's new federal drug pricing law, known as *AMNOG*, launched in January 2011 and is designed to generate savings of $2.32 billion (€1.7 billion) in 2011 and annual savings of $2.73 billion (€2 billion) thereafter by tying a drug's price to the value it provides.

Under Roche's proposed German contracts, if Avastin was shown to not slow tumor progression for a patient, Roche would reimburse the hospital or the public insurer the cost of the drug, a company spokesman says.

The pay-for-performance arrangement could potentially ease government concern over use of the drug in the wake of a May 2011 report by a regional medical group in the country questioning Avastin's value. The agreement covers the use of Avastin for breast, lung, kidney, and colorectal cancers and is complementary to a price-capping program for Avastin already in place in Germany.

Roche is offering contracts including the refund arrangement now because such contracts were not possible in the German healthcare system, the spokesman told *Reuters*. The new pay-for-performance plans are available for both health insurers and hospitals. ∎

*Figure 5.3* TOTAL PER CAPITA HEALTHCARE EXPENDITURES, BY COUNTRY IN 2009

Amount in USD purchasing power parity

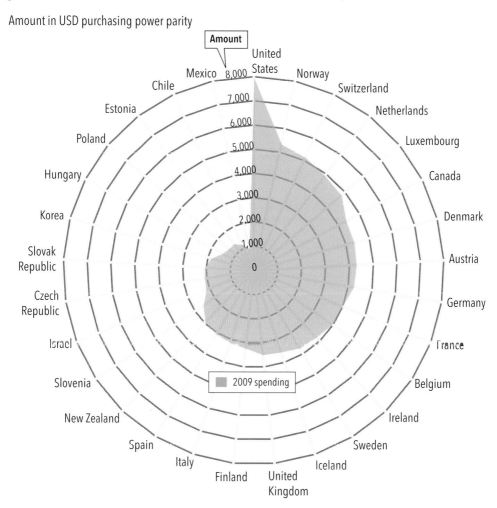

Source: OECD Health Data 2011

at the end of 2010. And Turkey in 2010 imposed price cuts on prescription drugs ranging from 11 to 23 percent [SEE FIGURES 5.1 AND 5.2].

Though the United States has not imposed price controls, the bipartisan **Joint Select Committee on Deficit Reduction**, the so-called Congressional Super Committee, which was charged with finding $1.2 trillion in cuts over the next 10 years, considered imposing a government-mandated pricing formula on both patented and generic medications provided through the Medicare prescription drug benefit known as *Medicare Part D* before the committee's work ended in failure. The issue of price controls, though, didn't end with the Super Committee. The **Independent Payment Advisory Board**, established by the *Patient Protection and Affordable Care Act*

in the United States, has a mandate to cut costs of the Part D prescription program and has broad authority to do so.

Efforts to contain costs come in response to the simple fact that the growth in healthcare costs continue to rise and take a greater share of the GDP of both developed and developing nations [SEE FIGURES 5.3, 5.4, AND 5.5]. Public healthcare spending as a percent of GDP is expected to rise by 3 percentage points by 2030 in advanced economies and by 1 percent in emerging nations, according to projections from the **International Monetary Fund**.

### The drivers of rising costs

Across the globe, rising standards of living, increasing longevity and improved healthcare is

*Figure 5.4*  **Total Expenditures on Healthcare as a Percent of GDP in 2009**

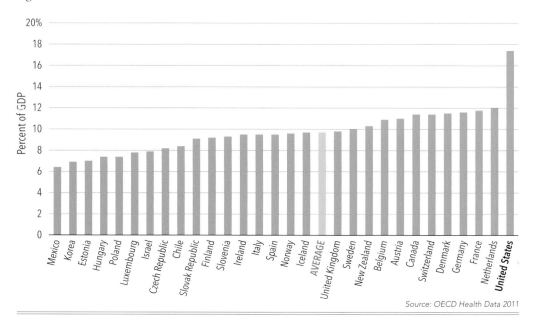

Source: OECD Health Data 2011

good news [*See Figure 5.6*]. But those developments, along with changing lifestyles, are also helping fuel demand for healthcare and placing pressures on healthcare systems across the globe [*See Sidebar Countries*]. Governments and payers are wrestling with how to contain costs, which continue to rise. Though not the only driver of healthcare, the rising incidence of chronic disease is becoming a critical issue in both developed countries and emerging markets [*See Figure 5.7*].

An April 2011 report from the **World Health Organization**, the first worldwide assessment of non-communicable disease, found that non-communicable diseases are the leading killer today and are on the rise. The WHO found that in 2008, 36.1 million people died from conditions such as heart disease, strokes, chronic lung diseases, cancers, and diabetes. Perhaps most shocking is that nearly 80 percent of these deaths occurred in low- and middle-income countries. In these countries, about 30 percent of the deaths from non-communicable diseases are among people 60 or younger.

"These premature deaths are all the more tragic because they are largely preventable," says Ala Alwan, WHO Assistant Director-General for Non-communicable Diseases and Mental Health. "This is a great loss, not just at an individual level, but also profoundly affects the fam-

ily and a country's workforce. For the millions struggling with poverty, a vicious circle ensues." WHO Director-General Margaret Chan says chronic non-communicable diseases deliver a two-punch blow to development because they cause billions of dollars in lost national income, and they push millions of people below the poverty line every year. While these diseases have reached epidemic proportions, the report says they could be significantly reduced through the reduction of their risk factors, early detection, and timely treatments. "The rise of chronic non-communicable diseases presents an enormous challenge," says Chan, who released the report at the WHO conference on non-communicable diseases in April 2011 in Moscow. "For some countries, it is no exaggeration to describe the situation as an impending disaster; a disaster for health, for society, and most of all for national economies."

The cost of healthcare is straining governments and individuals around the globe. WHO says that part of the solution lies in focusing on ways of financing healthcare. It argues that smarter spending could increase global health coverage by anywhere between 20 percent and 40 percent. And governments need to think about new sources of tax revenue to fund healthcare. Ghana, for example, has funded its national health insurance partly by increasing

*Figure 5.5*  **Increase in Years of Life Expectancy by Country from 1960 to 2009**

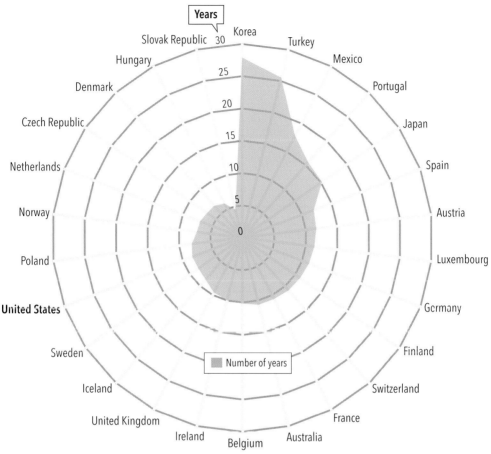

Source: OECD Health Data 2011

its value-added tax by 2.5 percent. A review of 22 low-income countries shows that between them, they could raise $1.42 billion through a 50 percent increase in tobacco taxes. India could generate $370 million per year by implementing a levy of just .005 percent on foreign exchange transactions.

"At a time when money is tight, my advice to countries is this: before looking for places to cut spending on healthcare, look first for opportunities to improve efficiency," wrote Chan. "All health systems, everywhere, could make better use of resources, whether through better procurement practices, broader use of generic products, better incentives for providers, or streamlined financing and administrative procedures."

While the report identifies ten areas where greater efficiencies are possible, ranging from purchasing generic drugs to addressing hospital-related inefficiencies, it says governments need to

*Figure 5.6*  **The Cost of Chronic Disease**

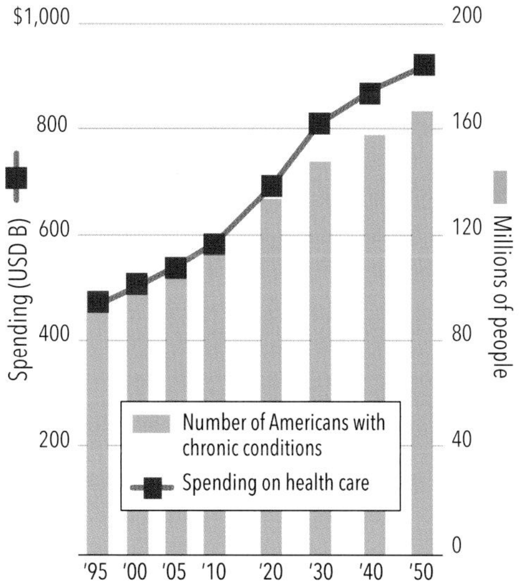

Legend:
- Number of Americans with chronic conditions
- Spending on health care

Source: Robert Wood Johnson Foundation

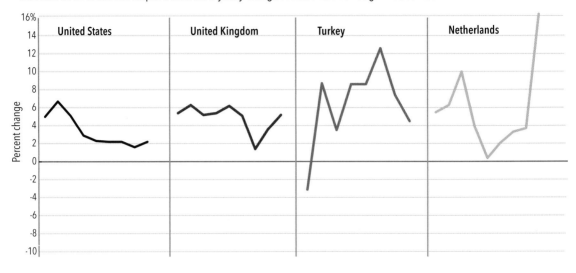

*Figure 5.7*   ANNUAL GROWTH RATE PER CAPITA OF TOTAL HEALTHCARE EXPENDITURE **2000-2009**

Selected OECD countries. Graphed lines show yearly change FY 2000-2001 through FY2008-2009

# Affordable Care Act Paying Dividends

## Reform extends coverage to 2.5M young adults

The healthcare legislation signed into law by President Obama in 2010 has helped as many as 2.5 million young adults gain medical coverage over the last year, new data released by the federal government indicates.

The data is much more telling when considering that earlier this year, government and private estimates showed that only about 1 million Americans aged 19-25 had gained health insurance coverage. The large increase in numbers, administration officials say, was due to more precise data-gathering that aimed to conclusively pinpoint the impact of the healthcare provision.

Young adults have traditionally been the most likely demographic to be uninsured. Some are making the switch from school to work while others are holding down low-wage jobs that don't usually provide healthcare. Because of the *Patient Protection and Affordable Care Act*, young adults can now remain on their parents' insurance plans through age 26. The provision has spurred families to sign up young adults transitioning to the workforce in a difficult economic environment.

The **National Center for Health Statistics** in a brief said that the new data from the June 2011 *National Health Interview Survey* showed that from September 2010 to June 2011, the percentage of adults 19-25 with insurance coverage increased to 73 percent from 64 percent.

Allowing young adults to remain on their parents' health plans is not nearly as expensive as expanding coverage to other demographics because young adults are generally healthy. But the rise in the number of young people who are relying on their parents for healthcare coverage may actually underscore how bad our economy is, says Paul Fronstin, senior research associate at the **Employee Benefit Research Institute**.

"If you have all these young adults who can't find jobs, they can't get health coverage on their own," he told *The Los Angeles Times*. "I don't know if we would have seen the same effect if unemployment was down below 4 percent." ■

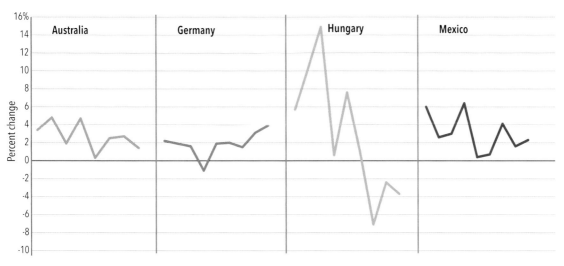

Source: OECD Health Data 2011

think about how to make healthcare more avail able and affordable. Countries such as Japan, which ensures health services are available to the entire population, have done so by reducing dependence on direct, out-of-pocket payments and increasing prepayment—generally through insurance or taxes or a mix of the two. The funds raised are then pooled, so that it is not just those who are unlucky enough to get sick that bear the financial burden. The report said this is the model used in many European countries, with Chile, Colombia, Mexico, Rwanda, Thailand, and Turkey all making significant progress in the last decade—along with Brazil, China, Costa Rica, Ghana, Kyrgyzstan, and the Republic of Moldova. "As the evidence shows, countries do need stable and sufficient funds for health, but national wealth is not a prerequisite for moving closer to universal coverage," says Chan. "Countries with similar levels of health expenditure achieve strikingly different health outcomes from their investments. Policy decisions help explain much of this difference."

## Healthcare reform passes, but costs rise

Despite the passage of the Affordable Care Act, the landmark U.S. healthcare reform legislation in 2010 which is headed to the **U.S. Supreme Court** in March 2012 to determine its constitutionality, healthcare costs continue to rise in the United States [*See Sidebar Suprema*]. Average annual spending on healthcare in the United States will outpace the growth of the GDP by 1.1 percent and reach $4.6 trillion by 2020, nearly 20 percent of the nation's expected economic output by then, according to a 2011 study by economists and actuaries at the **Centers for Medicare and Medicaid Services** and published in *Health Affairs*. It projects healthcare spending will grow at an average annual rate of 5.8 percent from 2010 to 2020. That will push healthcare spending to 19.8 percent of GDP by 2020, compared to 17.6 percent in 2010.

Healthcare spending was expected to have grown at a historically low rate of 3.9 percent in 2010, but the study attributed that low level of growth to losses in employment and health insurance coverage [*See Figures 5.8, 5.9, and 5.10*].

The 2010 healthcare reform legislation is actually expected to accelerate the pace of spending growth to an average of 5.8 percent a year, compared to 5.7 percent, between 2010 and 2020 as the new law expands coverage and increases demand for prescription drugs, physicians, and clinical services [*See Sidebar Healthcare*]. As healthcare spending grows, the government is expected to carry a greater share of the burden. The report says that by 2020 federal and state government sources will foot nearly half the bill,

*Figure 5.8* **U.S. Healthcare Expenditures: Where the Money Came From**

### Expenditures by source of payment in 2010

Total national health expenditures in 2010 = $2.6 Trillion

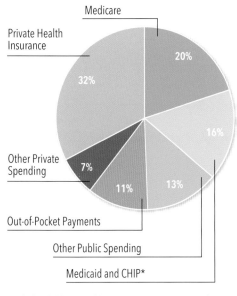

Medicare

Private Health Insurance

20%

32%

16%

Other Private Spending

7%

11%

13%

Out-of-Pocket Payments

Other Public Spending

Medicaid and CHIP*

\* Includes Children's Health Insurance Program (CHIP) and Children's Health Insurance Program expansion (Title XIX).

*Source: Health Affairs, January 2010*

up from 44 percent in 2009. About two-thirds of that amount is ultimately expected to be paid by the federal government.

"Health spending financed by governments at all levels in the U.S. will increase over the next decade as a result of expansions of health insurance coverage through Medicaid and subsidized private health insurance under the Affordable Care Act, as well as Medicare, as more Baby Boomers enter the program," says Sean Keehan, lead author of the study. While households' share of healthcare spending is expected to remain stable at 26 percent from 2014 to 2020, business spending will drop as a share, falling to 18 percent from 20 percent during that period, the study predicts.

A separate report from the **Congressional Budget Office** points to certain provisions of the Affordable Care Act that will drive government spending on healthcare higher. These include payments to health insurance plans for risk adjustment and reinsurance. In Congressional testimony following the release of the report, CBO Director Douglas Elmendorf said that if that rising level of spending is coupled with revenues that are held close to the average share of GDP that they have represented for the past 40

# Supreme Court to Review Healthcare Law

## Arguments slated for March 2012 with a June 2012 decision date set

The **U.S. Supreme Court** announced on November 14, 2011 that it will consider several challenges to President Obama's healthcare reform law. After four appellate court rulings on the healthcare law so far, the Supreme Court's decision should bring to an end questions of the law's constitutionality.

The court set a June 2012 date for its decision following a closed-door meeting of the justices. At the heart of the case is the constitutionality of the law's individual mandate, which requires virtually every U.S. citizen to have health insurance by 2014 or face financial penalties.

Opponents of the Act have said the mandate violates Congressional authority granted by the constitution both in its authority to regulate interstate commerce and a Constitutional prohibition on taking private property without just compensation.

**Sen. Chuck Grassley**
*R-Iowa*

The court could uphold the law; rule that the individual mandate is unconstitutional, but allow the rest of the law to stand; decide the individual mandate is unlawful and throw out the entire act because of it; or avoid a definitive decision by asserting that the mandate is a tax, making a ruling premature until someone is required to pay it.

As of the end of 2011, four appeals courts ruled on the healthcare law. Three appellate courts re-

years, the resulting deficits will increase federal debt to unsupportable levels. "To prevent that outcome, policymakers will have to substantially restrain the growth of spending for those programs, raise revenues above their historical share of GDP, or pursue some combination of those two approaches," he says.

The United States spends more per capita and spends a greater share of its GDP on healthcare than any other nation, but doesn't necessarily produce superior results for that spending, according to the **McKinsey Center for U.S. Health System**. The United States lags behind many other members of the **Organization for Economic Cooperation and Development** in measures of outcomes, despite its higher levels of spending, McKinsey notes. For instance, life expectancy at birth in the United States is 77.9 years, below the OECD average of 78.6 years. It's ranked for 21st behind the likes of Luxembourg, Denmark, and the Republic of Korea [*SEE FIGURE 5.12*].

The deep recession of recent years along with other changes helped slow the growth in spending in 2009—the eighth consecutive year of slowing growth in healthcare spending. In fact, in 2010, the rate of growth fell even further to 3.9

*Figure 5.9* **U.S. HEALTHCARE EXPENDITURES: WHERE THE MONEY WENT**

**Expenditures by healthcare sector in 2010**

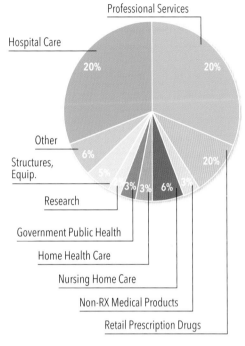

Source: Centers for Medicare & Medicaid Services, Office of the Actuary, National Health Statistics Group.

jected the argument that the mandate is unconstitutional while the one said that the mandate should be overturned.

The justices will also consider the legality of the section of the law that calls for the withholding of Medicaid funds to states that fail to cover anyone earning up to 133 percent of the federal poverty limit, part of the law's effort to expand coverage to people who are uninsured today.

**Rep. Nancy Pelosi**

*D-California, House Minority Leader*

Challengers have maintained that placing significant financial conditions on a state's behavior exceeds Congress' spending power. The **11th Circuit Court of Appeals**, the only appellate court to address the issue of Medicaid expansion, struck down the challenge. The justices have decided to rule on this case as well.

Finally, the issue of jurisdiction will be argued. Two appellate courts have maintained that the time is not right for the Supreme Court to even consider the law is constitutional because an 18th century law prevents individuals from challenging their taxes until after they've been paid. The justices will have to decide whether the law's penalty for not buying insurance functions enough like a tax that this rule applies.

In all, the Supreme Court has agreed to hear three appeals, two from the challengers of the law and the third from the Obama administration itself. Republican Senator Chuck Grassley of Iowa has asked Chief Justice John Roberts to allow the arguments in the case to be televised. House Minority Leader Nancy Pelosi, D-San Francisco, has said she supports that request. ■

*Figure 5.10* **Actual and Projected U.S. Healthcare Spending**

**Selected Years in 1993-2019**

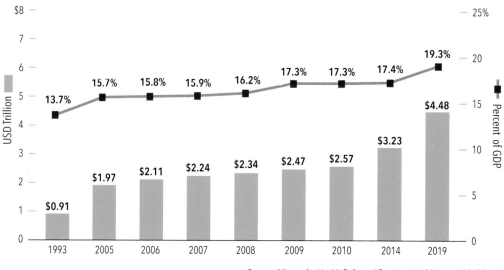

Source: Alliance for Health Reform; "Covering Health Issues, 5th Edition"

percent, the lowest level of spending growth in 50 years, according to McKinsey. At the same time, between 2007 and 2009, the number of people with employer-sponsored insurance also fell by nearly 10 million to 64.5 percent, the lowest level in 20 years of census records while the percent-

*Figure 5.11* **U.S. Spending on Pharmaceuticals**

**Per capita spending on pharmaceuticals including all medical non-durables**

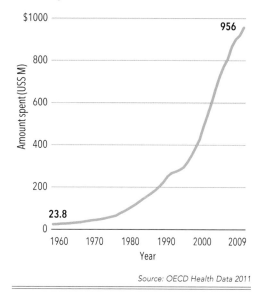

Source: OECD Health Data 2011

age of people receiving public assistance and the percentage of uninsured people both hit record highs.

Though the slowdown in spending occurred in all major healthcare sectors between 2006 and 2009, inpatient care, pharmaceuticals, and healthcare administration and insurance, historically among the fastest areas of growth in spending, experienced significant slowdowns in spending. Spending on prescription drugs slowed to a growth rate of 4.4 percent between 2006 and 2009. That compares to a 7.9 percent growth rate between 2003 and 2006. McKinsey said that reflects a stabilization of enrollment into the Medicare Part D prescription drug program and the growing use of generic drugs. Generics now account for 68 percent of all retail prescriptions, up from 55 percent in 2006. While that trend has been fueled by a number of factors, McKinsey notes one primary reason is that new drug launches have not kept pace with patent expirations on branded pharmaceuticals [*See Figure 5.11*].

The report said that the movement toward a focus on value is still in its early stages in the United States, but the combination of a reimbursement system that "pays for value over volume" and consumers that make value-based buying decisions, could drive improved performance. "The shift toward paying for value has also

*Figure 5.12* LIFE EXPECTANCY VS. HEALTHCARE EXPENDITURE

**Per capita healthcare expenditures compared to life expectancy by country in 2009**

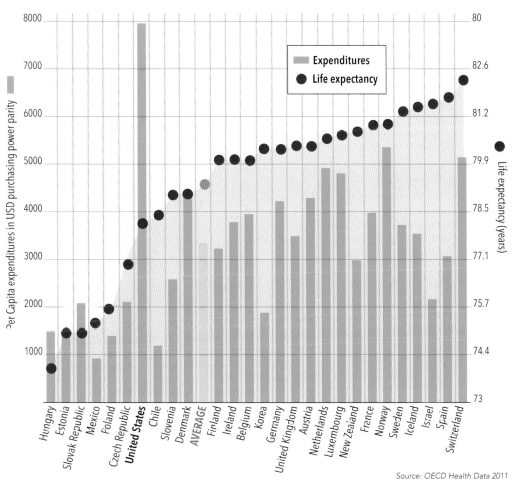

Source: OECD Health Data 2011

been accompanied by the emergence of health-care consumers—patients and their families—as an increasingly important factor in purchasing decisions," writes McKinsey. "There is a reason to believe that value-conscious consumers, armed with greater choices in how and where they purchase healthcare, will demonstrate a willingness to alter spending and consumption patterns and place a greater emphasis on what they are getting for their healthcare dollar."

### Innovation as cost driver

More than any other single factor driving healthcare costs in the United States during the past 40 years or so is technological innovation, according to a 2008 report from the **Congressional Budget Office**. While the report says technological innovation can reduce costs and typically

does so for many goods and services, within the healthcare arena its effects tend to drive costs higher. In fact, a CBO review of economic literature led it to conclude that over the past several decades about half of all of the increase in healthcare spending is attributable to advances in medical technology. Even when medical technological advances provide savings on a given procedure, they can add significant costs to the system if they are deployed broadly enough. Add to that the reality that innovations that extend life can increase overall spending simply by allowing people to live longer and require more healthcare services.

Consider coronary bypass surgery, which became possible in the 1960s with the advent of heart and lung machines. The CBO notes these lifesaving procedures, at first quite risky, grew

*Figure 5.13* **GROWTH IN PER CAPITA SPENDING BY COUNTRY 1960 TO 2010**

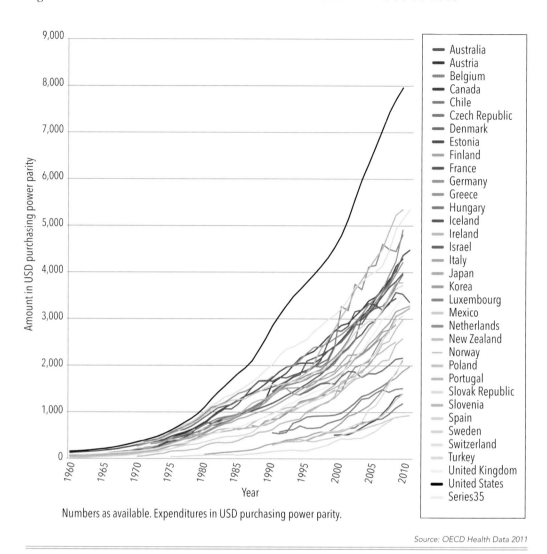

Numbers as available. Expenditures in USD purchasing power parity.

*Source: OECD Health Data 2011*

in popularity as techniques advanced. Improvements in the procedure allowed patients once considered too frail for the procedure to have it performed. In the 1970s, angioplasty, began to be used as an alternative means to restore blood flow through blocked arteries. It's similar to bypass surgery, but cheaper. But the CBO said it did not reduce costs because patients who otherwise might not have had open heart surgery chose to have angioplasty. Because blockages often recurred in the early days of the procedure, patients would return for second angioplasties. Sometimes, if an angioplasty was unsuccessful, patients would undergo bypass surgery. Spending on patients with heart disease increased after angioplasty was introduced. As improvements

were made to imaging agents to avoid adverse reactions, these new contrast media, meant to help physicians see the blockages, grew significantly more expensive. In the 1990s, patients with acute heart disease where treated with new clot-busting biologics. This provided a small improvement over older thrombolytic agents, but, the CBO notes, at several times the price.

Other examples of medical technology that have driven costs include neonatal intensive care, joint replacement, diagnostic imaging, and bone marrow transplantation. Innovative technology is a prime target of efforts to control healthcare spending because it is the biggest contributor to growth in spending. "An effective long-term strategy for controlling healthcare spending will

*Figure 5.14* INFANT MORTALITY VS. HEALTHCARE EXPENDITURE

Per capita  healthcare expenditures compared to infant mortality, 2009, by country

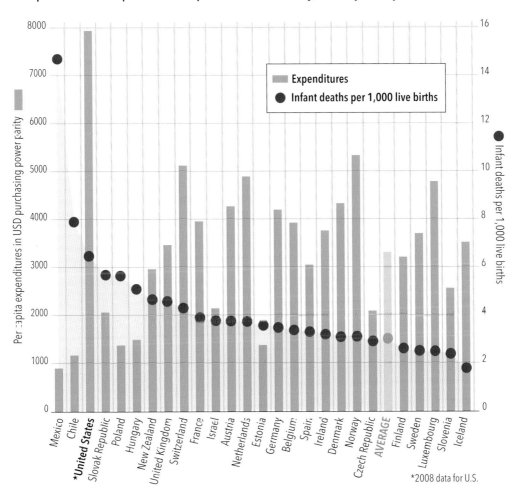

*2008 data for U.S.

Source: OECD Health Data 2011

probably have to address the healthcare systems' way of incorporating new technologies into practice," the CBO said. That would entail making more selective decisions about which new technologies to adopt. "Although this approach would mean that fewer medical services were available, evidence suggests that savings are possible without a substantial loss of clinical value," the CBO said.

## Comparative effectiveness takes hold

Comparative effectiveness analysis of new technologies is the means by which the CBO suggests the cost of new technologies can be controlled. It suggests that future technologies, as well as expensive ones in use today, should be adopted only when they provide clinical benefit that can't be provided by cheaper alternatives. Of course, there would have to be some way to implement the findings of comparative effectiveness research to change physician and patient behavior. That, it notes, would require altering reimbursement policies of insurers and Medicare.

The 2009 economic stimulus provided $1.1 billion for comparative effectiveness research with $300 million going to the **Agency for Healthcare Research and Quality**, $400 million going to the **National Institutes of Health**, and $400 million going to the Secretary of the **U.S. Department of Health and Human Services**. That was further advanced with an additional $800 million under the Patient Protection and

HEALTHCARE

5

# Countries Struggle with Cost, Access, and Delivery

| COUNTRY | TOP STORIES |
|---|---|
| Australia | • Healthcare expenditure is projected to drop to $122.7 billion in 2012 from $132.7 billion in 2011, a 7.6 percent drop<br>• Enacted R&D Tax Incentive that provides small and medium sized companies a 45 percent refundable tax offset; larger companies offered a 40 percent refundable tax offset |
| Brazil | • Pharmaceutical expenditure is projected to grow 22 percent in 2012, while healthcare expenditure is expected to grow 24 percent in 2012<br>• In September 2011, the MOH announced it would invest $881 million in R&D by the end of 2014 |
| Canada | • The healthcare costs in Canada are on the rise with an average of 40 percent of the budget.<br>• Canadian provinces are cutting generic drug prices, eliminating incentive fees to generic drug manufacturers, and paying hospitals on a fee for procedure basis |
| China | • China's healthcare spending accounted for 4.24 percent of GDP in 2011<br>• Government of China initiated a $124 Billion, three-year investment plan to fund universal coverage and build rural infrastructure and community health centers<br>• Plan to expand on medical insurance program designed to offer increased financial assistance for children suffering from heart disease and leukemia in all rural areas |
| France | • As part of a $85 million austerity plan, France announced that healthcare spending will be reduced to 2.5 percent year-on-year growth for 2012 |
| Germany | • Government has pledged to reform the country's healthcare system by announcing a $4.4 billion cut in healthcare spending and an increase in charges for state healthcare in order to generate savings of $7.6 billion<br>• The reorganization of the Pharmaceutical Market Act (AMNOG) in January 2011 |
| India | • Public health expenditure is expected to only reach 1.8 percent of GDP by the end of the 11th five year plan despite a target of 3 percent of GDP<br>• Government considering launching a universal health insurance scheme that it plans to partially fund |
| Japan | • Japan operates a universal social health insurance system with more than 3,500 insurers<br>• In order to cope with its large and continually growing elderly population, policymakers have stressed the importance of prevention and wellness as a means of reducing healthcare costs<br>• Since 2008, annual checkups have become obligatory for those aged between 40 and 74 |
| Mexico | • Healthcare spending Mexico is projected to rise to more than $100 billion by 2014, representing a compound annual growth rate of 13.1 percent in U.S. dollar terms<br>• The government continues to ensure that the entire population is covered and provides access to more than 51 million people, approximately 45 percent of Mexico's population |
| Republic of Korea | • Though healthcare spending as a percentage of GDP is among the lowest for OECD countries, it is expected to rise to about 6.5 percent of the GDP by 2014<br>• A universal health-insurance system—financed by employer and employee contribution, and government subsidies—covers 96.3 percent of the population<br>• In early 2010, the government indicated that it would reduce maximum drug prices by 15-25% |
| Russia | • Russia has more physicians, hospitals, and health care workers than almost any other country inthe world according to the World Health Organization<br>• Russia embarked on large-scale healthcare reform in 2011 and pledged to allocate more than 300 billion rubles ($10 billion) over the next few years to improve the health care system<br>• Putin also called for the raising of the obligatory medical insurance tax paid by companies for compulsory medical insurance from 3.1 percent to 5.1 percent in 2011 |
| Saudi Arabia | • The Ministry of Health is the major government provider of health care services, comprising 60 percent of total health services in the country with the private sector accounting for 21 percent<br>• The country's healthcare system has been burdened by a shortage of health care and high-rates of turnover because the majority of health professionals in Saudi Arabia are expatriates<br>• The underutilization of electronic health systems in the country prompted the MOH to allocate $1.1 billion into the budget to develop e-health services in the public sector |
| Singapore | • Singapore's healthcare system mandates that everyone has 6.5 to 9 percent deducted from their incomes for a medisave account that is used for hospitilized medical expenses |
| United Kingdom | • The United Kingdom's coalition government has identified drug prices as an area of focus and aims to implement a new value-based pricing system that will replace the current Pharmaceutical Price Regulation Scheme, which is due to come to an end in 2013 |

Source: Business Monitor, WHO World Health Statistics, OECD, The Commonwealth Fund: International Profiles of Healthcare Systems, Medical Protection Society, Reuters News

Affordable Care Act, which establishes the non-profit **Patient-Centered Outcomes Research Institute** to indentify comparative effectiveness research priorities and conduct research to establish how clinical benefits of different therapies compare. Known as PCORI, the organization began to take shape in 2011. Joe Selby, who served as the director of the division of research for **Kaiser Permanente, Northern California** for 13 years, became PCORI's first executive director in May 2011. Months later, the organization also announced a $26 million **Pilot Projects Grant Program**, its first major funding program. It is intended to fund the collection of preliminary data that will serve as a platform for the organization's research agenda as it evolves. Though the organization expects to make about 40 grants under the program, it received 856 proposals. The pilot grants focus on projects designed to develop research methods, patient-oriented outcomes instruments, decision-making strategies, and methods for translating research findings into clinical practice.

But while the introduction of formalized comparative effectiveness in the United States has long been the subject of discussion, there's some question about how much of an affect PCORI will actually have in shaping or altering policy, or at least bending the cost curve. That's because by design, PCORI will focus on comparative effectiveness research as opposed to cost-effectiveness research. Controversy surrounding its creation and fear that the government would deny people access to life-saving treatments because of cost issues led to language in the Affordable Care Act to establish prohibitions on Medicare's use of comparative effectiveness research. It also states that PCORI "shall ensure that the research findings not be construed as practice guidelines, coverage recommendations, payment, or policy recommendations."

Writing in the **American Medical Association's** *Journal of Medical Ethics*, Jason John Luke, a medical oncology fellow at **Memorial Sloan-Kettering Cancer Center**, says that analysis of efficacy by cost is specifically disallowed by the legislation, but generation of cost data is not. "Thus, it is reasonable for this information to be available to the public," he says. "The cost analysis could then be undertaken by non-governmental bodies such as professional societies, insurance companies, and patient advocacy groups. If the analysis influenced the development of professional guidelines, compendia listings, or routine patient care, it would eventually be reflected in Medicare reimbursement as standard-of-care treatment."

Industry and its advocates are concerned about the dampening of innovation comparative effectiveness threatens to have. The concern is that rather than guiding healthcare providers to the treatments that will work best, it will be used as a blunt instrument to block use of more expensive therapies in favor of less expensive ones regardless of the consequence to patients. They also fear, in the absence of clear understanding of how comparative effectiveness will be measured, by whom, and how it will implemented, what its consequence will be on development costs and eventual reimbursement of new technologies.

The industry-friendly **Center for Medicine in the Public Interest** offered one of the most dire assessments of comparative effectiveness research's effect on innovation in a May 2011 report when it argued that comparative effectiveness could lead to dramatic cuts in R&D spending, shorten life expectancy of Americans, and cost the U.S. economy trillions of dollars. "Our

HEALTHCARE

5

108

analysis suggests that because [comparative effectiveness research] will lead to a loss of innovation, Americans will live shorter lives, and in poorer health than would otherwise be the case," the group wrote. "Simply put, we will produce less health. People will be less productive and less able to enjoy life."

The reality is that comparative effectiveness will be playing a greater role in healthcare decision making going forward and this will put new pressures on industry to not just demonstrate the safety and efficacy of their products, but establish that they deliver value as well. "High-value innovation is not merely to introduce new medicines, but to introduce better ones—pharmaceuticals and devices that are proven to provide greater therapeutic benefit, safety, improved quality of life and/or convenience for patients or providers," wrote John Doyle, vice president and practice leader of **Quintiles Consulting Solutions** in a white paper from the contract research organization. "The overall treatment process or outcome must be shown to be a significant improvement; and for commercial viability, innovation must adapt to market realities."

## Quality, not quantity

It would be difficult to blame medical technology for the rising costs of healthcare absent of looking at the system in which it is used. Some would argue that the problem is not the availability of new medical technologies, but rather that the healthcare systems incentivize the misuse and overuse of medical technology by paying for procedures, thereby rewarding the use of more expensive procedures, and not providing financial incentives to keep people well. The problem, they say, is doctors and hospitals are paid for quantity, not quality.

In discussing the perverse incentives in the healthcare system, Susan DeVore, CEO of Premier, a national alliance of hospitals and healthcare organizations, points to one hospital executive who complains that in return for making a $2 million investment in care delivery innovation to manage chronic disease, his hospital lost $20 million in revenues. That's because in a fee-for-service world, hospitals make money for providing services to sick people. When they make improvements that keep people healthy and out of the hospital, it means lost revenues. Accountable Care Organizations, or ACOs, are viewed as a way

> In a fee-for-service world, hospitals make money for providing services to sick people. When they make improvements that keep people healthy and out of the hospital, it means lost revenues.

of changing the equation to align provider and patient interests while improving quality and cutting costs. "ACOs are the most significant change in Medicare since its creation," DeVore wrote in November 2011 in the *Charlotte Observer*. "They can align these incentives, moving our system away from volume-based, fee-for-service reimbursement."

Built into the Affordable Care Act, ACOs address the issue of incentives in healthcare by changing the way providers are compensated. Rather than paying on a fee-for-service basis, providers that form accountable care organizations agree to accept a flat fee to care for a particular patient or treat a particular condition. If they can keep the patient healthy and do so in an economically efficient way, they stand to make a greater profit and earn bonus payments.

In October 2011, the U.S. Department of Health and Human Services released its ACO regulations. It was the second go around for the regulations after they were widely panned by providers when first released in March 2011. The final version of the guidelines make ACOs more attractive to providers by reducing risks, simplifying quality measures, and eliminating a provision that would have allowed CMS to withhold portions of earned bonuses. "Today's rules represent the direction in which the hospital field is moving—toward better coordinated patient care across care settings," said **American Hospital Association** president and CEO Rich Umbdenstock in response to the final rules. "The hospital field is actively working on ways to improve care delivery and the final accountable care organization rule provides hospitals a better path to do so."

# Survey Finds Care is Often Poorly Coordinated

United States lags behind other high-income countries

**A**dults with serious illnesses or chronic conditions in the United States are far more likely to go without care because of the cost than people with similar ailments in other high income countries, a new study finds.

The report, published in *Health Affairs*, found that 42 percent of sicker adults in the United States forego care because of costs, triple the percentage of Switzerland, the next closest country. The study was based on findings from a 2011 *Commonwealth Fund International Policy Survey*.

Though half of U.S. adults under 65 went without care because of costs, only 19 percent of adults aged over 65 skipped care. The authors suggest that Medicare has a significant effect on minimizing cost as a barrier to care.

In administering the survey, the **Commonwealth Fund** aimed to better understand the needs of adult patients with complex care needs, especially in a climate where many high-income countries are seeing a disproportionate share of national health spending going towards the sicker adult demographic.

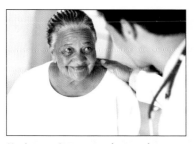

**Having a primary care doctor who coordinates care received from other providers and knows the patient's medical history mitigates some of the challenges of providing care for the chronically ill.**

A total of 18,000 sick adults participated in the Commonwealth survey in Australia, Canada, France, Germany, Norway, the Netherlands, New Zealand, Sweden, Switzerland, the United Kingdom, and the United States. The study found that across all countries, coordination gaps, lapses in communication between providers, and missed opportunities for engaging patients in management of their own care presented challenges in providing care to sicker adults.

Having a primary care doctor who coordinates care received from other providers and knows the patient's medical history mitigated many of these challenges.

"Chronically ill patients encounter failures of providers to communicate with each other or coordinate care," says Cathy Schoen, Commonwealth Fund senior vice president. "Yet in each country, patients with primary care practices that help them navigate the care system and provide easy access are far less likely to encounter delays and failures to share important information."

To address the problems laid out in their analysis, the authors of the study suggested that countries try to learn from one another and find ways to redesign primary care, develop care teams accountable across multiple sites of care, and manage transitions and medications better. ■

## Healthcare's Changing Dynamic

As with healthcare providers who often operate in a world of perverse incentives, individuals are often insulated from the economic consequences of their behavior. That's changing as individuals are bearing an increasing share of the cost of their own healthcare. The cost of employer-sponsored family health coverage rose 9 percent in 2011 to $15,073, the **Kaiser Family Foundation/Health Research & Educations Trust** found in their *2011 Employer Health Benefits Survey*. On average, workers pay $4,129 and employers pay $10,944 toward those annual premiums.

The study also found a growing number of people covered under consumer-driven plans.

These plans feature high deductibles and include a tax-preferred savings option, such as a health savings account. The survey found that in the past two years, the percent of workers enrolled in these types of programs more than doubled to 17 percent from 8 percent in 2009.

Employers are also seeking to cut the cost of healthcare by keeping their employees healthier. In 2010, employers increased their spending on such programs by 35 percent to about $220 per employee compared to 2009, according to **Buck Consultants**. The survey, which included 1,200 organizations with more than 13 million employees in 47 countries, found that 66 percent of respondents had a formal wellness strategy, up from 47 percent in 2007. The Affordable Care Act is expected to help fuel this trend as it increases the incentives corporations can offer their employees [SEE SIDEBAR GETTING]. As of 2014, employers can offer financial incentives up to 30 percent of premiums, up from 20 percent under current law. As these programs have matured, they are shifting from rewarding employees for participation to rewarding them for results and maintaining improvements in their lifestyles [SEE FIGURE 5.15].

For instance, the grocery chain **Safeway**, widely considered an innovator in employee wellness programs, provides employees rebates on their health insurance premiums for maintaining healthy behaviors. In 2010, the company began offering certain non-union employees as much as $800 in rebates on premiums depending on their compliance for meeting measures on certain risk factors including smoking, obesity, blood pressure and cholesterol. A 2010

# Getting Rewarded to Stay Well

## HHS announces $100 million in Affordable Care Act grants to prevent disease

It makes sense to pay people to stay healthy because it will save healthcare costs in the long run. That is the thinking behind the *Patient Protection and Affordable Care Act*—that spending on prevention today will save on healthcare costs tomorrow.

A new $100 million program, recently announced by the **U.S. Department of Health and Human Services**, will allow states to offer incentives to Medicaid enrollees who adopt healthy behaviors, such as quitting smoking or losing weight.

"Keeping people healthy is an important goal of the Affordable Care Act," says HHS Secretary Kathleen Sebelius. "One way to reach that goal is to encourage all Americans to make better choices about diet, exercise, and smoking to avoid potentially disastrous outcomes down the road like heart disease, cancer, or diabetes."

States may apply to the **Centers for Medicare & Medicaid Services** for grants to fund programs that demonstrate changes in health risk and outcomes, including the adoption of healthy behaviors.

Research has shown that one way to encourage people to embark on difficult changes in unhealthy habits is to offer economic incentives to those who reach stated goals. With that in mind, CMS will encourage states to adopt such strategies as rewarding Medicaid enrollees who meet goals established for them such as weight loss, smoking cessation, or diabetes prevention or control. Rewards could range from direct cash incentives, gift cards to grocery stores and other retailers, reduced Medicaid program fees, or offering services not normally available through Medicaid.

"With the right incentives, we believe that people can change their behaviors and stop smoking or lose weight," said then-CMS Administrator Donald Berwick. "Not only can preventive programs help to improve individuals' health, by keeping people healthy we can also lower the nation's overall health care costs."

Preventing an increase in the number of people with chronic health conditions is a key goal of

**For every person who dies from a smoking-related disease, about 20 more people have at least one serious illness related to smoking.**

*Washington Post* story found that Safeway overstated claims about the financial success of the *Health Measures* program, but reported it did produce improvements in the health of its participants. In 2009, the company saw a 5 percentage point drop in the number of employees who were obese, and a 1 percentage point decline in the number of overweight employees. Of the employees and their spouses who failed their blood pressure tests in 2008, 40 percent passed in 2009. Some 30 percent of one-time smokers said they were tobacco-free, and 17 percent of the people who failed cholesterol test in 2008, passed in 2009.

Wellness programs reflect a broader shift in healthcare out of the doctor's office to the places where patients work, live, and play. A digital health revolution is taking advantage of the ubiquity of wireless connectivity, smartphones, and inexpensive sensor technology to empower consumers to take command of their own health in bringing it into the homes. [*SEE CHAPTER 4 DIGITAL HEALTH*]. New means of accessing care are improving convenience and lowering costs.

Consider retail clinics, healthcare clinics providing a limited set of services often housed within pharmacies and grocery stores. The number of retail clinics grew tenfold between 2007 and 2009, according to a **Rand Corporation** study published in the *American Journal of Managed Care*. The study found that of 13.3 million commercially insured people, 3.8 million made a visit to at least one such clinic between 2007 and 2009.

Though the biggest predictor of whether the Affordable Care Act, passed almost a year ago. The new program focuses on those behaviors that can cause some of the most critical chronic conditions affecting millions of Americans—tobacco use, overeating, and physical inactivity.

Despite a decline in tobacco use, one in five American adults and teenagers still use tobacco. It is responsible for more than 430,000 deaths each year and for every person who dies from a smoking-related disease, about 20 more people have at least one serious illness related to smoking.

An estimated 26.7 percent of adults in the U.S. reported being obese in 2009, up 1.1 percentage points since 2007, and approximately 300,000 deaths per year may be attributable to obesity. In 2008, the annual healthcare cost of obesity in the United States was estimated to be as high as $147 billion.

More than one-third of adults have two or more of the major risk factors for heart disease, a leading cause of morbidity, mortality, and health care utilization and spending. Diabetes is the seventh leading cause of death in the United States and accounted for $116 billion in total U.S. healthcare system costs in

In 2008, the annual healthcare cost of obesity in the United States was estimated to be as high as $147 billion.

2007, and almost 24 million Americans have diabetes, including 5.7 million who don't know they have the disease. This includes about 186,300 people younger than 20 years who have type 1 or type 2 diabetes.

Commercial insurance program experience has shown that financial incentives can be effective in the short run for simple preventive care and distinct behavioral goals, but this demonstration will attempt to identify the most effective strategies for major, long-term changes in unhealthy habits.

"We are hopeful that these approaches will help to sustain patients' behavior change over their lifetime, especially in the areas of physical activity, nutrition, and smoking cessation," said Berwick. "We need to take aggressive steps to help give everyone the tools they need to improve their health." ∎

*Figure 5.15* **UNHEALTHY BEHAVIORS: TOBACCO AND OBESITY IN THE U.S. 1960 TO 2010**

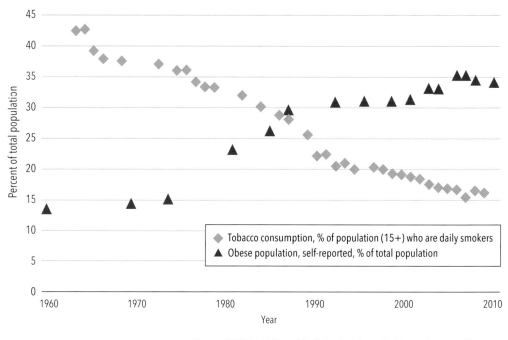

Source: OECD Health Data 2011, Gallop Poll, Center for Disease Control and Prevention

someone went to a retail clinic appears to be their proximity to one, Rand found women were more likely to go than men, higher income individuals more likely than lower income individuals (apparently for convenience because they value their time), and people who were in generally good health more likely than people who

## Components of a Rational Healthcare System

■ **Validated evidence**
(what works)

■ **Mechanism of action**
(why it works)

■ **Personalized medicine**
(who it works for)

■ **Comparative effectiveness**
(what works best)

■ **Best practices guidelines, standard-of-care, and malpractice**
(when should it be used optimally)

Source: Burrill & Company and George Poste

suffer from chronic diseases. Though the study did not determine whether these visits to retail clinics represented visits that would have otherwise occurred at a doctor's office or were additive because patients would have otherwise stayed home, the opportunity to provide substantial savings is compelling. Care initiated at retail clinics was 30 to 40 percent less expensive than similar care provided at a doctor's office. What's more, this care was 80 percent less expensive than care provided through an emergency room.

New models are changing the way care is accessed and delivered [*SEE SIDEBAR SURVEY*]. These models are taking forms such as telemedicine that connects patients in remote areas to specialists and the burgeoning medical tourism industry that **Deloitte** forecasts will treat 1.6 million patients in 2012 for elective surgical procedures. The patient-centered medical home model, an approach that uses a team of specialists coordinated by a primary care physician that oversees all aspects of a patient's care, is one approach boosted in part by the Affordable Care Act, which allocates funds for pilot projects. The expectation is that such an approach will cut costs while improving quality. With those efforts are experiments in payment models, such as pay-for-performance, or flat monthly fees for patients.

All of this represents a wave of disruptive innovation that is sweeping across healthcare. It is changing the way care is accessed, delivered, and paid for in an effort to address long-term problems healthcare systems face. At the heart of these changes are patients, who are no longer passive participants in their own care. They are empowered through unprecedented access to information and are facing an increasing share of the cost burden. As efforts are put in place to change incentives for both patients and providers, a shift is under way, putting greater focus on quality of care rather than on quantity.

The U.S. Supreme Court will weigh in on the constitutionality of the Affordable Care Act in 2012. At the time of this writing, it is unclear whether the court will take steps to strike down any or all of the law should it find that the individual mandate that requires people to purchase health insurance is not only unconstitutional, but so essential an element of the law that it collapses without it.

The reality, however, is that with or without the healthcare reform legislation, sweeping changes are underway. Efforts in the United States and throughout the rest of the world to find more economical ways to deliver care and keep people healthy are unfolding with remarkable speed. It is a time of great experimentation driven by the enormous pressure governments are feeling from the rising costs of healthcare. Payers, providers, patients, and technologies are driving changes to healthcare at a rapid pace regardless of the legislation. Key to the success

We cannot maintain an infinite demand for health care when our resources are finite. Without cost-cutting innovation, our choices are economic unsustainability or rationing of health care.

of new business and payment models will be a realignment of financial incentives that punish waste and unnecessary procedures and reward quality and results. At the heart of these changes will be the emergence of empowered consumers who no longer play a passive role in their own healthcare, but are actively engaged in decision making with an eye toward both their long-term health and the cost of care. In the absence of innovation-driven solutions, the rationing of care will be inevitable. ■

# A Balancing Act

There is a growing sense among life sciences innovators that regulatory barriers in the United States have made the process of bringing new drugs and medical devices to market too unpredictable, burdensome, and perilous. Finding new ways to balance risk and benefits will be essential to maintaining the brisk pace of medical innovation on which developed nations have come to rely. But while new regulatory frameworks and user fee programs awaiting approval in 2012 hold the promise of supporting some of the changes necessary to support the development of new and groundbreaking medical care in the United States, commitments to bold and daring action will be required of all parties to usher potentially life-saving therapies from lab to market. The increasing ability of companies to navigate global regulatory pathways means that there are more opportunities than ever to route around the U.S. Food and Drug Administration. But Washington is responding. Crucial patent reforms, tax changes, and new approaches to regulation and policy are gradually changing the map on which companies both small and large are plotting their future.

# Chapter 6:

# A BALANCING ACT

As **Orexigen Therapeutics** prepared in June 2011 to update shareholders on the U.S. regulatory progress of its experimental obesity drug, Contrave, the company faced a bleak and challenging picture. It was one of three drugmakers that had applied for approval of experimental obesity therapies in 2010. Many venture investors, once enthusiastic backers of daring drugs to fight big diseases, were starting to retreat from the sector. Long and costly development sagas and unpredictable regulatory hurdles added to mounting reimbursement risks, leaving investors to wonder if it is still possible to generate attractive returns from life sciences companies.

The **U.S. Food and Drug Administration** reviewers raised concerns about the risk of adverse cardiovascular events in obese people treated with Contrave. They wanted an additional trial to demonstrate that the risk of using the drug didn't exceed its benefits. While Orexigen proposed a trial of 12,000 to 15,000 patients, with a planned interim analysis in early 2013, the FDA countered with a proposed trial Orexigen believed would require enrolling 60,000 to 100,000 patients. Orexigen chose to put further clinical development of its obesity programs in the United States on hold until a clear and feasible path to regulatory approval could be identified.

The company called the FDA's request "unprecedented" and claimed it would generate significantly more information than was neces- sary or feasible. The agency said it would hold a general advisory committee in 2012 to discuss cardiovascular assessment for obesity drugs, and that any agreement reached on the design of a cardiovascular outcomes trial would be subject to change following its interpretation of the input received then. As Orexigen's shares lost nearly half their value, the company began exploring opportunities for its products outside the United States.

Signaling just how important regulatory delays can be, shares of numerous small life sciences companies, including **Transcept Pharmaceuticals**, **NuPathe**, and **Adventrx Pharmaceuticals** crashed during 2011 when the FDA declined to approve applications to begin marketing new drugs without additional safety data to support

# Strong Growth in FDA Approvals of Biologics

## Study says it will be challenging to maintain pace of past ten years

**U**nited States regulatory approvals for new biopharmaceuticals nearly doubled in the last decade, compared to the 1990s, according to the **Tufts Center for the Study of Drug Development**. But maintaining that pace will be challenging for drug developers notes the study's author.

During the ten years between 2000 and 2009, 65 biopharmaceutical products received marketing approval from the **U.S. Food and Drug Administration**, up from 39 in the 1990s and 13 in the 1980s.

"While the strong growth in approvals is positive news for biotech companies and patients alike, biopharmaceutical development remains complex and developers face substantial challenges if they are to continue winning approvals at the pace of the last decade," says Janice Reichert, research assistant professor at **Tufts University** and author of the recently completed Tufts study.

The challenges to securing new drug approvals, including regulatory and payer hurdles, become higher over time as more innovative products are approved, says Reichert.

As the pharmaceutical industry increases its capabilities in biologics, she says, biologics are no longer treated as fundamentally different from small molecules.

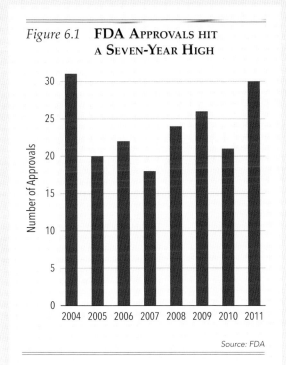

*Figure 6.1* **FDA Approvals hit a Seven-Year High**

Number of Approvals

*Source: FDA*

This is borne out in the study's analysis of drug approvals over the past 30 years, which finds that it now takes as much time to develop a new biologic as a new small molecule drug, about 95 months. In the 1980s it took less than 60 months from the start of clinical trials to the approval of a new biologic drug.

"Development times for new chemical entities have not been getting shorter, but they have increased since the 1980s for biologics because approvals in the 1980s included a number of recombinant versions of well-understood products such as insulin and human growth hormone," says Reichert.

The study found that new biopharmaceutical approvals between 2000 and 2009 were more evenly distributed in six therapeutic categories, compared to the periods between 1980 and 1989 and those between 1990 and 1999.

The Tufts analysis also found that neither orphan nor fast track designations had a substantial impact on the average time from initiation of clinical study to FDA marketing approval for new biopharmaceuticals approved between 2000 and 2009.

"Moving forward, developers will be under pressure to further streamline the development process to assure greater consistency across compounds and within disease areas," Reichert says. ◼

their applications.

Industry's frustration has grown over the agency's increasingly cautious, risk-averse posture, which at times has left drug developers feeling like the risks of new treatments are given more weight than their benefits to patients. The balance that had been struck during the late 1980s and early 1990s when patient groups pushed for faster access to new medicines has been eroded, critics in industry say, and is being replaced instead by a regime in which it has become increasingly difficult to, as Jonathan Leff, a managing director for the venture capital firm **Warburg Pincus** puts it, "make the math work for investment in novel therapeutic product development."

A survey of 150 members of the **National Venture Capital Association** found broad concern that the FDA was putting the United States at risk of losing its leading position in biomedical innovation. Regulatory challenges posed by

*Figure 6.2*    NEW MOLECULAR ENTITIES AND BIOLOGICS APPROVED BY FDA's CDER IN 2011

| DRUG NAME | ACTIVE INGREDIENT | DATE APPROVED | WHAT IT'S USED FOR |
|---|---|---|---|
| Eylea | aflibercept | 11/18 | To treat patients with wet (neovascular) age-related macular degeneration (AMD), a leading cause of vision loss and blindness in Americans ages 60 and older. |
| Erwinaze | asparaginase Erwinia chrysanthemi | 11/18 | To treat patients with acute lymphoblastic leukemia (ALL), who have developed an allergy to E. coli derived asparaginase and pegapargase chemotherapy drugs used to treat ALL. |
| Jakafi | ruxolitinib | 11/16 | To treat patients with the bone marrow disease myelofibrosis. |
| Onfi | clobazam | 10/24 | For use as an adjunctive (add-on) treatment for seizures associated with Lennox-Gastaut syndrome in adults and children 2 years of age and older. |
| Ferriprox | deferiprone | 10/14 | To treat patients with iron overload due to blood transfusions in patients with thalassemia, a genetic blood disorder that causes anemia. |
| Xalkori | crizotinib | 08/26 | To treat certain patients with late-stage (locally advanced or metastatic), non-small cell lung cancers who express the abnormal anaplastic lymphoma kinase gene. |
| Firazyr | icatibant | 08/25 | For the treatment of acute attacks of a rare condition called hereditary angioedema. |
| Xarelto | rivaroxaban | 7/10 | To reduce the risk of blood clots, deep vein thrombosis, and pulmonary embolism following knee or hip replacement surgery. |
| Adcetris | brentuximab vedotin | 08/19 | For the treatment of Hodgkin lymphoma and systemic anaplastic large cell lymphoma. |
| Zelboraf | vemurafenib | 08/17 | To treat patients with late-stage or unresectable melanoma, the most dangerous type of skin cancer. |
| Brilinta | ticagrelor | 07/20 | To reduce cardiovascular death and heart attack in patients with acute coronary syndromes. |
| Arcapta Neohaler | indacaterol inhalation powder | 07/01 | For the long term, once-daily maintenance bronchodilator treatment of airflow obstruction in people with chronic obstructive pulmonary disease including chronic bronchitis and/or emphysema. |
| Nulojix | belatacept | 06/15 | To prevent acute rejection in adult patients who have had a kidney transplant. |

the agency were identified as the main factor for declining investment in experimental drug and device startups in the United States and a shift toward investment in Europe and Asia. More than 40 percent of firms expected to decrease investment in biopharmaceutical and medical device companies, the survey found, while almost half of firms expected to increase their investment in non-FDA regulated healthcare services and healthcare information technology companies.

"Regulatory uncertainty, longer drug development timelines, and an increasing regulatory and Congressional focus on risk instead of reward in pharmaceutical innovation deters limited partners from investing in biotech venture capital firms and subsequently deters venture capitalists from investing in biotechnology discovery companies," said Paul Hastings, president and CEO of **OncoMed Pharmaceuticals**

| DRUG NAME | ACTIVE INGREDIENT | DATE APPROVED | WHAT IT'S USED FOR |
|---|---|---|---|
| Potiga | ezogabine | 06/10 | For use as an add-on medication to treat seizures associated with epilepsy in adults. |
| Dificid | fidaxomicin | 05/27 | For the treatment of Clostridium difficile-associated diarrhea. |
| Incivek | telaprevir | 05/23 | To treat certain adults with chronic hepatitis C infection. |
| Edurant | rilpivirine | 05/20 | For the treatment of HIV-1 infection in adults who have never taken HIV therapy. |
| Victrelis | boceprevir | 05/13 | To treat certain adults with chronic hepatitis C. |
| Tradjenta | linagliptin | 05/02 | An adjunct to diet and exercise to improve glycemic control in adults with type 2 diabetes mellitus. |
| Zytiga | abiraterone acetate | 04/28 | In combination with prednisone to treat patients with late-stage (metastatic) castration-resistant prostate cancer who have received prior docetaxel. |
| Caprelsa | vandetanib | 04/06 | To treat adult patients with late-stage (metastatic) medullary thyroid cancer who are ineligible for surgery. |
| Horizant | gabapentin enacarbil | 04/06 | A once-daily treatment for moderate-to-severe restless legs syndrome. |
| Yervoy | ipilimumab | 03/25 | To treat patients with late-stage (metastatic) melanoma, the most dangerous type of skin cancer. |
| Gadavist | gadobutrol | 03/14 | For use in patients undergoing magnetic resonance imaging of the central nervous system. |
| Benlysta | belimumab | 03/9 | To treat patients with active, autoantibody-positive lupus who are receiving standard therapy. |
| Daliresp | roflumilast | 02/28 | To decrease the frequency of flare-ups (exacerbations) or worsening of symptoms from severe chronic obstructive pulmonary disease. |
| Edarbi | azilsartan medoxomil | 02/25 | To treat high blood pressure (hypertension) in adults. |
| Viibryd | vilazodone hydrochloride | 01/21 | To treat major depressive disorder in adults. |
| Natroba | spinosad | 01/18 | For the treatment of head lice infestation in patients ages 4 years and older. |
| Datscan | ioflupane i-123 | 01/14 | An imaging drug used to assist in the evaluation of adult patients with suspected Parkinsonian syndromes. |

*Source: FDA*

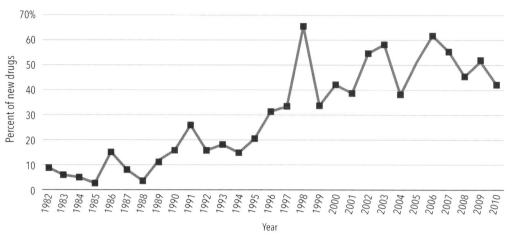

Source: Scrip, Pharmaprojects, FDA

to a Congressional committee during a hearing in July 2011.

Despite gradual improvement in the working relationship between industry and the FDA, on average, the agency still takes 37 months to approve a drug and only half of product applications are approved during the first review cycle, according to the **Biotechnology Industry Organization**. A desire to achieve the promise of biotechnology by advancing innovative therapies to market and building lasting value remained the goal of companies and sector investors in 2011. Despite 30 NMEs being approved in 2011, the chances of any given product going into the FDA and coming out with its blessing seemed to many drugmakers dimmer and less predictable than ever [*See Figures 6.2 and 6.4*].

The tensions built as the FDA turned the tables on the industry by pointing to the failings of companies to turn the massive investment in research and development into approvable products. "The past two decades have been marked by steadily increasing investments in basic research and development, with more than $95 billion in combined R&D by industry and the **National Institutes of Health** in 2010 alone," the agency pointed out in a September 2011 report. "And yet," it continued, "these investments have not translated into a parallel increase in novel products submitted to the agency for approval."

"I know that in some circles regulation is viewed as a roadblock to innovation and eco-

nomic growth," says FDA Commissioner Margaret Hamburg. "But in actuality, when done right, regulation isn't a roadblock; it's the actual pathway to achieving real and lasting innovation."

It was against this backdrop that negotiations began between industry and the FDA on renewal of the *Prescription Drug User Fee Act*, a critical piece of legislation governing the relationship between the interdependent partners.

## PDUFA takes center stage

The Prescription Drug User Fee Act, PDUFA for short, provides drugmakers assurances of timely action on drug reviews in exchange for providing funding to conduct those reviews. Before PDUFA was enacted in 1992, the FDA's drug review process was understaffed, unpredictable, and slow. "FDA lacked sufficient staff to perform timely reviews, or develop procedures and standards to make the process more rigorous, consistent, and predictable. Access to new medicines for U.S. patients lagged behind other countries," says Hamburg.

To overcome those problems, the agency used initial PDUFA funding to hire about 600 new reviewers. It also built in accountability, setting goals and a built-in check on the process, a requirement to renew the law in five years so that the agency could be held accountable when it came time to rewrite the law. With the clock ticking toward the five-year expiration date of PDUFA IV at the end of September 2012 and the rapid evolution of new therapeutic approaches

> The Prescription Drug User Fee Act, PDUFA for short, provides drugmakers assurances of timely action on drug reviews in exchange for funding to conduct those reviews.

during the past five years, changes are needed.

Much progress had been made toward meeting the needs of both industry and the FDA in past PDUFA negotiations, but there is still much left to be accomplished in PDUFA V. The growing complexity of new drug applications and original biologics license applications combined with the agency's greater attention to early safety signals has created problems that were failing to be caught ahead of the submission of those applications and caused significant delays later in the review process. Furthermore, advances in science have been outstripping the FDA's capacity to keep up with them, especially in high-priority areas, such as the adoption of patient-reported outcomes and adaptive trial designs.

BIO has expressed consistent support of reauthorization of PDUFA, but not without expressing several significant concerns as well. "Anyone will tell you that companies are still enormously frustrated with the process," said Jim Greenwood, president and CEO of BIO. "It takes too long. It is not sufficiently transparent. It's too bureaucratic."

Furthermore, the group wants to see the driving idea behind PDUFA reinforced: namely that providing additional financial resources will enable the hiring of staff for human drug and biologic reviews, promote performance management, and improve the efficiency of the review process. After what Greenwood characterized as "a long and technical negotiation," that focus was retained in the form of a final recommendation delivered to Congress in January 2012.

If enacted as negotiated, PDUFA fees paid by industry would increase by approximately 6 percent, and the FDA would commit to review 90 percent of applications for standard new molecular entities and biologics within 10 months. The program would provide the FDA with additional funding for five years, starting with $712.8 million per year in fiscal 2013 and adjusted upward annually to account for inflation. That money, together with revenue generated from several new user fee programs undergoing Congressional review in 2012, could account for nearly half the FDA's $4.5 billion budget in fiscal 2013. In fact, industry user fees would fund almost all of the agency's proposed 17 percent budget increase.

"These are austere budget times, and the FDA budget request reflects this reality," says Commissioner Hamburg. "Our budget increases are targeted to strategic areas that will help speed the availability of new medical products, address the challenges of increased globalization and allow the FDA to fulfill its public health duties more efficiently."

The key elements of PDUFA V that will support that mission include plans to extend review periods, in part by increasing the communication between the FDA and drug sponsors during

*Figure 6.4* **PERCENT OF NDAs AND BLAs APPROVED ON FIRST REVIEW CYCLE**

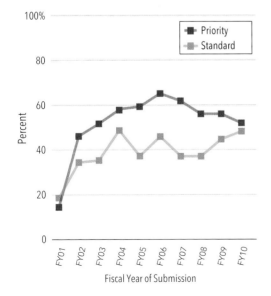

Fiscal Year of Submission

*Source: FDA*

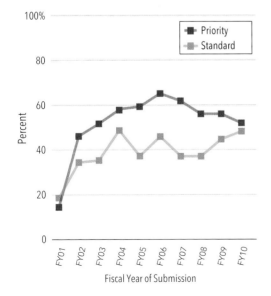REGULATION & POLICY

6

"Anyone will tell you that companies are still enormously frustrated with the process. It takes too long. It is not sufficiently transparent. It's too bureaucratic."

**Jim Greenwood,** President and CEO, BIO

a new 60-day window for sorting out application problems and other outstanding issues informally before the review clock officially starts; plans for better meta-analysis of completed studies to explore drug benefits and risks; an augmentation of the agency's ability to evaluate use of pharmacogenomic data and biomarkers in applications; better assessment of measures quantifying drug benefits from the patients' perspective; and better support for development of drugs to treat rare diseases.

Efforts to improve communications with drug sponsors could be a particularly important element in smoothing the relationship between the agency and drug sponsors, a relationship that BIO's Greenwood notes has been strained at times by a lack of informal communication channels.

While such systems had existed in the past, legal concerns and resource constraints at the agency gradually eroded them to the detriment of small companies, especially first-time filers. As Greenwood puts it, "You have to be able to pick up the phone and say, 'Hey, let's work this out, scientist-to-scientist.'"

PDUFA V would also establish two post-market, safety-focused initiatives. One initiative would standardize risk evaluation and mitigation strategies, also known as REMS. The idea behind a REMS plan is to help ensure the benefits of a drug outweigh its risks. But while the idea has helped better manage and monitor risks, FDA has found that in some cases, REMS plans so burdened healthcare providers that they ended up limiting patient access to important therapies. Standardized REMS programs, which are likely to become more commonly used, will be important to ensuring their utility while also driving down the cost of implementing them. Another longer-term pro-

gram supported by PDUFA, the Sentinel Initiative, will build a national electronic system for monitoring the safety of FDA-approved medical products.

By most measures, changes in the regulatory process brought about by earlier incarnations of PDUFA have been positive. During 2011, many notable drugs won approval, including **Vertex Pharmaceutical's** oral hepatitis C drug Incivek; **Bristol-Myers Squibb's** melanoma drug Yervoy, the first new melanoma drug in 13 yearsand the first to extend the lives of patients with late-stage disease; and **Human Genome Sciences'** lupus drug Benlysta, the first new lupus drug in 50 years [*SEE FIGURE 6.3*].

A preliminary analysis of Scrip data in 2011 provided by the agency showed that nearly half of all new active drug substances were first launched in the United States. The FDA approved a total of 30 new drugs and biologics, the most in seven years, during the 2011 calendar year. In fiscal 2011—October 2010 through September 2011—of the 35 innovative drugs approved during fiscal 2011, FDA approved 24 before any other regulatory agency in the world, including the European Medicines Agency [*SEE FIGURE 6.5*].

A study published in the journal *Health Affairs* looking at cancer drugs approved by the FDA and the European Medicines Agency between 2003 and 2010 also showed the United States in the lead. During that period the two agencies approved a total of 35 cancer drugs, with the FDA approving 32 of these products and the EMA approving 26. For the FDA, the median time of review for approved drugs was 182 days. Of the 32 cancer drugs it approved, the FDA approved 20 of those products within 184 days while three of the drugs took more than a year to approve. By contrast, the EMA took a median time of 350 days to review the 26 cancer drugs it approved. The study's authors attributed the U.S. advantage to improvements brought about by PDUFA.

To encourage a smooth transition from PDUFA IV to PDUFA V and discourage any diversion of resources from reviews, industry would like to see a quick renewal of the legislation with minimal amendments. But there remains plenty of potential for a rocky ride as the legislation winds its way through a divided Congress during an election year.

The importance of a timely passage of a "clean" PDUFA "free of extraneous additions that bring new costs and burdens to the FDA" is important, says **The Campaign for Modern Medicines**, an industry group sponsored by **Eli Lilly**. In 2007, the group points out, PDUFA IV was passed only a few days before it would have expired in late September of that year, causing disruptions in FDA staffing and the collection of user fees in both the months preceding the

*Figure 6.5* **SELECTED EUROPEAN APPROVALS IN 2011**

| COMPANY | PROPRIETARY NAME | ESTABLISHED NAME | INDICATION |
|---|---|---|---|
| Pfizer | Vyndaqel | tafamidis | Amyloidosis |
| DuoCort Pharma | Plenadren | hydrocortisone | Adrenal insufficiency |
| Astellas Pharma | Vibativ | telavancin | Cross infection pneumonia, bacterial |
| Boehringer Ingelheim International | Trajenta | linagliptin | Diabetes mellitus, type 2 |
| Orion Corporation | Entacapone Orion | carbidopa/levodopa | Parkinson's disease |
| Teva; Merck Serono | Zoely | nomegestrol/estradiol | Contraception |
| Novartis | Tobi Podhaler | tobramyin | Respiratory tract infections; Cystic fibrosis |
| Merck | Victrelis | boceprevir | Chronic hepatitis C |
| Bristol Myers Squibb | Yervoy | ipilimumab | Metastatic melanoma |
| Eli Lilly | Bydureon | exenatide | Type 2 diabetes |
| Bristol-Myers Squibb | Nulojix | belatacept | Preventing organ rejection in kidney transplants |
| Bristol-Myers Squibb; Pfizer | Eliquis | apixaban | Prevention of venous thromboembolic events in adults following a hip or knee replacement operation |
| Laboratoires SMB | Pravafenix | pravastatin and fenofibrate | High risk of heart disease |
| CSL Behring | Hizentra | immunoglobulin | Primary immunodeficiency syndromes, chronic lymphocytic leukemia |
| Novartis | Rasilamlo | Aliskiren and amlodipine | High blood pressure |
| GlaxoSmithKline; Valeant Pharmaceuticals | Trobalt | retigabine | Partial-onset seizures |
| Eisai | Halaven | eribulin mesylate | Metastatic breast cancer |
| Sanofi-Aventis | Jevtana | cabazitaxel | Hormone refractory metastatic prostate cancer |
| GlaxoSmithKline | Pumarix | Pandemic influenza vaccine (h5n1) (split virion, inactivated, adjuvanted) | Pandemic flu |
| InterMune | Esbriet | pirfenidone | Idiopathic pulmonary fibrosis |

*Source: Burrill & Company, European Medicines Agency*

*Figure 6.6* **AUTHORIZED BIOSIMILARS IN EUROPE**

| NAME | ACTIVE SUBSTANCE | THERAPEUTIC AREA | DATE AUTHORIZED |
|------|------------------|------------------|-----------------|
| Abseamed | epoetin alfa | Kidney Failure, Chronic Anemia, Cancer | 08/28/2007 |
| Binocrit | epoetin alfa | Kidney Failure, Chronic Anemia | 08/28/2007 |
| Biograstim | filgrastim | Hematopoietic Stem Cell Transplantation, Neutropenia Cancer | 09/15/2008 |
| Epoetin alfa Hexal | epoetin alfa | Kidney Failure, Chronic Anemia, Cancer | 08/28/2007 |
| Filgrastim Hexal | filgrastim | Neutropenia Cancer Hematopoietic Stem Cell Transplantation | 02/06/2009 |
| Filgrastim ratiopharm | filgrastim | Neutropenia, Hematopoietic Stem Cell Transplantation, Cancer | 09/15/2008 |
| Nivestim | filgrastim | Hematopoietic Stem Cell Transplantation, Cancer, Neutropenia | 06/08/2010 |
| Omnitrope | somatropin | Turner Syndrome, Dwarfism, Pituitary Prader-Willi Syndrome | 04/12/2006 |
| Ratiograstim | filgrastim | Neutropenia, Cancer, Hematopoietic Stem Cell Transplantation | 09/15/2008 |
| Retacrit | epoetin zeta | Cancer, Anemia, Kidney Failure, Chronic Blood Transfusion, Autologous Cancer | 12/18/2007 |
| Silapo | epoetin zeta | Anemia, Blood Transfusion, Autologous Cancer, Kidney Failure, Chronic | 12/18/2007 |
| Tevagrastim | filgrastim | Neutropenia Cancer Hematopoietic Stem Cell Transplantation | 09/15/2008 |
| Valtropin | somatropin | Dwarfism, Pituitary Turner Syndrome | 04/24/2006 |
| Zarzio | filgrastim | Cancer, Hematopoietic Stem Cell Transplantation, Neutropenia | 02/06/2009 |

*Source: European Medicines Agency (June 2011)*

deadline and the months afterward. But even with the incremental improvements negotiated with industry and patient representatives in place, not everyone is ready to close the door on possible additions or changes to PDUFA V.

Allan Coukell, director of Medical Programs at **Pew Health Group**, still sees room in the PDUFA reauthorization talks to better address drug safety risks inherent in the current global supply chain. Since the ingredients of so many U.S drugs are now made overseas, Pew says it would like to see the FDA update rules to require more frequent inspection of domestic and foreign drug manufacturing facilities to improve drug safety.

Diane Dorman, vice president of public policy for **The National Organization for Rare Disorders**, says that while mechanisms currently exist for patients and others to provide input to the FDA on how much risk they're willing to tolerate in exchange for the potential benefits of new drugs, those opportunities don't necessarily occur at the time that the agency is making key risk tolerance and other critical drug access decisions.

David Gollaher, president and CEO of the **California Healthcare Institute**, and others have pointed out a need for more granular information to be collected about reviews "in order to understand where things are working and where they need improvement." Gollaher noted that "there are significant deviations in average review times, depending on a product's therapeutic area," and hopes that fresh data might help clarify what explains differences in performance from one therapeutic area to another. Industry's biggest fear is that fresh amendments to PDUFA V would create additional responsibilities for the FDA without the requisite appropriations to pay for the added work. How much Congress is willing to alter PDUFA is still an unknown.

> Because biosimilars may be manufactured with different processes, cell lines, raw materials, and equipment than the biologics they copy, the FDA may require one or more clinical studies, as well as further information to determine that, in fact, a follow-on biologic can be considered biosimilar at all.

## Making room for biosimilars

After PDUFA, few areas of U.S. regulatory development were more closely watched in 2011—and remain more uncertain in 2012—than the new pathway created for the approval of biosimilar therapeutics by the U.S. Food and Drug Administration. The reasons for excitement among payers and drugmakers is straightforward. If follow-on biologics can be developed and produced at a lower cost than was borne by innovators, they can be sold for less too. That would create new chances for drugmakers to compete with established biologics while potentially saving government and other payers billions of dollars each year.

Biosimilars, drugs that mimic original biologics without being exact copies, are the generic medicines of the biotech world. But unlike generic drugs which are chemically synthesized copies of easily reproducible small molecules, protein-based biosimilars are more complex and unlikely to be structural twins of the therapeutics they copy.

Biosimilars legislation has been in place in the European Union since 2003 [*SEE FIGURE 6.6*]. In November 2010, the European Union made further progress when the **European Medicines Agency Committee for Medicinal Products for Human Use** adopted draft guidelines for approving biosimilars of marketed monoclonal antibody products. But in the United States, regulatory development has proceeded at a much slower pace. *The Biologics Price Competition and Innovation Act of 2009*, a provision of the *Affordable Care Act*, created an abbreviated approval pathway for biosimilars when health care reform was signed into law in 2010.

Under the provision, the FDA cannot approve an application for a biosimilar product until 12 years after the original brand product was approved. That represented a big win for industry,

which had argued for a 14-year exclusivity period even as others, such as **House Energy and Commerce Committee** chair Rep. Henry Waxman, D-California, had sought to cut that period to just five years, arguing that the shorter window of exclusivity granted small molecule drugs under the *Hatch-Waxman Act* had helped give rise to a thriving business in generic pharmaceuticals.

For many biologics, this 12-year exclusivity period has expired or is nearing expiration. Yet, as **Momenta Pharmaceuticals** put it to shareholders in a November 2011 regulatory filing, "the new law is complex and is only beginning to be interpreted and implemented by the FDA. As a result, its ultimate impact, implementation, and meaning will be subject to uncertainty for years to come."

That uncertainty stems from the complexity of protein-based products and its ramifications for consumer safety, which lead the FDA to spend 2011 engaged with industry, hashing out the details of how to establish biosimilar safety. Finally, in February 2012, the FDA issued a series of draft guidances on the subject. One part of the guidances addresses the scientific considerations for demonstrating biosimilarity to a reference biologic while another tackles qualitative issues, such as when a biosimilar can be considered interchangeable with its reference product. To establish that two protein products are similar and substitutable, the sponsor of a follow-on product would need to demonstrate through de novo clinical trials that repeated switches from the follow-on product to the referenced product (and vice versa) have no negative effect on the safety or effectiveness of the products.

Because even minor structural differences can significantly affect a protein's safety, purity, and potency, notes the FDA, getting them approved may require one or more clinical studies. Furthermore, because biosimilars may be manufactured

126

with different processes, cell lines, raw materials, and equipment than the biologics they copy, the agency may require further information to determine that, in fact, a follow-on biologic can be considered biosimilar at all.

For drugmakers facing patent expirations on blockbuster biologics, the rise of biosimilars and the approach regulators take toward their approval have tremendous implications. Biologics accounting for $20 billion in annual sales are expected to face patent expirations by 2015. Not only will biosimilars create new competition for established biologics, their global adoption will also create new market opportunities for savvy innovator companies moving to leverage their manufacturing prowess to get a head start on potential competitors. In the United States, biologics were estimated to account for approximately $57 billion in sales during 2011. In 2010, they made up 28 percent of new molecular entities approved in the United States, and by 2014 they could comprise as much as 60 percent of the top-ten selling drugs suggests a **Deloitte** analysis of **IMS Health** revenue values and market life cycle projections. By 2020, an IMS Health analysis projects that biosimilars will create a global market worth up to $25 billion, with the majority of demand driven by the United States.

Big Biotech companies such as **Amgen** are already anticipating greater competition from biosimilars, including from manufacturers with biosimilar products approved in Europe that may seek to quickly obtain U.S. approval. In the European Union, where regulation of biosimilars is ahead of most markets, the company has already met such competition, with biosimilars makers leaping in to develop alternatives to Aranesp, Epogen, and Enbrel.

Furthermore, as cash-strapped governments seek new ways to save money on healthcare, there is a growing likelihood that many will establish preferences for biosimilar products or reduce the amount of reimbursement they provide for innovator biologics when a biosimilar competitor is available. Biotech companies, though, see this not only as a threat, but an opportunity as well. Amgen formed a collaboration with generic drugmaker **Watson Pharmaceuticals** in December 2011 to develop and commercialize several biosimilar oncology antibody drugs, closing a year of similar deals made by the likes of **Bio-**

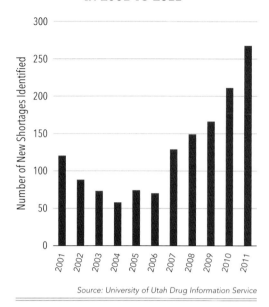

*Figure 6.7* **NATIONAL DRUG SHORTAGES IN 2001 TO 2011**

Source: University of Utah Drug Information Service

gen Idec and **Samsung**, **Merck** and **Hanwha**, and **Baxter**, and **Momenta**. While companies hoping to move biosimilars to market in the United States have plenty of questions, the biosimilars guidance introduced in 2012 and the unveiling of a new biosimilar user fee program in January 2012 will have provided at least some of the answers.

The *Biosimilar and Interchangeable Products User Fee* program, introduced in tandem with PDUFA, will provide the FDA with the resources needed to support development-phase meetings with sponsors of biosimilar biological product candidates and establishes a schedule of fees in line with those charged for the review of other biologics established under PDUFA. These include a biosimilar product development fee equal to 10 percent of the fee established for a human drug application under PDUFA, marketing application fees, establishment fees, and product fees.

In the near term, fiscal years 2013 and 2014, FDA says it will strive to review and act on 70 percent of original biosimilar product application submissions within 10 months of receipt. By fiscal 2017, it anticipates being able to respond to 90 percent of submissions within that time frame.

Despite all the work done in 2011 to develop the biosimilars approval pathway and the ongoing work introducing it in 2012, a singular uncertainty overshadows the whole show: the challenge to healthcare reform in the **United States Supreme Court**.

Even without interference from the Supreme Court, the ability of drugmakers to achieve success with biosimilars will be hampered, at least at first, by the high level of investment that will be needed to develop and manufacture these complex therapeutics. Executives surveyed by Deloitte suggested that development costs could run anywhere from $30 million for less complex biosimilars to as much as $250 million for trickier-to-copy drugs. Furthermore, doctors, patients, and insurers are likely to be slower to adopt biosimilars, which provide significantly less savings than generic drugs do.

Biotechnology innovators fearing the encroachment of new competition from less expensive biosimilars also face the problem that President Obama still wants to reduce the exclusivity period on brand name biologics to seven years from 12—a proposal that the president first advanced in a deficit reduction plan in September 2011. Reducing the exclusivity period would save federal health programs $4 billion over ten years, the President says.

Obama introduced his plan, which has found support in some quarters of Congress, as part of a larger scheme to wring $320 billion from federal healthcare expenses in the decade ahead as part of an effort to generate $3.5 billion in savings by shortening the data exclusivity period for brand name biologics beginning in 2012. Government projections suggested that savings from the changes would first begin to accrue in 2015 and ramp up through 2021, a year in which federal actuaries anticipate savings would reach $1 billion.

Such a change would encourage faster development of biosimilars while striking a balance between promoting affordable access to medications and encouraging innovation, the government argued. The biotech industry was not as convinced, viewing the current 12-year data exclusivity period as a boon for jobs, national competitiveness, and innovation.

> Among the goals set in GDUFA is elimination of the agency's backlog of applications within five years. That would be no small feat, since the FDA receives 800 to 900 new generic-drug-related applications annually and the applications are increasingly complex.

## Clearing the backlog

It was also an eventful year for the generic drug industry, which faces a number of crucial issues including patent reform, fights with the **Federal Trade Commission** over so-called pay-for-delay settlements, and the institution of FDA user fees for generic drugs.

In 2011, generic drugmakers, long opposed to paying to speed regulatory review of their medicines in the United States, collectively agreed to pay the FDA nearly $300 million per year so the agency can add new staff and resources to clear a backlog of generic drug applications awaiting its action.

Nearly 78 percent of all the prescriptions dispensed in the United States are filled using generic drugs, though generics consume just a quarter of total drug spending according to the **Generic Pharmaceutical Association**. But while consumers and payers alike realize substantial savings from using generics, the association argues that even more would be saved if the FDA were to approve generic medicines faster.

The FDA's **Office of Generic Drugs** had a reported backlog of close to 2,000 applications seeking approval to market generic versions of approved drugs in early 2012. The average approval time for an application is more than 30 months, five times longer than the statutory six-month review time called for by the Hatch-Waxman act, the 1984 law that established an accelerated pathway for approving generic drugs.

While the size of that backlog is big, it is also somewhat misleading argues the FDA. That's because many applications are held up by factors outside of the agency's control. The FDA also says that as many as 90 percent of generic medicines are approved for marketing as soon as the patent on the original branded drugs expire. But it also has admitted that, with greater and more predictable funding, the current backlog could be cleared faster.

Under the proposed *Generic Drug User Fee Act* (GDUFA), the FDA will receive $299 million per year over five years, or about $1.5 billion in total. There will be two types of user fees: one associated with applications and another tied to facility inspections. Payments made under the program will support not just new hires, but also the inspection of overseas drug manufacturing facilities to ensure the safety of medicines made abroad. Fees would be adjusted annually to account for inflation.

Among the goals set in GDUFA is elimination of the agency's backlog of applications within five years. That would be no small feat, since the FDA receives 800 to 900 new generic-drug-related applications annually and the applications are increasingly complex.

Another goal is to ensure that the FDA can inspect all drug facilities, domestic and foreign, at an increased frequency. With facility fees built into GDUFA, the FDA expects it will be able to achieve parity between surveillance inspections of foreign and domestic establishments by the 2017 fiscal year.

"The potential impact on revenue and profitability from reduction in review time could be significant and may result in savings for businesses of all sizes, expedite availability of generic drugs, and achieve a risk-based biennial (good manufacturing practice) inspection program for both foreign and domestic facilities," the agency wrote in a summary of its negotiations with representatives of the generics industry. A final draft of the proposed GDUFA performance goals, as well as legislative language, was sent to Congress in January 2012, where legislators will have a final say on the new fee program.

## Pay-for-delay scrutinized

Despite the progress made by the generics industry with the FDA, it had a less cordial year with the Federal Trade Commission, which struck out at so-called pay-for-delay deals. These arrangements, made between pharmaceutical companies and generic rivals grew by more than 60 percent in fiscal 2010, according to a May 2011 report from the Federal Trade Commission, which continues to push to outlaw such agreements. The agency says the deals come at a hefty price tag to taxpayers who pay billions of dollars more than necessary for drugs because they delay the entry of lower-priced

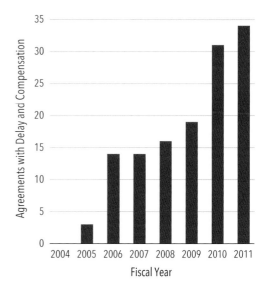

*Figure 6.8* **Pay-for-Delay Settlements**

Agreements with Delay and Compensation — Fiscal Year

generics into the market [*See Figure 6.8*].

"Pay-for-delay" settlements resolve patent challenges brought by generic drugmakers against their branded drug competitors. The branded companies provide payments as part of the agreements that delay the introduction of generic competition to the market. The FTC says such settlements that include a payment delay generic entry by 17 months longer on average than those that do not include a payment.

> The FTC has challenged a number of pay-for-delay agreements in court, contending that they are anticompetitive and violate U.S. antitrust laws.

The FTC found that 31 final settlements reached during fiscal 2010 between branded and generic drugmakers included both compensation to the generic drugmaker and restrictions on the generics company's ability to market a product. The agency says these agreements involved 22 different brand-name pharmaceutical products with combined

# FDA Surveys Import Risks

## Globalization, growing complexity demand a new model, agency says

The growing amount of imported food and drugs produced by complex and often-opaque supply chains threatens America's public health, the **U.S. Food and Drug Administration** said in 2011.

The agency's report on the problem, "Pathway to Global Product Safety and Quality," says that FDA-regulated imports have quadrupled since 2000, spurring a need for it to adopt an international operating model capable of matching the scope of the industries it regulates.

The agency's new approach, already implemented in certain areas, calls for using four core building blocks to improve the safety of everyday food, drugs, cosmetics, and devices. It advocates creating global coalitions of regulators, improving global data systems to track information about regulated products, expanding market intelligence and risk analysis, and leveraging public-private efforts.

The agency has already increased the number of foreign drug manufacturing inspections by 27 percent between 2007 and 2009 and has opened a series of international offices in key locations, including China and India, where a growing share of generic medicines are being manufactured. Furthermore, President Barack Obama's proposal for the agency's fiscal 2013 budget contains $10 million to support closer collaborations with the FDA's Chinese counterparts with the goal of strengthening the safety of the food and drugs produced in China for export to the United States.

On the inspections front at least, some relief may come from the agency's recent decision to join an international information-sharing collaboration that will provide it with access to information on pharmaceutical facility inspections conducted by its international counterparts.

But with as much as 80 percent of active pharmaceutical ingredients used in medications sold in the United States being manufactured in other countries, there's still much to be done. Adulterated Heparin, diverted and counterfeit glucose monitor test strips, contaminated glycerin, and low quality titanium implants have all raised public health concerns in recent years. "Global supply chains, international trade, foreign sourcing, and terrorism," the report notes, "remind us daily that the rest of the world will not stop and wait for regulators to catch up." ■

annual U.S. sales of about $9.3 billion. "Collusive deals to keep generics off the market are already costing consumers and taxpayers $3.5 billion a year in higher drug prices," said FTC Chairman Jon Leibowitz in a May 2011 statement issued by the commission. "The increasing number of these deals is a win-win proposition for the pharmaceutical industry, but a lose-lose for everyone else."

The FTC has challenged a number of these patent settlement agreements in court, contending that they are anticompetitive and violate U.S. antitrust laws. The agency also has supported legislation in Congress that would prohibit settlements that increase the cost of prescription drugs. President Obama also stepped into the fray, suggesting twice during the year that "pay for delay" agreements be stamped out through an authori-

zation for the Federal Trade Commission to stop companies from entering into the agreements. The administration estimates doing so would generate $11 billion over ten years in savings to federal health programs.

But pharmaceutical industry trade groups have fought such efforts and dispute the conclusions of the FTC as to the effects these settlements have on taxpayers and consumers. The Generic Pharmaceutical Association called the FTC's understanding of patent settlements "flawed" and says it misleads consumers. "The FTC is continuing to perpetuate the myth that pro-competitive, pro-consumer patent settlements are harmful to consumers—an unsubstantiated position that has repeatedly failed to receive support in both Congress and the courts," the orga-

# FDA Wants Companion Diagnostics To Be Approved with Paired Drugs

## Draft guidance to help development of personalized medicines

The **U.S. Food and Drug Administration** said in July 2011 it would like to see more companion diagnostics—tests used to determine whether a drug is appropriate to treat an individual patient—approved with new therapies. But because the agency worries that erroneous test results could lead to withholding appropriate medicines or, just as bad, administration of inappropriate therapies, it wants to see careful attention paid to their accuracy.

To that end, it has issued draft guidance on in vitro companion diagnostic devices (IVDs) explaining its perceived need for oversight and providing guidance for industry and FDA staff on possible premarket regulatory pathways for the tests.

Drug-diagnostic pairings featured prominently in a string of FDA new drug approvals in 2011, including **Pfizer's** Xalkori for treating non-small cell lung cancers in people who express the abnormal anaplastic lymphoma kinase gene, and Zelboraf, developed by **Roche** and **Plexxikon**, now part of **Daiichi Sankyo**, for the treatment of patients with melanoma whose tumors express a gene mutation called BRAF V600E. But the agency would like to encourage even more such pairings in the future.

"These proposed guidelines support the development of innovative new targeted medicines and their corresponding diagnostic tests and are intended to provide manufacturers with greater predictability," says Jeffrey Shuren, director of the FDA's **Center for Devices and Radiological Health**. "It is the agency's goal to help stimulate early collaborations between drug and device makers so they can develop the best medical products for treating patients."

The agency's growing expectation for companion diagnostics to be used in better matching patients and innovative new therapies is already resonating among drugmakers seeking to launch new medicines in the United States. Speaking at the *JPMorgan Global Healthcare Conference* in January 2012, Pascale Witz, president and CEO of **Medical Diagnostics** said, "We know that more than 80 percent of the drugs in the pipelines of the pharma industry are actually being developed with biomarkers, so the need for companion diagnostics is only going to grow and it's going to be here to last."

Still, the draft guidance raised questions and concerns for many companies. One of the most common questions was about exactly which tests will be considered companion diagnostics and which will not. FDA says that any test, even diagnostic kits and laboratory-developed tests, will be regulated as companion diagnostics, reported the *Personalized Medicine Bulletin*.

Other concerns reflected anxiety about the use of companion diagnostics to guide treatment. Plexxikon, in comments filed to the FDA, expressed dismay about "negative consequences on patient care when decisions are based solely on the results of a single IVD, rather than a combination of test results in conjunction with a healthcare team's expertise," and the "high logistical and economic barriers to the development, precise requirements and timely availability of companion IVDs, especially for orphan indications."

The **American Society for Clinical Pathology** also expressed concerns in comments it submitted. Its worry is that the FDA's desire for a therapeutic and its corresponding companion diagnostic to be developed and tested at the same time and in the same trials as the therapeutic "could delay implementation of new tests, stifle innovation, increase development costs, and thus limit patient access to potentially beneficial assays."

The FDA anticipates releasing its final *Guidance for In Vitro Companion Diagnostic Devices* in the second quarter of 2012. ∎

## Figure 6.9  BIG PHARMA AVOIDS THE PATENT CLIFF

Worldwide Pharmaceutical Sales in 2010 (USD B)

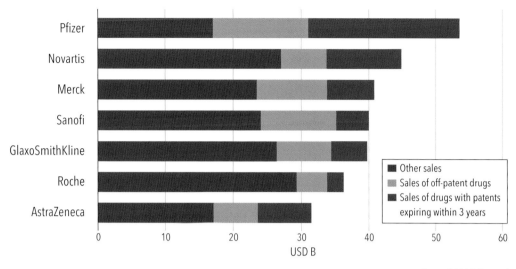

Source: BAS-ML Research

nization says. "Patent settlements have never prevented competition beyond the patent expiry, and generally have resulted in making lower-cost generics available months and even years before patents have expired."

Pointing to a **Royal Bank of Canada** analysis, the association argued that such settlements increase savings because, without them, litigation would lead to greater delays in bringing generic drugs to market. RBC found that generic drugs came to market prior to patent expiration in 48 percent of cases that were litigated compared to 76 percent for cases that ended in settlements.

Not surprisingly, the GPhA's prescription to Washington is if it wants to get serious about saving money it should stop worrying about the settlements and instead focus on initiatives to promote the use of generics for federal and state government funded health care programs and accelerate the approval of more affordable generics by increasing funding for the Office of Generic Drugs—something GDUFA will accomplish.

### Protecting Lipitor sales

Another generics controversy was ignited in 2011 with the landmark expiration of Lipitor's patent at the end of November 2011 [SEE FIGURE 6.9]. Pfizer's strategy for protecting the market share of branded Lipitor, through agreements with pharmacy benefit managers and insurers,

managed to ruffle Congress briefly.

To protect at least some of the blockbuster's revenue, a haul that totaled $10.7 billion in 2010, Pfizer sought to offer Lipitor to payers and patients at or below the cost of the generic versions during the 180 day period that **Ranbaxy** had an exclusive right to market the only generic rival to Lipitor. But while Pfizer sought to protect its lucrative franchise, Montana Democrat Max Baucus, Iowa Republican Chuck Grassley, and Wisconsin Democrat Herb Kohl expressed concerns that agreements between the drug giant and pharmacy benefit managers would undercut the sale of generic versions of Lipitor. The senators requested that Pfizer, the benefit managers, and the insurance companies provide copies of all agreements between the companies, all documents and communications pertaining to the agreements and all presentations describing the agreements or contracts. Kohl says he hoped the request would bring scrutiny to the business practices and "will restore fairness and open the gates to affordable prescription drug choices and tremendous cost savings."

### Accelerating medical device approvals

The **Institute of Medicine** at the end of July 2011 issued a report that calls for the U.S. Food and Drug Administration to scrap a 35-year-old process for approving medical devices not con-

*Figure 6.10* Average Time for Medical Device (510k) Submissions To Clear

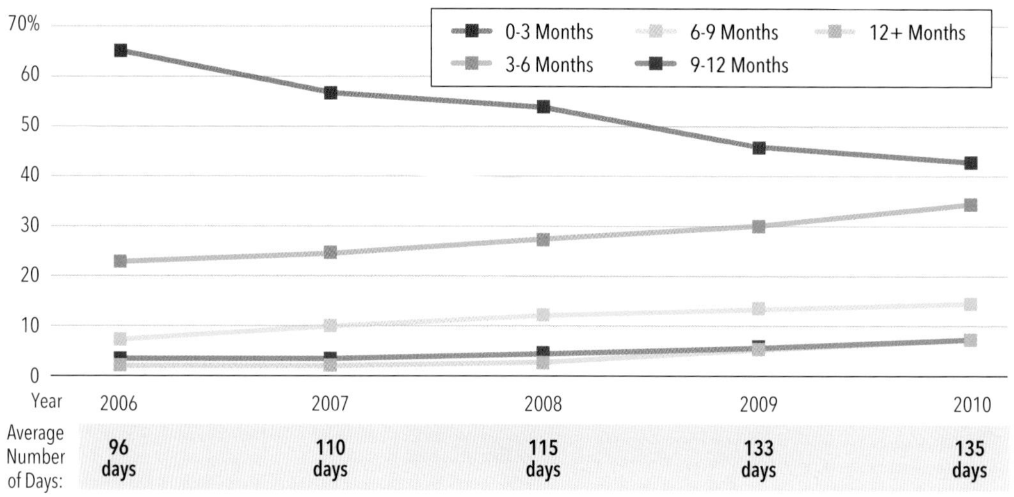

| Year | 2006 | 2007 | 2008 | 2009 | 2010 |
|---|---|---|---|---|---|
| Average Number of Days: | 96 days | 110 days | 115 days | 133 days | 135 days |

Source: EmergoGroup

sidered to be high-risk. The report says the current process cannot assure that devices reaching the market are safe and effective.

In January 2012, medical device industry trade groups and the U.S. Food and Drug Administration reached a tentative agreement to speed up and improve the agency's review process as part of the third reauthorization of the *Medical Device User Fee Act*, or MDUFA. "The tentative new user fee agreement puts in place a framework that will benefit FDA and industry, but most importantly patients by accelerating the development and approval of safe and effective treatments and diagnostics," says Stephen Ubl, president and CEO of the trade group **Advanced Medical Technology Association**, also known as AdvaMed. "The improvements in the agreement provide FDA and medical technology companies the tools needed to improve the efficiency and consistency of the review process."

On average, there's been a 37 percent increase since 2006 in the time it takes medical devices to win premarket clearance from the U.S. Food and Drug Administration, according to an analysis by **Emergo Group**, an Austin-based consulting firm that assists medical device manufacturers with regulatory compliance. While more than half of applications cleared in less than three months and more than 80 percent cleared within six months, on average the agency took 37 percent longer to clear a device in 2010 than

in 2006—132 days last year compared to 96 days in 2006.

What the analysis showed is that "the average length of time from when a 510(k) premarket notification application is submitted by a manufacturer to when it is cleared by FDA has increased pretty substantially since 2006," says Chris Schorre, vice president of Global Marketing for Emergo Group [*See Figure 6.10*].

Schorre suggested that one explanation may be that FDA reviewers are requesting more clinical performance data from a higher percentage of manufacturers submitting 510(k) applications. "This would, in turn, lead to an overall increase in 510(k) clearance times because manufacturers need to respond to those additional requests from the FDA," he says.

The agreement in principle, a result of more than a year of negotiation, includes authorization for the FDA to collect $595 million in user fees over five years, double the $287 million it collected during the previous five years. It will allow the FDA to hire more than 200 additional employees and result in a reduction in average total review times, greater accountability, predictability, and transparency through such improvements as a more structured pre-submission process and earlier interactions between the FDA and applicants, says the agency. "Reauthorization of this important program is an essential component for advancing medical device innovation," says

FDA Commissioner Margaret Hamburg.

Besides reduction of review times for pre-market applications and 510(k) submissions, the new agreement provides for the FDA to meet with applicants halfway through the review process to give them time to respond to reviewers' questions. It also includes a "leave no submission behind" provision requiring FDA to meet with companies if a performance goal on a premarket application or 510(k) is missed and work out a plan for completing work on the submission.

The user fee program for medical device makers was established by Congress 10 years ago with the Medical Device User Fee and Modernization Act of 2002, prompted by growing concerns about the capacity and performance of the medical device review program. It authorized the FDA to collect user fees for certain medical device applications, for the registration of certain medical device establishments, and for certain other purposes. Small businesses could have their fees waived on certain submissions or quality for a reduced fee.

The five-year program, reauthorized in 2007, is set to expire on September 30, 2012, before which it will need to be reauthorized by Congress. AdvaMed will work with members of Congress, the FDA, and other stakeholders to help make sure the agreement wins approval before the September 30 deadline, says Ubl.

## Beyond User Fees

Of course, user fees alone were never meant to fund the FDA—although they make up an increasingly large slice of its budget. They were designed to address a need for resources to ensure a timely review of new drugs. But core funding for the agency comes from Congress. That funding was jeopardized in 2011 when legislation designed to shake $100 billion in savings from the president's fiscal 2011 budget request sought to slash $220 million in funding from the FDA's annual budget, along with $1 billion from the **National Institutes for Health**.

Fortunately for both agencies, neither suffered the deep cuts other agencies endured. President Obama proposed roughly flat federal funding of $4.5 billion for the FDA for fiscal 2013, with a 17 percent raise over the agency's fiscal 2012 budget accounted for almost entirely by user fees.

The NIH came out with a recommended $31

> The new device approval agreement provides for the FDA to meet with applicants halfway through the review process to give them time to respond to reviewers' questions.

billion appropriation, including new grant management policies to increase the number of new research grants awarded. Such policies, making it easier for small companies to secure funding from government, can make a tremendous difference. The intention of such programs – to spur innovation – was echoed in a variety of initiatives and legislative changes that debuted in 2011.

In December 2011, the NIH established the **National Center for Advancing Translational Sciences**, or NCATS, with a budget of $575 million. The development highlights the need to re-engineer the process of translating scientific discoveries into new drugs, diagnostics, and devices. While many observers feared NCATS could become, essentially, a government-sponsored drug company, NIH Director Francis Collins said its purpose will be to work closely with partners in the regulatory, academic, nonprofit, and private sectors, striving to identify and overcome hurdles that slow the development of effective treatments and cures.

## Opening the door for innovation

An especially important legal change made in 2011 that will support innovative companies came in the federal small business funding program signed into law as part of the *National Defense Authorization Act.* It restored access to a funding program which historically had been a major source of seed funding for biotechnology companies but had been denied to companies majority-owned by venture capitalists.

The changes allow the NIH, the **U.S. Department of Energy**, and the **National Science Foundation** to award as much as 25 percent of funds allocated to the *Small Business Innovation Research* program to small businesses that

The National Institutes of Health has recommended a $31 billion appropriation, including new grant management policies to increase the number of new research grants awarded. Such policies, making it easier for small companies to secure funding, can make a tremendous difference for them.

are majority-owned by venture capital operating companies. Other federal agencies will be allowed to award as much as 15 percent of their SBIR funds to VC-backed companies.

The changes "will help to ensure that small U.S. venture-backed companies have increased access to capital for meritorious cutting edge early-stage research," wrote the NVCA, in a letter to Senate Majority Leader Harry Reid and Senate Minority Leader Mitch McConnell.

The *Small Business Innovation Research Reauthorization* extended the SBIR program for six years from its December 16, 2011 expiration. Nearly a third of the 252 companies that have developed FDA-approved biologics have received at least one SBIR or Small Business Technology Transfer award, according to BIO. "At the very earliest stages of development, alternate sources of financing, such as SBIR grants, have been instrumental in fur-

thering research and development in biotechnology," says Jim Greenwood, BIO's president and CEO.

### New tax credits for biotechs

In August 2011, a bipartisan group of House lawmakers introduced legislation that would provide new tax credits for investments in research and development, and create an opening for life sciences companies to repatriate foreign earnings at a reduced tax rate. The *Life Sciences Jobs and Investment Act of 2011* would allow companies engaged in life sciences research to either double their R&D tax credit on the first $150 million invested or repatriate foreign earnings at a reduced tax rate up to that same limit when used exclusively for job creation and research in the United States.

"American preeminence in the life sciences industry is threatened by the erosion of investment capital, the departure of highly educated workers, and intense global competition," the bill's sponsors wrote in a statement explaining their reasons for introducing the legislation. "Many of our competitors, including China and India, are aggressively expanding academic training and research capacity. Meanwhile, that capacity is shrinking in the United States."

The bill's backers represent California, Pennsylvania, and New Jersey. Together, they assert that reducing the tax burden on the mostly small- and medium-sized companies responsible for life sciences research in the United States would encourage new hiring of scientific personnel in the sector, new research at American universities and state-sponsored incubators, and investment in new laboratory and related life sciences research facilities.

Another way that Washington hopes to make things easier for small and medium-sized companies to succeed is through bipartisan legislation intended to make it easier for small and medium-sized companies to go public and raise capital through public markets. New York Senator Charles Schumer and Pennsylvania Senator Pat Toomey say their bill, the *Reopening American Capital Markets to Emerging Growth Companies Act of 2011*, would reduce the administrative and compliance hurdles that have become an obstacle to companies pursuing an initial public offering by phasing in many of the costliest obligations of being a public company while maintaining key investor protections.

"During difficult economic times, it is critical that we give growing innovators the breathing room that they need to access public markets," says Schumer. "The vast majority of job creation occurs after companies go public so it makes sense to make the IPO process easier for emerging firms."

From 2001 to 2010 there were 478 IPOs of venture-backed companies. That compared to 1,975 IPOs of venture-backed companies from 1991 to 2000, according to the NVCA. The Schumer-Toomey bill would establish a new category of issuers, called "emerging growth companies" that have less than $1 billion in annual revenues at the time they register with the **U.S. Securities and Exchange Commission** and less than $700 million in publicly-traded shares after their IPO.

Under the proposed law, these companies would have up to five years or until they reached the $1 billion in revenue or $700 million in publicly traded shares to reach full regulatory compliance with regulations phased in over that period. An estimated 11 to 13 percent of companies representing 3 percent of total market's capitalization would qualify for this so-called "on ramp" status if the provisions were in effect today, the senators said.

Among the high-cost compliance issues that these companies would be exempted from is a section of *Sarbanes-Oxley* that requires public companies to pay an outside auditor to attest to a company's internal controls and procedures, although CEOs and CFOs would still be required to personally certify that the internal controls and procedures are adequate, exposing them to personal liability.

The proposals would update restrictions on communications to account for advances in modes of communication and the information available to investors. The bill would allow investors to have access to research reports about emerging growth companies prior to the IPO. It would also permit emerging growth companies to gauge preliminary interest in a potential offering by expanding the range of permissible pre-filing communications to institutional investors, and allow for filing a registration statement with the SEC on a confidential basis. Additionally, the bill would exempt emerging growth companies from the requirement to hold a stockholder vote on executive compensation arrangements, including golden parachutes.

## Patent Reform

Among the most critical pieces of legislation to pass in 2011 was the *Leahy-Smith America Invents Act*, hailed as the most significant changes to patent law since 1952. The legislation won bipartisan support in a year marked by divisive partisanship. Passed in September 2011, the Act introduced a number of key measures supportive of entrepreneurship in general and the biotechnology sector in particular. The law seeks to better harmonize the U.S. patent system with other systems around the globe, speed the pace of patent reviews, and reduce litigation.

The law introduced a "first-to-file system," which takes the place of America's current "first-to-invent" system on March 16, 2013. While on its surface the change seems straightforward, eliminating the complex and costly interference proceedings now used to sort out who first conceived of an invention and reduced it to practice, in reality it created a "first-to-file, with an asterisk" system, says Courtenay Brinckerhoff, a partner with **Foley & Lardner** and editor of the Foley blog *Pharma-PatentsBlog.com*. That's because it allows an inventor a grace period of up to one year in which he or she can disclose an invention before filing a patent application without losing rights to the patent.

Filing dates and pre-filing disclosures of proprietary information will be more important than in the past says Brinckerhoff. But even though it will be somewhat easier to have uniform prior art standards across global patent authorities because drugmakers often seek patents internationally, every country will still have its own variations and grace periods. That means there will still be differences between countries in what qualifies as prior art.

More significant are changes in post-grant review, says Brinckerhoff. These changes will allow pharma and biotech companies an opportunity, within nine months of a patent's grant date, to challenge the patent within the patent office, without litigation. Furthermore, the new law directly and immediately will address the plague of false marking—instances in which companies mark a product as being protected by a patent when it is not—and make the legal system less hospitable to patent troll cases.

In recognition of the importance intellectual property portfolios play in the chances a startup can secure venture financing, the reform establishes a fast track option to expedite patent processing, intended to reduce to 12 months the average three-year wait applicants face at the U.S. Patent and Trademark Office. It also will introduce fees to support additional resources at the USPTO to trim the current patent backlog, which stood at nearly 680,000 applications when the Act was passed. The patent office released a proposal for those fees in February 2012.

## The Year Ahead

The events of 2011 have contributed to a growing sense within industry of regulatory barriers

> The events of 2011 have contributed to a growing sense within industry of regulatory barriers that are unpredictable, burdensome, and counterproductive.

that are unpredictable, burdensome, and counterproductive. In a global economy, companies are already looking beyond the United States for more flexible regulators and easier access to markets. "The globalization of science, people, and capital is accelerating," say the authors of a February 2011 **California Healthcare Institute** and **Boston Consulting Group** report assessing the current environment for innovation. "As organizations become adept and then expert at conducting research and development, clinical trials and business globally, their comfort with regulators around the world grows."

Finding new ways to balance risks and benefits in the years ahead will be essential to maintaining the vitality of medical innovation throughout the world, but so too will more meaningful collaborations between regulated industry and regulators.

In the United States, the development of a *National Bioeconomy Blueprint* is one platform supporting the formation of that partnership. The blueprint envisions a future in which reforms speed up commercialization, open new markets, encourage strategic R&D investments to accelerate innovation, reduce unnecessary burdens on innovators, and better develop the strength of public-private partnerships.

"Big, bold and daring thinking" will be required to create new models to encourage investment in innovation and to speed up the discovery of scientific breakthroughs, wrote Jim Greenwood in a letter offering the government BIO's ideas. In an age of global innovation, where world-changing medicines are being developed at ever-increasing speed along the paths of least resistance, nothing short of a revolution may do. ∎

# Tackling Fraud

## Government recovers billions from false healthcare claims

**A**lthough it may seem at times that government is too deeply involved in the affairs of industry, U.S. regulators likely feel justified in keeping a close eye on drugmakers. In 2011, the pharmaceutical industry was the number one source of payments made to resolve state and federal legal claims, according to the **U.S. Department of Justice**.

Federal authorities say that they recovered $4.1 billion in fraudulent healthcare payments during 2011, the largest amount ever collected in a single year. DOJ enforcement actions alone recovered nearly $2.2 billion in civil claims against the pharmaceutical industry in fiscal year 2011, including $1.76 billion in federal recoveries and $421 million in state Medicaid recoveries.

Altogether, eight drug manufacturers, including **EMD Serono** and **Novo Nordisk**, paid $900 million to resolve allegations that they had engaged in unlawful pricing to increase their profits, according to the agency.

Additionally, **GlaxoSmithKline** paid $750 million to resolve criminal and civil allegations that it had knowingly submitted, or caused to be submitted, false claims to government healthcare programs for adulterated drugs and for drugs that failed to conform to the standards of strength, purity or quality specified by the FDA.

Fraud against federal health programs, primarily Medicare and Medicaid, accounted for $2.4 billion of settlements and judgments in civil cases involving fraud against the government. With criminal and other cases taken into account, the government's healthcare fraud prevention and enforcement efforts recovered nearly $4.1 billion in taxpayer dollars during fiscal 2011.

Assistant Attorney General Tony West attributed the agency's success in part to the passage of the *Affordable Care Act* in 2010, which amended the *False Claims Act* to provide new incentives for whistleblowers to report fraud and strengthened the provisions of the federal health care *Anti-Kickback Statute*. More stringent practices enacted by the HSS Health Care Fraud Prevention & Enforcement and the Medicare Strike Force teams to review billings of the federal health programs also helped stem fraudulent claims.

"Fighting fraud is one of our top priorities and we have recovered an unprecedented number of taxpayer dollars," said HHS Secretary Kathleen Sebelius. "Our efforts strengthen the integrity of our healthcare programs and meet the president's call for a return to American values that ensure everyone gets a fair shot, everyone does their fair share, and everyone plays by the same rules."

The $4.1 billion recouped has been paid back to either the **U.S. Treasury** or the **Centers for Medicare and Medicaid Services**, transferred to other federal agencies that administer healthcare programs, or been paid to private individuals who were victims of fraud, the government says.

While newer fraud protection practices are making in-roads in curbing healthcare fraud, they remain only a stepping-stone towards eliminating rampant healthcare fraud, a problem that the government has said accounts for nearly 10 percent of all Medicare claims. ∎

> "Fighting fraud is one of our top priorities and we have recovered an unprecedented number of taxpayer dollars."

**Kathleen Sebelius**
*U.S. Secretary of Health and Human Services*

REGULATION & POLICY

6

# The Rise of the BRICs

After decades in which the United States, Europe, and Japan represented the drivers of economic growth, the tide has shifted to developing nations in Asia, Latin America, and other parts of the world where a rising middle class is fueling an economic boom. Although vastly different from one another, these emerging markets—China, India, Brazil, af sales growth in the coming years. Companies are investing in research and development around the world to take advantage of low cost talent, local expertise, and proximity to new markets. In turn, this global movement of technology and innovation has helped boost the economies of emerging countries, which are reaping its benefits and moving toward becoming their own centers of innovation. They are investing in education, infrastructure, and healthcare, and ensuring the growth of high-return, knowledge-based industries such as biotechnology. They see innovation as the way to transform their societies for the better, never more so than amidst the austere economic conditions and global challenges facing the world today. Globalization has dissolved borders, making cooperation rather than competition the driving force for economic well-being.

## Chapter 7:

# THE RISE OF THE BRICS

It's a heady time for life sciences in China. Flush with cash, the country is no longer content to be considered the world's low-cost manufacturer. Instead, it is investing heavily in research and education, aiming to become the world's leading innovator—a position it will attain by 2020, says Steve Yang, **AstraZeneca's** head of research and development in Asia and emerging markets.

China's *12th Five Year Plan*, ratified in March 2011, aims to double biomedical R&D innovation funding from the previous plan to $300 billion. It seeks to make China the second largest pharmaceutical market by 2020. At the same time, its government is moving to provide basic healthcare services to at least 90 percent of its 1.3 billion citizens. "China is a lot of fun and there is a huge sense of urgency," says Jinzi Wu, CEO of **Ascletis**, a privately funded company based both in the United States and China that launched in 2011 with $100 million in backing to discover and develop new treatments for cancer and infectious disease—both significant unmet medical needs in China [*SEE SIDEBAR ASCLETIS*].

Wu is one of many Chinese expatriates who are returning to their homeland to conduct research and create companies. Wu calls himself a sea gull because he is constantly travelling between China and the United States as he works to create a Chinese biopharmaceutical company

*Figure 7.1*   EMERGING MARKETS LEAD
GLOBAL GROWTH

Real GDP: Quarterly percent change from one year earlier

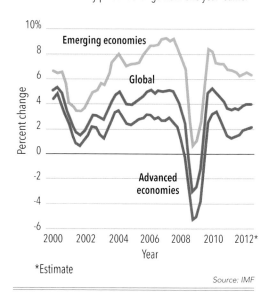

*Estimate

Source: IMF

141

with Western-style managerial expertise.

China's fervor is infectious and emblematic of the growing emerging markets focus among major pharmaceutical and biotech companies, which are not only offshoring manufacturing to China and other emerging markets, but also partnering with local firms, building local R&D facilities, and beefing up sales staffs to take advantage of opportunities to both grow revenue and conduct relatively low-cost clinical research and development. At the same time, the center of innovation is shifting away from Western markets to emerging markets, which are shaping new technologies, often originating in the West, to meet local needs.

China is not the only developing country embracing innovation. Indian companies are gaining a reputation for low-cost vaccines, boasting the only flu vaccine manufactured in cell culture instead of eggs in the developing world. Brazil is gaining a strong reputation in agricultural innovation and has developed its own genetically modified soybeans. And Russia is using its oil revenue to build its life sciences sector through internal investment in infrastructure and external investment in innovation.

South Korea's drug agency approved the first therapeutic using allogeneic stem cells in January 2012. The product, called Cartistem, was developed by Seoul-based **Medipost**, to help regenerate knee cartilage using stem cells derived from umbilical cord blood. In September, South Korea's president promised $89 million in funding for stem cell research over the next year, describing it as a "new growth engine."

The governments of these emerging countries are playing a critical role in this innovation shift as they seek to move their economies to high value industries from a dependence on lower value commodities and manufacturing. They see biotechnology and other medical technologies as important drivers of economic growth and are investing heavily to develop homegrown industries to serve the needs of their people and take their economies to the next level.

## Growth shifts to developing nations

After decades in which the United States, Europe, and Japan were the principal drivers of economic growth, the tide has shifted to developing nations in Asia, Latin America, and other

*Figure 7.2*   **REAL GDP PER CAPITA**

Percent change, Q4 2007 to Q2 2011

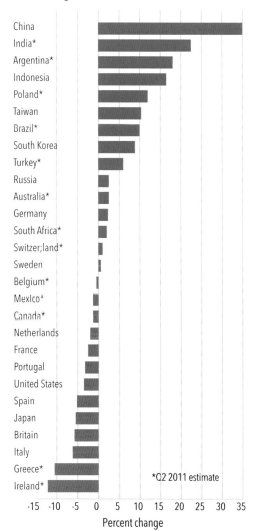

*Q2 2011 estimate

Percent change

Sources: Economist Intelligence Unit; Haver Analytics; IMF; JPMorgan; The Economist

parts of the world where a rising middle class is fueling an economic boom. These are the emerging markets—China, India, Brazil, Russia, South Korea, and Turkey, among others—targeted by the life sciences industry as the primary source of sales growth in the coming years.

As economic growth in the Western world slows, economic growth in the emerging markets is accelerating. Since the financial crisis of 2007, the economic performance of nations, as measured by GDP per capita, has soared in Asia at the same time as it has slowed in the United States and most of Europe [SEE FIGURE 7.2]. As

When he coined the term BRIC in 2001, to denote Brazil, Russia, India, and China, Goldman Sachs' Jim O'Neill believed their combined economies were likely to equal the combined economies of the G7—the world's top economies—within the next 40 years .

export-driven markets, many of the developing countries experienced a major economic slowdown in the second half of 2011 due to the sovereign debt crisis in Europe and the economic stumble of the United States. After accounting for inflation, however, China's GDP rose 9.2 percent in 2011, India's rose 7.3 percent, Rus-

sia's GDP rose between 3 and 4.5 percent, and Brazil's rose 3 percent, according to **Morgan Stanley** research. The U.S. economy grew 1.8 percent in 2011 and outside of Germany, most European economies remained at a standstill or turned sluggish [*SEE FIGURE 7.1*]. At the rate it is growing, China's economy is on track to be almost double the size of the United States' economy by 2050, according to **Goldman Sachs** [*SEE FIGURE 7.3*].

### BRICs exemplify emerging markets

When he coined the term BRIC in 2001, to denote Brazil, Russia, India, and China, Goldman Sachs' Jim O'Neill believed their combined economies were likely to equal the combined economies of the G7—the world's top economies—within the next 40 years and were, therefore, good investment opportunities [*SEE FIGURE 7.4*]. China had just been accepted into the **World Trade Organization** in 2001 and Russia had begun to privatize its industries. Other than their economic potential, however, they shared little in common. Their demographics, governments, politics, economic structures, per capita income, and cultures were quite disparate.

Today BRIC nations routinely trade with each other and have held three summits to discuss and strengthen their relationships. But they remain very different in many ways. Russia's and Brazil's economies are commodity-driven, heavily dependent on the strength of their natural resources; China's government controls its banking system; India and Brazil suffer from poor infrastructure and high inflation. Yet they are all becoming wealthier—economic heavyweights in a world dominated over the last 100 years by the United States, Europe, and Japan. BRICs are striving to sustain their economic growth and better provide for their populations, including investing in education, infrastructure, and healthcare, and

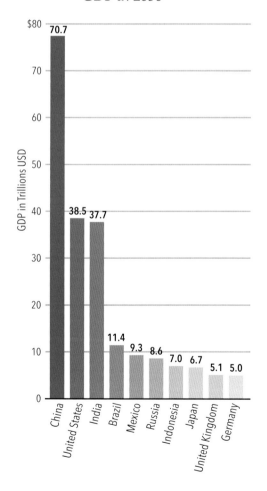

*Figure 7.3* **TOP TEN ECONOMIES BY GDP IN 2050**

GDP in Trillions USD

China 70.7
United States 38.5
India 37.7
Brazil 11.4
Mexico 9.3
Russia 8.6
Indonesia 7.0
Japan 6.7
United Kingdom 5.1
Germany 5.0

*Source: Goldman Sachs*

ensuring the growth of high-return, knowledge-based industries such as biotechnology.

Business regulations in these countries vary widely, according to the **World Bank's** *Ease of Doing Business Index*. Singapore and Hong Kong (one of China's two Special Administrative Regions) are ranked at the top of the list of 183 nations, while China stands at No. 79, compared to the United States at No. 5. India's rank is in the list's bottom third at No. 134 because it is considered to have a difficult environment for starting new ventures [*See Figure 7.5*].

China ranks much higher in *The Global Venture Capital and Private Equity Country Attractiveness Index*, a measure meant to guide institutional investors' decisions about where to allocate capital. While the United States continues to command the top ranking, China is ranked No. 20 among 80 countries, close behind Hong Kong and South Korea. India ranks No. 30, with Russia at No. 41 and Brazil at No. 43. The report finds that much of the attraction of the BRICs from an investment perspective is based on their expected economic growth and is already priced into new investments. The Index also ranks the BRIC countries relative to each other [*See Figure 7.6*].

Ten years after O'Neill coined the acronym, an influx of foreign capital, a rising middle class, and a shared government-driven strategy of growing their life sciences sectors have made the BRIC countries, along with the next generation of emerging nations, a strategic focus of global biopharmaceutical firms [*See Figure 7.7*].

> The United States remains the leader in the number of published patent applications, but published patent applications from China are likely to exceed the United States by 2015.

### Increasing innovation

It has been said that the 21st century will belong to the BRICs. Certainly they are catching up fast in terms of measures of innovation such as growth of R&D, research papers published

*Figure 7.4*   **Money Magnets – Foreign Direct Investment in BRIC**

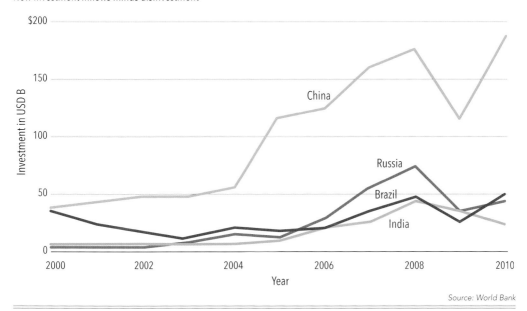

**Overall inbound foreign investment by country**

New investment inflows minus disinvestment

*Source: World Bank*

*Figure 7.5*   **EASE OF DOING BUSINESS INDEX IN 2009 AND 2010**

Countries ranked according to World Bank standards, with rank of 1 indicating the most business-friendly regulations

Change in rank, 2010 vs 2009

unchanged   improved   reduced

| COUNTRY NAME | RANK, 2009 | RANK, 2010 |
|---|---|---|
| Singapore | 1 | 1 |
| Hong Kong SAR, China | 2 | 2 |
| New Zealand | 3 | 3 |
| United Kingdom | 4 | 4 |
| United States | 5 | 5 |
| Denmark | 6 | 6 |
| Canada | 9 | 7 |
| Norway | 7 | 8 |
| Ireland | 8 | 9 |
| Australia | 10 | 10 |
| Saudi Arabia | 12 | 11 |
| Sweden | 18 | 14 |
| Korea, Republic | 15 | 16 |
| Japan | 19 | 18 |
| Thailand | 16 | 19 |
| Malaysia | 23 | 21 |
| Germany | 21 | 22 |
| France | 28 | 26 |
| Switzerland | 24 | 27 |
| Israel | 30 | 29 |
| South Africa | 32 | 34 |
| Mexico | 41 | 35 |
| Colombia | 38 | 39 |
| Chile | 53 | 43 |
| Turkey | 60 | 65 |
| Vietnam | 88 | 78 |
| China | 78 | 79 |
| Egypt, Arab Rep. | 99 | 94 |
| Indonesia | 115 | 121 |
| Russia | 116 | 123 |
| Brazil | 124 | 127 |
| India | 135 | 134 |

*Source: World Bank*

and cited, and intellectual property patents filed. While the United States continues to lead the way in research and development spending, China has risen quickly through the ranks to become the world's second largest spender. [*SEE FIGURE 7.8*].

For example, backed by $1.5 billion in government funding, China's **BGI**, formerly known as **Beijing Genomics Institute**, has become the world's largest sequencer of genomes. It is initiating new collaborations with private and public institutions at a rapid rate. In October 2011 it teamed up with U.S. advocacy group **Autism Speaks** to sequence the entire genomes of more than 2000 families with two or more autistic children, including Chinese patients. The non-profit is funding the sequencing of the first 100 genomes, with additional funding coming from government donors and public and private sources [*SEE BGI SIDEBAR CHAPTER 3*].

Other measures of innovation highlight the rapid strides occurring in emerging countries. Although the United States continues to lead in the number of research papers published in peer-reviewed journals, China, Brazil, and India are rapidly gaining ground. China was ranked second after the United States in terms of the number of published peer-reviewed papers in the biomedical sciences by the **National Science Foundation** in 2010 [*SEE FIGURE 7.9*].

The latest report from the **World Intellectual Property Organization** found that intellectual property patent filings rebounded strongly in 2010 after a considerable decline in 2009. The number of filings grew 7.2 percent amid an economically volatile year, with China and the United States accounting for 80 percent of the growth. The **U.S. Patent and Trademark Office** received the largest number of applications (490,226 filings), followed by China (391,117 filings), which overtook Japan (344,598 filings). The change mirrored wider economic trends that propelled China to surpass Japan as the world's second largest economy in 2011.

Although the United States remains the leader in the number of published patent applications, data from **Thomson Reuters** suggests that published patent applications from China are likely to exceed the United States by 2015. This is also evident in the subcategory of biomedical patent applications. Analysis of WIPO data for the ten years from 2000 to 2009, the latest year for which data is available, show that China has experienced a 768 percent surge during that time in the number of patent applications filed in the fields of chemical technologies (including biotechnology and pharmaceuticals) and medical technologies and devices [SEE FIGURE 7.10].

While the volume of applications does not speak to their quality, it is evident that Chinese companies are becoming more innovative as they transform themselves into producers of more sophisticated branded products.

## Innovation goes global

Boosting innovation is increasingly seen as the best way to transform societies for the better, never more so than amidst the austere economic conditions and global challenges facing the world. Innovation is also becoming more global in nature as companies invest in research and development around the world to take advantage of low-cost talent, local expertise, and proximity to new markets. In turn, this global movement of technology and innovation has helped boost the economies of emerging countries, which are reaping its benefits and gradually becoming centers of innovation in their own right.

One yardstick of this change is the *Global Innovation Index*, a collaborative effort headed by **INSEAD**, one of the world's largest business schools, with input from partners including the **Confederation of Indian Industry**, **Alcatel-Lucent**, **Booz & Company**, and the World Intellectual Property Organization among others. It ranks countries based on the conditions and qualities that allow innovation to thrive [SEE FIGURE 7.6]. Switzerland was ranked at the top of a list of 125 countries, and the United States held its position at number 7 in the 2011 rankings, behind several Nordic countries, Singapore, and Hong Kong. Three of the BRICs—China, Russia, and Brazil moved up the ranks from the previous year: China's ranking at No. 29, up from No. 43 in 2010, Brazil moved to No. 47, up from No. 68, and Russia moved to No. 56, up from No. 64. India fell in the rankings to No. 62, dropping from No. 56 in 2010 and No. 41 in 2009.

*Figure 7.6* **INVESTMENT ATTRACTIVENESS**

The business-friendliness of countries in terms of various economic factors, compared to the U.S. Scale of 1-200, with 200 being the most attractive.
U.S. rank of 100 on all measures

### The countries vary on a host of issues

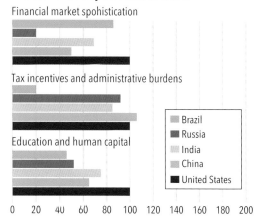

### Risks vary from country to country

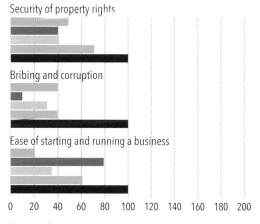

### Innovation prowess varies too

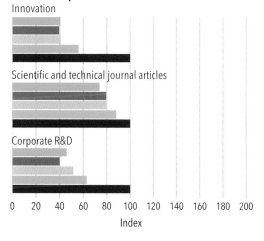

Index

Source: Global VCPE Country Attractive Index-2011 annual

EMERGING MARKETS

7

## Engines of drug spending

As they develop, these emerging countries are struggling with the same constraints of their more developed neighbors, including aging populations, growing incidence of chronic disease, and the rising cost of increasing access to healthcare for their citizens. With their huge populations, India and China alone account for almost 2.5 billion people and represent a vast and largely untapped market for life sciences companies seeking new revenue opportunities.

Global spending on medicines will reach about $1.1 trillion by 2015, up from $856 billion spent in 2010, with much of the growth coming from emerging markets, according to drug research firm **IMS Health** [*See Figure 7.11*]. Much of that growth will come from China, which is expected to contribute 22 to 28 percent of the total growth [*See Figure 7.13*].

Over the next five years, emerging markets are expected to nearly double their spending on drugs to between $285 billion and $315 billion, or about 28 percent of the total amount spent on pharmaceuticals. That compares to $151 billion in 2010. Strong economic growth and governments' commitment to expanded healthcare access is fueling the rise in spending. About 80 percent of spending in emerging markets will be for generics rather than innovative therapies. By 2015, IMS Health expects emerging market countries to become the second largest geographic segment globally in spending on medicines—surpassing Germany, France, Italy, Spain, and the United Kingdom combined, and approaching the level of the United States, and by 2020, drug sales in emerging markets are expected to account for half of global pharmaceutical sales [*See Figure 7.12*].

## Pharma targets emerging markets

The pressure on Big Pharma has intensified as many of its blockbuster drugs lose patent protection. Between 2011 and 2015 alone, some $120 billion in revenue is expected to be lost to competition from generic drugs. This lost revenue will not be offset by sales of new drugs coming onto the market. Total spending for branded drugs is expected to remain unchanged from 2010, as generics are increasingly preferred to existing or new brands. Emerging markets will be the key drivers of new spending over the next

*Figure 7.7* **A Tectonic Shift: Asia's Middle Class**

**The middle class in Asia will make a big jump in spending by 2030, says an OECD estimate**

Shares of global middle class spending by region, in trillions

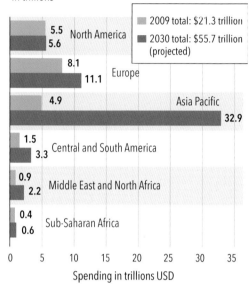

Spending in trillions USD

*Source: OECD; PwC*

five years, accounting for 70 percent of revenue growth [*See Figure 7.14*].

Selling into emerging markets is one of the ways to extend product life after loss of exclusivity in established markets. These markets have a high regard for brands, giving the originator a leg up over generic competitors. They also have an exploding middle class expected to number more than 1.8 billion people by 2014, all seeking increased access to medicines and healthcare services commensurate with their improved lifestyles [*See Figure 7.15*]. Lifestyle changes accompanying this new affluence and increased longevity will also impact the burden of disease in emerging markets, where a growing incidence of chronic disease is already underway. The frequency of type 2 diabetes has surged in emerging markets. The **World Health Organization** estimates that India and China will make up nearly one third of the world's total patients with diabetes in 2030, with more than 150 million people afflicted with the disease by then.

Targeting emerging markets has become one of the pharmaceutical industry's key strat-

## Figure 7.8 RELATIVE WORLD R&D IN 2011

Size of circle represents relative amount of country's annual R&D spending. Position on grid shows R&D spending as percent of GDP and number of scientists and engineers per million population

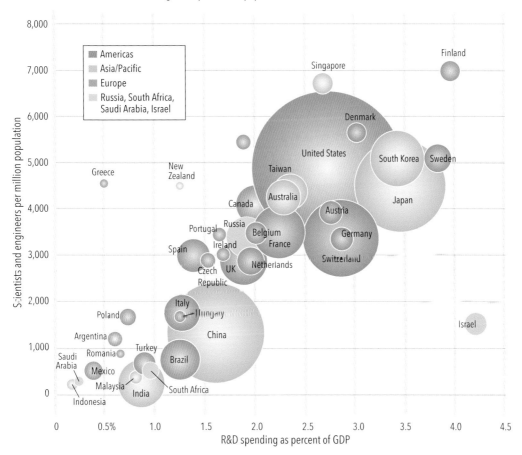

Source: Battelle, R&D Magazine: 2012 Global R&D Funding Forecast

egies for growth. In fact, for many companies, these markets are becoming more and more established. Analysis by accounting firm **KPMG** based on IMS Health data finds that revenue growth in emerging markets, mostly from volume growth of branded generics, could result in these countries together contributing as much to global profits as the United States by 2020 [*SEE FIGURE 7.17*]. Every multinational pharmaceutical company now has a presence in the major emerging markets countries. Europeans— **Sanofi**, AstraZeneca, and **GlaxoSmithKline**— were some of the first drugmakers to establish a foothold, but American pharmaceutical firms have fast followed suit [*SEE FIGURE 7.18*].

Most of Big Pharma's dealmaking in emerging markets in 2011 involved collaborative relationships with local firms as these companies worked to integrate several acquisitions made in 2010. These included Sanofi's $520 million acquisition of **BMP Sunstone** to position the French pharmaceutical as a leading consumer healthcare company in China; **Abbott Laboratories'** $3.7 billion acquisition of **Piramal's** branded generics business that catapulted the U.S.-based firm into position as the largest pharmaceutical in India; **Pfizer's** generics push into Brazil through its purchase of a 40 percent stake in **Laboratorio Teuto** for $240 million; and GlaxoSmithKline's similar push into Argentina through the acquisition of the generic drugmaker **Laboratorios Phoenix**.

## A China-centric strategy

U.S. biopharma **Merck** says it expects emerging markets will account for 25 percent of

*Figure 7.9* **BRICs See Rise in Scientific Articles**

Growth in number of articles published
in peer-reviewed journals

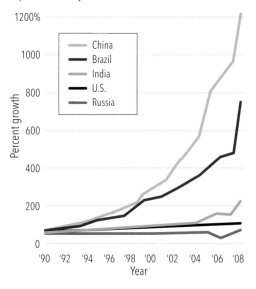

*Source: Thomson Reuters: Web Science Database*

*Figure 7.10* **China's Biomedical Explosion**

Published biomedical patent applications 2000 to 2009

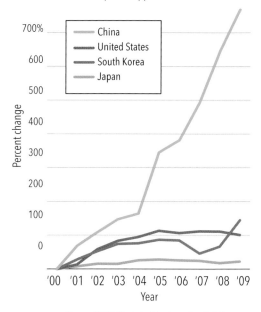

*Source: WIPO Statistics Database, Burrill & Company*

its global pharmaceutical and vaccine sales by 2013, from about 18 percent in 2011. The company's top emerging target markets are China, Mexico, and South Korea. Sales are improving in Brazil and it sees potential in Russia and India, countries in which it wants to establish a stronger presence. It plans to introduce existing drugs to treat unmet needs in these markets and to access their growing innovation to develop drugs for the global market.

Merck sees collaboration with local companies and the establishment of a local presence in each market as key elements of its strategy. In 2011 Merck entered into two joint ventures to expand its reach: in China with **Simcere** to expand into areas of China where it did not have a sales presence; and in India with **Sun Pharma** in order to enter India's growing market for branded generics. It also licensed technology from the South Korean firm **Hanwha Chemical** to expand its biosimilars portfolio, taking advantage of South Korea's growing expertise in the area [*See Sidebar Biosimilars*].

Merck's approach is just one example of the strategy being pursued by other multinational pharmaceutical companies in emerging markets. China is the cornerstone of most of these

companies' plans. Hardly a week went by in 2011 without an announcement of a deal or investment in the country. As Big Pharma announced cuts to its sales staff in the United States and Europe, it replaced them with additional people on the ground mainly in China and India. As R&D facilities were being closed in Western

> As R&D facilities were being closed in Western nations, new R&D facilities were being planned or built in China.

nations, new R&D facilities were being planned or built in China.

Even **Roche**, which has a global strategy rather than a China-centric one, has felt the improvement in its bottom line from sales growth in these countries, particularly from diagnostics sales in China. "China is absolutely critical to our global strategy," says Joe McCracken, global head of business development at Roche, in an October 2011 interview

*Figure 7.11* **GLOBAL PHARMACEUTICAL MARKET FORECAST**

**Pharmaceutical Sales and Growth in Emerging Markets**

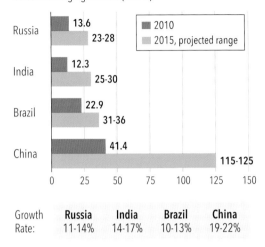

Sales in emerging markets (USD B)

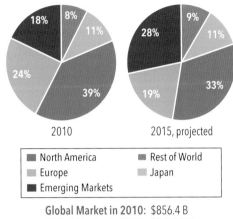

Breakdown of sales in world market

| Growth Rate: | **Russia** 11-14% | **India** 14-17% | **Brazil** 10-13% | **China** 19-22% |
|---|---|---|---|---|

Global Market in 2010: $856.4 B
Global Market in 2015: $1.1-1.2 B

Source: IMS Health, Market Prognosis, April 2011

with *ChinaBio Today*. "It is a source of innovation. We have a dedicated partnering team in Shanghai. It is a key source of talent. And we have our own R&D team in Zhangjiang." The company is building a new facility in Shanghai to expand its R&D and manufacturing capabilities. As its third largest market, Roche wants to triple its personnel in China by 2020.

The emerging markets push isn't limited to Big Pharma or China. In April 2011, U.S. biotech giant **Amgen**, entered the Brazilian market with its $215 million acquisition of **Bergamo** and the reacquisition of drug rights it had sold to the Brazilian pharmaceutical **Hypermarcas**.

Besides major U.S. and European drugmakers, other multinational biopharmaceutical firms have also targeted emerging markets for growth. It was one of the major reasons behind **Takeda's** $13.7 billion acquisition of **Nycomed**, a Swiss biopharmaceutical with a portfolio of branded and over-the-counter drugs. Nycomed has an established presence in Brazil and Russia and recently acquired a major stake in China's **Guangdong Techpool Bio-Pharma**. Emerging markets account for more than half of its global pharmaceutical growth.

Israeli generic drugmaker **Teva** has also emphasized expansion in emerging markets. In 2011, it took a roundabout route to staking

*Figure 7.12* **INDUSTRY GROWTH BY GEOGRAPHIC MARKET**

Forecasted growth rates, 2010-2015
CAGR=Calculated Annual Growth Rate

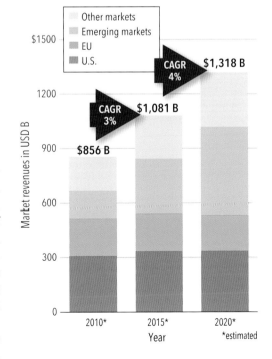

Source: IMS Health Prognosis, KPMG

a claim in emerging markets with its acquisition of U.S biopharma **Cephalon** for $6.8 billion. With Cephalon, the generics powerhouse acquired Swiss generic pharmaceutical **Mepha**, which Cephalon had bought in late 2010, giving it an immediate and strong presence in Eastern Europe, Africa, and Latin America.

### Tapping local innovation

The question for Big Pharma no longer lies in whether or not to enter or expand in these growth markets, but rather how they will execute their plans. Collaborative efforts to design drugs for diseases prevalent in developing countries are one way of expanding in these regions [*See Sidebar AstraZeneca*].

In late 2010, **Bristol-Myers Squibb** partnered with Chinese pharmaceutical Simcere to develop a preclinical compound that showed promise as a treatment for cancers prevalent in Asian popu-

## Capital Efficient Innovation

### Cross-border startup Ascletis wins $100 million in backing

What began for Jinzi Wu with a casual summer dinner conversation with a real estate mogul in China has resulted in a new multinational biopharmaceutical startup seeking to combine U.S. drug development know-how with China's cost-efficient and skilled scientific workforce, backed by $100 million in initial funding from private entrepreneurs in China.

Wu, formerly vice president of global HIV drug discovery at **GlaxoSmithKline**, is president and CEO of the new venture, **Ascletis**. Backers of the company include Jinxing Qi, a self-made billionaire who built his fortune in China's real estate market, and other private entrepreneurs in China, the United States, and elsewhere.

Ascletis will house key executive staff at offices in **Research Triangle Park**, North Carolina and scientific staff in Hangzhou, China, west of Shanghai. Ascletis has built a team of key executives, who are veterans of the pharmaceutical industry. Starting with a staff of six people at the company's facility in China, Wu expects to grow that to about 50 in 2012 and 100 within two years.

The company has what Wu calls a two-pronged strategy. Ascletis plans to in-license drugs for development for the growing market in China as a near-term route to revenue. At the same time, it will seek to discover and in-license early-stage drug candidates that it will develop to proof-of-concept and then partner with major pharmaceutical companies on a global basis. The company is also in discussions with several large pharmaceutical companies to in-license China rights to late-stage drug candidates.

While Ascletis is not the first attempt to marry U.S. expertise in drug development with capital efficiency promised by turning to affordable talent in China, Wu says he hopes to seize on opportunities created by cultural differences between China and the United States that may allow the company to in-license some promising products that have been shelved by pharmaceutical companies because they were viewed as too inconvenient or undesirable to compete in developed markets. For instance, Wu said while Americans want pills rather than injections, that's not a problem in China.

"We have some interesting leads with injectables, but we are looking at other things. People in the U.S. will not take twice-a-day pills, even if it has the same efficacy [as a once-a-day pill]," says Wu. "If GSK or Merck have something like that, they will put it on hold. People in China don't care about that. They care more about pricing and efficacy and safety. That's the angle we are looking at." ∎

lations. Simcere has exclusive development and commercialization rights in China and will run and fund the research through proof-of-concept. Bristol-Myers has retained exclusive rights in all other markets and sees the partnership as a creative approach to accelerating a preclinical oncology compound to clinical proof-of-concept, by leveraging the complementary strengths of a Chinese pharma and a global pharma. Just one year later, the companies expanded their partnership to include a similar co-development agreement in another therapeutic area. The agreement covers a pre-clinical small molecule in Bristol-Myers' pipeline that could potentially raise good cholesterol levels and help prevent cardiovascular disease.

Merck has taken the joint venture route with Simcere. The companies are working together in China's Jiangsu Province to help meet the country's fast-growing healthcare needs. Their immediate focus is on selling branded drugs for cardiovascular and metabolic diseases, two areas of rising incidence of disease and unmet need in China. Merck is also establishing an Asian R&D headquarters for innovative drug discovery and development located in Beijing as part of a $1.5 billion commitment the company is making to invest in R&D in China over the next five years.

Despite the tremendous revenue growth opportunities in emerging markets, there are numerous challenges inherent in working with different cultures, customs, and regulatory regimes. Many emerging market countries have just begun to address the basic healthcare needs of their citizens and their governments generally pay only for basic medicines, with specialist drugs and treatments paid by patients out-of-pocket. Governments are likely to curb drug prices even more going forward as they seek to contain rising costs. And while Big Pharma has successfully introduced branded prescription and generic drugs into these markets, it is likely to feel increased competition from local companies, who are fast adapting Western technology for local needs.

Many emerging markets governments are focused on building their domestic life sciences industry and favor domestic over foreign players. For foreign companies, local facilities staffed by local talent are often a must. Building R&D centers and collaborating with local scientists is important in gaining trust. Companies must be patient and persistent, work with the government, and

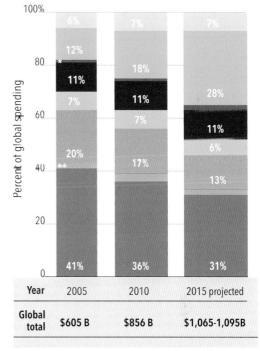

*Figure 7.13* **EMERGING MARKETS LEAD GLOBAL SPENDING GROWTH**

Between 2005 and 2015, the U.S. and EU5 share of total global spending is projected to decline significantly, while emerging markets will reach 28% of global spending.

Legend:
- Other markets
- Emerging markets
- South Korea
- Japan
- Non-EU Europe
- EU
- Canada
- United States

| Year | 2005 | 2010 | 2015 projected |
|---|---|---|---|
| Global total | $605 B | $856 B | $1,065-1,095B |

*South Korea: 1%, 1%, 2%

**Canada: 2%, 3%, 2%

Source: IMS Health, Market Prognosis, April 2011

marry their global expertise with local experience and interests to build trust and gain acceptance in foreign markets. However, the opportunities and challenges vary from market to market, and companies must be willing to adapt their strategies to local conditions.

## CHINA

### Economic power rises

Among the BRICs, China stands out as having the biggest economic engine, with $3.2 trillion in foreign reserves at the end of 2011. Its economy surpassed Japan's in 2011 and could equal, if not surpass the United States by 2040. Its lure for life sciences firms is not only its huge market size, but also a concerted government effort to become a leader in the sector through investment in R&D, education, and infrastructure, and favorable lending, real estate, and tax policies [*See Sidebar China*]. The government also pledged $124 billion in 2010 to strengthen its healthcare system in an effort to provide access to healthcare for 90 percent of its citizens.

At the same time that China is dealing with the challenges of rapid economic growth, an influx of people into cities has led to inflation, a potential real estate bubble, and strained its government-controlled banking system. Its currency is still not readily convertible and is not traded in the global market. China's economy is still very much export-driven—tied to demand from Europe and the United States. Economists worry that the growth of China's domestic market won't make up for the drop-off in export demand from debt-ridden Western nations.

Even more troubling is that China's old age dependency ratio—the ratio of non-working to

### CHINA AT A GLANCE

Population: 1.34 B
Growth rate: 0.48 percent
GDP: $11.3 T
Health Expenditure as share of GDP: 4.3 percent
Pharmaceutical market size: $41.1 B
Market growth rate: 20.1 percent

*Source: WHO, CIA World Factbook, IMS Health, Research and Markets*

working people—has reversed. Increasing longevity has come at the same time as its one-child policy, which has caused its birthrate to fail to keep pace with the expansion of its population of elderly people. This could lead to labor shortages and weaken domestic growth. People over 65 are expected to make up 22 percent of China's population by 2040. These people tend to save more and spend less.

China's policy to make life sciences a pillar of its economic growth and its promotion of innovation could counter some of the effect of its aging population. The country is rapidly building out its innovation infrastructure and boasts four major clusters of innovation centered near its largest cities; 100 life sciences parks; 200 life science incubators; and 500 universities and institutes that graduate more than 150,000 life sciences majors each year. In addition, China sends about 160,000 students to study abroad in U.S. universities. Two-thirds of those students return to China to start or run businesses there.

China is also luring foreign universities to set up campuses in the country to help improve its own schools through incentives that range from paying for the construction of buildings to free rent for several years. The foreign university must form a partnership with a local institution or get government permission to establish a presence. For example, in November 2011 the **University of California**, **Berkeley's College of Engineering** announced it was planning to open a research and training center in **Zhangjiang High-Tech Park**, in Shanghai. The Shanghai government and the park operators will build a 50,000 square foot building at no cost to U.C. Berkeley and provide a five-year, rent-free lease. The company running the park has also agreed

*Figure 7.14* **Key Drivers of Pharma Spending**

Sources of Pharma revenue, 2010-2015

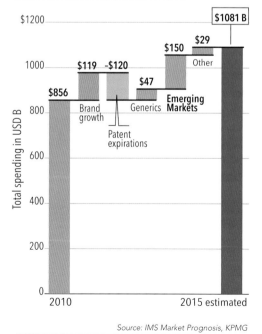

*Source: IMS Market Prognosis, KPMG*

to raise $10 million each year to support collaborative research between Chinese and Berkeley scientists. **New York University** and **Duke University** are also opening campuses in Shanghai and **Stanford University** is building a research center on the campus of **Peking University** in Beijing.

China's ambitious targets to ramp up its innovative capabilities have helped propel the country to become an intellectual property powerhouse [*SEE FIGURE 7.16*]. For many years, companies had been hesitant about bringing intellectual property or developing products in China because of weak enforcement of regulations. But China's entry into the **World Trade Organization** ten years ago and the growth of its domestic innovators, have pushed it to play by global rules. Strengthened protections are paying off. In 2011, China surpassed the United States and Japan in the total number of patent applications filed. Even if quantity does not necessarily translate

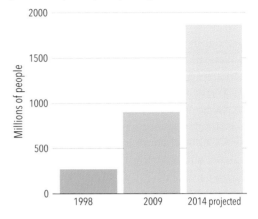

*Figure 7.15* **AN EXPLODING MIDDLE CLASS IN EMERGING MARKETS**

**A 21% growth in the BRIC middle class**

Population with household income above $5,000

(BRIC=Brazil, Russia, India, China)

*Source: Economist Intelligence Unit, 2010, China NSBA, Indian NFHS, RAND, Brazil PNAD*

# China Renews Commitment to Biotechnology

## Government will spend more than $300 billion on sweeping program to boost science and technology over the next five years

Flush with cash, China's government is going to put $308.5 billion (2 trillion yuan) to work to boost science and technology with a major priority on biotechnology, which is targeted as a "strategic pillar" for economic growth.

"The development priorities of the *12th Five-Year Plan* – biopharmacy, bioengineering, bioagriculture, and biomanufacturing – will bring benefits to Chinese people," said Chinese State Councilor Liu Yandong at an expo on the bioeconomy in Tianjin, reported the state-run news service *China Daily* in June 2011. The motto of the Tianjin expo was "develop the bio-economy, improve people's livelihoods."

China's **National Center for Biotechnology Development** says the sector is expected to add a million new jobs over the next five years and reduce emissions from pollution by 10 percent. The plan allocates more than $1.5 billion toward innovative drug development, with three quarters of the funds to be disbursed at the provincial and municipal levels.

Goals over the next five years include using biotech innovations to guarantee domestic standards are met in a variety of areas including healthcare and nutrition, food and drug safety, environmental protection, and climate change. China wants to add a year of life expectancy for its citizens and reduce its infant mortality rate by 12 percent.

Under the plan, healthcare expenditures are expected to grow to 5 percent of GDP in 2015, compared to 1.5 percent in 2010. The plan also targets the development of innovative medicines, the prevention and control of infectious diseases—especially hepatitis—and the development and cultivation of biotech crops. ∎

154

into quality, this tremendous growth speaks to the nation's commitment to develop its innovative capabilities.

## Pharma's top growth market

China's pharmaceutical market has seen exponential growth, averaging 24 percent a year from 2006 to 2010, and expects to continue growing by 17.2 percent between 2010 and 2015. Most of the market growth will come from prescription branded generics, an area in which multinational pharmaceutical companies expect to realize new value from their innovator drugs that have lost exclusivity elsewhere.

China's pharmaceutical market has grown steadily in the ranks with sales that could reach $60 billion in 2011. By 2015, it is expected to overtake Japan to become the world's second largest pharmaceutical market with sales set to reach as much as $115 billion, according to IMS Health. It is expected to represent 13 percent of global pharmaceutical sales by then, compared with 3 percent of the global pharmaceutical spending in 2007 [SEE FIGURE 7.19]. Most multinational pharmaceutical companies have already established a presence in China through acquisitions and joint ventures with domestic players. They have beefed up sales staff, and invested in R&D and infrastructure, which stood at about $2.5 billion in 2011 and will likely triple over the next five years [SEE FIGURE 7.20].

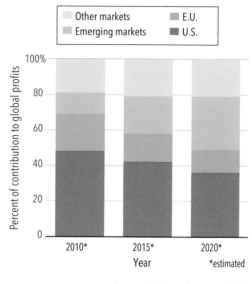

Figure 7.17 CHANGING GEOGRAPHIC CONTRIBUTION TO PHARMA PRE-R&D OPERATING PROFIT

Source: IMS Market Prognosis, KPMG

AstraZeneca has established a strong presence in oncology, with $1 billion of sales in China in 2010, according to Steve Yang, AstraZeneca vice president and head of R&D for Asia and emerging markets. The drugmaker invested $100 million in an R&D center in Shanghai in 2006. It conducts cancer research focusing on Chinese patients, biomarkers, and genetics. In

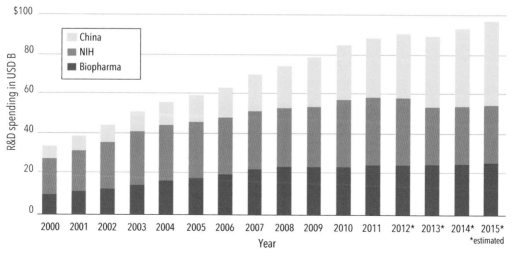

Figure 7.16 CHINA R&D SHOULD EXCEED NIH BUDGET BY 2020

Source: FactSet, Goldman Sachs Research, NIH, OECD

*Figure 7.18*     **SELECT PHARMA AND BIOTECH DEALS IN EMERGING MARKETS IN 2011**

| PHARMACEUTICAL COMPANY | EMERGING MARKET TARGET/ PARTNER | DEAL VALUE (USD M) | DEAL TYPE | PRINCIPAL FOCUS |
|---|---|---|---|---|
| Abbott Laboratories | Lupin (India) | N/A | License | Pharmaceuticals |
| Amgen | Bergamo (Brazil) | 215 | M&A | Pharmaceuticals |
| AstraZeneca | Guangdong BeiKang Pharmaceutical | N/A | M&A | Pharmaceuticals |
| | Hutchison China MediTech | 140 | License | Cancer |
| Bayer HealthCare | Zydus Cadila (India) | N/A | Joint Venture | Pharmaceuticals |
| | Yunona (Russia) | N/A | Joint Venture | Pharmaceuticals |
| Biogen Idec | Samsung (South Korea) | 300 | Joint Venture | Biosimilars |
| Bristol-Myers Squibb | WuXi PharmaTech (China) | N/A | Collaboration | CRO |
| | Simcere (China) | N/A | Partnership | Cardiovascular disease |
| GlaxoSmithKline | GSK-Neptunus Biologicals (China) | 39 | M&A | Vaccines |
| Janssen (Johnson & Johnson) | ChemDiv (Russia) | N/A | Collaboration | Drug discovery |
| | Jubilant BioSys (India) | N/A | Alliance | Drug discovery |
| | BeiGene (China) | N/A | Partnership | Cancer |
| Merck | Hanwha (South Korea) | 720 | License | Biosimilar technology |
| | Simcere (China) | N/A | Joint Venture | Biopharmaceuticals |
| | BGI (China) | N/A | Collaboration | Biomarkers |
| | Sun Pharmaceutical Industries (India) | N/A | Joint Venture | Branded generics |
| | Serum Institute of India | N/A | Collaboration | Pneumococcal vaccine |
| Pfizer | Shanghai Pharmaceutical (China) | N/A | Agreement | Pharmaceuticals |
| | Zheijiang Hisun Pharmaceuticals (China) | N/A | Joint Venture | Pharmaceuticals |
| | ChemRar (Russia) | N/A | Collaboration | Therapeutics |
| Sanofi | Glenmark Pharmaceuticals (India) | 613 | License | Autoimmune disease |
| Shionogi (Japan) | C&O Pharmaceutical Technology (China) | 182 | M&A | Pharmaceuticals |
| Valeant Pharmaceuticals | Sanitas (Lithuania) | 446 | M&A | Generics |

*Source: Burrill & Company*

EMERGING MARKETS

7

Figure 7.19 **China's Pharma spending 2001 to 2015**

China is becoming a larger part of the global Pharma market

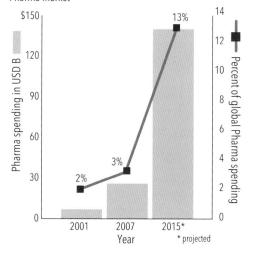

Source: IMS, Goldman Sachs

2011 AstraZeneca broke ground on a $230 million manufacturing facility in **China Medical City** in Taizhou, Jiangsu province. Yang says it is the pharma's largest ever investment in a single manufacturing facility globally. Expected to be completed in 2013, it will produce both intravenous and oral drugs to be sold in China and will enable AstraZeneca to expand the availability of its medicines to both urban and rural communities, which traditionally have had limited access to established medicines.

## Opportunities offset by challenges

China's huge market opportunities are balanced by equally big market challenges. Multinational pharmaceutical companies have to compete in a highly fragmented and complex market with more than 5,000 domestic and 1,000 multinational pharmaceutical companies battling for market share. Although China has adopted capitalism and more than half its companies are private, state-owned or controlled enterprises still dominate the list of top pharmaceutical companies [*See Figure 7.21*].

Consolidation, especially in the drug sector, fueled a 24 percent increase in China's life sciences M&A to more than $4 billion in 2011 [*See Figure 7.22*]. Most of the activity was between Chinese buyers and targets. Drug companies dominated with 91 percent of the deals by value and 77 percent by number of deals. Many involved consolidation of distributors. For example, China's largest drugmaker **Sinopharm** acquired a 60 percent stake of two businesses belonging to **Le Ren Tang** for $197 million, giving it control of a drug distributor and retailer with a 30 percent share in the province of Hebei. The central government encourages consolidation as a way to build "national champions."

Possibly the biggest challenge for foreign drugmakers is ongoing price cuts by the government as part of China's reform of the healthcare system. Begun in May 2007, China's **National Development and Reform Committee** has since mandated price cuts four times, including twice in 2011 [*See Figure 7.23*]. On top of price cuts mandated by the central government, several provinces have introduced a tendering or auction system for local contracts based on cost rather than quality or brand. Companies are forced to bid or be left out as 80 percent of drugs are procured by provinces to be dispensed by hospitals. It has become known as the Anhui system, because it has worked to lower the cost of medicines in the Anhui province, one of the poorest regions of China. Many other provinces have adopted similar tendering systems, according to the **Ministry**

*Figure 7.20* **Growth in China's BioMedical R&D Spending**

Growth of Chinese R&D has more than doubled 2008-2010 and is set to nearly triple in the next five years

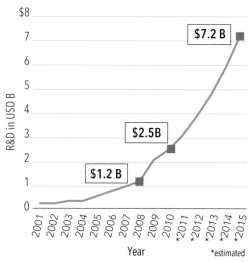

Source: ChinaBio Consulting, China Science & Technology Statistics

*Figure 7.21*    TOP CHINESE PHARMA COMPANIES BY MARKET CAP

| COMPANY NAME | STATE RELATED | MARKET CAP USD B | REVENUE USD M |
|---|---|---|---|
| Sinopharm | ✓ | 8.20 | 6,886.52 |
| Shenzen Hepalink | | 8.13 | 325.41 |
| Jiangsu Hengrui Medicine | ✓ | 6.52 | 544.95 |
| Shanghai Pharmaceuticals | ✓ | 6.35 | 5,512.73 |
| Yunnan Baiyao Group | ✓ | 6.12 | 1,044.34 |
| Sichuan Kelun | | 5.52 | 590.32 |
| Shandong Don-E E-Jiao | ✓ | 4.88 | 301.72 |
| Kangmei Pharmaceutical | | 4.88 | 346.98 |
| Harbin Pharmaceutical | ✓ | 4.09 | 1,552.77 |
| Hualan Biological Engineering | | 4.07 | 178.25 |
| Shanghai Fosun | ✓ | 3.74 | 563.60 |

*Source: BMI China Pharmaceutical report, 2011 Q1*

**of Health** and prices for drugs on those lists have dropped an average of 25 percent.

Price controls have hit domestic pharmaceutical companies hardest, but multinationals are adjusting to the fact that their profit margins will be smaller. Based on the lower prices for many drugs, IMS Health lowered its growth forecast for China to 17 percent from its previous forecast of 22 percent. Still, many believe that economies of scale and low costs of drug development will trump the shrinking profit margins. The sheer volume of the Chinese market is able to more than compensate, Sanofi CEO Chris Viehbacher told *Bloomberg* in November 2011.

Lead times for getting a new drug approved for marketing in the country can often take up to two years. And a drugmaker must have a local manufacturing facility to be considered the owner of the drug. Doing business in China is not for everyone, says Ascletis CEO Wu. "China has many opportunities and challenges. You must work with the system," he says, "and be adaptable and persistent. In China, the government is everywhere."

Despite the challenges, an increasing number of global companies are bringing assets into China to develop for the China market [*SEE FIGURE 7.24*].

### Biotech sales see strong growth

Biologics and biosimilars account for 10 percent of China's total pharmaceutical market today, but their share is growing at an annual rate of 32 percent [*SEE FIGURE 7.25*]. China is making headway in growing its biotech sector. **China National Biotech Group**, a subsidiary of Sinopharm, is China's largest biotech company

*Figure 7.22* **M&A ACTIVITY IN CHINA 2007 TO 2011**

Overall M&A in China increased 24% 2010-2011 though average deal value was down.

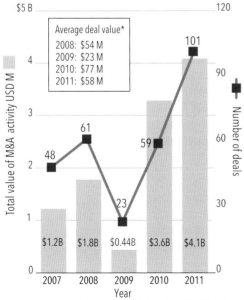

Average deal value*
2008: $54 M
2009: $23 M
2010: $77 M
2011: $58 M

*Financial data were not disclosed for all M&A deals

*Source: ChinaBio Consulting*

## Figure 7.23 POLICIES TO CUT DRUG PRICES, REDUCE HEALTHCARE COSTS

**Recent government-mandated price cuts**

| DATE | TARGET | AVERAGE PRICE DROP |
|------|--------|--------------------|
| May 2007 | 260 drugs (excl. TCM) | −19% |
| Nov 2010 | 176 drugs | −19% |
| March 2011 | 162 anti-infective and circulatory drugs | −21% |
| Sept. 2011 | 128 drugs; hormone treatments, endocrine and neurological drugs | −14% |

**Hospital cost-capping policies**

| TYPES OF CUTS | SAMPLE LOCATIONS |
|---------------|------------------|
| Overall budget paid to hospitals | Zhejiang |
| Diagnosis-related group | Chengdu, Beijing |
| Prescription capping | Wuhan, Shanghai |
| Ratio of drug spending to total spending | Multiple provinces |

*Source: NRDC, Sanofi*

and the world's fourth largest maker of vaccines and blood products. In November, it was reported to be planning an IPO in Hong Kong in the first half of 2012 to raise between $1.5 billion and $2 billion. The company is comprised of six institutes located in major Chinese cities and makes more than 200 drugs, vaccines and diagnostics. The company also collects about 25 percent of China's total output of plasma. In 2010, it reported $789 million (5 billion RMB) of revenue and profits of $114 million (722 million RMB).

The first half of 2011 was very strong for initial public offerings of Chinese life sciences companies, with more than $4 billion raised. This included $2 billion raised by **Shanghai Pharmaceuticals** on the Hong Kong exchange in May. China's second largest drug distributor already traded in China before listing in Hong Kong. IPO activity dropped in the second half of the year, however, ending with 30 life sciences companies raising $5.2 billion, compared to 33 companies raising $5.9 billion in 2010.

In August, Shanghai Pharmaceuticals said it was looking to make a major acquisition in the next six to 12 months to grow its patented products business and increase its competitive-

ness, according to a report in the *China Securities Journal*. With a rich balance sheet, bolstered by its recent $2 billion capital raise, the target would likely be a midsized U.S. or European company with a portfolio of patented drugs. It said it already has a list of potential takeover candidates that it is considering. "We hope to make structural improvements to our product portfolio by raising the proportion of innovative drugs, so as to better weather industry risks in the future," says Lu Mingfang, chairman of Shanghai.

Shanghai Pharma sees the development of innovative drugs as a hedge against the eroding drug prices for generics. It is partnered with Pfizer to promote the pneumonia vaccine Prevnar in China. In April 2011, the partners signed a memorandum of understanding to develop and commercialize an undisclosed Pfizer product in China and to explore other possible partnerships. Pfizer then invested $50 million in Shanghai Pharma's Hong Kong offering. With its intention to acquire an overseas innovator company, Shanghai Pharma is both following in the footsteps of its multinational competitors and raising the status of Chinese drugmakers in the global marketplace.

### Growing local innovation

The Chinese government is very serious

## Figure 7.24 CHINESE PARTNERSHIPS BY TYPE

Type and number of partnering deals; percent of total represented by each type

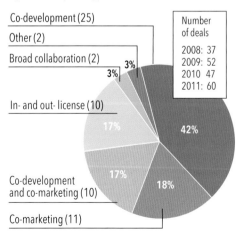

Co-development (25)
Other (2)
Broad collaboration (2)
In- and out- license (10)
Co-development and co-marketing (10)
Co-marketing (11)

| Number of deals |
|-----------------|
| 2008: 37 |
| 2009: 52 |
| 2010  47 |
| 2011: 60 |

3%
3%
17%
42%
17%
18%

*Source: ChinaBio Consulting*

*Figure 7.25* **CHINESE BIOTECH MARKET**

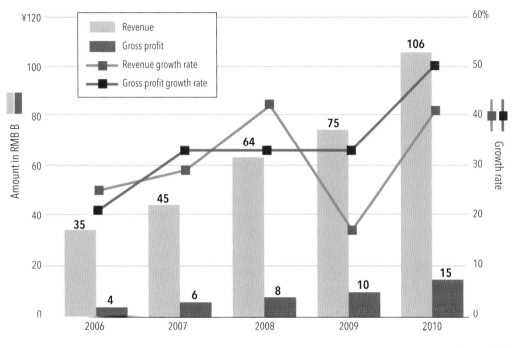

Source: NSBC

about building innovation capability in China to develop drugs. Major changes are happening in the country aided by returning Chinese expatriates trained in the West who have returned to help develop local innovation. **Hua Medicine** secured $50 million in a first round of financing with plans to become a premier Chinese drug developer. Hua plans to in-license promising Western drug candidates to develop and commercialize in China, and also to discover new medicines in China that can be developed globally.

The new company is co-founded by its CEO, Li Chen, who returned to China in 2004 to set up an R&D lab for Roche, and Ge Li, who also founded **WuXi PharmaTech**, one of China's biggest contract research organization, and a new investor in Hua through its corporate venture fund, which participated with a syndicate of U.S. and Chinese investors. "Hua is focused on building a new and better way to develop and commercialize drugs, leveraging the best of what the Eastern and Western worlds have to offer," says Chen.

In an interview with *ChinaBio Today*, Chen says the time is right for Chinese pharma startups because of the changing ecosystem in the country, which he credited to government sup-

port and the returnee phenomenon. The new company can leverage the lower-cost yet higher-quality drug discovery capabilities available in China, while partnering or licensing the most promising drug assets from Asia, the United States, and Europe.

The company has already looked at more than one hundred potential in-licensing candidates and picked five it hopes to develop. Hua announced its first program in December—a Roche program for the treatment of diabetes, a major unmet medical need in China. Because drug approvals in China take up to four years, even for drugs already approved elsewhere, the company hopes to launch its product by the end of 2015.

**BeiGene** was founded in 2010 to discover and develop new oncology drugs in China, marrying the talent of U.S. trained management and Chinese research expertise. The company's strategy focuses on taking novel small molecules and biologics, both in-licensed and developed in-house, to proof-of-concept, and then partnering them for further global development. The startup received a significant equity investment and debt commitment from Merck to support its efforts.

# When Being Down Under Actually Puts You on Top

## Australia's Queensland is positioned as a gateway to emerging markets

**Mario Pennisi**
*CEO, Life Sciences Queensland*

Many people refer to Australia as the "Land Down Under" – however, given Australia's geographic location in South East Asia, and its relative proximity to the economic powerhouses of China and India, it is hardly surprising that it is an economy that prospers with strong trading and economic ties with China, as well as with regional leaders including Japan, South Korea, and Taiwan.

Australia—a landmass equivalent in size to the U.S. (without Alaska)—is a resource-rich continent with an abundance of minerals, coal, and iron ore. It's a powerhouse of agricultural production too.

The northern part of Australia is above the Tropic of Capricorn – which situates about half of the continent in the tropics – and leads to it having an abundance of significant rainforests, coral reefs, and biodiversity. While these features attract tourists, governments in Australia have sought to build further economic diversity by nurturing knowledge-intensive industries that leverage our natural resources, capabilities, and features.

None have been more successful at seizing this opportunity than the State of Queensland. The State Government has invested heavily (more than AUD 3.5B) to develop the physical infrastructure required to attract world-class talent.

These world-class, innovative researchers now call Queensland home. They have helped establish links and develop collaborations across the world in a way that has transformed Queensland into a leading and influential life sciences center in the region recognized by the **World Bank** as a global innovation hot spot.

Queensland is in the right place, at the right time. With the infrastructure, expertise, innovative output, people, and global networks in place, it is positioned

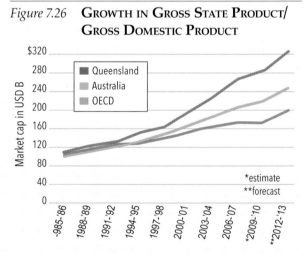

*Figure 7.26* **GROWTH IN GROSS STATE PRODUCT/ GROSS DOMESTIC PRODUCT**

Source: Queensland in the 21st Century, Queensland Treasury, OECD Economic Outlook.

to leverage the opportunities generated by the continued growth of the Asian economy and the development of the Tropics (South East Asia, Latin America, and Africa).

Research and business activities already underway in Australia addressing tropical health, agriculture, and environmental sciences will form the basis of significant opportunity in the tropics.

Queensland's *Smart State Strategy* led to the establishment of the southern hemisphere's most substantial research facilities, 66 institutes, and the employment of some 18,000 research-related roles. Now the *Queensland R&D Investment Strategy 2010-2020* is ensuring that the investment in R&D provides a strong, green, and innovative economy attractive to international investors and collaborators.

**A resource rich land with world class research**

This sustained commitment to the sector has not only benefited local **Australian Securities Exchange** listed companies such as **Alchemia**, **Qrxpharma**, **Impedimed** and **Tissue Therapies**, but has also seen continued investment by international companies:

■ The U.S. medical devices company, **Cook Group**, through their Australian entity, **Cook Australia**, recently developed new plant and facilities to service their Pacific Rim and Southeast Asia customers.

■ The multinational pharmaceutical company, **Sanofi Consumer Healthcare**, is currently expanding their Brisbane plant and facilities in order to best meet the needs of their growing Asian business.

Other exciting and important initiatives include ventures as diverse as:

■ A biofuels pilot facility in Mackay, in Regional Queensland's sugarcane industry

■ Groundbreaking malaria research

■ Pain killers being developed from shellfish found on the Great Barrier Reef

■ **Bill and Melinda Gates Foundation's** interest in the modification of bananas for sub-Saharan Africa

■ A new medical device for vaccine delivery using a nanopatch/microneedle technology that will revolutionize the way that vaccines are distributed and provided across the world.

In 2012, the **Queensland Institute of Medical Research** will double its capacity. **The Translational Research Institute**, established with assistance from the State and Federal Governments, and **The Atlantic Philanthropies** will also open its doors. The Institute will enhance and accelerate the translation of medical research breakthroughs into better patient care. Also due for completion in 2012 will be the **BioPharmaceuticals Australia** scale-up biologics manufacturing facility, established with **DSM Biologics**. This continued investment also leverages previous initiatives such as the **Queensland Clinical Trials Network**. The Queensland government's investment in a venture capital fund and the federal government's recent establishment of a 45 percent R&D tax credit scheme in Australia to further assist collaborators in accessing world quality researchers and infrastructure to reduce their times to market.

Queensland's fast-growing, highly skilled workforce makes it an ideal environment for a broad range of research-driven endeavors. The number of scientists and researchers working in Queensland per 1,000 people is now greater than the OECD average, and has increased at a rate 1.6 times that of the United Kingdom and 1.8 times the rest of Australia.

With more than 100 core biotechnology companies in the state, many of the industry stakeholders determined that it was time for a local industry organization to be established in Queensland to provide a single voice, a higher profile for the greater life sciences sector, and to ensure that the investment to date would be taken to the next level with a focus on outcomes that would provide a return on those investments. **Life Sciences Queensland Ltd.** (www.lsq.com.au) was established in 2011 to fill this role with bi-partisan political support, and the financial backing of leading stakeholders from industry, academia, professional firms, and state government.

LSQ is working to enhance Queensland's role and reputation as the primary point of contact for domestic and international organizations that are seeking to engage with Queensland and the region, serving as a stepping stone to the rest of Australia, the growing Asian economies and the future opportunity that is the Tropics. ■

*Life Sciences Queensland Ltd is a Burrill & Company content partner*

# Singapore is Asia's Innovation Hub

Centrally located in the heart of Asia, the city-state of Singapore is a preferred hub for multinational pharmaceutical companies seeking to do business in Asia, a list that includes **Johnson & Johnson**, **Pfizer**, **GlaxoSmithKline**, **Merck**, **Bayer**, **Roche**, **Sanofi**, and **AstraZeneca**. The industry in Singapore produced almost $16.6 billion worth of medicines and medical devices in 2010, according to Singapore's **Economic Development Board**.

Singapore topped the **World Bank's** *Ease of Doing Business Index* in 2009 and 2010 because of its stable political system, strong intellectual property protections, and extensive research and academic facilities that foster scientific talent and business expertise. Starting a business in Singapore is easy. It takes 15 minutes to register a business online, three weeks to receive approval for clinical trials, and 24 to 36 months for a manufacturing facility to be operational.

A push for research excellence has helped Singapore rank among the world's most R&D-intensive countries. A 2010 assessment of intellectual property coming out of government research based on quality and quantity ranked **A*STAR**, Singapore's government research organization, in tenth place, behind venerable institutions in South Korea, the United States, and France.

Besides being a manufacturing hub with more than 30 facilities that produce innovative medicines for the global market, Singapore is also favored as a location for public-sector research institutes and corporate R&D labs such as the **Novartis Institute for Tropical Diseases**, which houses more than 100 researchers from 18 nationalities.

In October, Merck's international subsidiary **MSD** and the Singapore Economic Development Board jointly announced that MSD would invest $1 billion in its operations in Singapore, including more than $250 million over the next ten years to improve its manufacturing facilities and expand its biotech operations to support new product launches. Some $550 million will be spent to strengthen its research capabilities, including collaborations with local universities.

Singapore's biomedical R&D is focused on translational and clinical research, with the goal of turning promising ideas into revenue-generating products. Its science and technology arm A*STAR is charged with fostering Singapore's scientific research and talent, harnessing it to build a knowledge-based and innovation-driven economy. Under its most recent 5-year plan for the years 2011 through 2015, the government has allocated $5 billion to A*STAR and its objectives.

In April 2011, French biopharma **Servier** entered into a three-year partnership with A*STAR's **Singapore Immunology Network** research unit to develop drug candidates targeting tumor-initiating cells to treat breast cancer. The network will discover monoclonal antibodies against the cells, while Servier has an option to acquire worldwide rights to any compounds discovered under the deal following the discovery work.

Innovation in Singapore is also taking place at the small company level. In January 2011 Novartis' **Alcon Pharmaceuticals** obtained exclusive North American rights to Singapore-based **MerLion's** finafloxacin specifically for treating ear infections. Besides an upfront payment, milestones, and sales-based royalty payments to MerLion, Alcon also has the option to expand the compound's use for ophthalmic applications and add additional territories.

**Aslan Pharmaceuticals** in-licensed two investigational cancer drugs that have the potential to address unmet needs in Asia, a HER2 / EGFR inhibitor from U.S.-based **Array BioPharma** and a small molecule inhibitor of the MET receptor tyrosine kinase from **Bristol-Myers Squibb**. Both compounds will be developed to treat gastric and lung cancers in Asia. ∎

BeiGene is being built with an effort to be a Chinese company, says CEO John Oyler. If you want to be supported by the government, work with it, he says, and be successful. Ultimately, the government wants to build Chinese companies, and you need to be a Chinese company—add value to the Chinese economy and the Chinese people. Oyler says building a business in China is complex, hard, and takes a lot of effort. The government intent is real, he says, and doing something for the country and being part of the local environment are imperative.

BeiGene, like Hua Medicine, and Ascletis, was formed to take advantage of a renewed interest in Chinese innovation, fueled by a return of expatriates trained abroad who are starting Chinese companies and combining the best of what the East and West have to offer. China offers a low-cost, high-quality workforce and the United States offers the managerial experience. The trend has received strong support from venture capitalists, who pumped $572 billion into Chinese companies in 2011, compared to more than $1 billion invested in 2010, according to **ChinaBio Consulting** [*See Figure 7.26*]. Greg Scott, CEO of ChinaBio, thinks the drop-off in funding in 2011 could be due to the fact that venture capital-

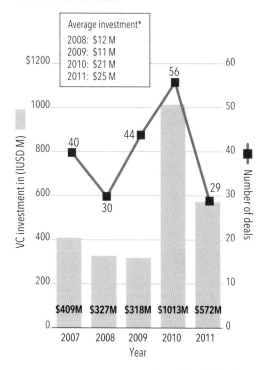

*Figure 7.27* **Venture Capital Investment in China**
VC investment in China is down 44%, though the average deal size set a new record

Source: ChinaBio Consulting

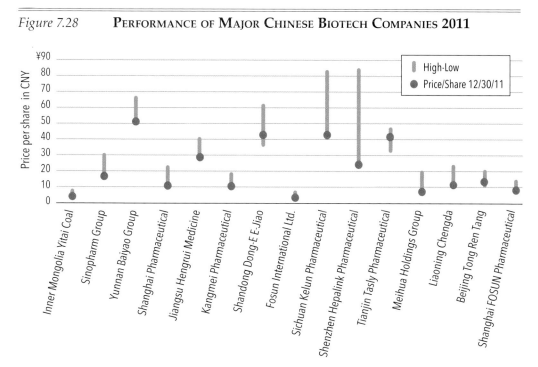

*Figure 7.28* **Performance of Major Chinese Biotech Companies 2011**

Source: Burrill & Company, S&P Capital IQ

# Taiwan Aims to be an International Player

Taiwan is leveraging its location between Korea, Japan, and the emerging Asia Pacific countries to build a gateway to life sciences markets in the region, especially China and its booming biomedical market. The nation of 23 million people is separated from China by the Taiwan Strait, which is only 100 miles wide at its narrowest point. Despite deep political differences, relations with China have been thawing.

At the end of 2009, biomedical companies in both countries reached agreements to cooperate on ten projects. In May 2010, representatives of Taiwan and China met in Taipei, Taiwan and signed two landmark agreements to open the door to bilateral trade between the two countries. The *Economic Cooperation Framework Agreement* set forth prospects for regulatory harmonization and cooperative ventures that will promote the growth of biomedical industries on both sides of the strait.

Since then Taiwanese companies have been investing in China, entering into collaborations with the intent of serving its growing medical market, and as a source of global clinical trials that will be accepted by mainland Chinese regulators for approval of drugs in China. **TaiGen Biotechnology** has a business model that connects global pharmaceutical companies with Taiwan and China. The company also in-licenses promising early-stage molecules, which it develops to proof-of-concept before out-licensing them to Big Pharma for late-stage development and global commercialization while keeping rights to the Chinese market. In December it regained worldwide rights for the antibiotic nemonoxacin from **Warner Chilcott**. Previously, TaiGen had shown the antibiotic to be effective in eradicating MRSA in two mid-stage clinical trials.

Long known for its strong information and communication technology industry, Taiwan's government has thrown its full support behind its growing biomedical industry through the *Taiwan Biotechnology Take-off Diamond Action Plan*, approved by the Executive Yuan, its main governing body, in 2009. The plan established the **Taiwan Food and Drug Administration** to provide a more efficient, transparent and reliable pathway for the approval of drugs and devices in the country while ensuring their safety; the **Supra Incubator Center** to assist startups with turning scientific discoveries into marketable products; and the $1.9 billion **Biotech Venture Capital Fund** that will support early-stage innovation in conjunction with private investment. The fund will provide 60 percent of invested capital with 40 percent coming from private investors.

Taiwan's biomedical industry, including biotechnology, pharmaceuticals, and medical devices reached $7.7 billion in revenues in 2011, a 16.7 percent increase from the $6.6 billion in 2010, according the **Ministry of Economic Affairs**. The government's long-term objective is for Taiwan to hold 3 percent of the global market. Government support has helped local companies receive Investigational New Drug approvals for approximately 20 products from the **U.S. Food and Drug Administration**, four of which are entering late-stage clinical trials.

Although most of Taiwan's healthcare related companies are still small enterprises, they are moving ahead rapidly. **Taiwan Liposome Company** is a specialty pharmaceutical that is developing and commercializing a series of new chemical entities and improved generics using its proprietary drug delivery and formulation technologies, with several products already on the market. The company listed on the **Taiwan Stock Exchange** in October 2011, a precursor to becoming a publicly traded company in Taiwan. **Burrill & Company**, publisher of this book, is an investor in the company. Its listing followed the IPO of **ScinoPharm Taiwan**, a global supplier of active pharmaceutical ingredients, in the first half of 2011. ScinoPharm's IPO at $1.50 a share gave it a market capitalization of almost $1 billion, making it the biggest drugmaker in Taiwan. ∎

ists are focused more on later-stage investments, something that there aren't many opportunities to choose from yet in China. "There just aren't many companies that have phase 2 compounds or later in the clinic or product already on the market," he says.

# INDIA
## A generics powerhouse

While China is pushing to become a center of innovation, India has established a thriving pharmaceutical industry and a rapidly growing biotech sector that excels at producing low-cost copies of off-patent innovator drugs. It has positioned itself to benefit from the rising global demand for generic drugs and opportunities for biosimilars. Indian companies produce 20 percent of the world's supply of generic drugs and 30 percent of U.S. consumption of generics. The major pharmaceutical companies, including **Ranbaxy Pharmaceuticals**, **Cipla**, **Dr Reddy's Laboratories**, **Sun Pharmaceuticals**, **Lupin Pharmaceuticals**, **Glenmark Pharmaceuticals**, and **Cadila Pharmaceuticals**, have collectively invested $2.5 billion toward building new manufacturing facilities in the last three years and raised the number of new drugs awaiting approval [*See Figure 7.28*]. They are also developing their own innovative molecules and vaccines in order to be able to sell them in the global market.

India's middle class is rising rapidly, projected to include one third of its 1.2 billion population by 2020, from just 5 percent in 2001. As their wealth grows, they will demand and be able to afford more Western medicines. Indians are expected to spend 9 percent of their overall disposable income on healthcare by 2015, more than double what they spent in 2005, making the healthcare market opportunity in India very compelling. At the same time, the government is aiming to raise public expenditure for health-related R&D to 2 to 3 percent of GDP from its current rate of 1 percent and has placed a priority on improving its healthcare infrastructure and increasing access to medical care in rural areas where 70 percent of its population still lives. However, the country still must contend with a high poverty rate and poor infrastructure.

Although India's markets were volatile in

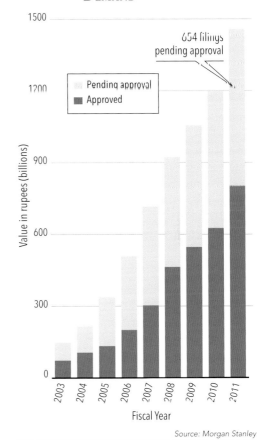

*Figure 7.29* **Indian Pharma Prepared to Meet Global Generic Demand**

Source: Morgan Stanley

2011, it did not impede India's drugmakers, which saw steady growth due to increased spending [*See Figures 7.29 and 7.30*].

India's pharmaceutical market was valued at $12 billion in 2010, according to IMS Health, and will grow to $49 billion by 2020, by **PwC** estimates. Rising rates of chronic conditions such as

*Figure 7.30* **B**URRILL **I**NDIA **I**NDEX VS. **BSE**

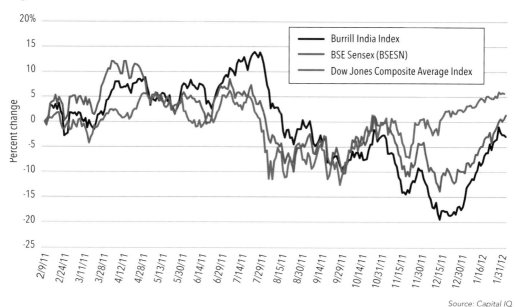

Source: Capital IQ

diabetes, heart disease, and cancer have fueled the steady 14 percent annual increase in pharmaceutical sales in the country since 2005.

India is viewed by global medical technology firms as a great test market for frugal innovation, adapting high cost medical technology to fit the needs of a much poorer population. For example, **GE Healthcare** is designing low-cost products for India and other developing countries. Rather than trying to push its existing products into the

Indian system, where 80 percent of medical care is paid for out-of-pocket, GE looked to see what products would be most beneficial to the local population under circumstances that included constant power outages, heavy use of equipment, and lower spending capacity. With cardiac disease being a frequent cause of death, GE devised a hand-held electrocardiogram, which is effective, but simpler in design. It costs just $800 compared to $2000 for a conventional machine and

*Figure 7.31* **P**ERFORMANCE OF **M**AJOR **I**NDIAN **B**IOTECH **C**OMPANIES IN **2011**

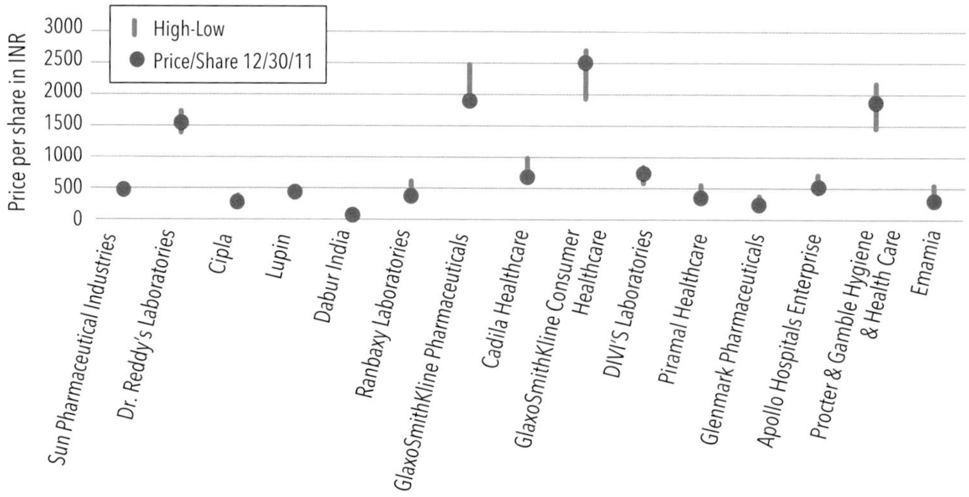

Source: Burrill & Company, S&P Capital IQ

# Indian Drugmakers Seek International Markets

## Western companies eyed as potential targets

**W**hile rumors swirled that Big Pharma was eyeing big pharmaceutical acquisitions in India during 2011, a number of Indian pharmaceutical companies looked outside their borders for possible acquisition targets. Although only a handful of deals were consummated, it is part of a trend likely to grow in the coming years. India's drugmakers, like larger global pharmaceutical companies, are seeking diversification and growth outside their traditional markets. Speculation heated up after Indian pharmaceutical firm **Piramal** said in September 2011 that it was looking at branded U.S. and European acquisition targets to grow its business.

One year after selling its generic drugs business to **Abbott Laboratories** for $3.7 billion, Piramal is looking to become India's first global drug developer through outside acquisitions. Chairman Ajay Piramal said the conglomerate planned to acquire struggling mid-size biotech companies and patents, as well as enter joint ventures with bigger pharmaceutical companies looking to reduce the cost of drug development, according to a report in the *Financial Times*. Piramal's expansion strategy is focused mainly in North America and Europe.

"We are looking to invest $1.5 billion in biotech companies that don't have enough money to expand," Piramal told the *Financial Times*. He said he also wanted to buy patents for drugs that companies have shelved because of financial constraints.

"We want to become a major player," said Piramal, "which means we will buy and form partnerships with existing global companies." The plan is not to relocate the companies it buys but to build Piramal's drug development business outside India.

Piramal hopes to achieve its goals by combining India's research capabilities with innovative technology coming out of Western firms. Its subsidiary, **Piramal Life Sciences**, already has a pipeline of novel drugs in development in areas that include cancer, inflammation, diabetes, and infectious diseases. But developing all of them in India is difficult.

India is well known for its generic pharmaceutical industry, but it lacks the intellectual property regime and expertise necessary for obtaining regulatory approval in global markets, the company's ultimate goal. Piramal is looking outside India to address this obstacle.

Piramal sees India as a growth market, and anticipates maintaining his company's over-the-counter focus there while conducting drug development activities in the West. He thinks that other Indian companies will follow suit, looking for patents and tie-ups with western companies. ∎

has reduced the cost of an ECG test to just $1.

India is adept at low-cost innovation. **Serum Institute of India's** mission is to make high quality, low cost vaccines. Its vaccines are distributed in 140 countries and it is now the fifth largest vaccine maker in the world. It estimates that one out of every two children immunized in the world is vaccinated by a vaccine manufactured by Serum Institute. In August 2011, it teamed up with Merck to develop and commercialize a pneumococcal conjugate vaccine for use in emerging and developing nations.

**Biocon** started as a brewing enzyme business for the beer industry in the early 1970s. Now it is India's top biotech company with 2010 revenues of $293 million and Asia's leading producer of insulin. In October 2010, Biocon signed a $350 million supply agreement with Pfizer for four generic insulin products to be sold initially in developing countries and eventually in the United States. Pfizer paid Biocon $200 million upfront.

For many years, India was not seen as a good place for foreign companies to do business because of weak intellectual property protections. But after the government instituted widespread reforms in the 1990s, the door opened to multinational companies to enter India's huge drug market. Until 2011, they met little government resistance as they entered India's drug market, mostly through acquisitions. But several government agencies moved to protect the country's generics industry.

This protectionist stance came under fire during the summer of 2011 when the government considered making it harder for foreign firms to acquire domestic companies in the wake of Abbott Lab's $3.8 billion acquisition of Piramal Healthcare, the generics business of Piramal Industries. Abbott's acquisition of Piramal Healthcare gave it the lion's share of India's generics market and followed several years of other marquee acquisitions that began with Japanese pharma **Daiichi Sankyo** taking a majority stake in Ranbaxy in June 2008 for $4.6 billion.

To the dismay of India's **Department of Industrial Policy and Promotion** and its **Health Ministry**, a government panel decided not to restrict foreign direct investment in the pharmaceutical industry by capping the number of foreign acquisitions of Indian pharma companies. It did recommend, however, that all transactions in the sector be cleared by the country's anti-monopoly watchdog, the **Competition Commission of India**. The **Foreign Investment Promotion Board**, which sets foreign investment policy, had said it wanted to cap foreign holdings in the sector to 49 percent. As of this writing, it was set to continue to clear transactions until mid 2012 when they would have to be cleared by the Competition Commission. These rules are likely to hinder more foreign acquisitions of Indian drugmakers.

The government has also proposed a pricing scheme that could slash prices on foreign drugs, a scheme that has met with opposition from industry groups. Under its proposed rules, a foreign company would have to price its drug at the average price of its three top-selling competitors, which are usually generics. For example, Novartis' cancer drug Glivec, which it sells for $2,450 per month, would be cut to $980 per month if it was among the top three drugs in its category and to $245 per month if it was not among the top three drugs by sales volume. The policy is still in

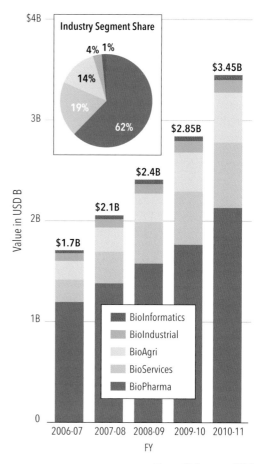

*Figure 7.32* **INDIA'S BIOTECH INDUSTRY**

Growth by Industry Sector

Source: BioSpectrum, ABLE

draft form but it highlights the challenges faced by Western drugmakers seeking to sell their off-patent innovator drugs in developing countries.

## Partnering becomes preferred route

India is an attractive market opportunity for Big Pharma not only because of its size, but also because of its low-cost and well-established expertise in medicinal chemistry and clinical research. In 2011, most Big Pharma companies preferred partnering to take advantage of India's pharmaceutical opportunities. **Aventis Pharma Limited's** acquisition of **Universal Medicare Private's** branded health and nutrition supplements business in India, was the only major acquisition. The $109 million deal expands the presence of Aventis, which is majority owned by Sanofi, in

# Novartis Blood Test Instructive in Understanding Brazil

## Gaining market share means working with partners and government

Blood donated in Brazil is estimated to have a ten times higher incidence of carrying hepatitis C, hepatitis B, or HIV than blood donated in the United States. Worsening the blood safety problem is the fact that an estimated 7 to 8 percent of people who donate blood in Brazil do so because they fear they may be infected with one of these diseases and use blood donation as a means of getting free testing.

Though donated blood is routinely tested in the country, traditional tests used to screen for these infectious diseases may not detect their presence quickly enough because they screen for antigens, which take time to appear in the blood. It could be as much as eight weeks before someone who is infected would begin to produce detectable antigens.

**Novartis'** Procleix Ultrio assay, which employs so-called NAT or nucleic acid testing, screens for genetic material unique to HIV, HBV and HCV and allows for detection of infected blood that might otherwise pass screeners. So it's not surprising the company sees great value in bringing its tests to Brazil. Across its business, the company has targeted emerging markets such as Brazil as important drivers of growth as their rapid economic expansion and growing prosperity drives demand for better access and higher quality medical care.

But the issues Novartis faces in bringing its blood test to Brazil illustrates the challenges in gaining access to such markets. First, Novartis' product faces high taxes—a total of 53 percent, according to the company. "There's already a significant hurdle on that end," says Peter Maag, president of **Novartis Diagnostics** and site head for Emeryville, California. "It was quite surprising because other countries go the other way by trying to reduce tax burdens on essential healthcare services."

But a bigger challenge is the government's control over the market. While Novartis has made inroads into selling its product to private hospitals and private blood banks, public hospitals currently are required instead to use a so-called homebrew diagnostics created and performed by individual hospitals and blood banks. About 75 percent of the 3.5 million to 4 million blood donations a year in Brazil are made in public hospitals and blood banks and being able to sell to these institutions will be critical to success.

The problem, says Celso Bianco, executive vice president of **America's Blood Centers** in Washington, D.C. and a Brazilian native who has provided training to blood banks in his home country, is money. "Brazil pushed very hard to start manufacture of their own antiviral therapies and they offer antiviral therapies for patients with HIV through the public systems," says Bianco. "They made deals that allow them to kind of get a cut in terms of patents and drop prices so they could afford those medications for the whole population and I suspect they are using the same approach for NAT testing."

Brazil did in 2001 mandate NAT testing for blood, but discontinued that requirement six months later because of the cost implications around the time Novartis started offering its first NAT tests in Brazil. Unlike many developed countries, they do not mandate such testing today.

Maag says the key is to approach Brazil and other emerging countries not as a supplier, but as a partner, something that the company has already done in places such as India, China, South Africa, and Indonesia. It's also done this in Brazil around vaccines, partnering with the government and transferring key technology. In September 2009, the company's vaccines and diagnostics division began construction on a new vaccine manufacturing facility in Goiana, in the Pernambuco region of Brazil. The manufacturing plant is aligned with the government's goal to become self-sufficient in vaccine production. The facility, which Novartis expects to invest $300 million in, will open at the end of 2014.

"A similar strategy needs to be in place for blood screening," says Maag, who notes the company is already in talks with the government and potential partners around its blood testing. "You go into Brazil not as a supplier, but you go in as a company being a leader in transfusion medicine where you say, 'Let's focus on blood safety and have a broader view on this than just being a supplier. What can we do to increase how we are treating the nation, increase the quality of the donor pool and increase the quality of standards in laboratories and so on?' We have done that in other countries around the diagnostics." ∎

the fast-growing consumer healthcare segment of the Indian market and adds a new segment to its portfolio of pharmaceuticals and vaccines.

Sanofi has expanded rapidly in India since it took an 80 percent stake in Indian vaccine maker **Shantha Biotechnics** in July 2009 for $784 million. In its other key deal in India in 2011, the French biopharma was granted a license by Indian pharmaceutical **Glenmark** to develop and commercialize a novel monoclonal antibody to treat Crohn's disease and other autoimmune disorders, which could result in as much as $613 million for the Indian pharma. Sanofi paid $25 million upfront for the first-in-class investigational therapeutic that had just completed a phase 1 dosing study. Sanofi has exclusive rights in most of the Americas, Europe, and Japan, while Glenmark retains the rights in India and the rest of the world. Glenmark and Sanofi also partnered in 2010 to develop a chronic pain therapeutic for which Glenmark received $20 million upfront and is eligible for up to $325 million in milestone payments.

Despite their dominance in generic drugs, Indian pharmaceutical companies are moving beyond their traditional focus to become innovators of new therapies and vaccines. They are also actively seeking overseas partnerships and acquisition opportunities, especially for innovative compounds. Glenmark has five research centers located worldwide and eight new investigational drugs in its pipeline. Glenmark's deal with Sanofi is one of five deals over the past five years that the drugmaker has signed with Western pharmaceutical companies [*See Sidebar Indian*].

## Biotech sector shows strong growth

India's biotechnology industry grew 21.5 percent to reach almost $4 billion in revenue in fiscal year 2010-11, which ended March 31, 2011. The biopharma sector, including vaccines, diagnostics, and biologics, rose 20.7 percent to make up 62 percent of the total revenue while agricultural biotechnology was the fastest growing sector with revenue rising 28 percent over the previous year [*See Figure 7.31*].

Vaccine sales are growing in the range of 10 to 13 percent a year and accounted for about $700 million in revenue in 2010. The industry boasts the only flu vaccine manufactured in cell culture instead of eggs in the developing world, an H1N1

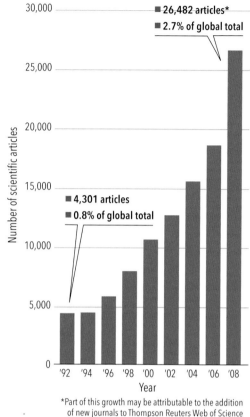

*Figure 7.33* **Scientific articles by Brazilian authors**

■ 26,482 articles*
■ 2.7% of global total

■ 4,301 articles
■ 0.8% of global total

*Part of this growth may be attributable to the addition of new journals to Thompson Reuters Web of Science

*Source: UNESCO, Biominas Brasil, PwC*

swine flu vaccine launched by **Bharat Biotech** in October 2010. Indian biopharmas have put a lot of effort into low-cost manufacturing of recombinant therapeutic products, of which 20 are approved for marketing in India. In May 2011, Dr. Reddy's Laboratories launched a generic version of Filgrastim priced 25 percent below the originator brand in India, and 95 percent lower that the U.S. price for pegfilgrastim. It has another 11 biosimilars in various stages of clinical development in its pipeline. With an integrated global manufacturing network, it is poised to benefit as the market for biosimilars grows.

## Startups face challenges

Although India's life sciences industry is growing, the financing environment for startup companies remains very challenging. India is not lacking in talent. It has a strong network of academic and research institutions but as they

*Figure 7.34*　**PERFORMANCE OF MAJOR BRAZILIAN BIOTECH COMPANIES IN 2011**

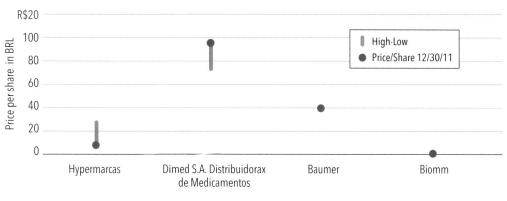

Source: Burrill & Company, S&P Capital IQ

are scattered throughout the country, few can take advantage of the synergies available in bioclusters. There is also a need for greater cooperation between companies and academic and research institutions to help translate ideas into products.

Indian investors tend to be risk averse and there are few options for startups. The government has been encouraging expatriates to return to India to start businesses, especially in rural areas, and is working on reforms to make it easier for foreign investors.

## BRAZIL
### A booming economy

Brazil is bustling with energy as it gets ready for hosting the **World Cup** in 2014 and the 2016 **Summer Olympics**. Once one of the most inequitable countries in terms of income, in recent years it has experienced a dramatic rise in its middle class, which now comprise more than half of its population of 200 million and fuel domestic consumption. Spurred by government reforms in all areas, the country's GDP has nearly tripled in the last ten years and, with the institution of state-funded universal healthcare, Brazil now spends close to 9 percent of its GDP on healthcare related activities.

Although the economic slowdown in the European Union and the United States has hit Brazil particularly hard and reduced domestic consumption due to fears about the global situation, it's still considered a booming market for life sciences, which are backed by a government committed to supporting education and homegrown

**BRAZIL AT A GLANCE**

**Population:** 194.4 M
**Population growth rate:** .9 percent
**GDP:** $2.3 T
**Health Expenditure as share of GDP:** 4.1 percent
**Pharmaceutical market size:** $22.9 B
**Market growth rate:** 12 percent

Source: WHO, CIA World Factbook, IMS Health, Research and Markets

high technology industries.

Brazil's drug market, at $22.9 billion, ranked the seventh largest in the world in 2010, and is growing at a rate of about 12 percent a year. Because of its growing middle class, the nation's disease profile has shifted from a prevalence of infectious diseases to increased incidence of chronic diseases such as cardiovascular disease and diabetes. Government policy has encouraged the growth of generics, which account for more than three quarters of its total spending on drugs.

Imported drugs account for 25 percent of the Brazilian pharmaceutical market. Anxious to reduce its reliance on imported drugs, the government, through the **Brazilian Development Bank BNDES**, has allocated more than $734 million since 2007 to support development of a domestic pharmaceutical industry. It has also worked to improve good manufacturing practices so it can compete in the global drug market and toughened its patent laws to encourage domestic innovation. At the end of 2010, the country's national health

172

# AstraZeneca Makes R&D Investment in Russia

## Research and manufacturing investments grow with opportunities

**A**straZeneca is establishing a new **Predictive Science Center** in Russia where it plans to leverage regional scientific talent to build software and systems for better predicting the safety and efficacy of potential new medicines.

The center is AstraZeneca's most significant research and development investment in Russia to date and represents the company's expectations for the industry's future growth in Russia, CEO David Brennan said during a speech at the **St. Petersburg International Economic Forum**. He noted that AstraZeneca plans to contribute $1.2 billion to the Russian economy over the next five years to support government efforts to modernize and grow its pharmaceutical sector.

Russia is the third largest contributor to overall clinical trial participation globally behind the United States and Japan, said Brennan. "Clinical development here is a very important part of the research base that we're involved in," he said.

Russia is also one of the very few countries where AstraZeneca is increasing its R&D investment because of the public health challenges the country faces, Brennan said.

Life expectancy for men in Russia is 63 years, 12 years less than for Russian women. By comparison, life expectancy is 78 years for men and 83 years for women in the United Kingdom, where AstraZeneca has its London headquarters. Heart disease is the number one cause of morbidity and mortality in Russia, accounting for 61 percent of deaths, according to Brennan. Premature deaths from heart disease, stroke, and diabetes alone are estimated to be an $11 billion drain on the overall Russian economy, he said.

Currently, AstraZeneca employs about 1,000 people in Russia in 68 cities and anticipates increasing that number to about 1,500 during the next three or four years. In early 2011, the company began construction of a new $150 million manufacturing facility in the Kaluga region to supply Russia with locally manufactured AstraZeneca medicines. By 2016 the company expects nearly three quarters of its products sold in Russia to be manufactured there.

In addition, AstraZeneca has established several partnerships with Russian development institutes, including the **Skolkovo Innovation Centre** and **Russia Venture Company**, to share its global R&D expertise through research collaborations, grant programs, and clinical trials. ∎

---

agency issued guidelines to pave the way for the approval of biosimilars, copycat versions of off-patent biologic drugs.

Many of the multinational pharmaceutical companies have invested in Brazil, mostly through acquisitions of local firms, and now account for the majority of branded and generic drug sales. For example, Sanofi acquired **Medley** and Pfizer took a 40 percent stake in **Laboratorio Teuto Brasileiro**. Amgen staked its claim in Brazil in April 2011, gaining immediate access to the country's fast-growing drug market with the acquisition of **Bergamo** for $215 million. It also bought back drug rights from Brazilian pharmaceutical **Hypermarcas** for its cancer therapeutic Vectibix and hyperparathyroidism medication Mimpara, both of which are already approved for the Brazil-

ian market, and two as yet unapproved treatments for cardiovascular disorders [*See Figure 7.34*].

The acquisition of a company with a significant local presence in Brazil may prove essential to Amgen's ultimate success in the country. For foreign firms, access to the Brazilian market can prove difficult because the federal government is the biggest buyer of goods and services and it can be challenging to win government contracts. As a leading manufacturer and supplier of medicines to Brazil's hospitals, the acquisition of Bergamo facilitates Amgen's entry into a significant market [*See Sidebar Novartis*].

### Pushing innovation

Most of Brazil's innovation takes place in its universities and research centers and the coun-

*Figure 7.35* **RUSSIA'S PHARMACEUTICAL MARKET**

Russian sales breakdown by company, showing proportion of government payment

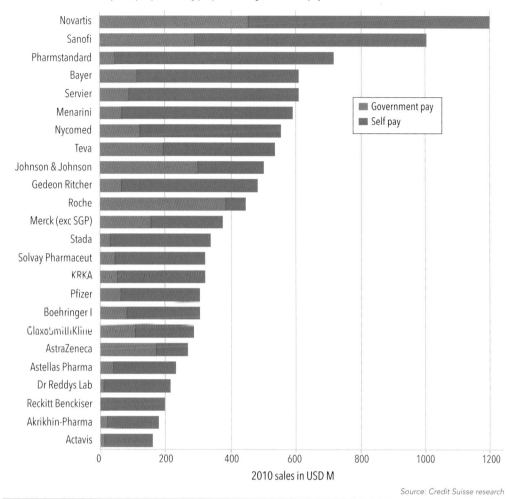

2010 sales in USD M

*Source: Credit Suisse research*

EMERGING MARKETS

7

try has been successful in greatly increasing its output of research papers [*SEE FIGURE 7.33*]. But it has been difficult to translate the innovation coming out of its 123 national institutes of science and 400 incubators into economic gain. More than half of biotechs surveyed by **Biominas Brasil** and PwC, said their greatest challenge over the next two years was raising funds. While the government has several programs for funding life sciences startups, Brazilian corporations have been slow to help young companies get off the ground.

The good news is that Brazil has begun to attract a lot of private capital, although most of it is going into Internet-focused startups and mobile technologies. Still, new funds focused specifically on life sciences companies are being set up. At

the beginning of 2012 **Burrill & Company**, the publisher of this book, announced a $125 million first close of an expected $200 million venture fund that will invest in the life sciences in Brazil, including early- to late-stage investments in therapeutics, diagnostics, medical devices, healthcare services, biofuels, and digital health.

BNDES has been a strong supporter of the domestic biofuels industry. In November 2011, it approved a $12.3 million project financing facility for **Amyris Brasil's** first industrial-scale production plant located in Piracicaba, São Paulo. "BNDES sees great potential in green-chemistry projects that add new technologies to the sugarcane sector, where Brazil is competitive and the world leader," says Roberto Zurli Machado, director of BNDES.

# GE Establishes Joint Venture in Russia

## Move is part of tech firm's global expansion strategy

**G**eneral Electric is expanding its presence in Russia with the establishment of a healthcare joint venture that could drive billions in sales of medical diagnostic equipment, part of the firm's strategy to expand its presence in emerging markets.

The joint venture with **Russian Technologies**, a government entity set up to help develop Russia's high tech industry, will focus on modernizing Russia's medical diagnostic equipment to improve healthcare in the country. GE and Russian Technologies will each have a 50 percent stake in the venture.

GE will exercise operational control of the businesses, with shared decision making by both partners on strategic matters. As is the case with most foreign companies seeking to establish a Russian presence, manufacturing will take place in Russia using GE parts, which over time will be sourced from qualified Russian suppliers.

Russian Prime Minister Vladimir Putin attended the signing ceremony, which took place during the **10th International Investment Forum** in Sochi, Russia. The healthcare joint venture agreement was signed by GE Chairman and CEO Jeffrey Immelt and Russian Technologies Deputy General Director Dmitry Shugayev.

"We welcome the signing of the agreement with GE, which provides for the future large-scale localization of production of high-tech medical equipment in Russia," says Shugayev.

The venture will start with the production of CT scanners, relying on GE's recently established manufacturing facility in Moscow. Production will eventually expand to other diagnostic equipment such as angiographs, MRI, ultrasound, digital X-ray, PET, and gamma cameras. **GE Healthcare** installed the first Russian-assembled 16-slice CT scanner in one of Moscow's hospitals in May 2010 and plans to supply 60 more CTs to hospitals all over Russia by the end of the year. The Russian government has targeted more than $30 billion over the next four years to modernize its healthcare facilities. GE estimates current Russian demand for CT scanners alone at 3,000 units.

GE is no newcomer to Russia, with more than 2,700 employees and 2010 revenues of $1.5 billion from operations there across a wide spectrum of industries. It has also established training centers for energy and healthcare in Moscow.

GE joins a growing list of health-related companies setting up joint ventures in Russia in the past year, including **AstraZeneca**, **Novartis**, and the Indian pharmaceutical **Aurobindo**. ■

**Russian Technologies Deputy General Director Dmitry Shugayev, Russian Prime Minister Putin, GE Chairman and CEO Jeffrey Immelt, and President of INTER RAO UES, Boris Kovalchuk (L-R) signed agreements to set up joint ventures in power production and medical technology.**

*Figure 7.36*    **RUSSIA BRINGS WESTERN INNOVATION EAST**

| WESTERN COMPANY | RUSSIAN INVESTOR | DEAL TYPE | FOCUS |
|---|---|---|---|
| Sequella | Maxwell Biotech | License | Tuberculosis |
| Panacela Labs (Cleveland BioLabs) | Rusnano | Joint Venture | Cancer immunotherapy |
| Pro Bono Bio (Celtic Pharma Holdings | Rusnano | Joint Venture | Nanomedicines |
| Lipoxen | SynBio | Partnership | Biopharmaceuticals |

*Source: Burrill & Company*

Blessed with rich biodiversity and abundant natural resources, Brazil's life sciences strength lies in agribusiness and biofuels [*SEE CHAPTER 8*]. Brazil grows more biotech crops than any other country in the world except for the United States. One of the most effective public private partnerships in the country has been that of **Embrapa**, the leading Brazilian research institution, and Germany's **BASF**. It highlights the effectiveness of partnering and developing products relevant to local needs. In 2010, the companies announced the approval for commercial cultivation of Cultivance, the first genetically modified crop developed in Brazil, from laboratory to commercialization.

In 2011 Embrapa and BASF entered into a five-year technical cooperation agreement to develop and bring new agriculture technologies and products to Brazilian growers. They will work together in the areas of biotechnology, genetic improvement, soil fertility and mechanization, plant protection, and physiology. Several projects are already in the development stage. The initial project, for example, evaluates the feasibility of using a bacterium to enhance nitrogen fixation for sugar cane plantations.

"We believe that the development of new technologies of this scale is only possible through partnerships such as this one, which enhances the exchange of knowledge between two key agricultural partners in Brazil," says Markus Heldt, president of **BASF Crop Protection**. "The scope of this initial project and the benefited crop was selected according to its relevance to Brazilian agriculture. The objective is to ensure the solutions we bring are relevant and needed."

**RUSSIA AT A GLANCE**

Population: 138.1 M
Population growth rate: -.48 percent
GDP: $2.4 T
Health Expenditure as share of GDP: 5.4 percent
Pharmaceutical market size: $13.6 B
Market growth rate: 14.2 percent

*Source: WHO, CIA World Factbook, IMS Health, Research and Markets*

## RUSSIA
### Moving into high-tech enterprises

The Russian Federation is one of the few emerging markets that didn't experience a slowdown in its economy during the second half of 2011. The country's drug market is expected to grow at a compounded annual growth rate of 13 percent and is forecast to reach $60 billion by 2020. Although its population of 142 million is not growing, the weakness of the domestic healthcare industry presents significant market opportunities for those who venture to do business there.

With Russia accepted as a member of the World Trade Organization in December 2011, it must modernize and develop its life sciences sector to compete on the world stage and make itself more attractive to international investors. Despite political unrest among Russia's middle class ahead of presidential elections in 2012, the country's abundant oil and gas resources have enriched its coffers. Like other economies heavily dependent on commodity exports, Russian

*Figure 7.37*    **CIVETS: The Next Generation of Emerging Markets**

### Turkey

**Population (2011 estimate):** 78.8 million
**Population growth rate (2011 estimate):** 1.24 percent
**GDP (2010):** $960.5 billion
**Total Health Expenditure (2009):** $36.5 billion
**Total Health Expenditure as proportion of GDP (2009):** 6.7 percent
**Size of pharmaceutical market (2009):** $4.5 billion
**Pharmaceutical market growth rate (2009):** 2.87 percent

### Colombia

**Population (2011 estimate):** 44.7 million
**Population growth rate (2011 estimate):** 1.1 percent
**GDP (2010):** $435 billion
**Total Health Expenditure (2009):** $17 billion
**Total Health Expenditure as proportion of GDP (2009):** 6.4 percent
**Size of pharmaceutical market (2010):** $3.44 billion
**Pharmaceutical market growth rate (2010):** 8.2 percent

### South Africa

**Population (2011 estimate):** 49 million
**Population growth rate (2011 estimate):** -.38 percent
**GDP (2010):** $524 billion
**Total Health Expenditure (2009):** $25.9 billion
**Total Health Expenditure as proportion of GDP (2009):** 8.5 percent
**Size of pharmaceutical market (2009):** $2.6 billion
**Pharmaceutical market growth rate (2009):** 14.7 percent

leaders are working to diversify the economy by focusing on high technology industries, including the life sciences.

Under an ambitious *Pharma2020* plan, launched in 2010, Russian Prime Minister Vladimir Putin pledged about $12 billion over ten years toward increasing the country's capacity to produce drugs and medical equipment, including the establishment of more than a dozen centers of innovation and the training of people to staff them. One of the main goals of the initiative is to reduce the country's dependence on imports by increasing domestic production. Russia's pharmaceutical market is the tenth largest in the world, with sales of about $13.6 billion in 2010, according to IMS Health. Generics make up 78 percent of the volume but only 20 percent of the market value. Russia's goal is to increase domestic market share to 50 percent by 2020, from 20 percent in 2011, and eventually to be a major exporter of medicines, a difficult task considering that less than 10 percent of the country's manufacturing facilities are GMP compliant.

Another problem the government has to overcome is that as its population has gotten wealthier, demand has shifted from cheap locally produced generics to more expensive branded generics from foreign companies [*See Figure 7.35*]. This is in spite of the fact that there is limited government reimbursement for most people who pay for medicines out-of-pocket. The government does exert control over drug prices, though, especially for drugs on its vital and essential drug list.

Sanofi and Novartis are the country's leaders by revenue, ahead of Russia's largest domestic pharmaceutical **Pharmstandard** [*See Figure 7.38*]. While growing demand for brands is an attractive opportunity for foreign drugmakers, it comes with a caveat—they must manufacture their drugs in Russia if they want to sell them to

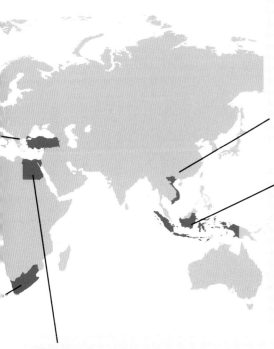

## Vietnam

**Population (2011 estimate):** 90.5 million
**Population growth rate (2011 estimate):** 1.08 percent
**GDP (2010):** $103 billion
**Total Health Expenditure (2009):** $5.7 billion
**Total Health Expenditure as proportion of GDP (2009):** 7.2 percent
**Size of pharmaceutical market (2009):** $1.71 billion
**Pharmaceutical market growth rate (2009):** 20 percent

## Indonesia

**Population (2011 estimate):** 245.6 million
**Population growth rate (2011 estimate):** 1.07 percent
**GDP (2010):** $1.03 trillion
**Total Health Expenditure (2009):** $14.8 billion
**Total Health Expenditure as proportion of GDP (2009):** 2.7 percent
**Size of pharmaceutical market (2010):** $3.9 billion
**Pharmaceutical market growth rate (2010):** 10 percent

*Source: WHO, CIA World Factbook, IMS Health, Research and Markets, BusinessWire*

## Egypt

**Population (2011 estimate):** 82.1 million
**Population growth rate (2011 estimate):** 1.96 percent
**GDP (2010):** $497.8 billion
**Total Health Expenditure (2009):** $8.6 billion
**Total Health Expenditure as proportion of GDP (2009):** 5.0 percent
**Size of pharmaceutical market (2009):** $2.48 billion
**Pharmaceutical market growth rate (2009):** 11.4 percent

Russians. Although not a de facto requirement, doing so clearly gives companies a competitive advantage because it supports the Pharma2020 plan's goal of raising the share of domestic production of "vital and essential drugs", which include several innovative cancer treatments, to 90 percent by 2020.

Big Pharma has responded to the challenge by increasing its investment in Russia through infrastructure investments, partnerships, and other agreements to help develop the domestic industry. For example, AstraZeneca began construction on a new $150 million manufacturing plant in the Kaluga region in April 2011. It has also pledged $1.2 billion over the next five years toward the construction of an R&D center in St. Petersburg. GlaxoSmithKline and Pfizer's HIV joint venture **ViiV** is launching manufacturing in the country in partnership with Russia's **Binnopharm**, which already collaborates with GSK to produce vaccines for the local market using intellectual property supplied by GSK.

Pfizer has signed a memorandum of understanding to collaborate with **ChemRar**, a Russian investment and R&D incubator, on the development of innovative drugs and vaccines in disease areas including cardio-metabolic, infectious, and oncology diseases. Pfizer is also working with other Russian academic and R&D institutes to help build their expertise in the sector [SEE SIDEBAR GE].

Indian generic drugmakers are also actively seeking to increase their sales in Russia. For example, **Aurobindo Pharma** formed a 50/50 joint venture with Russian healthcare products maker **Diod** called **Aurospharma** to make and market generic drugs and over-the-counter products in Russia, Belarus, and Kazakhstan. As part of their agreement, the joint venture will construct a new manufacturing facility in Russia for generics and over-the-counter products. This is in line with the Russian government's strategy of keeping costs of essential drugs under control by encouraging the use of generics and encouraging foreign companies that wish to do business in the country to establish manufacturing facilities in Russia.

## Building the Nation's Expertise

Russia's Pharma 2020 plan also calls for further investment in infrastructure, both in academia and high-technology centers that will spur home grown innovation. The government is investing heavily in centers such as Skolkovo, a technology park being built on the outskirts of Moscow. Skolkovo will house five technology clusters, with 90 companies participating in the biomedicine cluster at the end of December 2011.

As of September 30, 2011, **Skolkovo Foundation** had approved the issue of grant financing for 39 companies for a total amount of $155.5 million with individual grants varying from $100,000 to $10 million. Participating companies are focused on clinical research and healthcare, biotech, bioinformatics, and industrial biotechnologies. Skolkovo will also house a university and offer classes to improve Russians' managerial expertise. Russia's government is modeling Skolkovo after Silicon Valley, and it has been dubbed the "Silicon Valley of the East" [SEE SIDEBAR RUSSIA].

## Russia Imports Innovation

Russia is also importing innovation—leveraging its financial strength to gain international industry expertise. Government-backed investment firms made significant bets in innovative Western startups in 2011 that were willing to set up drug development and manufacturing facilities in Russia in an effort to jumpstart its ailing pharmaceutical industry and improve its healthcare infrastructure [SEE FIGURE 7.36].

Tuberculosis is an epidemic in Russia, with

# Russia Gets Innovative

## SynBio joint venture set up to create novel medicines

A group of Russian biotech companies have come together to establish **SynBio**, a joint venture to develop and produce first-in-class medicines and improved versions of existing pharmaceuticals, or "bio-betters."

The joint venture was initiated by the **Human Stem Cells Institute**, a public Russian biotech focused on cell-based gene therapies. SynBio has attracted the backing of **Rusnano**, Russia's government investment company, which is taking a 41.4 percent stake in the joint venture. HSCI has a 28.1 percent stake in SynBio. Rusnano's investment is part of Russia's government strategy to strengthen its pharmaceutical industry, which it sees as an important driver of economic growth.

SynBio's drug development focus will be in three areas: cell therapies for the treatment of liver cirrhosis; recombinant human Histone H1 for the treatment of cancer and other diseases; and sustained-release drugs containing polysialic acid to treat a variety of diseases ranging from diabetes and chronic kidney disease to Alzheimer's disease.

Speaking at a press conference to launch SynBio, HSCI director Artur Isaev said it's the first time a Russian company is the initiator of an international biotech project designed to serve both the Russian and global markets.

"The aim of this project is to bring to market a number of innovative drugs that will represent real progress in the treatment of socially significant diseases," he said.

The SynBio project is set up to be operational for seven years and will be funded with approximately $113 million. SynBio's first international R&D partner is the British biotech **Lipoxen**, which just acquired the German cancer drug developer **SymbioTec** with a lead drug in clinical trials in Russia. Although details have not been disclosed, SynBio will develop six of Lipoxen's drug candidates through proof-of-concept in Russia to prepare them for clinical trials in the United States and Europe. SynBio will continue to develop the drugs for the Russian market. ∎

more than 150,000 cases of active TB reported each year and over 43,000 cases of multi-drug resistant tuberculosis, making TB control a top priority of the Russian government. **Maxwell Biotech**, a privately owned firm in which the Russian government has a minority stake, found a potential answer to the problem at U.S. biotech **Sequella** and got an exclusive license to Sequella's lead experimental antibiotic for the treatment of tuberculosis in the Russian Federation and neighboring Commonwealth of Independent States countries. Sequella could get up to $50 million over the duration of the license in an equity investment, clinical trial supply purchase, milestones, and royalty payments. Maxwell is assuming all responsibility for further clinical development and regulatory approval in Russia and neighboring CIS countries, while Sequella retains rights in the United States and the rest of the world.

**Rusnano**, backed by $10 billion of government funding, has made several investments outside its borders in technologies ranging from microchips to medical diagnostics and vaccines, reflecting an ongoing effort by the Russian government to strengthen its pharmaceutical industry. It invested in three U.S. biopharmaceutical companies in 2011, taking an equity stake in two of them and forming a joint venture with the third.

Rusnano took an equity stake in two Massachusetts-based biotechs, **Bind Biosciences** and **Selecta Biosciences**. It also provided each company with up to $25.25 million to set up wholly-owned subsidiaries in Russia. Both companies are developing drugs based on nanotechnology platforms, Bind uses its nanoparticle technology to develop highly selective targeted therapeutics for oncology, inflammatory and cardiovascular diseases that are in early stage testing. Selecta's synthetic vaccine particle platform offers the potential for improved efficacy and safety over existing vaccines and is flexible enough to enable immune responses to all types of antigens. Applications include autoimmune diseases, allergies, and transplant rejection. Both companies plan to use their new Russian subsidiaries to advance clinical development of their pipeline candidates and accelerate their presence in emerging markets. They also expect that Rusnano's commitment will help them in their partnering efforts, as well as help them access global sources of funding.

Rusnano also formed two joint ventures with

As Russia's population has gotten wealthier, demand has shifted from cheap, locally produced generics to more expensive branded generics from foreign companies.

Western companies. **Pro Bono Bio**, a joint venture with U.K-based **Celtic Pharma**, has been set up to seek profit in European drug markets and give away drugs in Africa. The company will also support research into new medicines to aid Africa, and hopes to make a real difference to global healthcare at the same time as it delivers attractive shareholder returns, says John Mayo, founder of Celtic Pharma Holdings and CEO of Pro Bono. Pro Bono Bio is using nanotechnology to develop new treatments for a range of inflammatory conditions and infections. Rusnano, which has already invested around $477 million in Celtic's funds, will have more than a 40 percent stake in the new company.

Pro Bono's first prescription medicine, Flexiseq, is a new nanomedicine to treat osteoarthritis, launched in the United Kingdom at the same time the company was announced in Russia. Other products in its pipeline include treatments for inflammatory skin disorders, including psoriasis and eczema, blood factors to treat hemophilia, and novel antibiotics to treat serious infections. All of the products are based on Pro Bono's Sequessome

*Figure 7.38*　**Performance of Major Russian Biotech Companies in 2011**

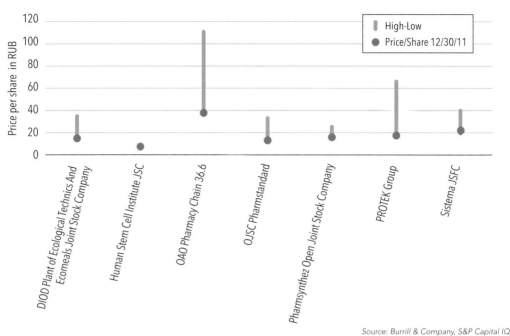

Source: Burrill & Company, S&P Capital IQ

technology, which absorbs and remove chemicals that are a key component in the pain and inflammation cascade. With Rusnano's backing, Pro Bono Bio intends to build a state-of-the-art pharmaceutical plant close to Moscow and a sister plant in the United Kingdom to comply with European regulations, which together will supply global markets.

Rusnano and **Cleveland BioLabs** are teaming up to form a joint venture to develop preclinical drug candidates against cancer and infectious diseases in Russia. Rusnano is investing up to $26 million over a four-year period in **Panacela Labs**, Cleveland BioLab's new subsidary, which will develop a portfolio of new preclinical drug candidates. The deal calls for $9 million upfront, with future investments based upon achievement of development milestones and attraction of new investments to the project. Cleveland BioLabs will contribute a $3 million initial investment. Cleveland BioLabs, **Roswell Park Cancer Institute**, **Cleveland Clinic Foundation**, and **Children's Cancer Institute Australia** are transferring IP for five preclinical drug candidates targeting cancer and infectious disease developed under the guidance of Andrei Gudkov, chief scientific officer of Cleveland BioLabs and an SVP at Roswell Park to Panacela Labs.

The compounds will first be developed and approved in Russia. After the drugs are introduced into clinical practice there, Panacela intends to seek licensing and approval in other global markets, including the United States, thus significantly decreasing its risk.

In June 2011, Rusnano's Board of Directors approved its participation in Burrill & Company's **Life Sciences Capital Fund IV**, a $500 million fund that will invest globally in healthcare, including early- to late-stage investments in therapeutics, diagnostics, medical devices, healthcare delivery, wellness, and digital health. Rusnano committed to the fund in its first close of $313 million in December. Burrill & Company, the publisher of this book, is setting up an office in Moscow in conjunction with the funding.

Rusnano also teamed up with U.S. venture capital firm **Domain Associates** in March 2012 in an effort to bring next-generation medicines, medical devices, and diagnostics to Russia. The two investment firms have agreed to jointly invest in innovative companies with an eye to transferring the technology to Russia and manufacturing it there. They will invest in approximately 20 U.S.-based companies that are developing technology that addresses unmet needs in Russia and complements Rusnano's focus on nanotechnology-based innovation. They will also jointly establish a drug and medical device manufacturing facility in Russia that meets GMP standards.

The joint venture will leverage the innovations created by the portfolio companies, and will obtain exclusive rights to manufacture and market products based on these innovations in Russia and the Commonwealth of Independent States. Rusnano and Domain's venture capital funds, together with other co-investors, are expected to invest approximately $760 million into portfolio companies and the manufacturing facility in Russia. The joint venture will manage advanced-stage clinical trials in Russia of new pharmaceuticals and other products that will support regulatory approval of these products in Russia, the United States and other markets.

"Life sciences portfolio companies constitute approximately 20 percent of Rusnano actual investments. We are working hard to spur development of innovative technologies in the Russian healthcare industry," says Anatoly Chubais, CEO of Rusnano.

"We expect Domain's collaboration with Rusnano to provide a significant boost to the modernization efforts of the Russian pharmaceutical and medical technology industry," says Brian Dovey, partner at Domain. "For our portfolio companies, this strategic relationship opens up new attractive avenues for financing. Finally, we are excited about the commercial potential of establishing a cutting-edge production facility in Russia."

## Challenges remain

Although Russia's government has implemented policies to make doing business easier, such as strengthening intellectual property protections and reducing regulatory uncertainties, it has also issued laws that could hamper business, such as recently introduced drug pricing measures. A law that went into effect in 2010 that was meant to make it easier to develop and register new drugs in Russia has instead hampered clinical trials and limited the number of drug approvals in 2011, according to a report from the industry group the **Association of**

> Globalization has minimized the importance of borders and we live in a world where cooperation rather than competition will be the driving force.

**Clinical Trials Organizations** in Moscow. The new law makes it mandatory that all medicines sold in Russia first undergo clinical trials in the country, even if they have already been approved elsewhere. The new law also specifies that new medicines that have been developed cannot first be tested in Russia, a provision that goes against many of the new investments by such firms as Rusnano.

"These changes in the guidelines happened at the moment when the country had invested so much in innovative drug development that there were quite a few drugs which were around the corner from starting phase I trials," Gudkov told the journal *Nature*. Companies are hoping the government will scrap the rule.

## New Models of Innovation

The world will be increasingly challenged in the years ahead as developing countries reach the status of developed countries. China will soon exceed the United States as the world's largest economy and new markets are emerging as more nations' move their economies forward to become important players on the world stage [*See Figure 7.37*].

Globalization has minimized the importance of borders and we live in a world where cooperation rather than competition will be the driving force. As we continue to partner and trade, nations' fortunes are tied more closely together. With limited resources we will have to find new ways to collaborate to ensure the well-being of all. ■

# SCALING UP

Energy security and food security are the two main drivers of an emerging bio-economy. In pursuit of a greener future, low-carbon-emitting technologies are helping mitigate the effects of climate change and preserve the environment for future generations. Innovative bioenergy companies are addressing these global challenges using the tools of biotechnology and engineering to improve food and feed crops and develop bio-based fuels and chemicals that can replace fossil fuels. These companies have proven their technologies in the lab and are now advancing toward commercialization. Along the way, they are doing what they must to raise the huge sums necessary to deliver on their promise through diversifying into high value chemicals, going global to access capital, striking strategic partnerships with the big oil, chemical, and consumer goods companies, and even entering the cosmetics, flavors, and fragrances markets. In the end, they will be judged on whether or not they deliver the biofuels, bio-products, and enhanced crops they are promising. Today the bio-based industry is in the same place the fossil fuel industry was one hundred years ago—just getting off the ground. The kimono is set to open at end of 2013 when the first plants become operational. Even if it takes longer to come to fruition, adoption of these technologies will play a critical role in solving the energy, food, and environmental challenges the world is facing today.

# Chapter 8:

# SCALING UP

At the beginning of 2011, **DuPont**, one of the world's biggest chemical companies, agreed to acquire **Danisco**, a global enzyme and specialty food ingredients company for $6.4 billion. As part of the deal it acquired **Genencor**, a Danisco subsidiary that makes enzymes used in the development and production of advanced biofuels and bio-based chemicals. It was a major bet on industrial biotech for the traditional chemicals company. DuPont beat several rival suitors to seal the deal and expand its presence in bio-based chemicals and biofuels. The company has set a goal to generate $1 billion of revenue from renewable materials and fuel technologies by 2015.

"This transaction is a perfect strategic fit with our growth opportunities and will help us solve global challenges presented by dramatic population growth in the decades to come, specifically related to food and energy," said Ellen Kullman, DuPont chairman and CEO, at the time. "In addition, biotechnology and specialty food ingredients have the potential to change the landscape of industries, such as substituting renewable materials for fossil fuel processes and addressing food needs in developing economies, which will generate more sustainable solutions and create growth for the company."

DuPont and Danisco already had an established joint venture, **DuPont Danisco Cellulosic Ethanol**, to develop advanced biofuels. DuPont also had an ethanol joint venture with **BP** and **British Sugar**, and a biobutanol joint venture with BP called **Butamax**. **Pioneer Hi-Bred**, DuPont's biotech seed division, provides seeds to farmers in more than 90 countries. "We have been in industrial biotechnology for 10, 15 years already, and so we are coming up that curve," Kullman told *Bloomberg Businessweek*. "There will be a tipping point."

Reinforcing Big Oil's growing interest in renewable fuels, **Royal Dutch Shell** and Brazilian ethanol producer **Cosan's** $12 billion joint

*Figure 8.1*  EMERGING ECONOMIES DRIVE GROWTH IN GLOBAL ENERGY DEMAND

Global energy demand increases by one-third from 2010 to 2035, with China & India accounting for 50 percent of the growth

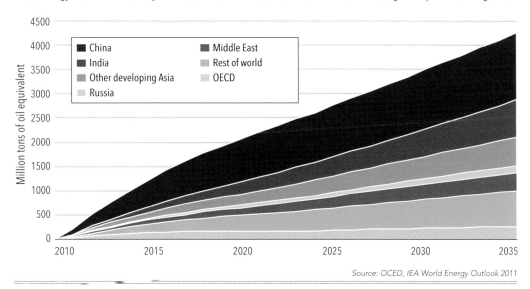

Source: OCED, IEA World Energy Outlook 2011

venture, **Raizen**, was launched in early 2011, consolidating a big chunk of ethanol operations in the country. The joint venture covers the whole supply chain from feedstock to pump for ethanol in Brazil. Shell is placing its renewable energy bets on biofuels, having let go of its wind and solar investments in recent years, to create the third largest ethanol producer in the world with 4,500 retail stations and annual production of 440 million gallons.

It was an auspicious start to a year that saw renewed interest by venture investors and major oil, chemical, materials, and consumer goods companies in advanced biofuels and bio-based technologies. In 2011, venture capitalists, private equity, and strategic investors poured more than $1.1 billion into companies engaged in producing bio-based alternatives to fossil fuels and chemicals. The capital markets also welcomed these biorenewables companies. Three of them in the United States—**Gevo**, **Solazyme**, and **Kior**—raised $500 million in initial public offerings.

Despite industry difficulties in the second half of the year, January 2012 saw another affirmation of the sector when Dutch materials and ingredients maker **Royal DSM** and U.S. biofuels developer **POET** teamed up in a joint venture to commercialize cellulosic ethanol. The 50/50 joint venture will start with an investment of $250 million toward the initial capital expenditure in Project

Liberty in South Dakota. Both companies expect it to be profitable in the first full year of operation, which is slated to be 2014. At an industry gathering in May, Royal DSM CEO Feike Sijbesma said that even though the fossil age still had one hundred years to go, his company would not wait until the last moment to make the switch. "The curve is heading towards the bio-based economy," he said.

"Together we shall deliver the key to unlock the cellulosic bio-ethanol opportunity," Sijbesma said when the joint venture was announced. "As the world is facing unprecedented challenges with a growing population making an ever bigger claim on the planet's resources, we need to accelerate the transition to a bio-based economy and this joint venture is a significant step in that direction."

### Challenges to delivering on the promise

Although no technology is yet deployed at commercial scale, major industrial users of petroleum see bio-based renewables as a significant part of their future mix of products. The price of oil will only get higher as demand in emerging markets grows and as dwindling global reserves get harder to tap [*SEE FIGURE 8.1*].

Industrial biotechs, having demonstrated that their technology works in the lab or in small pilot facilities, must now prove that their processes can work at commercial scale and produce high enough volumes at low enough costs to establish

8

*Figure 8.2* **FOOD PRICES ON THE RISE**

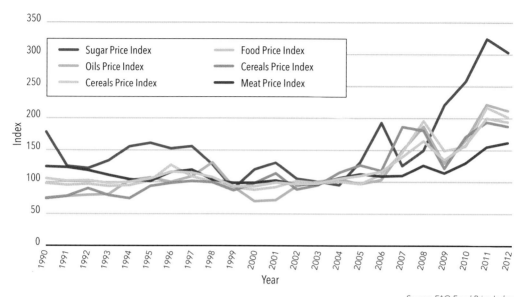

*Source: FAO Food Price Index*

viable businesses. To do so will take money. It will cost between $100 million and $300 million to cover capital expenditures to get a facility up and running.

Whether technologies will work at scale will probably not be answered until late 2013, when many facilities first come on line. Raising capital to get to that point and securing a reliable consistent supply of renewable feedstock is critical.

Big oil and chemical companies, conservative by nature, are interested and have provided significant funding, but they are willing to wait and see which technologies are proven at scale before making any acquisitions. Low expectations for achieving near-term M&A exits have forced many companies to become creative in sourcing capital. They are going global to get funding, forming joint ventures, securing supply contracts, tapping government grants and loan guarantees, and in many cases, selling their products into the specialty chemicals and personal care markets where they can command premium prices and move ahead with products that require less biomass [*SEE SIDE-BAR SMOOTHING*].

### Rapid growth leads to rising demand

Food and energy demand is rising rapidly, expected to grow more than 50 percent by 2030, according to the **U.S. Department of Energy**. Most of the demand is coming from the devel-

oping world, in which as many as 3 billion people are expected to move to the middle class by 2030. This emerging middle class, mostly from the rapidly expanding economies in India and China, will intensify demand for cars (doubling the number of vehicles on the road to 2 billion by 2050) and food. At the same time, finding new sources to supply these demands has become more difficult and expensive. There has been a 100 percent increase in the average cost to bring a new oil well on line over the past decade, according to **McKinsey & Company**, a global research and consultancy firm. As resources have grown more limited, commodity prices have reached an all-time high.

And it's not just oil and minerals that are becoming more difficult to extract. McKinsey's analysis finds increasing the supply of water and arable land as likely to present the biggest challenges. It estimates that the annual pace at which supply is added over the next 20 years in water and land would have to increase by 140 percent for water and up to 250 percent for land, compared with the rate of expansion over the past 20 years. This would lead to huge environmental degradation and intensify global climate change and its effects.

As the middle class grows, demand for higher nutrition, especially meat, is skyrocketing, adding to the need to grow more food. At the same

# Smoothing Fine Lines and Wrinkles

Solazyme develops a line of anti-aging creams

Thanks to biotechnology, consumers around the world may be able to erase the fine lines and wrinkles that define an aging face. A few months ahead of its May 2011 IPO, **Solazyme**, remade itself, moving from being an algal biofuels developer, to a renewable oils and bio-based products company. Its first target was the cosmetics market with the introduction in March 2011 of Algenist, a line of microalgae-based anti-aging products, which became available in the United States and seven European countries at **Sephora** stores and through home shopping network **QVC**.

Algenist anti-aging skincare products are formulated with alguronic acid, discovered unexpectedly by Solazyme's scientists while studying thousands of microalgae strains for renewable energy solutions. When researched for potential anti-aging benefits, alguronic acid demonstrated significant rejuvenating properties.

While Solazyme is pursuing the potential of algae-based oil as a fuel, it is also developing a cosmetic ingredient from algae as a way to create income without having to produce the volume necessary for commercially viable fuel.

The South San Francisco, California-based company started its business in 2004 with the idea of developing biofuels from algae, growing its genetically engineered microorganisms in closed tanks. It was a heady time for algae—the promise of a renewable fuel that harnessed the power of the sun and didn't depend on farmland. Microalgae produced prodigious amounts of oil that could be made directly into biodiesel. Soon the sector attracted a slew of venture investors, oil companies, the military and aviation industries, and even Bill Gates, who invested in a $100 million round for Solazyme's competitor **Sapphire Energy**.

But Solazyme and other advanced biofuels developers have realized that making money on biofuels is going to take some time. What worked in the lab is difficult to reproduce in commercial volumes. It's one thing to produce a few gallons of oil and quite another to produce the millions of gallons required for it to be successfully substituted for petroleum-based transportation fuels.

Without abandoning the biofuel strategy, Solazyme and many other advanced biofuels companies have refocused to use their technology to produce renewable chemicals and bio-based products, a higher value market requiring lower volumes of production.

Solazyme has been a leader in pursuing revenue opportunities in other sectors, having signed deals in 2010 to supply its oils to consumer products giant **Unilever** for use in soaps and to food ingredient maker **Roquette Freres**. In 2011, it entered into an alliance with **Dow Chemical** in which Dow would help Solazyme advance development of its algal oils for use in next generation, bio-based dielectric insulating fluids that are key for transformers and other electrical applications. Dow also signed a letter of intent to buy millions of gallons of the renewable oils in 2013 should the project be successful. ∎

China has begun to invest in the development of advanced biofuels made from agricultural residues. However, with one-fifth the world's population and only one-twentieth of its arable land, food security is an issue. The establishment of new ethanol plants using edible feedstock was banned in 2006.

# Advanced Biofuels in China

## Energy and food security issues drive growing bioenergy industry

China has ramped up its investment in bioenergy to meet rising demand for energy and food. With fuel consumption rising 10 percent annually, it has overtaken the United States in fuel imports, mostly from the Middle East. With one-fifth of the world's population but only one-twentieth of its arable land, its food imports have also increased dramatically.

To meet this demand, China has become a renewable energy powerhouse. With $49.8 billion invested in the development of renewable energy sources, it led the world in 2010, according to the **United Nations**. As part of its *12th Five Year Plan*, China's 2020 targets include 15 percent non-fossil fuel use in total energy consumption by 2020; 31 percent energy intensity reduction from 2010 levels; and 40 to 45 percent reduction in carbon emissions from 2005 levels.

Expert at commercializing technology developed elsewhere, as it did with solar energy, China has begun to invest in the development of advanced biofuels made first from agricultural residues, and eventually from municipal waste. The target is 10 million metric tons, equivalent to about 8 million barrels of oil, by 2020. That level will meet E5 standards, or 5 percent ethanol in the fuel mix, but will be only half its E10 goal. China banned the establishment of new ethanol plants using edible feedstock in 2006.

Leading biofuels projects are **COFCO**, China's largest food manufacturer and ethanol producer, and **CNOOC New Energy Investment**, a subsidiary of **China National Offshore Oil Corporation**. In May 2011, under two separate agreements, they partnered with U.K.-based **TMO Renewables** in the development of advanced biofuels produced from agricultural residues. After testing in pilot programs, the goal with both partnerships is to develop the country's first commercial advanced biofuels plants using residues and stalks from cassava, a major food crop in China.

China opened up the market for advanced biofuel production to private producers for the first time at the end of 2010, facilitating the deal that had been in the works for more than a year. New Zealand-based **LanzaTech's** joint venture with **Baosteel** is bringing a different technology to China. The joint venture will construct a 100,000 gallon a year demonstration facility of **LanzaTech's** fermentation technology that will use carbon waste streams from Baosteel's steel mill as feedstock to produce ethanol.

It is estimated that China may need as many as 300 new biorefineries built over the next ten years to meet its biofuels targets. While this may seem daunting to any other government, China has the resources and the will to make it happen. ■

*Figure 8.3*  NON-OECD ASIA BECOMES BIGGEST CARBON DIOXIDE EMITTER

Non-OECD Asia will account for almost 75 percent of the world increase in energy-related carbon dioxide emissions

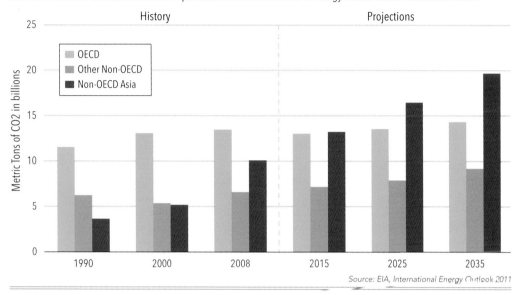

Source: EIA, International Energy Outlook 2011

time, the world population is headed toward 10 billion people by 2050. Arab Spring, the revolutionary wave of demonstrations in the Middle East and North Africa that started in 2011, was fueled in part by anger over escalating food prices. It was in December 2010 that a Tunisian street vendor set himself on fire after authorities seized his produce cart because he couldn't afford to pay bribes. The resulting riots toppled the government of Tunisian dictator Zine el Abidine Ben Ali in January 2011, and eventually spread across the Arab world. The turmoil in a prime oil producing region also led to increased oil price volatility and supply concerns.

Grain prices, and food prices in general, were at an all time high at the beginning of 2011, and had pushed 44 million more people into extreme poverty by the end of 2010, according to the **World Bank** [*SEE FIGURE 8.2*]. Crop-searing temperatures and droughts in many parts of the world and extreme flooding in other areas were blamed for the soaring prices of grains and it was feared that the dynamic would have an inflationary impact, especially in the developing world. Crop ecologists say that for every 1 degree Celsius rise in temperature above the optimum, farmers can expect a 10 percent decline in grain yields. The world is well on its way to at least a 2 degree Celsius rise in temperature by 2035 due

to carbon emissions from the use of fossil fuels, the main form of greenhouse gas emissions that contributes to global climate change.

Unfortunately, the nuclear disaster at Fukushima, and global economic concerns in the United States and Europe, kept most of the industrialized world from taking any meaningful action on energy policy to mitigate rising temperatures. $CO_2$ emissions rebounded to a record high in 2011 according to the **International Energy Agency's** annual outlook. The agency warns that unless action is taken within the next five years, the world temperature will rise above the 2 degree scenario. Coal was the big winner in the first decade of the century, fueling much of China's and India's economic growth. Any significant action, therefore, would have to involve emerging markets, as they will be the biggest consumers of energy and the biggest emitters of carbon dioxide in the years ahead [*SEE FIGURE 8.3*]. And although China has surpassed the United States as the top emitter of greenhouse gas emissions, it has moved to become a leader in bioenergy as well [*SEE SIDEBAR ADVANCED*].

Many innovative companies, especially in the United States and Europe, have risen to address these global challenges using the tools of biotechnology and engineering to improve food and feed crops and develop bio-based fuels and chemicals

# Making a Case for Biofuels

## IEA report says they can contribute to significant greenhouse gas reductions

With proper investments and policies, most biofuel technologies could become nearly cost-competitive with fossil fuels, or even be produced at lower costs in the longer term, according to a new report from the **International Energy Agency**.

Biofuels could represent 27 percent of all transportation fuels by 2050, compared to just 2 percent today, helping reduce CO2 emissions and boost energy security, according to the agency's new technology roadmap.

Countries will have to spend between $11 trillion and $13 trillion on biofuels over the next 40 years to meet the roadmap targets, depending on actual production costs, the IEA calculates. While this may seem like a large figure, even in a worst case scenario, it would only increase the total costs of transportation fuels by around 1 percent over the next 40 years, and could possibly lead to cost reductions, asserts the agency [*SEE FIGURE 8.4*].

The IEA, an autonomous organization created after the 1973 oil crisis to secure affordable and clean energy for its 28 member countries, prepared the roadmap in consultation with representatives of government, industry, academia and non-governmental organizations.

Expanding the role of biofuels is perceived in some quarters as compromising food security and providing limited environmental benefits. But the agency argues that biofuel consumption can be increased in a sustainable way and lead to significant reductions in greenhouse gas emissions when advanced technologies are deployed.

"While vehicle efficiency will be the most important and most cost-efficient way to reduce transport-emissions, biofuels will still be needed to provide low-carbon fuel alternatives for planes, marine vessels and other heavy transport modes, and will eventually provide one-fifth of emission reductions in the transport sector," says Bo Diczfalusy, the IEA's director of sustainable energy policy and technology.

The IEA says commercial-scale deployment of advanced biofuels has not yet happened, and is not expected to contribute much to the fuel supply until 2020.

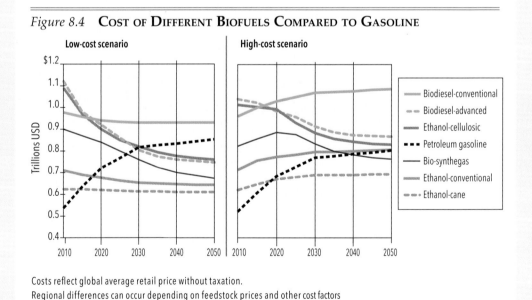

*Figure 8.4*  **COST OF DIFFERENT BIOFUELS COMPARED TO GASOLINE**

Costs reflect global average retail price without taxation.
Regional differences can occur depending on feedstock prices and other cost factors

*Source: IEA Biofuels Roadmap*

*Figure 8.5*   **Biofuels Consumption and Resulting Land Demand**

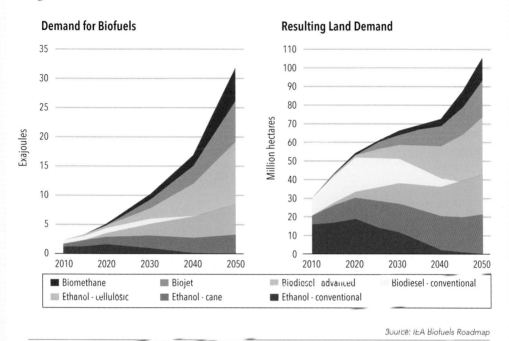

**Demand for Biofuels**

Exajoules

| | | | | |
|---|---|---|---|---|
| 2010 | 2020 | 2030 | 2040 | 2050 |

**Resulting Land Demand**

Million hectares

| | | | | |
|---|---|---|---|---|
| 2010 | 2020 | 2030 | 2040 | 2050 |

■ Biomethane    ■ Biojet    ■ Biodiesel - advanced    Biodiesel - conventional
■ Ethanol - cellulosic    ■ Ethanol - cane    ■ Ethanol - conventional

*Source: IEA Biofuels Roadmap*

"Further support for advanced biofuel research, development, and demonstration is still needed to improve conversion efficiencies and reduce costs," says Diczfalusy. "In addition, investments in commercial-scale production units will be a key to enable advanced biofuels to reach full market maturity."

> "Biofuels ... will eventually provide one-fifth of emission reductions in the transport sector."
>
> **Bo Diczfalusy**
> *IEA's director of sustainable energy policy and technology.*

Governments need to provide a stable, long-term policy framework for biofuels that allow for sustained investments in biofuel expansion. "Specific support measures that address the high investment risk currently associated with pre-commercial advanced biofuel technologies will be vital to trigger industry investments in first commercial plants," he says.

Efficient use of biomass through integrating biorefineries will be vital to reduce land competition and address food security issues as the world population swells by more than 30 percent to 9 billion people in 2050, the IEA report says.

IEA figures that three billion tons of biomass per year will be needed to reach the biofuels target envisioned in its roadmap, which would consist of one billion tons of biomass residues and wastes supplemented by production from about 100 million hectares of land—around two percent of total agricultural land. It estimates that crop yields could increase by a factor of ten through the use of more productive practices such as multi-season planting—rotating the planting of food and energy crops, and the improvement of crop yields [*See Figure 8.5*].

The report stresses governments should adopt mandatory sustainability standards for biofuels aligned with international standards to avoid acting as barriers to trade. It also calls for international collaboration and the reduction of tariffs and trade barriers to expand trade in biomass and biofuels to meet emerging demand in different regions of the world. ■

that can replace fossil fuels. New technologies are being deployed to capture carbon emissions from coal-fired power plants and feed them to microbes capable of turning them into fuels and chemicals. Wood residues from pulp and paper mills, agricultural residues, and municipal waste are also being used to make biofuels and bio-chemicals. Industry and government studies give a conservative estimate for biomass-derived biochemicals markets growing ten-fold over the next 15 years to more than $1.4 trillion, with a 16 percent compounded annual growth rate [*SEE FIGURE 8.6*].

### Betting on a bio-economy

Energy security and food security, the two main drivers of the emerging bio-economy, can address these concerns with low-carbon-emitting technologies to mitigate the effects of climate change and sustainability to preserve the environment for future generations [*SEE FIGURE 8.7*]. While many renewable technologies, such as wind and solar, can provide alternative sources of energy, biofuels are the only viable alternative to fossil fuels as a source of liquid transportation fuel, especially for the aviation, marine, and trucking industries, and the military.

The International Energy Agency in April 2011 published a report that makes a case for increasing the use of biofuels in transport. The report provides a roadmap for how global biofuel consumption can increase from 2 percent of total transport fuels to 27 percent in 2050 in a sustainable way—one in which production of biofuels brings significant life cycle environmental benefits and does not compromise food security [*SEE SIDEBAR MAKING*].

For most advanced biofuels developers in the United States, one of the biggest challenges is the lack of a cohesive energy policy. During a meeting of industry leaders in November in San Francisco, Brooke Coleman, executive director of the **Advanced Ethanol Council**, voiced industry concerns. "The policy outlook is bleak," he said. He argued against subsidies and for incentives to encourage adoption, including revising an outdated U.S. energy tax policy that benefits oil companies at the expense of renewables developers.

"The climate in Washington is not supportive of biofuels," said Michael McAdams, President of the **Advanced Biofuels Association**. He noted that

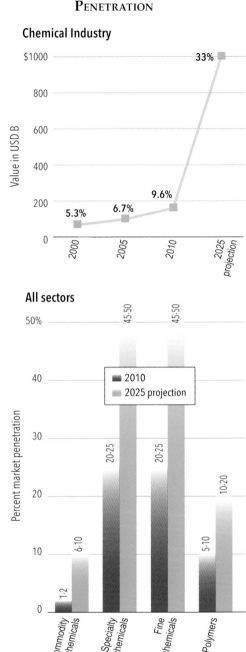

*Figure 8.6* **WORLD BIO-BASED MARKET PENETRATION**

Source: USDA, McKinsey, MBI

the subsidies, grant programs, and the *Renewable Fuel Standard* were under attack. Political dissension in Congress throughout the year exacerbated an already weak economy and made any kind of long-term energy policy unlikely. While Congress let stand preferential tax considerations for oil companies, it let the 45-cent per gallon ethanol blender credit known as *Volumetric Ethanol Excise Tax Credit*, or VEETC, lapse at the end of 2011.

In August 2011, a deal that would have scrapped VEETC while providing new tax incentives to biofuels producers as part of debt reduction negotiations died, leaving in question whether new incentives could be crafted to promote biofuels. The compromise proposal forged by Senators Dianne Feinstein, John Thune, and Amy Klobuchar, would have generated $2 billion in savings by immediately ending VEETC, but $668 million of the savings would go toward tax credit extensions to promote cellulosic and algae-based biofuels.

Some biofuels companies are concerned that government incentives are misplaced. In a letter sent to California Senators Barbara Boxer and Dianne Feinstein in June 2011, CEOs of six California-based biofuels companies including **Amyris, LS9, Sapphire Energy, Cobalt Technologies, Rentech**, and Solazyme expressed concern that fuel-specific infrastructure spending will come at the expense of future renewable fuels that are compatible with existing infrastructure. "Government support for renewable fuels and transportation should reward performance and compatibility rather than seeking to lock in ethanol, natural gas, or electricity as the fuel of the future," they wrote. "To that end, we support a feedstock agnostic approach that uses net carbon savings over petroleum as its primary metric."

"Our nation's economy is healing from a great recession and our companies have learned to do more with less," they wrote. "However, pulling back the policy mechanisms that provided advanced renewable fuel companies with appropriate incentives to bring promising technologies into the commercial energy market is the wrong kind of belt tightening and will further our reliance upon fossil fuels."

It will be difficult for biofuels developers to win new tax incentives going forward. The industry says while the Renewable Fuel Standard, which sets a requirement for a minimum number of gallons of renewable fuel in the transportation fuel supply each year, may be enough to ensure demand for first-generation corn ethanol, financial incentives are needed to provide investors confidence to put up the capital needed to scale and support advanced biofuels. "What we've seen over the past five years in the current form of the RFS is that the RFS by itself isn't enough to overcome the investment risk in these new technologies," says Matt Carr, policy director for the Industrial & Environmental Section of the **Biotechnology Industry Organization**. "That's where the tax code and other programs have a role."

The RFS establishes a market for renewable fuels. It mandates 36 billion gallons of renewable fuels be blended into the nation's fuel supply by

*Figure 8.7* **Non-Hydro Renewable Sources More Than Double 2010 to 2035**

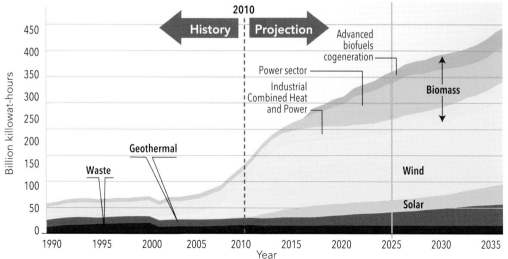

Source: EIA, Annual Energy Outlook 2012 Early Release

*Figure 8.8*   **GLOBAL POLICIES ENHANCE LONG-TERM DEMAND**

Select government mandates and subsidies

### UNITED STATES

| |
|---|
| Mandate of 36 billion gallons of biofuels by 2022 |
| $1 billion suport for second-generation technologies |
| Producer tax credit of $1.01/gallon for cellulosic biofuels |

### EUROPEAN UNION

| |
|---|
| 5.75 percent blending target by 2010 and 10 percent by 2020 |
| Airlines in CO2 emission cap in 2012 |

### CHINA

| |
|---|
| Target of 1.7 billion gallons of ethanol by 2010 and plans to substitute 20 percent of crude imports by 2020 |
| Investments in second-generation technologies by COFCO, PetroChina, and Sinopec |

### BRAZIL

| |
|---|
| Annual blending target for ethanol at 25 percent |
| Lower taxes for E100 than gasoline and FFV sales tax of 14 percent compared to 16 percent for gasoline-only vehicles |

### INDIA

| |
|---|
| Blending targets in current drafts of 5 percent by 2012, 10 percent by 2017, and 20 percent by 2020 |

*Source: Burrill & Company*

2022, and caps first generation biofuel at 15 billion gallons, with the rest coming from cellulosic and other advanced biofuels and biodiesel. Cellulosic ethanol did not meet the RFS targets in 2011, the third year it has fallen short. It is expected to continue to fall short of the goal through 2022, but exceed the 36 billion gallon target by 2030 [*SEE FIGURE 8.8*]. The **U.S. Energy Information Administration** projects cellulosic ethanol production, a subset of advanced biofuels, at almost 4 million gallons in 2012, short of the 8.6 million gallon target. U.S. biodiesel production topped 800 million gallons, more than double the previous year. However, production is expected to drop in 2012 due to the expiration of the tax incentive at the end of 2011.

## Government spurs innovation

At the end of March 2011, against a backdrop of Middle East turmoil, nuclear meltdown in Japan, and rising oil prices, President Barack Obama outlined his plan for America's energy security in a speech to students at **Georgetown University**. His goal, he said, is to reduce oil imports by one third from the 11 million barrels of imported oil a day when he was elected in 2008, within the next decade.

He also pledged renewed support for biofuels as part of the government's comprehensive national energy policy, *Blueprint for a Secure Energy Future*, to develop new sources of energy including natural gas, wind, solar, and biofuels. He pointed to Brazil as exemplifying the potential of biofuels, noting that he had just returned from a state visit there that had focused on establishing a cooperative agreement on energy needs of both countries. Half of the nation's automobiles can run on biofuels instead of petroleum, he said. Obama also commented on a test flight by the **U.S. Air Force** using an advanced biofuel blend. "If an F-22 Raptor can fly faster than the speed of sound on biomass, then I know the old beater that you've got, that you're driving around in, can probably do so too."

Obama's blueprint for energy security identifies expanding biofuels markets and commercializing new biofuels technologies as a key goal. The government will help entrepreneurs break ground for four next-generation biorefineries— each with a capacity of more than 20 million gallons per year, he said. He also pledged to look for ways to reform biofuels incentives to "make sure that they're meeting today's challenges and that they're also saving taxpayers money."

While government funding will continue to be important, Obama advocated a clean energy standard to drive private investment in innovation. "What it does is it gives cutting-edge companies the certainty that they need to invest," he said. He added it also lets companies know that they will have a customer for their clean energy products.

The U.S. military has been a strong supporter of renewable fuels with the Air Force working to get half its domestic jet fuel from alternative sources by 2016 and the **U.S. Navy** working toward getting 50 percent of its energy from low-carbon emitting renewable sources by 2020. The military spent about $15 billion on fuel in 2010 and accounts for almost 2 percent of the total annual U.S. energy demand [SEE FIGURE 8.9]. It is especially concerned with its ability to supply the energy needs of its troops on the ground, which can cost it upwards of $400 per gallon and carries mortal risks for its transport.

For the Navy, the main reason for focusing on alternative energy sources is military preparedness. "We're moving away from [oil] for one reason, that it makes us better war fighters," Secretary of the Navy Ray Mabus told *C-SPAN* in early February 2012. "It makes us a better military." Mabus said the military has certified all its Navy and Marine Corps aircraft to fly on biofuels. It's doing the same thing for its surface fleet. "We've got an F-18, the Hornet, that's flown 1.7 times the speed of sound using a 50/50 mix of biofuel and aviation gas," he said.

The main source of the biofuel used in the flight came from **Tyson Foods**—inedible chicken fat. Mabus said the Navy doesn't have a specific technology in mind. "We just need the energy," he said. The Navy will need 8 million barrels of biofuels per year to meet its 2020 goal and will be buying it from a lot of companies, says Chris Tindal, director of operational energy for the Navy. The Navy also plans to demonstrate a naval fleet, dubbed "Green Strike Group," on 50 percent renewables, which includes biofuels and nuclear energy, in 2012 and sail it around the world by the end of 2016.

Following up on the Blueprint for a Secure Energy Future, the Obama Administration in August announced a $510 million commitment by the **U.S. Departments of Agriculture, Energy**, and the Navy to advance commercialization of advanced biofuels for military use [*SEE SIDEBAR OBAMA*].

### Europe's carbon scheme affects aviation

The looming inclusion of aviation in the European Union cap and trade scheme at the start of 2012 has pushed airlines to look for alternatives to petroleum-based fuels. Under Europe's requirements, airlines will be required to introduce fuels blends that are 10 percent biofuels into transport fuel by 2012, with the requirement gradually rising to 40 percent by 2050. Penalties will cost airlines an estimated $1.9 billion in 2012 and up to $9.7 billion in 2020 if they do not comply.

In July, **ASTM**, a U.S.-based testing and standards board, approved an aviation biofuel blend, Bio-SPK, which allows up to 50 percent of the fuel to be hydrotreated oils, produced from renewable sources such as camelina, microalgae, cooking oil, or biomass. Since then, more than 10 commercial airlines have conducted test flights using the new aviation biofuel. The approval opens a $139 billion annual market for aviation fuels, according to **Bloomberg New Energy Finance**.

The approval of Bio-SPK gives the airline industry a green light to enable it to diversify its fuel sources and reduce its carbon emissions, which contribute about 2 percent to the global

*Figure 8.9* **THE PENTAGON'S FUEL MIX**

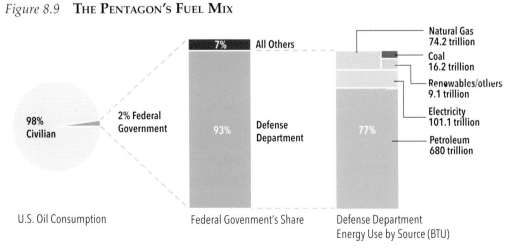

*Source: U.S. Navy, U.S. Department of Energy, The Wall Street Journal*

# Obama Commits $510 Million for Advanced Biofuels

Initiative calls for partnership with private sector
to fuel military and commercial transportation

President Obama in August 2011 said the U.S. government would partner with the private sector to speed commercialization of advanced aviation and marine biofuels that can make use of existing fuel infrastructure for military and commercial transportation. The United States will invest up to $510 million during the next three years in so-called "drop-in" biofuels through the **U.S. Department of Agriculture**, the **U.S. Department of Energy**, and the **U.S. Navy**, an amount that will require at least an equal match by the private sector.

Obama's initiative delivers on his pledge in March to boost the development of advanced biofuels as a means to reduce the country's dependence on foreign oil, strengthen America's rural economy, and provide a secure source of energy for the military.

The USDA, the DOE, and the Navy will share equally in funding efforts to address the issues hindering commercialization of these advanced biofuels. The USDA will oversee the mitigation of feedstock risk, supporting growers and providing incentives for growing energy crops; the DOE will support technology development; and the Navy will create the market for the end product. The Navy and **Air Force** have already worked with industry to test and certify that advanced biofuels meet their performance requirements.

Although increased use of advanced biofuels is a key component of the Obama's energy security agenda, lack of manufacturing capability for next-generation drop-in biofuels has been a major hindrance to its commercialization.

To accelerate the production of bio-based jet and diesel fuel for military and commercial purposes, Secretary of Agriculture Tom Vilsack, Secretary of Energy Steven Chu, and Secretary of the Navy Ray Mabus have developed a plan to jointly construct or retrofit several drop-in biofuel plants and refineries. Private industry is expected to contribute at least as much as the $510 million being provided by the government sources.

The biofuels initiative is being steered by the **White House Biofuels Interagency Work Group and Rural Council**, set up to encourage and coordinate public-private partnerships that can improve rural economics.

The aim of the advanced biofuels partnerships is to reduce U.S. reliance on foreign oil and create jobs while positioning American companies and farmers to be global leaders in advanced biofuels production. The United States spends more than $300 billion on imported crude oil per year. Producing a domestic source of energy provides a more secure alternative to imported oil and improves our energy and national security.

"By building a national biofuels industry, we are creating construction jobs, refinery jobs, and economic opportunity in rural communities throughout the country," says USDA's Vilsack. "As importantly, every gallon of biofuel consumed near where it is produced cuts transportation costs and, for the military, improves energy security."

The **Advanced Biofuels Association**, **Air Transport Association**, and the **Biotechnology Industry Association** all applauded the advanced biofuels initiative. "The military's leadership can drive the costs down and increase availability for the commercial sector," says Brent Erickson, executive vice president of BIO's Industrial & Environmental section. "This action will help move forward the commercialization of advanced biofuels and will further help develop the biofuels market. We need a basket of policy options to get the advanced biofuels industry to a large scale, and this joint effort is one more step in the right direction." ■

Many advanced biofuels companies, from Solazyme to Gevo, are developing aviation biofuels to take advantage of a market that could reach $68 billion assuming 2011 prices for kerosene, the standard jet fuel today

carbon dioxide emissions that contribute to climate change. Airlines will have spent $200 billion on jet fuel in 2011, according to **Carbon War Room**, a trade and advocacy group with a mission to accelerate the scale-up of a sustainable renewable jet fuel industry. Fuel costs typically represent between 25 percent and 40 percent of the commercial airline industry's operating costs, making it vulnerable to a highly volatile petroleum market.

**Boeing** sees sustainable aviation biofuels as critical to the health of its customers, says Michael Lakeman, regional director of biofuels and environmental strategy at the company. Boeing's goal is to see one percent of jet fuel from renewable sources by 2015, which translates to about 600 million gallons. The incentive for meeting this goal strengthened when Iran announced in mid-February 2011 that it was stopping shipments to the United Kingdom and France, sending oil prices to $120 per barrel, the highest they had been in more than eight months.

Many advanced biofuels companies, from Solazyme to **Gevo**, are developing aviation biofu-

els to take advantage of a market that could reach $68 billion assuming 2011 prices for kerosene, the standard jet fuel today. **Honeywell UOP** has emerged as a leader, developing a process that converts plant oils into jet fuel. The work was funded by a grant from the **U.S. Defense Advanced Research Projects Agency**. The fuel was used in some of the first test flights in 2010 and 2011.

Solazyme provided a 40/60 biofuel blend, refined by UOP, for **United Airlines'** first commercial flight in November 2011 from Texas to Chicago. It has also signed a supply agreement with Australia's **Qantas Airlines**. **LanzaTech** has partnered with **Virgin Airlines**, Gevo has an agreement with United and a contract with the U.S. Air Force for up to 11,000 gallons of alcohol-to-jet fuel, and Cobalt is working with the U.S. Navy. Amyris is forming a joint venture with **Total** to produce renewable diesel and jet fuel.

The **Federal Aviation Administration** has also gotten into the act, awarding $7.7 million in 2011 to eight companies, including Lanza-Tech, **Virent**, and UOP, to help them develop sustainably sourced renewable jet fuels that can be incorporated directly into the existing jet fuel supply chain.

Although the market for aviation biofuels exists, actually producing the advanced biofuels to fill the need is in its infancy. To date only about 12 million gallons of renewable jet fuel have been produced. "To meet demand, we are going to have to be building one new refinery per month for the next 20 to 30 years (a total of at least 290 plants)," says Charles Fishel, chairman of **BioJet**, a facilitator and distributor of renewable jet fuel. "With the capital cost of a biorefinery at $200 to $500 million each, the total investment requirement will be $58 to $145 billion."

Sustainability is also an issue, with concerns that finding enough acreage for energy crops will interfere with land that can be used for food crops. One way some companies are dealing with this issue is using waste streams. For example, LanzaTech's process is feedstock agnostic and can use the carbon gases emitted by steel mills as the feedstock for its alcohol-to-jet fuel. The company has teamed up with Chinese steel producer **Baosteel** in a joint venture that is building a biorefinery adjacent to a steel mill to make more than 30 million gallons of advanced biofuels from industrial waste gases.

# Biofuels Boom in Brazil

Opportunities and challenges in store for companies heading south
to commercialize ethanol-production technologies

As U.S. and European renewable fuel and chemical companies move aggressively to commercialize their technologies, the future for many lies in Brazil, where sugar is king and the ethanol industry is well developed. Brazil boasts access to plentiful feedstock in the form of sugarcane and a market where more than half the cars are flex-fuel enabled, and all fuel stations have ethanol pumps.

"They have the best potential short-term feedstock supply and the capability to grow more without any detrimental deforestation and unwanted environmental impact," says Ed Dineen, CEO of South San Francisco-based renewable fuels and chemicals company **LS9**, which has opened an office in São Paulo and is collaborating with Brazilian engineering and vehicles manufacturing company **MAN** to test LS9's renewable diesel in trucks and buses.

One potential benefit from using sugarcane as a feedstock is its purity. "If you haven't yet figured out how to make your magic bug process complex sugars well, then cane sugar is desirable," says Jim Lane, editor of the online publication *Biofuels Digest*.

Most Brazilian sugarcane processors are family-owned businesses that have been there for generations. "It's a pretty insular market," says Jim Lane, editor of the on-line publication Biofuels Digest.

But sugar, which has gotten a lot more expensive, isn't the only thing attracting companies. There's also the abundant bagasse, the cellulosic part of the sugarcane that is currently burned to power the sugar mills and ethanol plants. That's where the opportunity lies for companies such as LS9, **Amyris**, **Virent**, and **Codexis**, because such companies have the ability to take the bagasse and convert it into higher-value renewable chemicals and fuels, rather than just burn it to power existing plants. Although Brazil has a well-developed sugarcane processing industry, it has invested little in advanced biofuels technology. Companies there are seeking partners that can give them access to such technology.

That's the strategy behind Amyris' "capital light" policy of partnering with existing Brazilian sugar and ethanol producers to build "bolt-on" facilities adjacent to their mills. Amyris has been an early mover in Brazil, and its first production facility, a joint venture with **Usina São Martinho**, was operational in May. It plans to use the facility to first produce renewable chemicals, while it fine-tunes its renewable diesel and jet fuel technology.

Another partnership, the $12 billion joint venture **Raizen**, links **Shell** and sugarcane and ethanol producer **Cosan**. It is helping enzyme maker Codexis gain a stronger foothold in the country through its partnership with Shell. In September Codexis entered into a joint development agreement with Raizen to use its directed evolution technology platform to improve Raizen's current process for producing ethanol from sugar. Codexis will retain commercialization rights and Raizen will receive preferential commercial terms. The agreement could also be expanded to include bio-based chemicals.

Brazil began developing a biofuels policy in 1938 with mandatory ethanol blends to all gasoline in the country. Over time it has abandoned mandates in favor of a combination of policies to support the use of biofuels, mainly by reduced taxes on flex-fuel vehicles and ethanol fuels. But while Brazil offers the benefits of a pro-renewable energy environment, cheap and plentiful feedstock, complementary partnering opportunities, distribution infrastructure, and a vibrant market, there are challenges.

The main challenges, according to Jim Lane are cultural. Most sugarcane processors are family-owned businesses that have been there for many generations. "It's a pretty insular market and it's not crawling with entrepreneurs and people who understand the five-person, entrepreneurial spirit—local companies are not impressed," says Lane.

Companies looking to partner must also make sure that existing ethanol plants are connected to the electrical grid; they must be modern. Many of the existing ethanol plants are severely undercapitalized, says Lane. "The big ethanol plants haven't been able to modernize in many cases," he says. "There's a lot of consolidation going on right now. They're trying to find new capital structures that work for what they know they need to do in terms of investment. So there's a lot of instability."

In June 2011, the sugarcane industry trade group **Unica** warned that the sugar and ethanol industry needed $80 billion of new investment in the next 10 years to meet global demand. In a show of support, Brazil's state development bank **BNDES** said in January 2012 that it would lend $2.2 billion to the industry to increase its sugar harvest and boost ethanol production by up to 17 percent.

There's also the issue of the labor environment in the sugarcane industry. "There's been several investigations and fines," says Lane. "You need to be careful when you pick your partner."

Despite these challenges companies big and small have been flocking to Brazil and other Latin American countries to take advantage of the biofuels opportunities. Players range from big agriculture conglomerates, such as **Archer Daniels Midland**, **Bunge**, and **Cargill**, to Shell, **BP**, and **Total**. Brazil's state-run energy company **Petroleo Brasileiro**, or **Petrobras**, has also been pumping money in the sector, acquiring a 46 percent stake in **Acicar Guarani**, one of Brazil's largest sugarcane millers. It also partnered with U.S. advanced biofuels developer **KL Energy** and Dutch company **BIOeCON** to optimize its cellulosic ethanol process technology to use sugarcane bagasse feedstock.

Biofuels companies must still get their products to compete on price and performance, produce enough volumes, and having the right partner. For the near-term, Brazil offers plenty of opportunities for making it happen. ■

Ethanol plants run by companies such as LS9, Amyris, Virent, and Codexis have the ability to convert the cellulose from sugar cane into higher-value renewable chemicals and fuels, rather than just burning it to power existing plants.

*Figure 8.10* **INVESTMENT IN CLEAN ENERGY BY REGION**

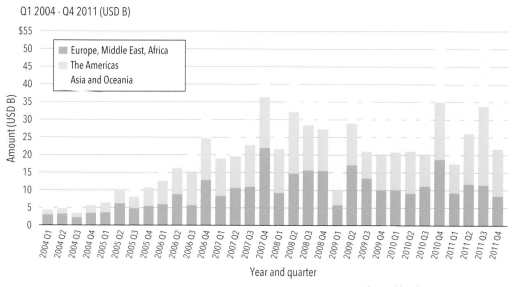

Q1 2004 - Q4 2011 (USD B)

*Source: Bloomberg New Energy Finance*

## Makers of consumer goods go green

Besides governments, the military, and the aviation industry, the market pull for these technologies is growing from commercial sectors with direct ties to consumers such as **The Coca-Cola Company**, **P&G, and DSM**, to name a few [*SEE FIGURE 8.12*]. For example, Procter & Gamble, the world's largest packaged goods company, has a long-term goal to use only recycled or renewable materials to make the packaging for its products. To achieve this goal, the company has entered into collaborative agreements for bio-based chemicals with LS9 in 2009, Amyris in 2010, and **ZeaChem** in 2011.

Coca-Cola entered into partnerships with three industrial biotechs to accelerate the development of plastic bottles made entirely of plant-based materials. The company has already distributed more than 10 billion first-generation recyclable polyethylene terephthalate (PET) beverage bottles that have 30 percent bio-based materials. After an intensive two-year analysis of different technologies, Coca-Cola picked Virent, Gevo, and **Avantium** as partners.

"While the technology to make bio-based materials in a lab has been available for years, we believe Virent, Gevo, and Avantium are companies that possess technologies that have high potential for creating them on a global commercial scale within the next few years," says Rick Frazier, vice president of commercial product supply at Coca-Cola. "This is a significant R&D investment in packaging innovation and is the next step toward our vision of creating all of our plastic packaging from responsibly sourced plant-based materials."

"New technologies need champions. The Coca-Cola Company is in a unique position to drive and influence change in the global packaging supply chain with this development," says Patrick Gruber, CEO of Gevo. All three companies expect to have full-scale commercial capability within the next couple of years. The global market for PET is 54 million metric tons and has a value of $100 billion, with approximately 30 percent used for plastic bottles.

## It's all about diversification

Many advanced biofuels companies seeking to find sustainable business models are finding that the quickest way to market is diversification through renewable chemicals. "Why make a $2 fuel when you can make a $5 chemical?" asked former-Cobalt Technologies CEO Rick Wilson at an industry event in March 2011.

In October, Cobalt partnered with French specialty chemical company Rhodia to develop bio n-butanol refineries, initially in Brazil. They will start with a demonstration plant located next to a **Rhodia** power generation facility to demonstrate that Cobalt's technology using sugarcane bagasse feedstock works in larger volumes. If successful, they will build plants next to sugarcane mills throughout Latin America to produce bio n-butanol for the chemicals and fuels markets [SEE SIDEBAR BIOFUELS].

Although the specialty chemicals market is small—about $400 billion annually compared to $1 trillion for jet fuel, according to Jeri Hilleman, CFO at Amyris—it provides higher margins and requires lower volumes. There is also a ready market for these chemicals in everything from plastic packaging to new carpet fibers.

One recent effort reflecting corporate giants' interest in renewable chemicals is a large-scale joint venture in Brazil between **Dow Chemical** and Japanese conglomerate **Mitsui**, established in November 2011 to build ethanol and biopolymer plants.

Although the ultimate goal of the joint venture is to produce ethanol from sugarcane, Dow and Mitsui are also seeking to reduce their reliance on petroleum-derived chemicals. DuPont will also capitalize on the biotechnology it acquired through its $6.4 billion purchase of Danisco to develop new bio-based products and reduce its reliance on fossil fuel feedstocks.

Such a strategy is not only for big players like DuPont and Dow. Biofuels startups are also finding traction in the renewable chemicals space. Solazyme, an algae biofuels developer, jumped into the cosmetics market in March 2011, rolling out a new line of microalgae-based anti-aging products, which are available in the United States and seven European countries at **Sephora** stores and through home shopping network **QVC**.

Emeryville, California-based Amyris, began producing its first renewable chemical Biofene, a biochemical precursor for use in creating lubricants, cosmetics, polymers and plastics additives, and flavors and fragrances.

Smaller companies pursuing such a strategy are attracting both strategic and venture investment. In January, **PTT Chemical Group**, Thailand's largest petrochemical producer, made a $60 million strategic equity investment in **Myriant Technologies**, developer of renewable bio-based chemicals. And in July, **Elevance Renewable Sciences** landed $50 million to support its technology for taking plant-based oils and turning them into specialty chemicals. **Hutchinson Worldwide** agreed in June 2011 to use Elevance's renewable products as an alternative to petroleum-based raw materials in its rubber production.

**BlueFire Renewables'** focus on bio-chemicals helped it attract funding from **China Huadian**, which agreed to help bankroll its 20 million-gal-

*Figure 8.11* **GLOBAL VC INVESTMENT IN BIOFUELS AND BIOMATERIALS**

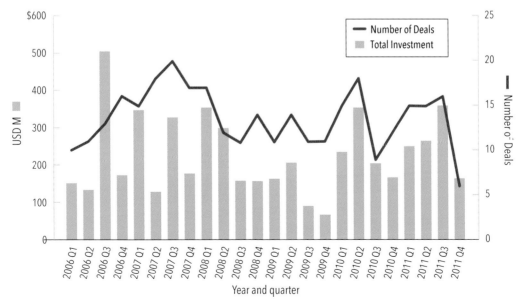

*Figure 8.12*    **Select Renewable Chemical Deals in 2011**

| INDUSTRIAL BIOTECH | PARTNER | DEAL TYPE | PRINCIPAL ASSET/RATIONALE |
|---|---|---|---|
| Amyris | Givaudan (Switzerland) | Partnership | Givaudan will develop a derivative of Biofene, Amyris' renewable farnesene, to be used in its fragrance ingredients. |
| | Paraiso Bioenergia (Brazil) | Partnership | Amyris will build a specialty chemicals facility and cane-processor Paraiso will supply the juice from up to 1 million tons of cane per year. Plant is expected to be operational in 2012. |
| | Wilmar International (Singapore) | Partnership | Development and commercialization of a family of surfactants derived from Amyris' Biofene for use in multiple products as a replacement for nonylphenol ethoxylate surfactants, a $1 billion annual market. |
| | Kuraray (Japan) | Partnership | Development of innovative polymers from Biofene, which Kuraray will use to replace butadiene and isoprene in the production of certain polymers. |
| | Albemarle | Supply agreement | Albemarle's Fine Chemistry Services will serve as a custom scale-up and production partner for Amyris Biofene, which will then be marketed by Amyris and Cosan joint venture Novvi to finished lubricant manufacturers globally. |
| | Total (France) | Joint venture | Expansion of Total and Amyris' R&D partnership on Biofene and renewable diesel and formation of a 50-50 joint venture to develop, produce and commercialize a range of renewable fuels and bio-based products that will be marketed worldwide. |
| Avantium (Netherlands) | Coca-Cola Company | Agreement | Partnership to accelerate development of the first commercial solutions for PlantBottle packaging made 100% from plant-based materials. |
| BioAmber | Mitsubishi Chemical (Japan) | Partnership | BioAmber and its partner Mitsui will be the exclusive suppliers of bio-based succinic acid to Mitsubishi Chemical to use in its renewable, biodegradable polymers. |
| | PTTMCC Biochem (Thailand) | Partnership | BioAmber and PTT (a strategic investor) will build a biobased succinic acid plant in Thailand and supply PTTMCC (a joint venture between PTT and Mitsubishi) with bio-based succinic acid on an exclusive basis. PTTMCC will help secure biomass for the plant. |
| | Lanxess (Germany) | Partnership | Development of succinic acid based plasticizers that are both renewable and phthalate-free and can exceed the performance of phthalates at competitive prices. |
| | Mitsui & Co (Japan) | Partnership | Companies will build and operate a facility in Ontario, Canada, the first of three plants (including one in Thailand) expected to begin operating in 2013. BioAmber will be the majority shareholder. |
| | Celexion | License | Exclusive licensing agreement for technology related to the production of adipic acid and other chemical intermediates for the chemicals market. |
| Cobalt Technologies | Rhodia (France) | Alliance | Memorandum of understanding to develop bio n-butanol refineries in Latin America, starting with a demonstration plant, that will use sugarcane bagasse as feedstock. The parties will initially develop options for deploying Cobalt's technology at a sugar mill. |

*Continued on next page*

| INDUSTRIAL BIOTECH | PARTNER | DEAL TYPE | PRINCIPAL ASSET/RATIONALE |
|---|---|---|---|
| Codexis | Chemtex (M&G-Italy) | Collaboration | Broad deal to develop and produce sustainable detergent alcohols for use in the household products market, which includes development of second generation detergent alcohols from cellulosic biomass. |
| | Raizen (Brazil) | Agreement | Using the Codexis CodeEvolver directed evolution technology platform to improve Raizen's current process for producing ethanol made from sugar and explore producing chemicals. Codexis will retain commercialization rights and Raizen will receive preferential commercial terms. |
| Danisco | DuPont | Acquisition | DuPont acquires Danisco, a global enzyme and specialty food ingredients company, for $5.8 billion in cash and assumption of $500 million of net debt. |
| Genomatica | Waste Management | Agreement | R&D agreement to develop Genomatica's technology to enable production of renewable chemicals from syngas made from municipal solid waste. |
| | Tate & Lyle | Partnership | Strategic partnership to speed commercialization of Bio BDO, an intermediate chemical used to make spandex, automotive plastics, running shoes, insulation, and high-value downstream derivatives. |
| | Mitsubishi Chemical (Japan) | Collaboration | Memorandum of understanding for a joint venture for Bio BDO production in Asian and development of additional green intermediate and basic chemicals. |
| Gevo | Coca-Cola Company | Agreement | Partnership to accelerate development of the first commercial solutions for PlantBottle packaging made 100% from plant based materials. |
| Metabolix | CJ CheilJedang (South Korea) | Agreement | Joint development agreement to advance production technology and assess investment options for the commercialization of renewable C4 chemicals via fermentation. C4 chemical products are used in engineering plastics, fabrics and fibers, personal care products and in semiconductor manufacturing. |
| Segetis | Method Products | Partnership | Method Products, a maker of home cleaning and laundry products, will use Segetis' bio-based materials in a variety of its products. |
| Solazyme | Dow Chemical | Alliance | Advance the development of Solazyme's algal oils for use in next generation, bio-based dielectric insulating fluids key to transformers and other electrical applications and a non–binding LOI for Dow to buy up to 20 million gallons of Solazyme's oils for use in industrial applications in 2013 and up to 60 million gallons in 2015. |
| | Bunge | Agreement | Two-year joint development agreement to develop algal oils using Brazilian sugar cane feedstock and a joint venture to build a biorefinery in Brazil. |
| Virent | Coca-Cola Company | Agreement | Partnership to accelerate development of the first commercial solutions for PlantBottle packaging made 100% from plant-based materials. |

*Source: Burrill & Company*

lon-a year plant in Fulton, Mississippi with the possibility of investing in additional plants in the United States and China [SEE FIGURE 8.10].

The path to revenue through renewable chemicals remains a challenge, though, as companies must find the capital and partners to build demonstration capacity. Similar to the importance of diversification in portfolio strategies, diversity in sourcing capital, partners, and feedstock is important in helping companies meet the challenge of reaching scale.

## Financing the move to scale

Venture, private equity, and corporate investment in North American and European bio-based renewables companies increased 29 percent in 2011, compared to 2010, to reach $1.1 billion as companies needed increased capital to finance their commercialization projects [SEE FIGURE 8.11].

Industry analyst **Cleantech Group** reported that total global venture investment in companies developing renewable technologies was the highest it had been since the financial crisis of 2008 with close to $9 billion raised in 713 deals [SEE FIGURE 8.13]. Solar and energy efficiency drew the most investment.

Investors showed a lot of interest in waste-to-renewables companies in 2011 with several large financings that included a $75 million round for **Fulcrum Bioenergy** for its waste-to-ethanol process, $60 million for **Enerkem** for its waste-to-energy technology, $45 million for **Genomatica** for its waste-to-chemicals technology, and $51.7 million for **Harvest Power**, which converts organic waste to energy and fertilizer products. **Waste Management**, one of North America's largest municipal waste handlers, invested in the financing rounds of all these companies.

Enerkem's financing also included **Valero Energy** as an investor. The oil refiner already has investments in ten ethanol plants in the Midwest, buying several from ethanol producer **VeraSun** after it went bankrupt and closed its operations. As part of its investment in Enerkem, the two companies agreed to consider commercial opportunities together. The capital will support the company's rollout of current and future planned projects. In June 2011, Enerkem received a commitment of $130 million in financial support from the U.S. Department of Agriculture

*Figure 8.13* **GLOBAL VENTURE INVESTMENT IN RENEWABLES**

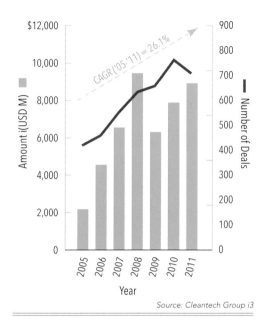

Source: Cleantech Group i3

and the U.S. Department of Energy for a plant in Pontotoc, Mississippi, which was expected to break ground by the end of 2012.

According to Bloomberg New Energy Finance analysis, venture capitalists and private equity firms have provided 60 percent, or $2.7 billion, of the total private investments made in advanced biofuels since 2004. However, the amount of money companies need to finance scale-up projects is beyond the scope of traditional venture capital financing [SEE FIGURE 8.14].

When they get to the demonstration stage, companies have to rely on a mix of corporate investors, strategic partners, and the government for funding or go public to raise the needed funds. Companies began to see serious funding from the U.S. government to support projects in 2011 [SEE FIGURE 8.15]. After a slow start, the USDA started to award loan guarantees under the 2008 farm bill *Biorefinery Assistance Program*. **Coskata**, Enerkem, **INEOS New Plant Energy**, and Sapphire Energy received USDA loan guarantees in 2011 worth more than $440 million. The DOE awarded loan guarantees to **Abengoa**, **Diamond Green Diesel**, POET, and **Mascoma** worth about $560 million.

Getting a government loan guarantee, though, does not guarantee success. This was made painfully clear by the failure of **Range**

*Figure 8.14* **Financing Biorenewables Projects**

| TECHNOLOGY STAGE | WHO FINANCES | HOW MUCH? | WHAT IS IT? |
|---|---|---|---|
| Laboratory | Grants, Angels, VCs | $1M-$5M | Proof in a 10L fermenter; patents; process outline |
| Pilot | Grants, VCs | $10M-$20M | Larger scale, integrated processes, feedstock, economics, engineering |
| Demonstration | Grants, Partners, IPO | $20M-$100M | All engineering—biology is over |
| First Commercial | Partnerships, IPO, Loan guarantees | $100M-$500M | A very large plant that employs a lot of people and uses a lot of feedstock |

*Source: Burrill & Company*

**Fuels** at the end of 2011. It was one of the first biofuels startups to attempt commercializing its technology to produce ethanol from wood chips and other biomass. The company received loan guarantees from DOE and USDA and more than $150 million from venture capitalists. It broke ground for a plant in Georgia in 2007 that was designed to produce 20 million gallons of cellulosic ethanol per year in the beginning, with greater volumes to come. Range said it would be operational by 2008 but immediately ran into problems with its technology. The recession derailed its ability to raise funding to address its problems. By 2010 it was producing some methanol at a loss and by 2011 it had stopped production. In early 2012 LanzaTech, another advanced biofuels developer, bought the plant for $5.2 million at auction.

> Waste Management has invested in a variety of technologies that can turn waste into commodities, and is working with them to develop their processes for turning municipal solid waste into higher value fuels and chemicals.

### Attracting strategic investors

Waste Management has been one of the most active strategic investors in bio-based renewable companies capable of maximizing the value of municipal solid waste, which Waste Management collects every day. It's a far cry from when trash collectors went door-to-door, collected the waste, and dumped it into a landfill. Now the waste can be fermented into alcohols, or converted into chemicals, biogas, or electricity. The company has invested in a variety of technologies that can utilize waste and turn it into commodities and is working with them to develop their processes for turning municipal solid waste into higher value fuels and chemicals.

Chemical companies are also active strategic investors. In January 2011, renewable chemicals startup Myriant Technologies closed a $60 million strategic equity investment from PTT Chemical Group. The funding will be used to further develop its technology and commercialize its succinic acid platform, including construction of a succinic acid plant in Louisiana, which will be the world's largest when completed.

Myriant and PTT Chemical also signed an agreement to establish a joint venture to deploy Myriant's technology in Southeast Asia. The joint venture will combine PTT Chemical's R&D capabilities and Myriant's technology to manufacture green chemicals using the abundant high quality bio-based feedstock available in Thailand and the Asian region.

Oil refiner Valero stepped in as a strategic investor in the advanced biofuel company Mascoma, pledging $50 million in November 2011. One month later, the two companies teamed up in a joint venture to develop and operate a 20 million gallon per year commercial scale cellulosic ethanol plant in Kinross, Michigan at an expected cost of $232 million. The facility will use Mascoma's proprietary consolidated bioprocessing technol-

206

*Figure 8.15*    **SELECT PUBLIC FUNDING FOR ADVANCED BIOFUELS IN 2011**

| COMPANY | AMOUNT USD M | PROJECT | STATE | GRANTING AGENCY |
|---|---|---|---|---|
| Advanced Biofuels companies | 156.0 | Advanced Biofuels | Several | USDA Bioenergy Program for Avanced Biofuels grants |
| Abengoa (Spain) | 134.0 | Cellulosic ethanol biorefinery | KS | DOE loan guarantee |
| AE Biofuels | 1.9 | Cellulosic biofuels | CA | California Energy Commission grant |
| BlueFire Renewables | 88.0 | Biorefinery | MS | US American Recovery & Reinvestment Act grant |
| Cobalt Technologies | 18.0 | Biorefinery | CA | DOE Integrated Biorefinery Program grant |
| Coskata | 250.0 | Biorefinery | AL | USDA loan guarantee |
| Diamond Green Diesel (Valero and Darling JV) | 241.0 | Renewable diesel plant | LA | DOE loan guarantee |
| EdeniQ | 20.5 | Biorefinery | CA | DOE Integrated Biorefinery Program grant |
| Enerkem (Canada) | 80.0 | Biorefinery | MS | USDA loan guarantee |
| General Atomics | 2.0 | Algal fermentation | CA | DOE grant |
| Genomatica | 5.0 | Conversion technology | CA | DOE grant |
| Gevo | 5.0 | Biojet fuel development | TX | USDA National Institute of Food and Agriculture grant |
| Virdia (HCL Cleantech) | 9.0 | Conversion technology | MS | DOE grant |
| Honeywell UOP | 1.1 | Renewable jet fuel | | Federal Aviation Administration |
| INEOS New Plant Energy | 75.0 | Biorefinery | FL | USDA loan guarantee |
| LanzaTech (New Zealand) | 3.0 | Renewable jet fuel | | Federal Aviation Administration |
| Mascoma | 80.0 | Cellulosic Biorefinery | MI | DOE cooperative funding agreement |
| POET | 105.0 | Cellulosic ethanol biorefinery | IA | DOE loan guarantee |
| Sapphire Energy | 43.6 | Algal biofuel demonstration | NM | USDA loan guarantee |
| Virent | 13.4 | Conversion technology | WI | DOE grant |
| Virent | 1.5 | Renewable jet fuel | | Federal Aviation Administration |
| ZeaChem | 40.0 | Cellulosic biofuels | OR | USDA grant |

*Source: Burrill & Company*

ogy platform to turn wood biomass into ethanol. It is expected to be operational by the end of 2013.

These companies are also moving to the sources of their feedstock—Brazil for sugarcane, Australia for microalgae, Chile and South Korea for seaweed, India for sugarcane and jatropha, and Southeast Asia for its abundance of all types of biomass. Many advanced biofuels companies are developing projects in the Southeast United States because the developed wood products industry there provides plentiful feedstock.

## The IPO route

The public markets embraced rising bioenergy companies in the first half of 2011, as three of them—Gevo, Solazyme, and Kior—completed successful IPOs at or above their target range, collectively raiseding $500 million. The price of oil was high, the market was on an upswing, and biorenewables were hot. Markets turned sour in the second half of the year though, due to the growing debt crisis in Europe and U.S. political machinations, which affected the markets in general, and the newly public bioenergy

*Figure 8.16* **THE BURRILL BIOGREENTECH IN INDEX 2011**

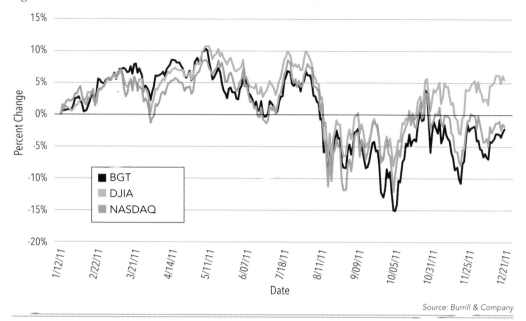

Source: Burrill & Company

companies in particular. The Burrill Biogreentech Index ended the year down 1.3 percent [SEE FIGURE 8.16].

But it has been a difficult time for the nascent bioenergy sector since the second half of 2011. Average returns from initial offering price for the five U.S. companies that went public in 2010 and 2011—Codexis, Amyris, Gevo, Solazyme, and Kior— were down an average of 42.8 percent as at the end of 2011. [See Figure 8.17]. These companies all completed their initial offerings in or

near their target price ranges and had a strong initial market reception.

The biggest selling points for investing in these companies was their broad set of strategic partners, faster routes to revenue through the renewable specialty chemicals market, and—for Amyris, Codexis, and Solazyme—their growing presence in Brazil. Gevo and Kior both have technologies that can feed directly into the existing fuel supply at high yields using low-cost feedstocks. Further, Gevo's isobutanol has a relatively

*Figure 8.17* **INDUSTRIAL BIOTECH IPOS NOT PERFORMING**

| COMPANY | TICKER | CAPITAL RAISED (USD M) | TARGET RANGE (USD) | PRICE/ SHARE (USD M) | PRICE 12/30/11 (USD) | RETURN FROM IPO 12/30/11 | MKT CAP 2/15/12 (USD M) | TECHNOLOGY |
|---|---|---|---|---|---|---|---|---|
| Codexis | CDXS | 78 | 13-15 | 13 | 4.55 | -59.2% | 164 | Enzymes, biocatalysts |
| Amyris | AMRS | 84.6 | 18-20 | 16 | 6.41 | -27.9% | 292 | Advanced fermentation using engineered yeast |
| Gevo | GEVO | 123.3 | 13-15 | 15.0 | 10.2 | -58.1% | 266 | Advanced fermentation using engineered yeast |
| Solazyme | SZYM | 227.2 | 15-17 | 18.0 | 11.6 | -33.9% | 691 | Renewable oil from microalgae |
| KiOR | KIOR | 150 | 19-21 | 15.0 | 12.0 | -32.1% | 1,220 | Cellulosic biomass conversion to renewable crude |
| **AVERAGE** | | | | | | **-42.8%** | | |

Source: Burrill & Company

quick route into the fuel market. Its model of building, owning, and operating the conversion of existing corn ethanol facilities gives it ownership flexibility with less capital cost.

In February 2012, Amyris, once considered the poster child for the emerging sector, announced that it would not meet its production goals for its renewable chemical, Biofene, due to consistency problems in moving to higher volumes. Its shares sank 29 percent on the news, a reminder of the difficulties of reproducing lab results in commercial volumes [SEE SIDEBAR AMYRIS].

Codexis, a developer of enzymes used in the production of biofuels, biochemicals, and pharmaceuticals, has also encountered difficulties. Slow progress in the scale up of cellulosic biofuel production has affected the company's bottom line. It abandoned its efforts to develop enzymes for carbon capture at coal-fired power plants and it has been unable to get a foothold in the public market, where its shares have failed to reach or exceed its $13 IPO price. "We're late to our own party," long-time CEO and company founder Alan Shaw told *Biofuels Digest* in late 2011, before resigning in February 2012 to pursue other inter-

# Amyris Scales Back

## Shares tumble as company finds scale-up more difficult than expected

Bio-based renewables company **Amyris** pulled back production plans in a major shift in strategy after running into problems scaling its technology. In a conference call with investors in February 2012, CEO John Melo admitted that although the company had proven its technology works at scale, it had learned that "it takes time to translate from peak yield levels in the lab to maintaining those yields over longer operational periods in the field."

The news sent Amyris shares tumbling 29 percent. Once a high flyer with shares trading for as much as $33.82, shares in the company fell the day after Melo's assessment to $6.99, having fallen lower in earlier trading. By February 15, 2012 Amyris was trading 60 percent below its IPO price and had lost 78 percent of its value in the past year, a reminder of the difficulty in translating achievements in the lab or at pilot scale into the commercial quantities in which bio-based renewables firms need to operate, especially if they are producing advanced biofuels.

Amyris was once held up as the model of how to build a bio-based renewable business. While most industrial biotech startups were just that, Amyris sought to become a full-fledged industrial concern in an industry dominated by big oil and chemical companies. It was one of the first to venture into Brazil to take advantage of the country's cheap feedstock, sugarcane.

For Amyris, partnerships are a major key to building a successful business. It has a capital-light strategy—partnering with existing facilities and sharing costs to ramp up production of its renewable technology. Based on a synthetic biology platform, its engineered microbes, primarily yeast, can convert plant-based sugars into renewable chemicals that can be used in an array of products such as cosmetics, fragrances, flavors, lubricants, and transportation fuels that can be directly "dropped in" to the established fuel supply. In June 2010, ahead of its September 2010 IPO, Amyris signed a flurry of partnering agreements that helped establish its position in the market and strengthened its feedstock and production capacity.

The company counts more than a dozen partners, both strategic and commercial, including oil company **Total**, sugarcane and ethanol producer **Cosan**; chemical companies **M&G** and **Kuraray**; flavors and fragrance producers **Givaudan** and **Firmenich**; cosmetics maker **Soliance**; and consumer goods manufacturers **Procter & Gamble** and **Wilmar**.

Although Amyris' IPO priced below its target range at $16 per share, the stock quickly climbed as the company continued its partnering activities and built its first commercial plant in Brazil plus signed agreements for one in Spain and the use of a **Tate & Lyle** facility in the United States.

In the conference call, Melo reported that the company only produced 1 million liters of its renewable chemical Biofene, for which it has several supply agreements with chemical, household

ests. While Shaw will serve as a special advisor to the Codexis' board, his resignation sent shares plummeting 19 percent to an all-time low.

Despite the risks inherent in scaling the technology, though, the need to raise capital has pressed biorenewables companies to add themselves to a growing queue of IPO hopeful. Two companies in the queue went public in the first two months of 2012. Biodiesel producer **Renewable Energy Group's** IPO in January 2012 was greeted with restrained enthusiasm, forcing it to slash its price by 29 percent to raise $72 million.

Energy crop company **Ceres** priced its initial public offering in February 2012 raising $65 million, the first agricultural biotechnology company to go public on a U.S. exchange since Monsanto in 2000. While Ceres had originally hoped to sell its shares for $21 to $23, it revised its range to $16 to $17 after starting its road show. But that range also proved too high and, after delaying its debut for a month, the company settled at $13 a share, 21 percent below the midpoint of its desired range. Existing shareholders were expected to purchase up to 1 million shares of the offering, or 20 percent, according to a regulatory filing days before it priced.

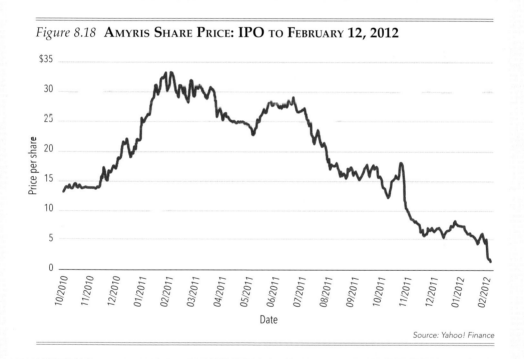

*Figure 8.18* **AMYRIS SHARE PRICE: IPO TO FEBRUARY 12, 2012**

Source: Yahoo! Finance

goods, and cosmetics and fragrance companies. Melo said Amyris would abandon previous guidance that it would produce 40 to 50 million liters of Biofene in 2012. It would discontinue issuing production targets, and instead give regular updates on performance. Melo also said that the company would not be cash flow positive in 2012 and was in the process of raising additional equity financing to cover the gap.

In light of its difficulties producing consistent yields at production quantities, Amyris is changing its focus to improving the quality of its products and the consistency of yields at commercial scale. He said he was "proud" of what the company has accomplished and "humbled by the lessons we have learned." But he insisted that the company's long-term plans hadn't changed and were still on track.

Amyris' experience will serve as a cautionary tale to the growing line-up of companies at the crucial stage of testing their technology at commercial scale. The challenges are many and include raising the capital to build the first commercial facility, retaining a consistent supply of feedstock, bringing the cost and quality of products to be par with conventional chemicals and fuels, and having a market in which to sell. ■

*Figure 8.19* **SELECT AGBIO PARTNERING IN 2011**

| DEAL TYPE | COMPANY/ LICENSEE | COMPANY/ LICENSER | PRINCIPAL ASSET/RATIONALE |
|---|---|---|---|
| Collaboration | BASF (Germany) | Evolva (Switzerland) | Joint research on the design of novel and optimised biosynthesis routes for selected natural products with crop protection potential |
| Collaboration | Bayer CropScience | Caprotec Bioanalytics (Germany) | Proprietary technology to profile the interactions of one of Bayer CropScience's undisclosed new active ingredients in the relevant biological system |
| License | Bayer CropScience | Fazenda Ana Paula (Brazil) | Exclusive worldwide license rights to the rice breeding program of the Brazilian company Fazenda Ana Paula, specialized in hybrid rice breeding |
| Collaboration | Bayer CropScience | KeyGene | Development of novel traits for crop improvement by applying KeyGene's KeyBase methodology to specifically target plant genome sequences for mutagenesis and develop traits using the DNA repair mechanism present in plant cells, with an initial focus on traits for new oilseed rape varieties |
| Collaboration | Monsanto | BASF (Germany) | Advancement of dicamba herbicide tolerant cropping systems |
| Collaboration extension | Monsanto | Evogene (Israel) | One-year extension to five-year R&D collaboration focused on identifying key plant genes related to yield, environmental stress and fertilizer utilization in corn, soybean, cotton and canola |
| Partnership | Monsanto | GrassRoots | Extension of an agreement for the development of gene promoters to enhance and protect crop yields in a broad range of crops, including corn, soy, cotton, and canola |
| Collaboration | Monsanto | Sapphire Energy | Multi-year collaboration that will leverage Sapphire's algae-based synthetic biology platform to discover genes that could be applied to agriculture, particularly in the field of yield and stress |
| Acquisition | Monsanto | Divergence | Monsanto acquires Divergence, a privately-held company with a focus on its work with parasitic nematodes, including developing biotechnology traits for nematode control and nematicides with novel modes of action and superior safety profiles |
| Alliance | Pioneer Hi-Bred (DuPont) | Biotique Systems | Next-generation sequencing management, biomarker analysis, and genotype to phenotype association to Pioneer Hi-Bred's agricultural research platform to develop improved crops |
| Collaboration | Pioneer Hi-Bred (DuPont) | Evogene (Israel) | Multiyear collaboration to improve resistance to soybean rust |
| Agreement | Pioneer Hi-Bred (DuPont) | Rosetta Green (Israel) | Identification of drought tolerance genes in corn and soybeans using Rosetta Green's proprietary technology and bioinformatics capabilities to identify microRNAs, unique genes that function as "main bio-switches" to control key processes in major crops such as corn, wheat, rice, soybean, cotton, canola and algae |
| License | SESVanderHave | Arcadia Biosciences | Exclusive global rights to the use of Arcadia's Water Efficiency technology in sugar beets. Builds on a 2007 deal for the development of Nitrogen Use Efficient sugar beets |
| Collaboration | Syngenta | BioLeap | Application of BioLeap molecular design technology to the discovery of Syngenta crop protection products. Syngenta Ventures makes an equity investment in BioLeap and gains exclusive license to any products discovered |

*Source: Burrill & Company*

In that filing, Ceres advised prospective investors that recent weather-related developments were likely to reduce yields of its sweet sorghum crops for the current growing season and could adversely affect demand for its seeds for the coming season.

Investments in bioenergy, as with biotechnology in general, come with significant risks, including the weather hazards, which could hamper Ceres. However, companies in the sector know that worldwide demand for their technologies—biotech, chemistry, and engineering—is only going to get stronger as global challenges force the world to move toward a bio-economy and away from one based solely on fossil fuels.

### Improving crops, increasing food supply

While companies like Ceres are focused on improving crop traits to make them more suitable as energy crops, other agricultural biotech companies have been hard at work developing crops that can increase the food supply and its quality while using less fertilizer and water. Although the industry is dominated by a handful of big companies such as Monsanto, **Syngenta**, DuPont's Pioneer Hi-Bred, **Dow AgroSciences**, **Bayer CropScience**, and **BASF**, many of these big companies look to partner with the smaller players to access innovative technology [*SEE FIGURE 8.19*].

The first GM crop technologies were focused on increasing crop yield through managing insect and weed invasion. Iterations of these two traits—insect resistance and herbicide tolerance—by the big agbiotechs ushered in enormous improvements in crop yields in the 15 years since they were first adopted mainly in four crops: soy, corn, cotton, and canola. Their adoption has grown rapidly to encompass close to 400 million acres planted by 16.7 million farmers worldwide, 90 percent of whom farm on less than one and a half acres [*SEE SIDEBAR DEVELOPING*].

Brazil has become a leading adopter of GM crops, specifically soybeans, introducing a variety in 2011 developed totally in-house by **Embrapa**, the state agricultural research institute. Brazilian farmers choose to plant GM soy even though the seeds command a high premium because when all the costs are factored in, they save almost $49 per hectare [*SEE FIGURE 8.20*].

*Figure 8.20* **WHY BRAZILIAN FARMERS CHOOSE GM SOY**

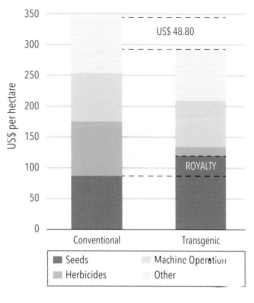

Source: Conab, Abrasem, Celeres, ISAAA, Kleffmann

Most GM seeds are developed and sold by multinational companies. Part of the reason is the enormous regulatory hurdles companies have to go through to get a trait approved for commercialization is difficult to bear for smaller companies. Still, many countries have begun developing their own seeds. India's first Bt-cotton seeds came from multinationals but it opened the way for four new varieties developed by Indian and Chinese companies.

Still, GM crops raise red flags in some parts of the world. Groups in India have blocked approval of a domestically developed GM eggplant and the federal government passed a rule in 2011 that makes it mandatory to get approval from local authorities before conducting field trials of GM crops.

The United States grows the most GM crops. Still there are strong pockets of resistance to GM technology in the United States for safety and economic reasons. In January 2012, a federal judge in the United States rejected challenges to biotech alfalfa and refused to overturn USDA approval for planting. Although the status of GM sugar beets is still uncertain, farmers can continue planting them pending appeal by environmental and organic seed groups, but they can't let the plants flower and produce seed.

# Developing Nations Lead in Biotech Crop Adoption

Spurned by Europe and Japan, genetically modified crops are being embraced by the world's small, resource-poor farmers

The global adoption of biotech crops continued its upward trajectory in 2011, as an additional 12 million hectares (29.6 million acres) were planted worldwide with genetically modified seeds, an 8 percent increase over 2010, according to the **International Service for the Acquisition of Agri-biotech Applications**.

The benefit of GM crops, according to the non-profit biotech advocacy group, is their contribution to food security, especially in the developing world where growing populations and a rising middle class are putting increased demand on food supplies. The research firm **PG Economics** found that between 1996 and 2010, increased crop production from the adoption of GM crops has led to reducing carbon dioxide emissions equivalent to taking nine million cars off the road; saved almost 1 billion pounds of pesticides from being used; and added $78 billion to the pockets of 15 million small farmers, who are some of the poorest people in the world.

GM crops were planted on 160 million hectares (395.4 million acres) during 2011 by 16.7 million farmers in 29 countries, of which 90 percent are small, resource-poor farmers in developing countries. These are farmers whose plots average half a hectare (1.2 acres). While the United States continues to lead the world with 69 million hectares (170.5 million acres) planted, adoption rates grew much faster in developing countries, with Brazil, Argentina, China, India, and South Africa leading the rate of adoption. In fact, for the first time developing countries' land planted with biotech crops was close to half of the total planted [*SEE FIGURE 8.21*].

Corn, soybeans, cotton, and canola make up the bulk of the GM crops planted [*SEE FIGURE 8.22*]. They have been modified through genetic engineering to resist insects and/or tolerate herbicides, reducing the need to use large amounts of insect or weed killers. The list of GM crops is growing, however, to include rice, and vegetables and fruits such as sugar beets and papaya. For example, China has developed two varieties of insect-resistant rice and a high-phytase corn designed to reduce methane production in animals that consume it. They have

*Figure 8.21* **BIOTECH CROP AREA: DEVELOPING COUNTRIES CLOSE IN ON INDUSTRIALIZED COUNTRIES**

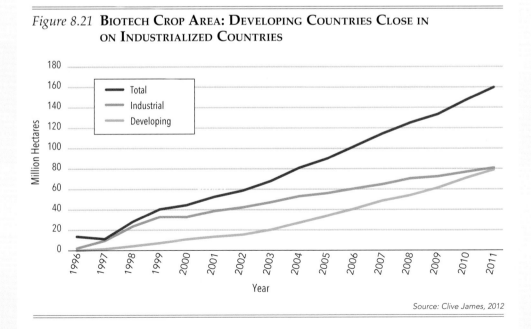

*Source: Clive James, 2012*

*Figure 8.22* **GLOBAL BIOTECH CROP AREA BY CROP**

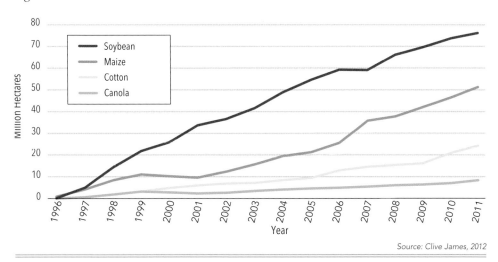

Source: Clive James, 2012

passed bio-safety standards and are awaiting marketing approval. For now the country ranks sixth in biotech crop acreage, with 7 million small resource-poor farmers growing insect-resistant cotton on a record 3.9 million hectares (9.6 million acres).

Brazil ranks second behind the United States in its adoption of GM crops, with more than 30 million hectares (74.1 million acres) planted with soybeans, corn, and cotton. The country has created a fast-track approval system that has allowed it to approve eight GM products in 2010 and an additional six GM products in the first nine months of 2011. Brazil approved the first soybean with both insect resistance and herbicide tolerance for commercialization in 2012. The country reached a milestone in 2011 with the marketing approval of a virus-resistant bean, developed in-house by **Embrapa**, a public agricultural research institution.

Despite the negative sentiment about genetically modified foods and crops, especially in Europe and Japan, people have been growing and consuming them for the past 15 years. As countries look for ways to feed their populations, many political leaders around the world are viewing the technology as a key part of the solution to critical social issues of food security and sustainability. At the same time, the big agbiotechs that have led in the development of GM technology are loosening the purse strings in order to allow poor farmers to increase their yields with less fertilizer, often through public/private partnerships.

Perhaps the most encouraging story is that after many years, golden rice is close to being approved for cultivation in the Philippines. Golden rice is genetically modified to contain enhanced levels of beta carotene. When first developed by plant biologists Ingo Potrykus and Peter Beyer in 1999 at the **Swiss Federal Institute of Technology**, it held hope as an answer to vitamin A deficiency, which can damage the retina and cornea of the eye and lead to blindness. It affects up to half a million children each year in developing regions of the world that often subsist on rice, killing about half of them, according to **World Health Organization** estimates.

Golden rice met with great resistance by anti-GM groups and eventually **Syngenta**, which held the research and license rights, donated those rights to the **Rice Humanitarian Board**. In the Philippines, the **International Rice Research Institute**, a non-profit group, continued its development and conducted field trials in 2010 and 2011. The golden rice trait has been inbred into several varieties with seeds that can be saved and replanted. The plan is to sell the rice at the same price as conventional varieties. Applications for regulatory approval are planned to be submitted in the Philippines in 2013 and in Bangladesh in 2015 and the hope is that it will be released for marketing in the Philippines by 2014. ■

*Figure 8.23*     BIOTECH CROPS UNDER CULTIVATION GLOBALLY

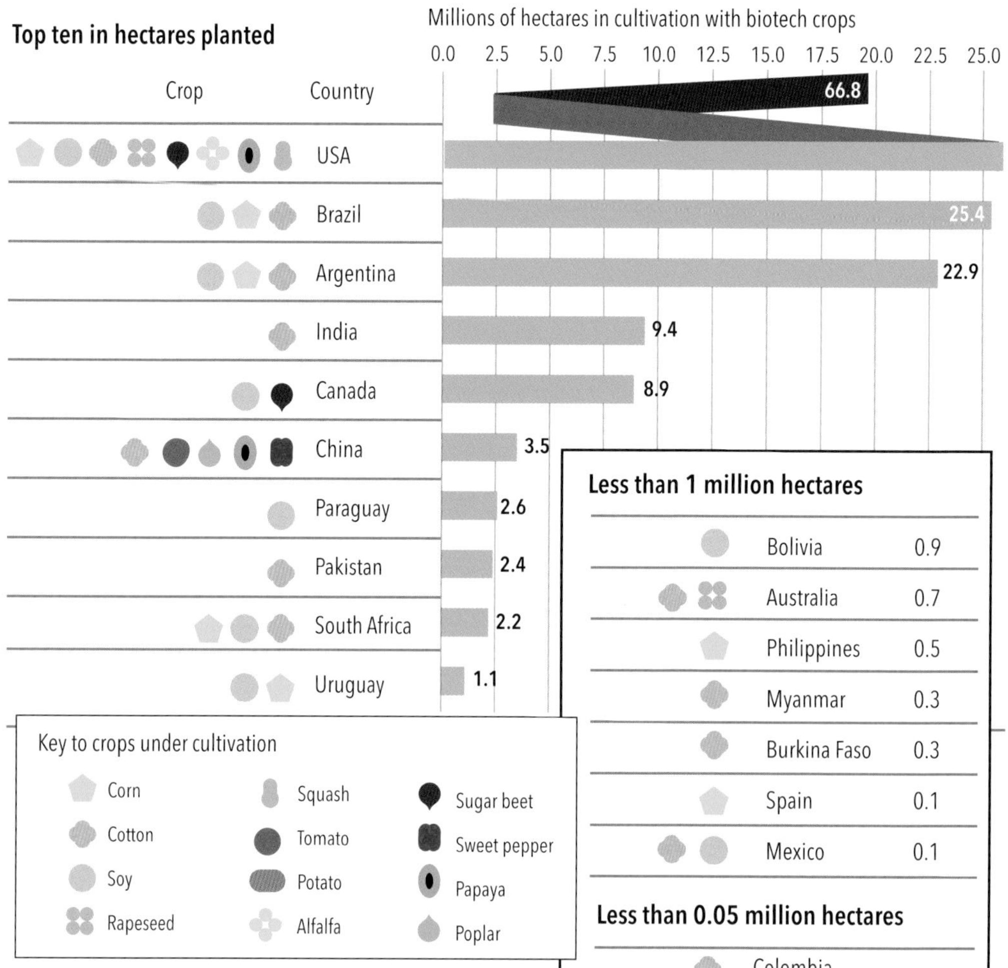

### Top ten in hectares planted

Millions of hectares in cultivation with biotech crops

| Crop | Country | Millions of hectares |
|------|---------|---------------------|
| 🌽🌾🫘✕●✚◉◗ | USA | 66.8 |
| 🌾🌽🌾 | Brazil | 25.4 |
| 🌾🌽 | Argentina | 22.9 |
| 🌾 | India | 9.4 |
| 🌽● | Canada | 8.9 |
| ◉●🌾◉■ | China | 3.5 |
| 🌾 | Paraguay | 2.6 |
| 🌾 | Pakistan | 2.4 |
| 🌽🌾🌾 | South Africa | 2.2 |
| 🌾🌽 | Uruguay | 1.1 |

**Key to crops under cultivation**

| Corn | Squash | Sugar beet |
|------|--------|------------|
| Cotton | Tomato | Sweet pepper |
| Soy | Potato | Papaya |
| Rapeseed | Alfalfa | Poplar |

### Less than 1 million hectares

| |  |  |
|--|---------|-------|
| | Bolivia | 0.9 |
| ◉✕ | Australia | 0.7 |
| | Philippines | 0.5 |
| | Myanmar | 0.3 |
| | Burkina Faso | 0.3 |
| | Spain | 0.1 |
| ◉● | Mexico | 0.1 |

### Less than 0.05 million hectares

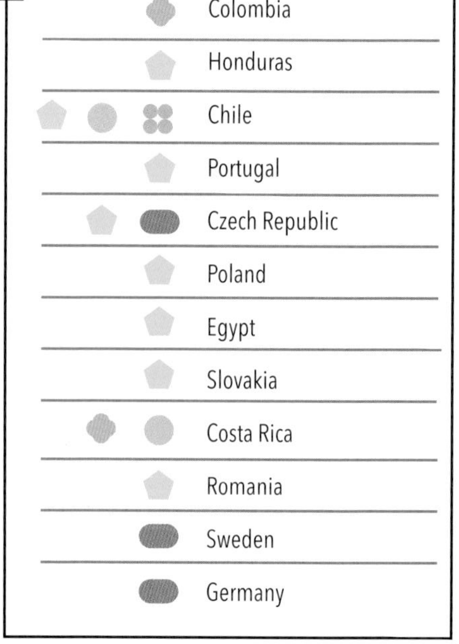

| |  |
|--|---------|
| | Colombia |
| | Honduras |
| 🌽◉✕ | Chile |
| | Portugal |
| 🌽▬ | Czech Republic |
| | Poland |
| | Egypt |
| | Slovakia |
| ●◉ | Costa Rica |
| | Romania |
| ▬ | Sweden |
| ▬ | Germany |

## Europe warned on slow pace

The most vociferous resistance to GM technology can be found in Europe. Genetic modification of food and feed crops has been a politically charged issue in Europe for a long time. Adoption of GM crops is growing in most of the world because of the benefits they offer to farmers in terms of reliability, productivity, and decreased use of pesticides, but most European consumers are still opposed to GM foods.

There is a problem, however, when it comes to feedstock for animals. Europe imported about 50 million tons of GM animal feed last year. Until recently, import of animal feed containing any unapproved GM material was prohibited. In July 2011, the European Union modified the rules to allow for a trace amount, just 0.1 percent, of unapproved GM product in imported feed in an effort to avoid a disruption in imports.

*Source: Clive James, 2012*

**EuropaBio**, a European biotechnology industry organization, says Europe needs to pick up the pace of its genetically modified crop approvals or risk the loss of needed agricultural imports vital to its food security. The group presented a report in October to European Union commissioners as they prepared to publish reforms to their *Common Agricultural Policy*.

GM crop authorizations in Europe take 15 to 20 months longer than in the three top GM exporter nations—the United States, Brazil, and Canada. "The EU authorization process for GM products takes substantially longer than comparable systems, despite the fact that government processes around the world to assess the safety and impact of GM products are essentially the same," the group wrote.

Europe's food security is at risk if it continues to rely on imports for a large part of its animal feed supply. Its backlog of GM crops awaiting approval has grown to 72 crops from 50 crops at the end of 2007, with 51 GM varieties awaiting approval for import and 21 for cultivation.

Although European commissioners have said that GM crop approval should only be based on scientific and safety considerations, the politicization of decision-making has left the region with only two approved GM crops for cultivation for feed and industrial use only, a corn-borer resistant maize variety from Monsanto and a potato called Amflora with extra starch for industrial use. A few other varieties are approved for import in animal feed only. This compares with 90 varieties approved in the United States and 28 in Brazil. Most of the European Union's imported animal feed is soybeans from the Americas, and is increasingly genetically modified.

The Common Agricultural Policy blueprint aims to strengthen the European Union's competitiveness and the sustainability of agriculture in member countries and allocates European Union funds for research and development to meet sustainability goals. EuropaBio recommended the Commission set targets in the plan to reduce the backlog of applications. It also said agricultural and industrial biotechnologies have an important role to play if Europe is serious about transitioning towards a sustainable bio-based economy.

"The bio-based economy offers Europe the potential to accelerate its transition to a more sustainable growth model while also developing a globally competitive sector capable of generating more jobs," says Nathalie Moll, secretary general of EuropaBio, commenting on the CAP proposal. "Farmers must also be given the choice to use the tools they need in food production. Access to biotechnology not only helps farmers become more productive, it helps them compete globally."

## Research encompassing more traits

Research is advancing in a broader range of crop improvement traits [*SEE FIGURE 8.24*]. These encompass agronomic traits that improve stress tolerance such as drought resistance and salt tolerance to improve yields in marginal lands. One of the most difficult and important qualities in development is nitrogen use efficiency, which could eliminate the massive need for fertilizers. A complex trait that involves more than one gene, its development could benefit from the growing use of genomic technologies in agricultural research.

## Agbiotech in the genomics age

Companies are looking beyond genetic modification to a host of advanced breeding technologies that take advantage of advances in genomic sequencing to develop superior hybrids without policy hurdles faced by genetically modified crops in many parts of the world. DuPont's Pioneer Hi-Bred introduced a new drought-resistant corn to

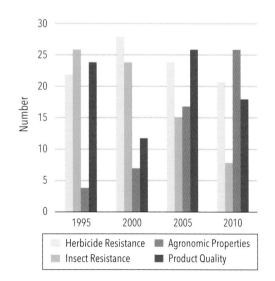

*Figure 8.24* **GM TRAITS IN DEVELOPMENT**

Source: Joyce Tait and Guy Barker, EMBO

Companies are looking beyond genetic modification to a host of advanced breeding technologies that take advantage of advances in genomic sequencing to develop superior hybrids without policy hurdles faced by genetically modified crops in many parts of the world.

the market in January 2011, developed through advances in its breeding technology rather than through genetic modification, thus avoiding regulators in bringing their seed to market. The company promises a 5 percent increase in yield above what farmers in arid parts of the Midwest United States have been able to achieve.

Monsanto is among many companies looking beyond genetic modification to the host of new breeding technologies enabled by advances in genomics. In April, Monsanto said it would partner with **Atlas Venture**, an early-stage venture capital firm, to explore investment opportunities in early-stage life sciences technology companies, especially those that support and complement agbiotech's increased focus on the

use of genomics, informatics, and biology in the improvement of crops. Monsanto would avail itself of Atlas' investment experience within life sciences while Atlas would benefit from Monsanto's technology expertise in R&D and support for investment decisions.

"As we work with farmers to help meet the needs of our growing planet, continued innovation is critical," says Steve Padgette, Monsanto's research and development investment strategy lead. "Our collaboration with Atlas will provide a great opportunity for us to get an early look at promising new technologies that could potentially be introduced into our biotechnology, breeding and agronomic practices work to drive yields even further."

Many of the new agronomic and quality traits will be difficult to achieve. As in complex diseases, they involve not just a gene, but a molecular pathway that must be found and then altered. This is where advances in genomics can make all the difference.

Monsanto recognized the power of genomics and DNA sequencing early on, investing in a $68 million funding round for **Pacific Biosciences** in April 2009. It invested in the synthetic biology platform of Sapphire Energy, an algal biofuels developer. Monsanto is also looking to the "cloud" to manage and analyze the massive amounts of data generated by its research activities. In October, it teamed up with **Cloudant**, a startup that provides solutions for "big data," to develop a next-generation data integration and visualization platform based on its technology.

### Delivering on the promise

In the end, bioenergy companies—industrial and agricultural—will be judged on whether or not they can deliver the biofuels, bioproducts, and enhanced crops they are promising. The analogy with the cost of sequencing the human genome is instructive. What cost $3 billion dollars just ten years ago can now be had for a few thousand dollars. Similarly, a gallon of biojet fuel that may cost 10 times as much as the same gallon of fossil fuel today, with constant improvement in technology, will also fall in price.

Today the bio-based industry is in the same place the fossil fuel industry was one hundred years ago—just getting off the ground. It is moving from small labs and pilot plants to commercial operations. The kimono is set to open at end of 2013 when the first plants become operational. It will take money, partnerships, and government backing to make it work. Even if it takes longer to come to fruition, adoption of these technologies is not an option, it is an imperative to finding solutions to the energy, food, and environmental challanges the world is facing today. ▥

# BUYING INNOVATION

Dealmaking to access innovation is driving large M&A activity, as pharmaceutical companies look beyond the patent cliff and embrace innovative products as the way to best build revenue growth in a world where they will need to not only demonstrate safety and efficacy, but value as well to be successful. The weak IPO market has also bolstered M&A activity as the most viable exit for investors in privately held biotechs. As the industry seeks to address its lack of R&D productivity, it is increasingly looking outside its own walls to research and discovery deals that lead to promising early-stage drug candidates. This was seen in the spate of alliances between academic institutions and industry, as well as a growing number of licensing deals centered on preclinical or early-stage compounds. There will be a continued bifurcation of partnering deals as companies seek research and discovery deals with small upfront payments plus options to license compounds at one end and big dollar, late-stage deals at the other end. Pharmaceutical and big biotech companies will not be afraid to pay top dollar for assets that have largely had their risks abated. But as the activity in 2011 showed, companies that produce true innovation will be richly rewarded.

# Chapter 9:

# Buying Innovation

In presenting **Sanofi's** annual results in February 2012, the company's CEO Chris Viehbacher began by recalling his first time standing at the podium discussing Sanofi's results for investors in 2008 after just one month on the job. The numbers painted an upbeat picture then, but what was ahead for the company was clear and Viehbacher laid out the strategy for contending with the steep patent cliff the Paris-based pharmaceutical giant faced. Now, the year that Viehbacher has long said he has had circled in red in his diary, had arrived.

Between 2010 and 2012, Sanofi expected to lose protection on products that generated about 34 percent of its 2007 revenue. In 2012, the company faces competition from generic drugmakers on its blockbuster anti-platelet drug Plavix, the world's second best-selling drug with sales of $9.8 billion shared between Sanofi and **Bristol-Myers Squibb**. It is also facing new generic drug competition for Aprovel, which is used to treat enlarged prostates, cancer drugs Eloxatin and Taxotere, which lost protection in 2010, as well as generic drug competition for its blood thinner Lovenox. Despite all of the dealmaking and cost cutting that led up to 2012, the Sanofi CEO soberly declared that earnings per share for the company are expected to fall 12 to 15 percent in 2012.

In recent years, Sanofi made a series of acquisitions culminating in its 2011 purchase of the

**Chris Viehbacher**
*CEO,*
*Sanofi*

storied biotech **Genzyme**. In fact, Sanofi has been the most active acquirer of biotech and pharma companies over the past three years with a total of nine acquisitions. [*See Figure 9.1*]. Like many Big Pharmas bracing for the loss of patent protection, much of its activity has been focused on adding new sources of revenue and expanding its geographic reach [*See Figures 9.2, 9.3, and 9.4*]. Sanofi has targeted everything from competitors to over-the-counter products and generic drugmakers in emerging markets. Sanofi in 2010 acquired China's specialty pharmaceutical **BMP Sunstone**, Poland's consumer healthcare company **Nepentes**, India's

*Figure 9.1*  MOST ACTIVE BUYERS OF PHARMACEUTICAL AND BIOTECH COMPANIES

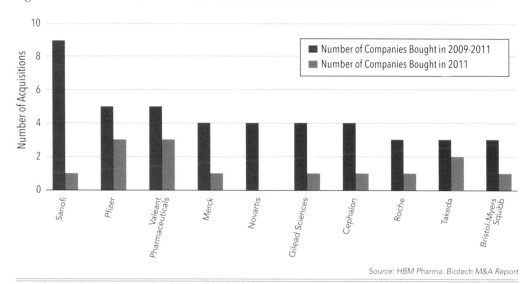

Source: HBM Pharma: Biotech M&A Report

**Shantha Pharmaceuticals**, and Brazil's **Medley** in an effort to become a leading consumer healthcare company in emerging markets. In 2010 it also acquired the over-the-counter products company **Chattam** with brands including Icy Hot and Gold Bond, for $1.9 billion.

This type of M&A activity defined Big Pharma acquisitions in recent years, driven by the need to replace revenue and establish a strong presence in emerging markets as a source of future growth. The strategy was evident in deals such as **Pfizer's** $66.7 billion purchase of **Wyeth** in 2009, **Merck's** $42.1 billion acquisition of **Schering-Plough** in 2009, and a sudden surge in deals in emerging markets in 2010. Even **Roche's** acquisition of the remaining part of **Genentech** it did not already own, while being used to remake Roche in a very real way today, was largely driven by Roche's concerns at the time about protecting revenue it derived from Avastin and other Genentech drugs moving forward. All three acquisitions also pushed each of the acquirers deeper into the business of biotechnology.

Unlike many previous acquisitions, the Genzyme buyout, while bringing in new sources of revenue to Sanofi, was driven by the need to tap into new sources of innovation. The deal, completed in 2011 for $20.1 billion deal plus contingent value rights worth up to $3.8 billion, reflects the attraction biotechnology products offer in the emerging healthcare regime where the leading companies are suffering from the bruising loss of

revenues, something they would like to insulate themselves from in the future. They must also contend with increasing pressure from payers to demonstrate the value of their products.

The agreement between Sanofi and Genzyme came after a long courtship in which the two companies had to bridge a gulf between what Sanofi was willing to pay for the company

*Figure 9.2*  **M&A BY BIG PHARMA ACQUIRERS 2007 TO 2011**

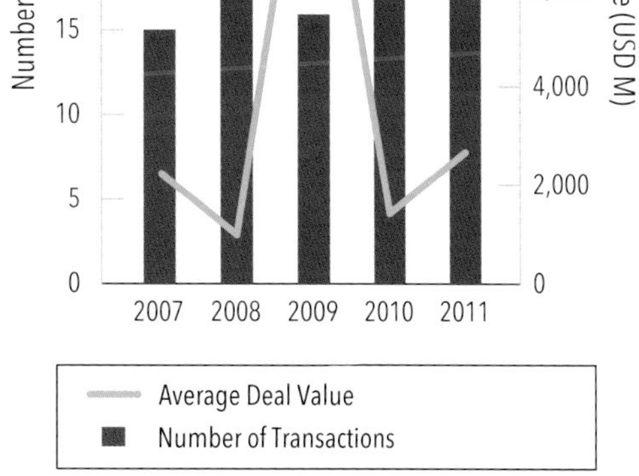

Average Deal Value

Number of Transactions

Source: Burrill & Company, Windhover

9

and what Genzyme believed it was worth. After seven months of wrangling, Sanofi raised its initial $18.5 billion, or $69 per share, offer for the company to $20.1 billion, or $74 a share, and ended the dispute over the value of the company by sweetening the deal with contingent value rights worth up to $3.8 billion, or up to an additional $14 per right, should Genzyme meet set milestones. The final price represented a 48 percent premium to Genzyme's shares when reports first surfaced that Sanofi was preparing to make an offer for the company. The agreement makes it the second largest acquisition of a biotech ever behind Roche's purchase of Genentech. The rights are publicly traded and will terminate on December 31, 2020 or earlier if the last sales milestone has been achieved. All but $1 of each right's value is tied to the multiple sclerosis drug Lemtrada. So far, the contingent value rights have proved to be of little value to shareholders. Trading in the contingent value rights closed the year at $1.17, a reflection of Wall Street's uncertainty of their value.

For Sanofi, Genzyme is positioned to play a critical role in the company's reinvention of its approach to research and development with a greater reliance on external research partners.

> **For Sanofi, Genzyme is positioned to play a critical role in the company's reinvention of its approach to research and development with a greater reliance on external research partners.**

Genzyme not only provides Sanofi with a portfolio of rare disease products and expertise in biologics, but a strong physical presence in one of the world's leading research hubs. While announcing Sanofi's 2011 results, Viehbacher discussed the company's decision to reorganize its research and development operations in the United States with Genzyme as its principal source of research in the country. "I think Cambridge is one of the most promising areas in the world today to do research and development," he

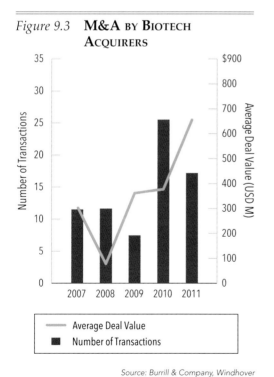

*Figure 9.3* **M&A BY BIOTECH ACQUIRERS**

Source: Burrill & Company, Windhover

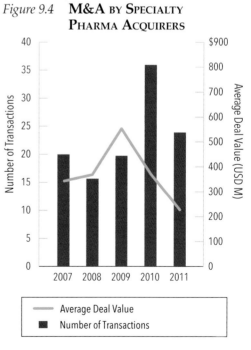

*Figure 9.4* **M&A BY SPECIALTY PHARMA ACQUIRERS**

Source: Burrill & Company, Windhover

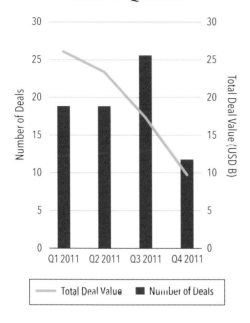

*Figure 9.5* THERAPEUTICS M&A DEAL VALUES BY QUARTER

Source: Burrill & Company, Windhover, S&P Capital IQ

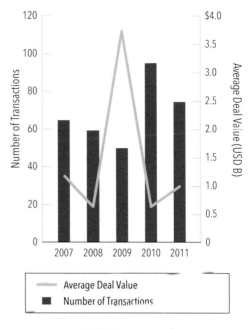

*Figure 9.6* THERAPEUTICS M&A IN 2011

Source: Burrill & Company, Windhover, S&P Capital IQ

said. "And with the acquisition of Genzyme, but also past acquisition of Campath, the creation of our oncology research and development, we are now the number one life sciences player in this very promising area."

### Targeting innovation

Overall, global M&A activity in the life sciences reached $159.7 billion in 2011, up 7.5 percent from $148.6 billion the previous year. Activity focused on U.S.-based targets climbed more dramatically than global activity overall, reaching a total of $95.2 billion in 2011, a 32.5 percent increase from $71.9 billion .

The number of therapeutics deals in 2011 was evenly divided between the first half of 2011 and the second half, but deal values fell steadily quarter-to-quarter throughout the year [*SEE FIGURE 9.5*]. Of the total $76.3 billion in transactions for these companies, nearly 65 percent was realized in the first half, and just 13 percent realized in the final quarter. The drop in total values reflected the sharp drop in market values of potential target companies triggered by the fight over the debt ceiling in the United States and the European debt crisis.

Overall, therapeutics deal volume fell to

76 deals in 2011, down from 97 in the previous year, but average deals values climbed to a little more than $1 billion [*SEE FIGURE 9.6*]. The 2011 average was buoyed by the acquisitions of Genzyme ($20.1 billion), **Nycomed** ($13.7 billion), and **Pharmasset** ($11 billion). M&A activity in all other value ranges fell from the previous year. North America was the source of half the acquirers and a little more than half the targets for the year, the lowest it's been for North American targets and acquirers during the past five years. It reflects the shift in activity from North America, Europe, and Japan, to emerging markets, which drove the rest-of-world category up to 17 percent of the total as an acquirer and 18.5 percent as a target, the highest level it's been over the past five years [*SEE FIGURE 9.9*].

The push for innovation drove M&A activity into development stage companies as large pharmaceutical and biotech companies sought to replenish their pipelines with promising drug candidates. M&A deal activity declined for companies with marketed products or only preclinical drug candidates compared to activity in 2010 [*SEE FIGURE 9.11*]. But companies that had clinical stage candidates were increasingly sought as acquisition targets. In fact, 37

# European M&A Up on Two Outsized Deals

## Activity seen in partnerships for drug discovery platforms

**E**uropean life science companies were still in demand in 2011, the target of 63 acquisitions by mostly U.S. and Japanese drugmakers. Although total deal values surged 141 percent over 2010 numbers, they were skewed by two outsized acquisitions that were valued in excess of $10 billion—both of which took place in May before the European debt crisis got out of hand and the euro was still fairly strong versus other currencies [*See Figure 9.8*].

Johnson & Johnson's $21.6 billion acquisition of Swiss orthopedic medical device maker **Synthes** and **Takeda Pharmaceuticals'** $13.7 billion buy of Swiss biopharma **Nycomed** accounted for 70 percent of the total dollar volume of transactions involving a European target. When these two deals are taken out of the mix, total deal values fell 28 percent compared to 2010, even as the number of deals rose by 13 percent, and resulted in a 32 percent drop in average deal value year-over-year.

Few of the larger deals were for biopharmaceutical innovators outside of two deals focused on central nervous system therapeutics. **Alkermes'** $960 million acquisition of **Elan Drug Technologies** gave it resources to back the development of its CNS drugs, and **Jazz Pharmaceuticals'** $525 million acquisition of Ireland-based Azur Pharma added to its pipeline of CNS drugs.

> ### When these two deals are taken out of the mix, total deal values fell 28 percent compared to 2010.

**Thermo Fisher Scientific** acquired Swedish diagnostics firm **Phadia** for $3.5 billion but most of the rest of the large deals were diversification plays for generics, over-the-counter drugs, and medical devices. Takeda's purchase of Nycomed was driven by its desire to access emerging markets, where Nycomed already had an established presence and where it got almost half its revenue.

**Sanofi's** purchase of U.S. biopharma **Genzyme** for $20.1 billion plus contingent value rights was the largest outbound deal of the year. Again, if this one deal is taken out of the numbers, European acquirers kept their money in-house, as total M&A values fell 64 percent from 2010 when there were several billion dollar deals by European drugmakers, including **Merck KGaA's** $7.2 billion acquisition of **Millipore**, Grifols' $3.4 billion deal for **Talecris Biotherapeutics**, and **Covidien's** $2.6 billion purchase of medical device maker **EV3**.

Dublin-based **Shire's** $750 million purchase of U.S. wound care specialist **Advanced BioHealing** in May 2011 on the eve of its IPO was one of a handful of acquisitions of innovators by European drugmakers during the year. Indeed, M&A activity stalled during the second half of the year as the European Union wrangled with resolving mounting debt among its members. Excluding the three outsized deals in the first half of the year, the second half of 2011 accounted for only a fifth of deals for European targets.

## Partnering focused on discovery platforms

Although total partnering deal values rose slightly in 2011, the number of deals involving European assets declined 4 percent. Most of the activity was centered on drug discovery research collaborations with Big Pharma that include licensing of compounds coming out of the collaboration. There were 10 such collaborations out of the 28 deals for European assets with disclosed deal values above $50 million [*See Figure 9.7*]. These deals usually involve risk-sharing, with small up-front licensing fees and milestones contingent both on the development of molecules and also on sales targets being met. The total deal value, therefore, is not a real reflection of the money coming to the licenser as few compounds ever reach commercialization.

Still these partnering deals are crucial for validating the biotech's platform technology and provide valuable capital for the development of its own pipeline. Swiss biotech **Molecular Partners** entered

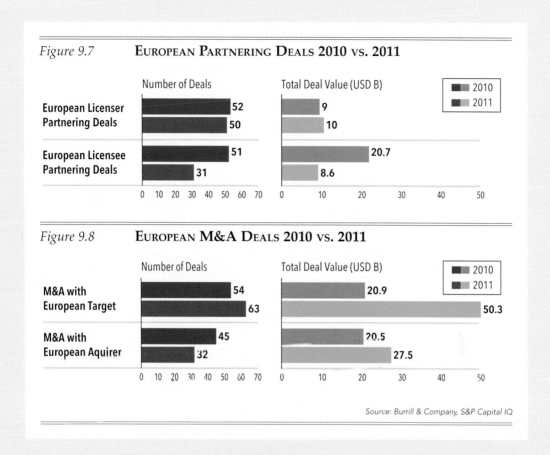

Figure 9.7    EUROPEAN PARTNERING DEALS 2010 VS. 2011

Figure 9.8    EUROPEAN M&A DEALS 2010 VS. 2011

Source: Burrill & Company, S&P Capital IQ

into such an agreement in December with **Janssen Biotech**, a division of Johnson & Johnson, worth up to $800 million. An expansion of a previous agreement, the companies will work together using Molecular Partners' DARPins technology to explore a set of targets in diseases where there are still no effective treatment options. Janssen has the option to exclusive license DARPin products generated from the research at which point it will take over development and commercialization activities. Molecular Partners retained the option to co-develop one product on a global basis.

There was a significant drop in European companies' in-licensing assets from outside the continent, predominantly from the United States. Deal values fell 58 percent in 2011 compared to 2010 with the number of deals dropping 39 percent and the average deal value down 33 percent. The biggest deal was Danish pharma **Lundbeck's** long-term agreement with Japanese pharmaceutical **Otsuka** for the global development and commercialization of up to five early- and late-stage compounds for the treatment of central nervous system disorders. The assets include two late-stage compounds from Otsuka, OPC-34712 and a depot formulation of aripiprazole, better known as Abilify. It is Otsuka's top-selling CNS drug in collaboration with **Bristol-Myers Squibb** with net sales in fiscal year 2010 of approximately $4.5 billion. The depot formulation is currently in late-stage trials in the United States as a once-monthly injection maintenance treatment for schizophrenia. Lundbeck paid Otsuka $200 million upfront and up to $1.6 billion in milestones. Both companies will share in the global sales, development and commercialization costs. The deal expands Lunbeck's presence in Asia and North America and Otsuka's presence in Europe.

Again, as in-inbound partnering, seven out of the 17 deals valued at more than $100 million focused on drug discovery or preclinical assets as the big European drugmakers looked to beef up their pipelines with outside innovation. Among the deals, **GlaxoSmithKline** paid U.S. biotech **Epizyme** $20 million upfront to use its platform focused on finding drugs that inhibit histone methyltransferases, epigenetic enzymes that regulate gene expression. The total deal value could be as much as $630 million. ■

*Figure 9.9*  THERAPEUTIC **M&A** IN **2011** BY ACQUIRER REGION AND TARGET REGION

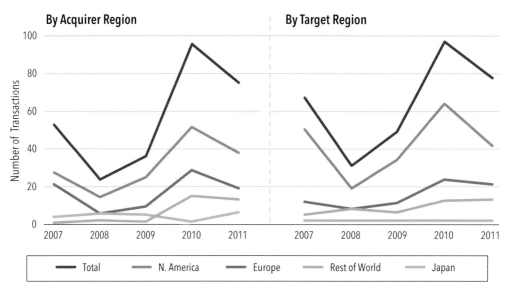

Source: Burrill & Company, Windhover, S&P Capital IQ

percent of transactions were for clinical stage companies, up from about 8 percent in 2010. Acquisitions for companies with marketed products fell to 58 percent compared to 86 percent the previous year.

The hunt to acquire innovative products in many ways shaped the year in M&A. Even generic drug powerhouse **Teva Pharmaceuticals** got in on the action when in October 2011 it completed the acquisition of **Cephalon** for $6.8 billion. Teva beat back a hostile offer for Cephalon from **Valeant Pharmaceuticals** by offering a 39 percent premium to Cephalon's stock price on March 29, 2011, the day before Valeant made its unsolicited bid. The acquisition fits into Teva's long-term strategy to grow its global generics business and transform and diversify its branded business. The deal is a game-changer

*Figure 9.10*  **M&A** DEALS BY VALUE RANGE **2007** TO **2011**

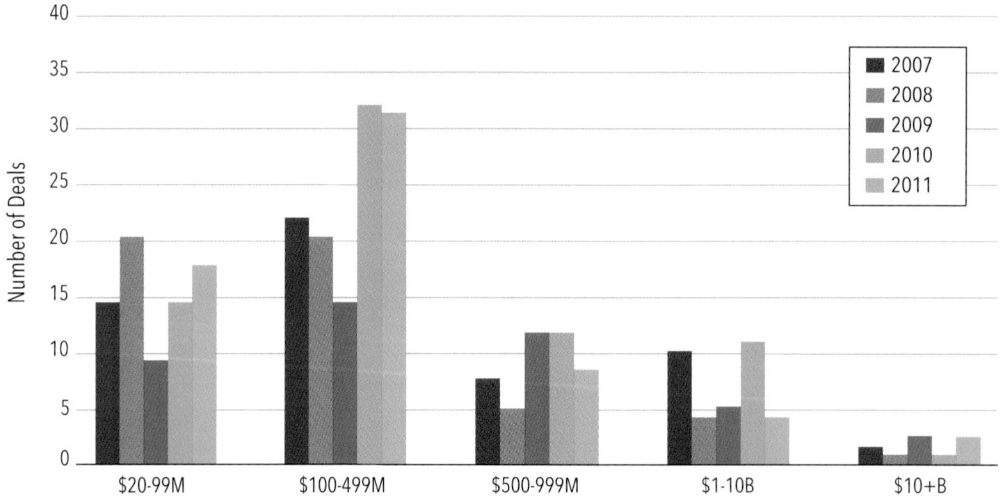

Source: Burrill & Company, Windhover

*Figure 9.11*    **M&A Deals by Latest Stage of Product Development 2007 to 2011**

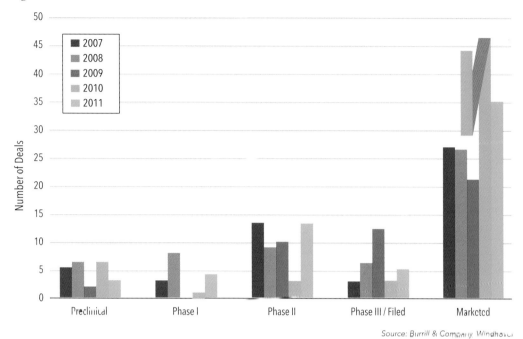

Source: Burrill & Company, Windhover

for the Israeli drug company, according to its CEO Shlomo Yanai, making it not only the world's largest generic drug company, but also one of the world's largest specialty pharmaceutical companies. With the purchase of Cephalon, Teva acquired a brand company with a generics component—**Mepha**, which has a strong presence in Switzerland, Eastern Europe, Africa, and Latin America. Teva had bought German generics firm **Ratiopharm** in 2010 for $4.9 billion to expand its European presence.

The Cephalon deal also helps Teva diversify its revenue stream, lessening its dependence on Copaxone, the multiple sclerosis drug that contributes 70 percent of its branded drug revenues. Cephalon's CNS and respiratory pipeline strengthens Teva's position and expands its foothold in these areas, and Cephalon's pain management and oncology business, where Teva has no established commercial franchise, expands its portfolio in these areas. Teva CFO Eyal Desheh, speaking at the **JPMorgan Healthcare Conference** in January 2012, said Teva expects revenues of about $22 billion in 2012 with generics generating about 55 percent of that, branded products 37 percent, and the balance coming from over-the-counter products. With the Cephalon acquisition, Teva actually will sell more branded

products in the United States than generics. "Teva is changing," Desheh said, according to a *SeekingAlpha* transcript. "It's changing rapidly and is going according to its strategic roadmap regarding execution and managing in a complex environment."

### The race for the new

The competition in the area of new hepatitis C drugs showed the willingness of companies to pay big premiums to access innovation. With an estimated 160 million to 180 million people infected with hepatitis C worldwide, rivalry to develop a market-leading treatment is fierce. Both Merck's Victrelis and **Vertex's** Incivek won approval as new hepatitis C therapies in 2011. These are new approaches that shorten the course of treatment and improve outcomes, but neither offer daily single dose regimens. As with HIV, the expectation is that the future of hepatitis C therapies will rely on cocktails of drugs. "It is increasingly clear that the future treatment landscape for HCV will be defined by regimens of oral antivirals that are safe and well-tolerated, simpler to use, and offer the best rate of cure for the largest segment of patients," says John Martin, chairman and CEO of Gilead, which is based in Foster City, California.

**Gilead Sciences**, already developing a pipeline

## Figure 9.12 M&A Deal Values by Primary Therapeutic Category

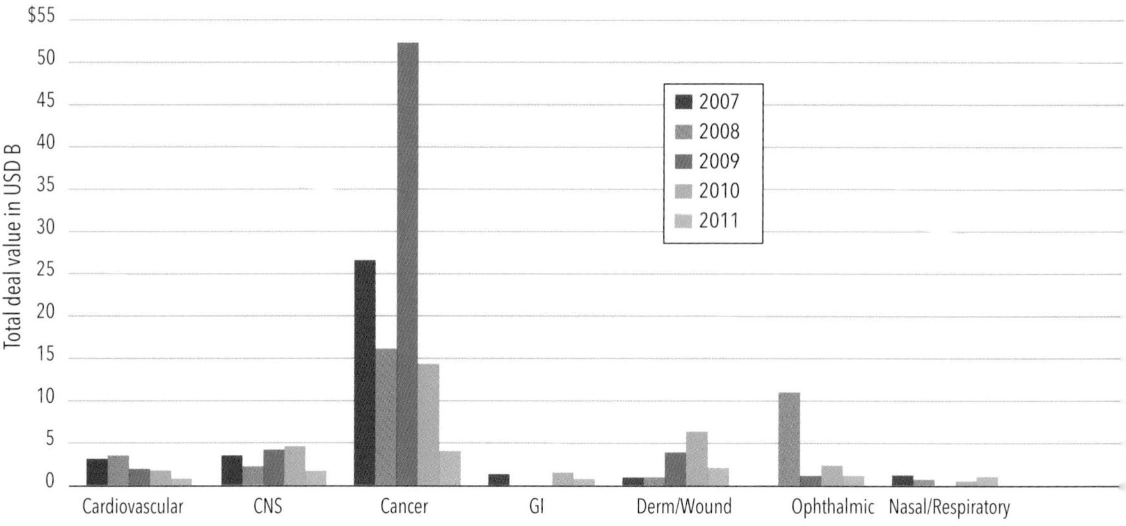

of hepatitis C drugs, acquired the clinical-stage hepatitis C drug developer **Pharmasset** for $11 billion in November 2011, an 89 percent premium over the close of the company's shares the day prior to the announcement. The deal alone explains the big jump in M&A activity around infectious disease therapies [*SEE FIGURE 9.12*]. The acquisition reflects Gilead's intensifying efforts to become the leading supplier of next-generation drugs to combat the virus. Having already built its success in HIV therapeutics, Gilead now sees an opportunity to parallel that victory with hepatitis C. Gilead estimates that more than 12 million people are infected with HCV in major markets, but fewer than 200,000 people are treated each year. Many people don't even know they're infected with the virus, exposing them to potential liver scarring or liver cancer.

"The acquisition of Pharmasset represents an important and exciting opportunity to accelerate Gilead's effort to change the treatment paradigm for HCV-infected patients by developing all-oral regimens for the treatment of the disease regardless of viral genotype," Martin says. Pharmasset

> Gilead estimates that more than 12 million people are infected with hepatitis C in major markets, but fewer than 200,000 people are treated each year.

shareholders received a cash payment of $137 per share for the company in the first quarter of 2012 when the deal closed. **Burrill & Company**, publisher of this book, was an investor in Pharmasset.

Gilead already has seven candidate molecules for the treatment of hepatitis C in various stages of development. One or several of those compounds could eventually be marketed as part of an all-oral treatment regimen, allowing patients to skip injections of pegylated interferon, which with ribavirin is currently part of the standard of care treatment for patients with chronic hepatitis C. The company sees the addition of Pharmasset's portfolio as an opportunity to accelerate progress toward the goal of an all-oral, once-daily dosing regimen.

Bristol-Myers Squibb also jumped into the fray at the start of 2012 with the announcement that it would pay $2.5 billion to buy **Inhibitex** and its lead drug INX-189, an experimental hepatitis C therapy in mid-stage trials. The acquisition, valued at $26 per share, offered a 150 percent premium to Inhibitex's pre-announcement mar-

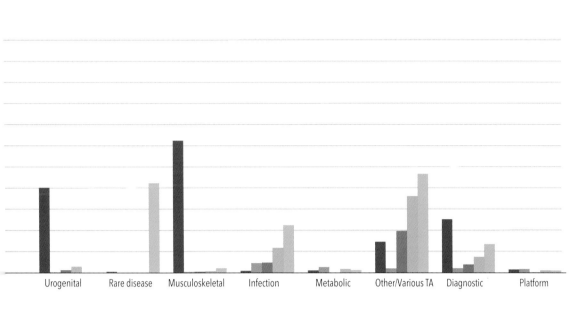

| Urogenital | Rare disease | Musculoskeletal | Infection | Metabolic | Other/Various TA | Diagnostic | Platform |

Source: Burrill & Company, S&P Capital IQ, Windhover

ket close. Commenting on both the Pharmasset and Inhibitex deals, incoming Vertex CEO Jeffrey Leiden told attendees of the annual JPMorgan Healthcare Conference in January 2012 that "these deals tell us there's a lot of demand and need in hepatitis C."

The demand has been for the new breed of hepatitis C nucleotides. It is in this new class of nucleotide inhibitor drugs that BMS is hoping to make a mark. INX-189 does not have to be used in combination with an injection that causes side effects for patients. Both Vertex's and Merck's hepatitis C drugs, which are oral protease inhibitors, are used in tandem with an interferon injection. "This transaction puts INX-189 and the company's other infectious disease assets in the hands of an organization that can more optimally develop them," says Russell Plumb, CEO of Inhibitex. "Bristol-Myers Squibb's expertise in antiviral drug development, and its existing complementary portfolio, will assure that the potential of INX-189 is realized."

The richest premium in a hepatitis C deal, though, came from Roche when in October 2011 it agreed to acquire **Anadys Pharmaceuticals**, a San Diego-based developer of small molecule therapeutics for the treatment of hepatitis C, for $230 million in cash, or $3.70 per share, a 256 percent premium to its closing price of $1.04 per share before the deal was announced. Anadys is another biotech that has struggled to develop its candidates.

The deals boosts Roche's pipeline with two hepatitis C candidates that could bring the pharma closer to a cure for the viral infection, or at least closer to an interferon-free treatment regimen. Setrobuvir, Anadys' most advanced drug candidate, is an oral drug in mid-stage clinical testing in combination with Roche's injectable pegylated interferon, Pegasys, and its brand of ribavirin, Copegus. The company is also developing ANA773, an oral, small-molecule inducer of innate immunity. That compound was in early-stage trials at the time of the announcement and may prove useful for treating hepatitis C as well as other chronic infections and cancer.

A new era of interferon-free hepatitis therapies creates both a short-term threat and a long-term opportunity for Roche. In 2010, the company made $1.8 billion (CHF 1.6 billion) from sales of Pegasys. But Pegasys loses patent protection in 2017 and a new wave of oral hepatitis therapies is likely to become the new standard of care by then, sparing patients from interferon's flu-like side effects and delivery method by injection.

Roche has been active in seeking to develop and promote new therapeutic combinations incorporating its own products. In May 2011, it agreed to help Merck promote its new hepatitis C therapy, Victrelis, which is taken with both a

M&A AND PARTNERING

9

230

## Figure 9.13 MEDIAN M&A PREMIUMS BY TARGET TYPE 2007-2011

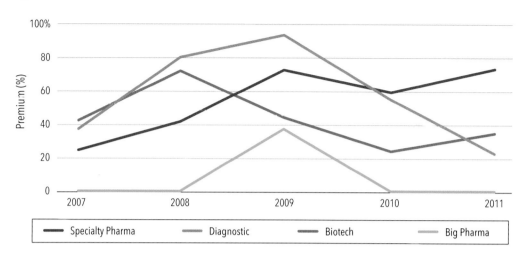

Source: Burrill & Company, S&P Capital IQ, Windhover

pegylated interferon and ribavirin, such as those in Roche's portfolio.

### A preferred exit

Overall, median premiums for biotech M&A targets rose in 2011 to 34 percent, up from 25 percent the previous year, but down from levels in 2007 to 2009 [*SEE FIGURE 9.13*]. M&A transactions of private companies in each of the past five years have outnumbered the M&A transactions where public companies were targets [*SEE FIGURE 9.14*]. Nevertheless, the percent of deals involving private targets was near its lowest level over the past five years with just 54 percent of transactions involving private targets.

M&A has become the preferred exit strategy for privately-held companies as the market for initial public offerings in recent years was at first effectively shut down by the global recession

and continues to be muted [*SEE FIGURE 9.15*]. About half of the life sciences companies that went public in 2011 had to significantly cut their expectations, selling their shares below the target price and selling more shares than originally anticipated to raise adequate capital. Some fund managers have complained that the most attractive companies too often are snapped up by Big Pharma before ever going public.

Consider **Advanced BioHealing**, maker of Dermagraft, an artificial skin made from living cells that is used to treat diabetic foot ulcers. The day before its initial public offering was to be consummated, **Shire** stepped in and nabbed the company for $750 million. The company was expected to price at the mid-range of its $14 to $16 target, which would have valued it at a market cap of $732 million. Stephen Bloch, a general partner at Canaan Partners, which held more

## Figure 9.14 PUBLIC VS. PRIVATE M&A TARGETS 2007 TO 2011

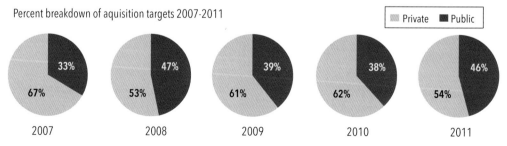

Percent breakdown of aquisition targets 2007-2011

Source: Burrill & Company, Windhover

*Figure 9.15* **A SHIFT TO M&A EXITS 1990 TO 2011**

Source: Thomson Reuters and the National Venture Capital Association

than a quarter of Advanced BioHealing's shares and a director of Advanced BioHealing at the time, told *The New York Times* that the regulatory complications of being a public company and the opportunity for Canaan to get a faster return helped push the decision in favor of the acquisition. *Bloomberg* noted that the Shire acquisition price came at 5.1 times Advanced BioHealing's previous year sales. That compared to a median price for medical products acquisitions of $500 million or more in the past five year's of three times prior year's sales.

Other notable acquisitions of privately held companies included **Amgen's** potential $1 billion purchase of **BioVex** and **Daiichi Sankyo's** potential $935 million acquisition of **Plexxikon**. The deal for Plexxikon, made when its lead asset Zelboraf was still a late-stage clinical candidate for malignant melanoma, included $805 million in upfront cash and $130 million more based on near-term launch milestones.

**Kathleen Sereda Glaub**
*President*
*Plexxikon*

The acquisition of the Berkeley, California-based company was in line with Daiichi Sankyo's strategy to address diverse unmet medical needs, including personalizing medicine to maximize patient benefits. Zelboraf was approved in conjunction with a companion diagnostic to identify patients expressing the BRAF mutation, the population most likely to benefit from the drug.

Less than two months before it was acquired, Plexxikon had agreed to co-promote then experimental PLX4032 in the United States with Roche's U.S. oncology division Genentech. Daiichi Sankyo is retaining the U.S. co-promotion rights following the acquisition. "This deal made a lot of sense to Daiichi," Kathleen Sereda Glaub, Plexxikon's president, told *Bloomberg* in an interview, noting that the ability to co-market PLX4032 "presented them with a near-term opportunity to jump-start what they wanted to do in oncology."

Besides PLX4032, Daiichi Sankyo will get a pipeline of oncology compounds and a scaffold-based drug discovery platform. Plexxikon will operate as a stand-alone unit of Daiichi Sankyo, and all its employees have been asked to stay.

The deal for BioVex, the creator of a late-stage cancer vaccine that has shown encouraging results in treating solid tumors, included $425 million in cash upfront and up to $575 million in additional payments upon the achievement of certain regulatory and sales milestones. The Woburn, Massachusetts company was already running late-stage pivotal trials to evaluate use of the experimental vaccine, called OncoVex, for the treatment of melanoma and head and neck cancer.

About 650,000 people are diagnosed with squamous cell head and neck cancer each year

M&A AND PARTNERING

9

worldwide, and around 350,000 die from the disease annually, according to BioVex. Melanoma was expected to kill about 8,700 people in the United States during 2010, according to the **American Cancer Society**.

Successful therapeutic cancer vaccines have proven difficult to develop, but have gained new attention following the approval of **Dendreon's** Provenge for the treatment of men with advanced prostate cancer. Such vaccines enlist the body's own immune defenses to selectively destroy cancer cells. OncoVex has already demonstrated encouraging anti-tumor activity in clinical studies for the treatment of melanoma and head and neck cancer, says Amgen's Perlmutter. "Amgen is ideally positioned to leverage the potential of OncoVex in multiple solid tumor indications given their impressive oncology franchise and expertise in biologics manufacturing and development," says BioVex CEO Philip Astley-Sparke.

### Demand for cancer drugs continues

Daiichi Sankyo's acquisition of Plexxikon follows other Japanese pharma moves into the oncology market, including **Astellas'** acquisition of **OSI Pharmaceuticals** in May 2010 and the recent acquisition of U.K. cancer drugmaker **Pro Strakan Group** by **Kyowa Hakka Kirin** for $474 million. Cancer drug sales are forecast to grow 12 to 15 percent annually, according to **IMS Health**. In addition, the strong yen versus the dollar before the Japanese tsunami in March 2011, made U.S. acquisitions attractive for Japanese pharmaceutical companies seeking growth outside their home-base where sales were forecast to grow at an anemic 1 to 1.4 percent, according to **Datamonitor**.

### A big deal for a private company

Takeda Pharmaceutical's acquisition of Swiss pharmaceutical Nycomed from its private equity owners was the largest deal for a privately-held company in 2011. The all cash deal, announced in May 2011, was valued at $13.7 billion (€9.6 billion), inclusive of Nycomed's debt. It is in line with Takeda's sustainable growth strategy, designed to offset declining sales in Japan and boost revenue before the patent expiry of its best-selling diabetes drug, Actos, which accounted for 27 percent of the company's 2010 revenue.

The Nycomed buy expands Takeda's global

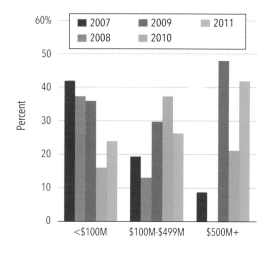

*Figure 9.16* **M&A Transactions with Milestones by Deal Size Range 2007 to 2011**

*Source: Burrill & Company, S&P Capital IQ, Windhover*

reach beyond Japan and the United States, where it currently gets about 85 percent of its revenue, to Europe and fast-growing emerging markets, which together made up 83 percent of Nycomed's 2010 revenue of $4.5 billion (€3.2 billion). Emerging markets account for more than half of Nycomed's global pharmaceutical growth. It has an established presence in Brazil and Russia and recently acquired a major stake in China's **Guangdong Techpool Bio-Pharma**.

The Swiss drugmaker's portfolio includes both established prescription pharmaceuticals as the primary growth driver, and over-the-counter products. Takeda expects major revenue growth to come from Nycomed's roflumilast, a recently approved first-in-class treatment for chronic obstructive pulmonary disease. Nycomed's U.S. dermatology unit is not included in the deal and will become an independent business owned primarily by its current private equity owners following Takeda's takeover.

### Sharing risks

In many cases, power at the negotiating table rested with acquirers as investors' risk-aversion in the current environment made it difficult for many life sciences companies to reliably access capital on attractive terms. Smaller life sciences companies, often without the luxury of lots of choices to fund the continued development of

# J&J Spends Big on Medical Device Maker

## With acquisition of Synthes, Big Pharma looks toward aging population

**J**ohnson & Johnson's $21.6 billion acquisition of Swiss orthopedic device maker **Synthes** reflected drug firms' positioning to address an aging customer base. Synthes is the leading maker of screws, plates, and other tools used to mend broken bones and address traumatic injuries. J&J's deal to buy Synthes in a cash and stock transaction, will give the healthcare conglomerate a dominant share of the market in orthopedic devices, a growing market estimated to encompass $37 billion in annual sales.

The acquisition was the largest purchase of a medical device maker in 2011. In fact, it was one of only seven deals in excess of $1 billion. For deals with disclosed terms, the overwhelming number of deals in the space—72 out of 100—were for less than $100 million [See Figure 9.17]. Nevertheless, the acquisition of Synthes pushed acquisition values for medical device companies in 2011 to an average of $540 million from $458 million the previous year. The number of deals, though, fell to 101 from 121 in 2010 and the total value of all medical device M&A transactions fell to $54.5 billion in 2011 from $55.4 billion the year before [See Figure 9.18].

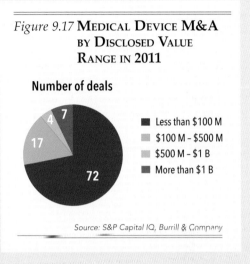

*Figure 9.17* **Medical Device M&A by Disclosed Value Range in 2011**

**Number of deals**

- Less than $100 M — 72
- $100 M – $500 M — 17
- $500 M – $1 B — 4
- More than $1 B — 7

*Source: S&P Capital IQ, Burrill & Company*

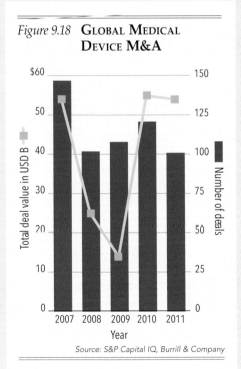

*Figure 9.18* **Global Medical Device M&A**

*Source: S&P Capital IQ, Burrill & Company*

In the case of the J&J acquisition, Synthes provides the company with new R&D capabilities and a global footprint, according to J&J's CEO Bill Weldon. Besides growing demands in emerging markets and a trend toward earlier intervention, J&J will be in a position to better address the desire of an aging customer base to remain active despite increasing rates of obesity and its resulting impact on joint disease.

J&J will integrate Synthes with its **DePuy** subsidiary, gaining 50 percent of the market for sales of materials and tools for repairing skeletal injury.

The percentage of people over the age of 65 in the United States has grown to 12.8 percent by 2009, up from 8.1 percent in 1950, according to a Congressional report on the nation's changing demographics. By 2050, it is expected that one in five people in the United States will be aged 65 or older. With its new acquisition, J&J will be well-positioned to address the needs of this growing customer base. ■

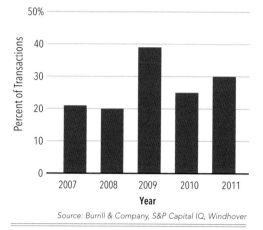

*Figure 9.19* **PERCENT OF M&A TRANSACTIONS WITH MILESTONES 2007 TO 2011**

Source: Burrill & Company, S&P Capital IQ, Windhover

their products, found acquirers unwilling to provide all cash offers, at least at rich enough prices. The result was that acquisitions often looked more like partnering deals in their structure with an upfront cash payment and performance-based milestone payments. While pharmaceutical companies may be anxious to get the novel therapeutics and technologies coming out of biotechs, they are increasingly unwilling to make the total payout upfront. Overall, acquisitions made through a combination of upfront and milestone payments had an average of 36 percent of their total value tied to milestones. Of 20 acquisitions for which companies disclosed both upfront and milestone payments, six had milestones in excess of the upfront value. Nevertheless, the deals may eventually provide handsome payouts—if the milestones are met. A total of 42 percent of the M&A transactions with total deal value of $500 million or more included a milestone payment, up from just 21 percent in 2010 [*SEE FIGURE 9.16, 9.19*].

Bristol-Myers Squibb said it would pay up to $475 million for **Amira Pharmaceuticals** to acquire its fibrosis program and its lead asset, AM152, that is ready for mid-stage trials for the treatment of idiopathic pulmonary fibrosis and scleroderma. Amira's investors will get $325 million upfront and potentially an additional $150 million in milestone payments. Based in San Diego, privately-held Amira is focused on the discovery and early development of small mol-

ecule drugs to treat inflammatory and fibrotic diseases. Besides AM152, BMS will also obtain Amira's preclinical autotaxin program, a potential treatment of neuropathic pain and cancer metastases. The drugmaker plans to retain Amira's researchers and its facilities in San Diego.

**Ventana Medical Systems**, a division of Swiss pharmaceutical Roche, said it would acquire German biotech **mtm Laboratories**, a developer of in vitro diagnostics with a focus on early detection and diagnosis of cervical cancer, the largest early detection market in oncology. Roche will pay $180 million (€130 million) upfront and up to $85 million (€60 million) based on performance-related milestones. mtm will be folded into Roche's Tissue Diagnostics business unit.

And **Allergan's** deal to acquire **Vicept Therapeutics** could be worth as much as $275 million, but Vicept's investors may have to wait a bit for all of it. Allergan is only paying $75 million upfront for the Pennsylvania-based dermatology company, with the remaining $200 million contingent upon achieving certain future development, regulatory, and sales milestones. Vicept's lead investigational product is a topical cream for the treatment of the redness associated with rosacea that has achieved positive results in two randomized, placebo-controlled mid-stage studies.

## Partnering to build an industry

Life sciences companies facing a difficult environment for fundraising in the United States are finding one cost-effective way to develop drugs is to get someone else to pay for it. Several transactions in 2011 show that by turning to partners in emerging markets, where governments are keen to develop a biopharmaceutical sector, companies can gain access to funding for development, while retaining rights to their products throughout most of the world.

Consider **Harbor BioSciences**, which in January 2011 granted Sinopharm subsidiary **China State Institute of Pharmaceutical Industry**, or **CIPI**, exclusive rights in China to three of its products in exchange for the Chinese government-owned pharmaceutical's agreement to develop them. The products are all metabolites or synthetic analogs of adrenal steroids that have been designed to restore the biological activity of cellular signaling pathways disrupted by disease and aging.

Under the agreement, Harbor retains the rights to the products outside China. CIPI will finance all of the product development in China to two mid-stage compounds and one pre-clinical compound for major indications including diabetes, cancer, inflammation and infectious diseases. Harbor will also receive milestone payments at the completion of specific stages of development, excluding infectious diseases, plus royalties on net sales of any commercialized product. A critical part of the agreement is that Harbor can use all of the pre-clinical and clinical data CIPI generates to seek marketing approval outside China. Harbor advances its products through development simultaneously without having to provide any financial support to do so.

By leveraging the needs in emerging markets, companies such as Harbor are obtaining access to non-dilutive financing, reducing development risk, and developing multiple compounds at once. For the emerging markets, these deals provide a means of building their economies, decreasing their dependence on drugs produced

> ## Life sciences companies facing a difficult environment for fundraising in the United States are finding one cost-effective way to develop drugs is to get someone else to pay for it.

outside their borders, increasing high-value skills and technical know-how, and addressing health needs of their populations.

Such agreements take on varying forms. **Rusnano**, Russia's government investment company, struck an agreement with **Cleveland BioLabs** in September 2011 to create a joint venture dubbed **Panacela Labs**, which will develop five preclinical drug candidates for cancer and infectious

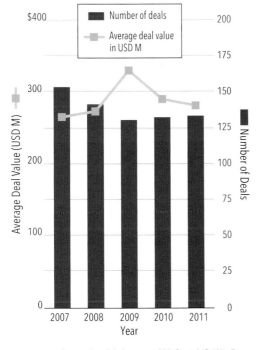

*Figure 9.20* **INDUSTRY-WIDE ALLIANCES: NUMBER AND AVERAGE DEAL VALUES 2007 TO 2011**

Source: Burrill & Company, S&P Capital IQ, Windhover

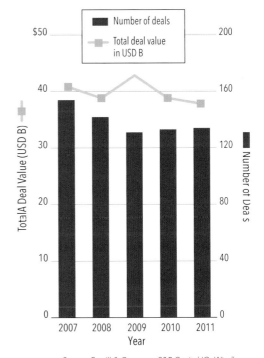

*Figure 9.21* **INDUSTRY-WIDE ALLIANCES: NUMBER AND TOTAL DEAL VALUES 2007 TO 2011**

Source: Burrill & Company, S&P Capital IQ, Windhover

*Figure 9.22* **PARTNERING DEALS BY TOTAL DEAL VALUE RANGE 2007-2011**

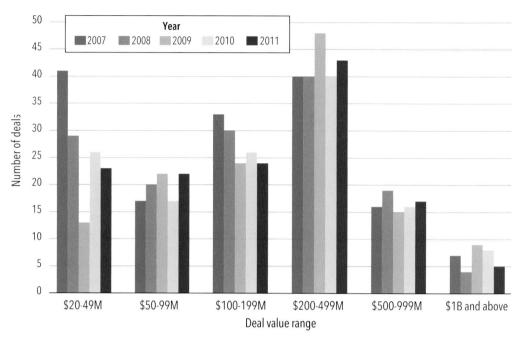

Source: Burrill & Company, S&P Capital IQ, Windhover

*Figure 9.23* **PARTNERING DEALS BY BIG PHARMA LICENSEE**

Includes all deals above $20M

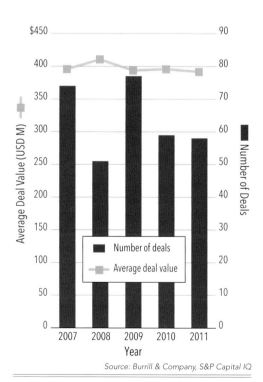

Source: Burrill & Company, S&P Capital IQ

disease for the Russian market.

Rusnano will invest up to $26 million over four years, with $9 million upfront and future investments based upon the achievement of development milestones and the attraction of new investments to the projects. While Rusnano will provide the majority of the funding, Cleveland BioLabs will contribute a $3 million initial investment and product candidates developed under the guidance of Andrei Gudkov, chief scientific officer of Cleveland BioLabs and a senior vice president of **Roswell Park Cancer Institute**, to Panacela Labs. The compounds will first be developed and approved in Russia. After the drugs are introduced into clinical practice there, Panacela intends to seek licensing and approval in other global markets, including the United States. Cleveland BioLabs will have an initial ownership of 55 percent of Panacela. Both Cleveland Biolabs and Rusnano will be granted warrants providing options to increase their investment at two and four years following initial investment.

The joint venture follows Cleveland BioLabs' strategy to create separate, independently funded entities to develop a broad pipeline of drug candidates. Cleveland BioLabs CEO Michael Fonstein says the agreement allows the company to move multiple drug candidates forward, with separate management teams focused on a smaller set of goals. For Rusnano, its investment in Panacela Labs provides Russia access to innovative therapeutics and global expertise, reflecting an ongoing effort by the Russian government to strengthen its pharmaceutical industry, which it sees as an important driver of economic growth.

In other cases, these agreements can take the form of more traditional looking partnering agreements. That's the case when Russia's **Maxwell Biotech Venture Fund** licensed Rockville, Maryland-based **Sequella's** lead experimental antibiotic for the treatment of tuberculosis. Maxwell, which is backed in part with investment from the Russian government, will fund a subsidiary called **Infectex**, a new biopharmaceutical company that will feature Sequella's compound as its flagship product alongside other assets Maxwell plans to bring in.

Tuberculosis is an epidemic in Russia, with infection rates more than three times what the

**World Health Organization** considers epidemic in some parts of the country, making TB control a top priority of the Russian government. Sequella's lead compound, SQ109, has been shown to be active against both drug-susceptible and drug-resistant TB bacteria in mid-stage efficacy trials in Africa. The Russian market for anti-tubercular drugs is more than $150 million per year, says Sequella, with total TB control costs estimated to be well over $1 billion.

For its investment, Maxwell gains rights to the drug in Russia and neighboring Commonwealth of Independent States countries, where it will assume responsibility for further clinical development and regulatory approval. For Sequella, the agreement provides a partner that can navigate the product through local regulatory agencies to get the drug registered and successfully commercialized. Sequella gets an equity investment, clinical supply purchase, and milestone payments worth up to $50 million, as well as royalties. And, the company retains rights to the drug in the United

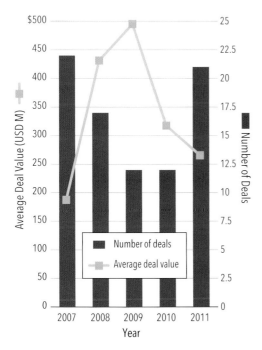

*Figure 9.24* **Partnering Deals by Biotech Licensee**

Includes all deals above $20M

*Source: Burrill & Company, S&P Capital IQ, Windhover*

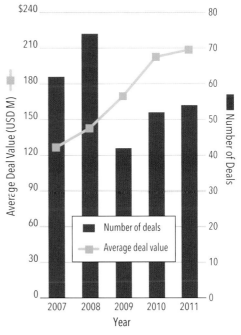

*Figure 9.25* **Partnering Deals by Specialty Pharma Licensee**

Includes all deals above $20M

*Source: Burrill & Company, S&P Capital IQ, Windhover*

States and the rest of the world.

Though such agreements may not seem all that groundbreaking relative to a long history of partnering deals, they show how companies can leverage an asset that they may be ill-prepared to commercialize in an emerging market, and use the needs in those countries to accelerate the development and cut the cost and risk of bringing those products to market in developed countries. How these deals ultimately turn out for both drug developers and the countries hoping to build out their own local industries remains to be seen, but given the current environment for funding and the hunger for innovative products in emerging markets, these agreements represent a reflection of what's likely to be many more deals to come.

## A push for discovery

One of the most dramatic changes to partnering activity in 2011 came in the rising interest for discovery deals and industry-academic alliances, a reflection of the growing pressure on an industry struggling with flagging R&D productivity to find innovative new products with less costs and risk. It represents a growing trend among large companies to look for promising product candidates outside of a company's own internal R&D operations. Overall, the number of disclosed partnering deals in excess of $20 million in 2011 was close to

the levels seen in 2010, with 134 deals announced worth a potential total of $37.8 billion [*SEE FIGURE 9.20, 9.21*]. That compares to 133 deals with a total value of $38.7 billion in 2010. Average deal values in 2011 fell to $282 million during the year, down from $291 million in 2010.

As a group, pharmaceutical companies made slightly fewer deals and spent less on partnering in 2011, but biotech increased its activity while specialty pharma increased its spending [*SEE FIGURE 9.23, 9.24, 9.25*]. In fact, as many pharmaceutical companies reorganized their R&D operations and reevaluated the therapeutic areas in which they would invest, they terminated existing partnerships that no longer filled their strategic focus [*SEE TABLE DEAL TERMINATIONS*]. In terms of total dollar volume, cancer led all other therapeutic areas for activity with $9.7 billion in deals, up from $6.3 billion in 2010. Metabolic disease rose to become the therapeutic category with the second greatest dollar total of activity, accounting for $7.4 billion in transactions from $6.5 billion the previous year. The total value of cardiovascular partnership deals fell for the third straight year to $1.4 billion, down from $3.6 billion from its peak in 2008 [*SEE FIGURE 9.26, 9.27*].

The sharpest increase in deal activity occurred in research-stage agreements with more than a three-fold increase to 33 deals in 2011, up from

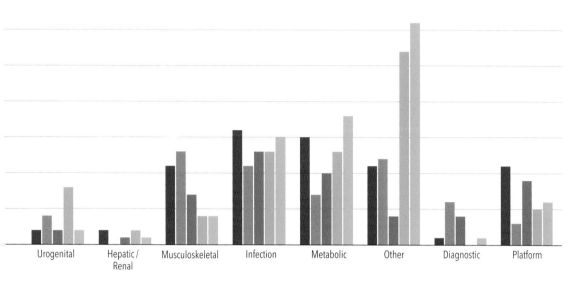

Urogenital    Hepatic /    Musculoskeletal    Infection    Metabolic    Other    Diagnostic    Platform
              Renal

Source: Burrill & Company, S&P Capital IQ

just 10 deals the previous year. The combined value of these deals reached $10.4 billion, up from $4.5 billion in 2010. Pre-clinical deal activity, the second most active area, also increased to 23 deals from 18 deals in 2010. It also represented the second highest total value as it reached $6.7 billion, compared to $5.6 billion in 2010 [*See* Figure 9.28]. Deal activity among mid-stage and late-stage products were the only areas that saw a decline in 2011. Mid-stage deal activity fell more than 60 percent as the number of transactions fell to just 15 in 2011 from 35 the previous year. Mid-stage deals, however, commanded the highest average value at $379 million, up from $316 million in 2010. Average deal values were down in every category other than early-stage and mid-stage [*See* Figure 9.29, 9.30, 9.33].

Pfizer is employing more of a shared-risk tactic—partnering instead of acquiring as it seeks new drugs to fill its portfolio. During January 2011, Pfizer entered into four discovery deals with biotechs and signed on seven research institutions as partners in its **Centers for Therapeutic Innovation**.

The Big Pharma also entered into several drug discovery collaborations with biotechs. Pfizer first expanded its discovery-stage global strategic alliance with Danish biotech **Santaris Pharma**, a partnership focused on the development and commercialization of RNA-targeted medicines using Santaris' locked nucleic acid drug platform. Pfizer will pay $14 million for access to the technology to develop RNA-targeted drugs. Santaris will be eligible to receive up to $600 million in milestone payments as well as royalties on sales of products that may be developed for up to ten new RNA targets selected by Pfizer.

Then, Pfizer struck a discovery-stage deal with **Seattle Genetics** for an upfront fee of $8 million for rights to utilize Seattle Genetics' antibody-drug conjugate technology with antibodies to a single oncology target. Pfizer will be responsible for research, product development, manufacturing and commercialization of any ADC

> (There is) a growing trend among large companies to look for promising product candidates outside of a company's own internal R&D operations.

M&A AND PARTNERING

9

*Figure 9.27* **Partnering Deal Values 2007 to 2011 for Selected Therapeutic Categories**

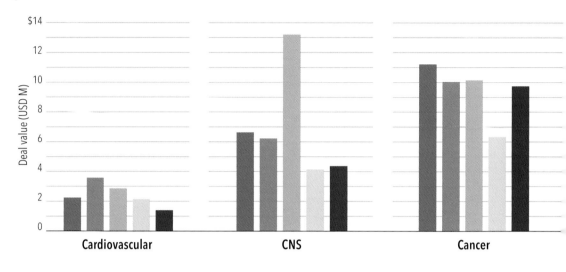

products under the collaboration. Seattle Genetics will be eligible to receive more than $200 million in progress-dependent milestones as well as royalties on worldwide net sales of any resulting ADC products.

In another discovery deal, Pfizer agreed to pay **Theraclone Sciences** as much as $632 million in milestones during the course of a multi-year partnership in which the pair hope to find promising monoclonal antibodies to battle infectious disease and cancer. Pfizer will use Theraclone's I-STAR technology to screen and identify natural human antibodies and find those with exceptional biologic activity against two infectious disease targets and two cancer targets. Pfizer will receive an exclusive worldwide license to any therapeutic antibodies discovered under the collaboration. Theraclone is eligible to receive undisclosed royalties on sales of any developed products and up to $632 million in research funding and milestone payments. Pfizer will be responsible for preclinical and clinical development of the antibodies.

### Back to school

Belt-tightening forced internal research and development cutbacks at many of the world's biggest drugmakers in 2011 even though demand for innovative ideas to fill product pipelines remains. To meet the demand for promising new drug candidates, diagnostics, and devices while simultaneously keeping costs in check,

healthcare companies, led by pharmaceuticals, have increasingly turned to academic centers for fresh fodder [*See Figure 1.6 in Chapter 1*]. Pharmaceutical companies see the formation of new alliances as a way to access commercially viable ideas early, bridging the gap between lab bench and patients. At the same time, academic centers view these agreements as a way to build stature and tap new sources of research revenue as well as the potential for license agreements.

In January 2011 seven major research-based medical centers in New York City had joined Pfizer's Centers for Therapeutic Innovation, a network of partnerships that aims to speed the translation of biomedical research into life-saving medicines. The effort is meant to leverage Pfizer's investment in discovery and early-stage drug development by funding preclinical and clinical development at leading centers.

They followed an agreement announced in November 2010 between Pfizer and the University of California, San Francisco that established the first of these centers for Pfizer. In exchange for providing funding for translational research, Pfizer offers what the company described as "equitable" intellectual property and ownership rights to support continued experimentation and exploration, as well as broad rights to publication.

Participating in the newly forged agreements are **Rockefeller University, New York University's Langone Medical Center, Memorial Sloan-**

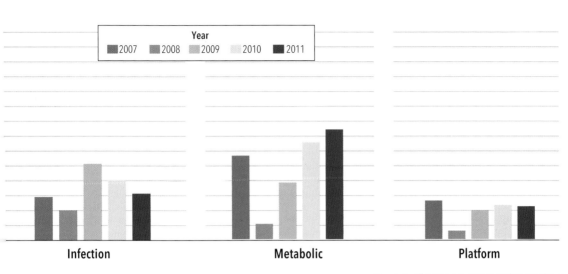

**Year**
■ 2007  ■ 2008  ■ 2009  ■ 2010  ■ 2011

| Infection | Metabolic | Platform |

*Source: Burrill & Company, S&P Capital IQ, Windhover*

Kettering Cancer Center, The Mount Sinai Medical Center, Columbia University Medical Center, Albert Einstein College of Medicine of Yeshiva University and **Weill Cornell Medical College**. Pfizer has leased research space at the **Alexandria Center for Life Sciences** in New York City to facilitate the collaborations. Investigators working with Pfizer will have access to the company's proprietary antibody libraries and advanced research tools along with technical support. Successful programs that advance to commercialization by Pfizer will be subject to license terms that will include milestone payments and royalties.

**Children's Hospital Boston** is also a participant in Pfizer's **Centers for Therapeutic Innovation**. To Nurjana Bachman, business development manager in the technology and innovation development office at Children's, the real importance of partnerships lies in the vitality of intellectual exchange and growth they engender. "If you really think about assets, the real asset is only fractionally in the patents we file. It's mostly in the people, the animal models, the infrastructure we have," she says. "The patents are a snapshot of a per-

son's research at a certain time. Even if the work goes on, the research continues to evolve."

As broad-based partnerships become more common, says Bachman, companies are changing the way they do business. As an example, she points to Children's work with Pfizer, in which the hospital is finding it has more flexibility in choosing what research to contribute to the partnership, and equally shares control of decisions about resource allocations, milestone definitions, and other executive choices within the scope of the partnership. "There's no such thing as a straight license anymore," says Bachman. "Pharma is externalizing more of its work through partnerships. They don't have the same impulse to bring stuff in-house and take control of it."

With access to willing partners, early-stage innovations, and intellectually curious researchers operating a step outside the pressures of corporate labs, such partnerships may offer some of the best hope for replenishing the industry's pipelines.

### Biosimilars fuel dealmaking

Biologics currently make up five of the world's ten best-selling

"The real asset is only fractionally in the patents we file. It's mostly in the people, the animal models, the infrastructure we have."

**Nurjana Bachman**
*Technology and Innovation Office, Children's Hospital Boston*

M&A AND PARTNERING

9

drugs. With an estimated $60 billion in biologics expected to lose patent protection through 2017, companies are jockeying into position to reap the potential revenue from biosimilars, copies of biotech drugs that go off patent. Dealmaking to secure technology and manufacturing capability took off in 2011, and included Amgen and **Biogen Idec**, two premier biotechnology companies that want to stake a claim in a market expected to exceed $2 billion annually by 2015, according to IMS Health. Unlike generic drugs, which are copies of small molecule drugs that are chemically synthesized, the molecular complexity of biologics and the fact that they are produced by living cells, means biosimilars are not truly identical to their branded counterparts.

Biosimilars have become an area of enormous interest within the biopharmaceuticals industry, especially for global markets where pricing is much more of an issue. Although few biosimilar products have been approved in the United States, the *Public Health Service Act* created an abbreviated pathway for biologics that are demonstrated to be "biosimilar" to or "interchangeable" with a U.S. Food and Drug Administration licensed biological product. The FDA in February 2012 issued draft guidance to provide a roadmap for companies seeking to

> Companies are jockeying into position to reap the potential revenue from biosimilars, copies of biotech drugs that go off patent.

navigate their way to participating in the space.

Merck and **Samsung** have been among the most aggressive in developing a biosimilars-based business, though other companies including generic powerhouse Teva Pharmaceuticals, **Hospira**, **Momenta**, and South Korean companies **Celltrion** and **Hanwha**, have also been developing technology to produce biosimilars in expectation of patent expiries. Merck hopes to be well-positioned to reap revenue from biosimilars. The company said in its 2010 annual report that it expected to have five biosimilar candidates in late-stage testing by 2011. The big pharma struck two deals in 2011 to strengthen its position. In January 2011, Merck teamed up with global contract research and services company **Parexel** to set the stage for its global

*Figure 9.28* INDUSTRY ALLIANCES: TOTAL REPORTED DEAL VALUE BY PHASE **2007** TO **2011**

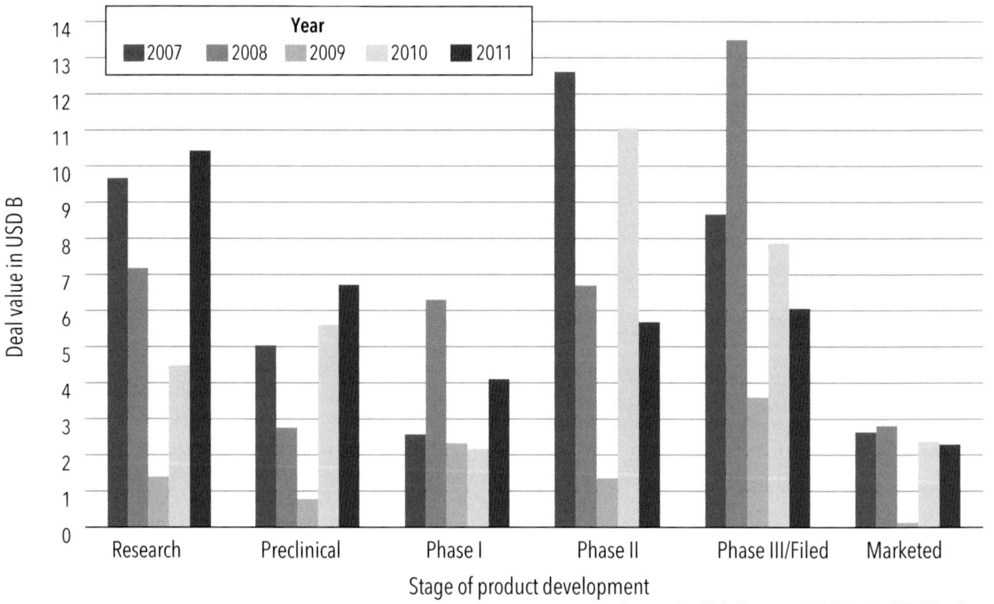

Source: Burrill & Company, S&P Capital IQ, Windhover

*Figure 9.29* **INDUSTRY ALLIANCES: DEAL NUMBER BY PHASE 2007 TO 2011**

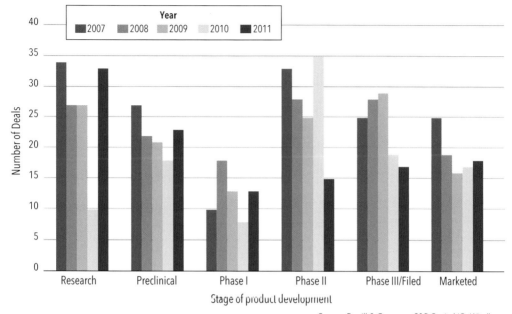

Source: Burrill & Company, S&P Capital IQ, Windhover

for its global development strategy for biosimilars. The Parexel alliance gives Merck access to global clinical development services for designated biosimilar candidates of **Merck BioVentures** and also includes access to a broad range of regulatory strategy and clinical development planning capabilities for the development of certain broad classes of biosimilars across various therapeutic areas, including exclusivity for certain candidates.

Merck followed up the Parexel alliance by entering into a deal with South Korea's Hanwha

*Figure 9.30* **INDUSTRY ALLIANCES: AVERAGE DEAL VALUE BY PHASE 2007 TO 2011**

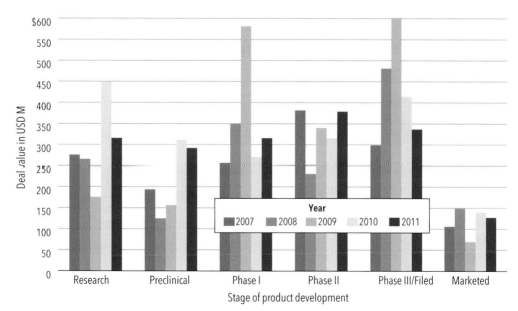

Source: Burrill & Company, S&P Capital IQ, Windhover

*Figure 9.31*　**STRATEGIC REALIGNMENT: BIG PHARMA TERMINATES PARTNERSHIPS IN 2011**

| LICENSEE | LICENSER | FOCUS/COMPOUND | ORIGINAL DEAL DATE |
|---|---|---|---|
| GlaxoSmithKline | Targacept | Neurology | 2007 |
| Merck | Portola Pharmaceuticals | betrixaban | 2009 |
| Pfizer | Rigel Pharmaceuticals | R343 syk inhibitor for allergic asthma | 2005 |
| Pfizer | Zealand Pharma | danegaptide | 2003 |
| Valeant Pharmaceuticals | Kyowa Hakko Kirin | istradefylline | 2010 |
| Roche | Chugai Pharmaceutical | CSG542 | 2007 |
| Bristol-Myers Squibb | Exelixis | XL-281 | 2008 |
| Novartis | Paratek Pharmaceuticals | PTK796 | 2009 |
| Merck | Addex Pharmaceuticals | ADX63365 | 2008 |
| Merck | BioDiem | Flu vaccine technology | 2004 |
| Genzyme (Sanofi) | PTC Therapeutics | ataluren | 2008 |
| Merck KGaA | Newron Pharmaceuticals | safinamide | 2006 |
| Abbott Laboratories | Emergent BioSolutions | TRU-016 | 2009 |

Chemical in June 2011 to bring a generic version of etanercept, better known as Enbrel, to market. Amgen's blockbuster biotech drug is used to treat autoimmune conditions such as rheumatoid arthritis and psoriasis and is going off patent in 2012. Enbrel had close to $6.2 billion in global sales in 2010, according to IMS Health. As part of their agreement, Hanwha's biobusiness unit and Merck's **Merck Sharp & Dohme Research** subsidiary will develop and commercialize HD203, Hanwha's biosimilar version of etanercept, together with Merck conducting clinical development and taking responsibility for manufacturing. Merck will commercialize HD203 globally except in Korea and Turkey where Hanwha has retained marketing rights.

Hanwha received an upfront payment from Merck and is eligible for additional payments associated with milestones for technology transfer and regulatory progress as well as tiered royalties on sales. Although specific financial terms of the agreement were not disclosed, it

| |
|---|
| GSK stops discovery research in depression and pain. |
| Returns anticoagulant in late-stage development following review of portfolio. |
| Pfizer returns full rights to phase 1 compound as a result of its decision to exit the allergy and respiratory therapeutic area within R&D. |
| Zealand regains rights to its gap junction modifier with potential in atrial fibrillation from former partner Pfizer, which gained it through its acquisition of Wyeth, because Pfizer is exiting cardiovascular research. Drug completed two phase 2 studies. |
| Valeant terminates 2010 deal with Biovail and returns North American rights for Parkinson's disease candidate istradefylline (KW-6002). According to Kyowa, the project no longer fits with the merged company's new R&D model. This is the last of 6 CNS deals struck by Biovail from 2008 to before its merger with Valeant that have been terminated by the merged company. |
| Roche returns ex-Japanese rights to diabetes candidate CSG452 after reviewing priorities of its development pipeline. The drug is in phase 3 testing in Japan for type 2 diabetes with regulatory submission planned for 2013. Chugai is majority owned by Roche. |
| BMS returns rights to XL-281 based on its overall research priorities and pipeline. XL-281 targets RAF kinases and has completed phase 1 testing. Exelixis was eligible for milestones of up to $315 million and sales milestones of up to $150 million plus royalties. |
| Novartis terminates deal, stops development, and returns all rights for aminomethylcycline antibiotic PTK796, which was in phase 3 testing to treat complicated skin and skin structure infections, citing its "strategy of prioritizing investments and focusing commercialization efforts on new product launches and core brands." |
| As part of its pipeline prioritization, Merck terminates 2008 deal and returns rights to positive allosteric modulator of metabotropic glutamate receptor subtype 5 (mGliR5), in preclinical development to treat schizophrenia. |
| Merck's Nobilon International unit returns worldwide rights, ex Russia and CIS, to BioDiem's live attenuated influenza vaccine (LAIV) technology as a result of its ongoing pipeline prioritization. The St Petersburg Institute of Experimental Medicine has Russian and CIS rights. |
| Genzyme returns its global commerical rights (ex-US and Canada) for PTC's protein restoration therapy due to a portfolio assessment. It retains option to commercialize ataluren in indications other than nonsense mutation Duchenne/Becker muscular dystrophy outside US and Canada. PTC had received $100 million upfront when original deal was signed in July 2008. |
| Merck Serono returns global rights to safinamide due to strategic considerations and re-prioritization of its R&D pipeline, not based on any new efficacy or safety findings. Drug was in late stage development as an adjunctive treatment for Parkinson's disease. |
| Abbott terminates it co-development and co-commercialization agreement for TRU-016 anti-cancer therapeutics as a result of its portfolio prioritization. Emergent retains worldwide rights and Abbott is obligated to provide certain transition assistance for a period of time. The anti-CD37 mono-specific protein is currently being evaluated in phase 2 studies. |

*Source: Burrill & Company*

was reported to be worth about $720 million to Hanwha over the life of the deal—13 years. Hanwha's HD203 was being tested in Korea in a late-stage trial to evaluate the equivalence in efficacy and safety of HD203 and Enbrel in combination with methotrexate in patients with rheumatoid arthritis. Clinical trials have yet to be initiated in the United States and could be delayed after Amgen, in December 2011, was issued a new patent on Enbrel that extended protection for another 16 years past its 2012 expiration date. While Merck can continue global development, the new patent will impact entry into the U.S. market, which accounts for almost half of Enbrel's global sales.

The new Amgen patent does not impact Hanwha, however, as development of biosimilars has the backing of the South Korean government, which has set a goal of snaring 22 percent of global market share by 2020. The government has already enlisted Samsung as a partner in its effort to develop the sector in Korea. Samsung, South Korea's largest conglomerate, first announced its intentions to enter the biosimilars market in 2009, targeting the biomedical market as a hot area for growth in light of the aging world population. In 2010, the maker of mobile phones and TVs said it would invest up to $1.9 billion over the next ten years to build up its biomedical business, with half of that intended to develop biosimilars and the other half used to build factories.

In February 2010, Samsung teamed up with **Quintiles Transnational**, a U.S.-based global contract services company, to form a biosimilars joint venture with plans to target Johnson & Johnson's arthritis drug Remicade and Roche and Biogen Idec's cancer drug Rituxan, among others. The joint venture would be funded with $266 million and would start building a plant

*Figure 9.32*     **BIOSIMILARS DEALS IN 2011**

| DEAL TYPE | PARTNER/ LICENSER | PARTNER/ LICENSEE | TOTAL DEAL VALUE (USD M) |
|---|---|---|---|
| License | Hanwha Chemical (Korea) | Merck | 720.0 |
| Collaboration | Momenta Pharmaceuticals | Baxter International | 452.0 |
| Collaboration | Amgen | Watson Pharmaceuticals | 400.0 |
| Joint venture | Biogen Idec | Samsung (Korea) | 300.0 |
| Joint Venture | Quintiles | Samsung (Korea) | 265.5 |
| Alliance | Parexel | Merck | N/A |
| License | NeuClone (Australia) | Lupin (Lupin) | N/A |
| Partnership | GH Genhelix (Spain) | Toyota Tsusho (Japan) | N/A |
| Joint Venture | Meiji Seika Pharma (Japan) | Dong-A Pharmaceutical (Korea) | N/A |
| License | Chemo Sa Lugano (Switzerland) | Natco Pharma (India) | N/A |
| Joint Venture | Fujifilm (Japan) | Kyowa Hakko Kirin (Japan) | N/A |

in Incheon, South Korea in the first half of the year to make biosimilars. **Samsung Electronics** and **Samsung Everland** each own a 40 percent stake in the venture, with **Samsung C&T** and **Quintiles** each holding 10 percent. The affiliates will focus on production, while Quintiles will help develop technologies. By April 2011 Samsung had set up **Samsung Biologics** with plans to begin supplying biosimilars in the first half

of 2013, as they come off patent, and sell them worldwide.

By December 2011, Samsung had agreed to set up another joint venture, this time with Biogen Idec to develop, manufacture and market biosimilars. Samsung is taking a leading role in the $300 million joint venture, with Biogen Idec contributing its expertise in protein engineering and biologics manufacturing and working with

---

**DESCRIPTION**

Merck licenses Hanwha's technology to produce biosimilars. Hanwha receives an upfront payment and is eligible for milestones for technology transfer and regulatory progress as well as royalties on sales. Merck will conduct clinical development and manufacture the biosimilar drugs, and will also market them in countries worldwide, except in Korea and Turkey, where Hanwha has retained marketing rights.

Collaboration to develop and commercialize biosimilars. Baxter will pay $33 million upfront to Momenta for up to six follow-on biologic compounds. Momenta is also eligible for milestone payments contingent to the development and approval of the compounds.

Collaboration to develop and commercialize several oncology antibody biosimilar medicines worldwide. Amgen will take primary responsibility for development, manufacturing and initial commercialization. Watson will contribute up to $400 million in co-development costs and share product development risks, plus lend its expertise in the global commercialization and marketing of products, which will be sold under a joint Amgen/Watson label. Watson will initially receive royalties and sales milestones from product revenues. Biosimilars of Amgen's proprietary products will not be pursued.

Companies establish a joint venture to develop, manufacture and market biosimilars. Samsung will take a leading role, with Biogen Idec contributing its expertise in protein engineering and biologics manufacturing. Samsung will contribute $255 million for an 85 percent stake and Biogen Idec will contribute $45 million for a 15 percent stake in the joint venture, which will be based in Korea.

Samsung Group establishes a joint biomedical venture with contract research and services organization Quintiles Transnational as part of its efforts to seek new businesses for driving growth.

Parexel will provide strategic access to global clinical development services for designated biosimilar candidates to Merck BioVentures, including strategic access to a broad range of regulatory strategy and clinical development planning capabilities for the development of certain broad classes of biosimilars across various therapeutic areas, including exclusivity for certain candidates. Parexel will also establish a dedicated Merck BioVentures unit within its organization.

NeuClone will provide an exclusive proprietary mammalian CHO cell line which will express a specific recombinant protein of interest in oncology to Lupin. Lupin will use the cell line to develop generic versions of blockbuster biologics going off patent in the next 5 to 8 years.

Toyota Tsusho will represent GH Genhelix exclusively in Japan in promoting its biosimilar products and contract research, development and manufacturing services for biopharmaceutical products. GH Genhelix is Spain's biggest monoclonal antibody manufacturer.

Companies will form a joint venture to develop and commercialize biosimilars, including DA-3111, a biosimilar of breast and gastric cancer drug trastuzumab. Meiji will be responsible for marketing products in Japan, while Dong-A will be responsible in Korea.

Natco Pharma will source four monoclonal antibodies from a unit of Chemo Sa Lugano to sell biosimilar products in India and other Asian countries. Natco will use the antibodies for manufacturing and commercialising finished dosages.

Companies form a joint venture to develop and commercialize biosimilars, taking advantage of Fujifilm's production technology and Kyowa's biopharmaceutical expertise. The joint venture hopes to begin a clinical trial of the first drug candidate by 2013.

*Source: Burrill & Company*

*Figure 9.33* **AVERAGE TOTAL UPFRONT PAYMENT BY STAGE OF DEVELOPMENT**

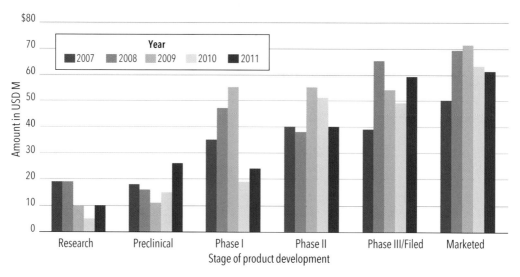

Source: Burrill & Company, S&P Capital IQ, Windhover

Samsung Biologics and Quintiles. Samsung is contributing $255 million to own 85 percent of the joint venture while Biogen is contributing $45 million, for a 15 percent stake. The venture will be based in South Korea and will contract with both companies for technical development and manufacturing services. It will not pursue any biosimilars of Biogen's proprietary products. (Burrill & Company, publisher of the Burrill Report, served as an advisor to Samsung in the agreement.)

Biogen CEO George Scangos had been keen to promote the prospects of biosimilars. In an interview with *Reuters* in May 2011, Scangos said that he believed a follow-on biologics business could gain more than a billion dollars a year in revenue and added that Biogen would be very interested in a partnership that allowed it to remain focused on manufacturing the drugs while the partner would handle clinical trials, commercialization, sales and marketing. That right partner was found in Samsung Biologics. "This

"We both have strengths that make sense for each other no matter how the market develops."

**Paul Bisaro,** *CEO,*
*Watson Pharmaceuticals,*
(speaking of Watson's
partnership with Amgen)

relationship will allow us to leverage our world-class protein engineering and biologics manufacturing capabilities while maintaining focus on our mission of Two weeks after Biogen Idec and Samsung announced their deal, Amgen said it would collaborate with generic drugmaker **Watson Pharmaceuticals** to develop and commercialize several biosimilar oncology antibody drugs. Amgen will assume primary responsibility for developing, manufacturing, and initially selling the biosimilars while Watson will provide its expertise in the commercialization and marketing of generic medicines. Amgen and Watson will split the costs of development roughly in half, with Watson providing up to $400 million. Watson will receive royalties and milestone payments on any sales of the drugs. Although neither company specified which drugs they plan to develop, they will not pursue biosimilars of any of Amgen's patented products. Speculation centered on the possibility that they would develop copycat versions of Genentech's cancer drugs Herceptin, Rituxan, and Avastin.

Amgen will initially do most of the development and marketing, but that role will change as the market for biosimilars matures. Eventually, the companies believe that the biosimilar market could become more like the market for conventional generic drugs, with competition focused around price. Should that happen, Watson's expertise would come into greater play. "Over time, the commercial relationship modifies," says Paul Bisaro, CEO of Watson. "We both have strengths that make sense for each other no matter how the market develops."

## The year ahead

Pharmaceutical companies moved away from internal R&D in 2011 to rely more on partnerships with biotechs and academic centers as sources of innovation. In 2012, there will be a continued bifurcation of partnering deals as companies seek research and discovery deals with small upfront payments plus options to license compounds at one end and big dollar, late-stage deals at the other end. Pharmaceutical and big biotech companies will not be afraid to pay big dollars for assets that have largely had their risks abated. There will also be an increase in non-competitive alliances between large companies seeking to cut the cost and risk of drug development through shared research. ∎

# 10

# Exit Strategies

The life sciences continue to attract new ideas and people dedicated to improving lives around the world. But financing life sciences companies is changing as new deal structures evolve to address the problems entrepreneurs and investors face in the risk-averse and often volatile financial climate that now exists. With capital scarce and expensive, companies need to be creative. Venture investors are structuring investments today with an eye toward exits, ensuring that they not only meet the needs of the companies they fund, but their limited partners as well. Public investors have also become quicker to both reward successes and punish companies that fail to meet their expectations. Both public and private companies need to focus their investments on clear paths to revenues, innovative products for unmet needs that push beyond incremental improvements, and disruptive solutions to containing healthcare costs. The industry will continue to raise a substantial amount of capital. Smart companies will raise money when they can and take advantage of financing opportunities that might be on more attractive terms in foreign markets hungry to tap innovation.

# Chapter 10:

# EXIT STRATEGIES

At the start of 2012, **Third Rock Ventures** and **Sanofi** unveiled a new company, **Warp Drive Bio**. It was launched with up to $125 million in committed funding, a partnership with Sanofi, and a built-in exit strategy for Third Rock. Sanofi, under the terms of the agreement, will acquire Warp Drive Bio if certain milestones are achieved.

The Warp Drive financing structure is designed to address the changing needs faced by startups, large pharmaceuticals, and venture capitalists. It comes at a time when access to funding for life sciences startups has never been more difficult, when venture capitalists in the life sciences are bemoaning the lack of exits and shrinking investment in the space, and when pharmaceutical companies are rethinking how they access innovation and ramp up the lagging productivity of their R&D operations.

In this new model, the startup gets funding to pursue its idea, the Big Pharma gets access to innovation with relatively limited risk, and the venture capitalist, if all goes as planned, gets an assured exit. Of the $125 million in funding for Warp Drive, $75 million is an initial tranched equity investment, with the remaining $50 million tied to the achievement of specified milestones.

The collaboration between Sanofi and Third Rock provides the opportunity to build significant value and the potential for venture capital

levels of return, says Alexis Borisy, a partner at Third Rock Ventures and interim CEO of Warp Drive Bio. "Importantly, it also enables us to advance and accelerate the development of our proprietary genomics platform, unlock 'nature's drugs' and, ultimately, create breakthrough therapies for patients."

Warp Drive Bio's founders include Gregory Verdine, professor of chemistry in **Harvard University's** department of stem cell and regenerative biology and a venture partner at Third Rock Ventures, **Harvard Medical School** professor of genetics and genomics expert George Church, and **University of California, San Francisco** professor of pharmaceutical chemistry and protein-protein interaction expert James Wells. The startup hopes to use the proprietary genomics search engine it is developing to identify potentially powerful therapeutics hidden within microbes. The idea is to pursue biological pathways that are currently considered undruggable.

"We created not only a company, but a process for Third Rock," said Sanofi CEO Chris

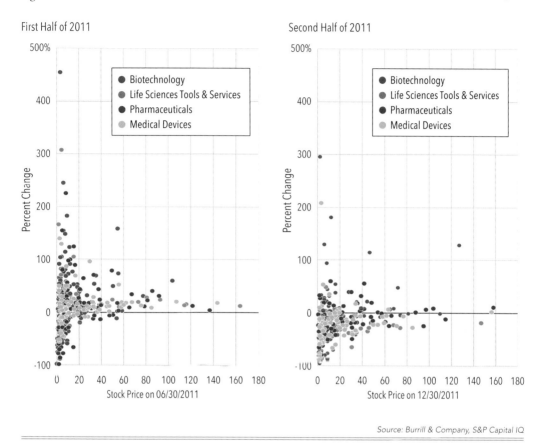

First Half of 2011

Second Half of 2011

Source: Burrill & Company, S&P Capital IQ

Viehbacher in a speech soon after the deal was announced. "Third Rock had the capability and funding; we brought a library of compounds."

Though the agreement assumes Sanofi will eventually acquire the Cambridge, Massachusetts-based startup, its partnership does not hinder Warp Drive Bio's ability to act as an independent company in the meantime and allows it to pursue other partnerships to advance its programs.

Warp Drive's technology is still in the early stages. If it is successful, the built-in exit may limit Third Rock's return on its investment, but the trade-off—assured liquidity—ameliorates the risk and may be worth the price. Viehbacher justified the benefit of such a deal structure for Sanofi in a presentation to investors in February 2012: "Sanofi is gaining accesses to potentially very innovative products from Warp Drive, but also maintains a close involvement and can therefore ensure that the products are developed to a pharma quality standard."

## Market turmoil roils second half of 2011

The formation of Warp Drive Bio is one example of a new model, structured from the start to deal with funding innovation in a constrained economy. It is one example of how financing is changing as deal structures evolve to address the problems entrepreneurs and investors face today. Despite a strong and promising start for life sciences in the first half of 2011, the slow pace of the economic recovery and highly charged political fighting over debt burdens in the United States and the soverign debt crisis in Europe weighed heavily on financial markets and overshadowed industry successes. Market volatility during the second half of the year wreaked havoc on share prices of publicly traded companies [SEE FIGURE 10.1].

The wild market swings not only hampered companies' ability to obtain funding in the second half of the year, but also raised the specter of cuts to governments' expenditures on healthcare and biomedical research. With capital scarce

*Figure 10.2* **PERFORMANCE OF PUBLICLY TRADED LIFE SCIENCES COMPANIES IN 2011**

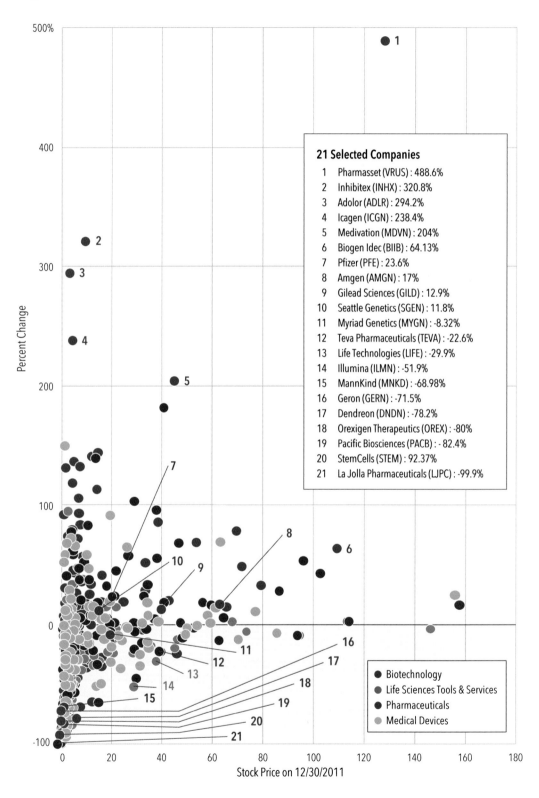

**21 Selected Companies**

| | | |
|---|---|---|
| 1 | Pharmasset (VRUS) | : 488.6% |
| 2 | Inhibitex (INHX) | : 320.8% |
| 3 | Adolor (ADLR) | : 294.2% |
| 4 | Icagen (ICGN) | : 238.4% |
| 5 | Medivation (MDVN) | : 204% |
| 6 | Biogen Idec (BIIB) | : 64.13% |
| 7 | Pfizer (PFE) | : 23.6% |
| 8 | Amgen (AMGN) | : 17% |
| 9 | Gilead Sciences (GILD) | : 12.9% |
| 10 | Seattle Genetics (SGEN) | : 11.8% |
| 11 | Myriad Genetics (MYGN) | : -8.32% |
| 12 | Teva Pharmaceuticals (TEVA) | : -22.6% |
| 13 | Life Technologies (LIFE) | : -29.9% |
| 14 | Illumina (ILMN) | : -51.9% |
| 15 | MannKind (MNKD) | : -68.98% |
| 16 | Geron (GERN) | : -71.5% |
| 17 | Dendreon (DNDN) | : -78.2% |
| 18 | Orexigen Therapeutics (OREX) | : -80% |
| 19 | Pacific Biosciences (PACB) | : -82.4% |
| 20 | StemCells (STEM) | : 92.37% |
| 21 | La Jolla Pharmaceuticals (LJPC) | : -99.9% |

Legend:
- Biotechnology
- Life Sciences Tools & Services
- Pharmaceuticals
- Medical Devices

Axis: Percent Change (y), Stock Price on 12/30/2011 (x)

*Source: Burrill & Company*

expensive, public companies needed to focus their investments on clear paths to revenues, innovative products for unmet needs that push beyond incremental improvements, and disruptive solutions to containing healthcare costs. It was clear at the beginning of 2011 that the old ways of conducting business would not work in the risk-averse economic climate that lay ahead. The need for true innovation moved companies and investors toward creative approaches to funding.

Biotech companies developing therapeutics were among the strongest and the weakest market performers during the year. Their shares often skyrocketed when they became acquisition targets or sank when sales or clinical trial results failed to meet investors' expectations [*See Figure 10.2*].

Four of the top five market performers in the sector in 2011 were targets of acquisitions. **Pharmasset**, shares of which surged almost 500 percent during the year, rose mostly on positive results of its investigational treatment for hepatitis C. It was acquired by **Gilead Sciences** in late November for $11 billion, at an 89 percent premium to its closing before the announcement. **Burrill & Company**, publisher of this book, was an investor in Pharmasset.

But for some one-time high flyers, 2011 delivered a drubbing. Investors hammered **Dendreon** in early August when sales of its newly approved cancer vaccine, Provenge, failed to live up to expectations. The company, which was one of the top performers in 2010, ended the year down 78 percent. Sequencing companies felt the sting of expected cuts in government and industry research budgets. **Pacific Biosciences** lost 82.4 percent of its value in 2011. **Illumina** fell almost 52 percent during the year and became a takeover target for biopharmaceutical **Roche** in early 2012.

## Biotech outpaces the Dow

The *Burrill Biotech Select Index* finished the year up 18.5 percent, handily outpacing the *Dow Jones Industrial Average*, which rose 5.5 percent, and the *Nasdaq Composite Index*, which closed in negative territory as it finished the year down 1.8 percent [*See Figure 10.24*]. The healthcare sector benefitted from strong growth and several new drug approvals in the

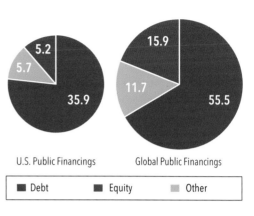

*Figure 10.3* **Public Financings in 2011**

U.S. Public Financings        Global Public Financings

■ Debt        ■ Equity        ■ Other

*Source: Burrill & Company*

first half of the year as an aging population drove the need for medicine and services. The *Burrill Mid-Cap Index* was the best performer in the Burrill family of life sciences indices, ending the year up 35.4 percent, while the *Burrill Personalized Medicine Index* was the worst performer, closing down 5.3 percent for the year [*See Figure 10.25*].

Market volatility in August, September, and October left investors wary and uncertain about the future. Major market indices along with the Burrill indices lost much of the gains they had made during the first half of the year [*See Figure 10.26*].

Taking a longer view, the *Burrill Biotech Select Index* has performed exceptionally well over the past five years compared to the *Dow Jones Industrial Average* and the *Nasdaq Composite Index*, up more than 40 percent since the beginning of 2007 [*See Figure 10.27*]. But most of the gains in the industry have come from the large and mid-cap companies. Most biotechs have market capitalizations less than $250 million. As a group they have underperformed the market during the past five years by about 40 percent [*See Figure 10.28*].

In the same five year period from 2007 through 2011, U.S. biotechnology companies, a category that includes therapeutics, diagnostics, tools and technology, and industrial and agricultural biotechs, have continued to raise increasing amounts of capital through financings and partnering deals [*See Figure 10.29, 10.31*].

### Public financings grow on debt

Life sciences companies across the globe raised a total of $83.2 billion in public financings during 2011, 28 percent more than the $65 billion raised in 2010. Debt dominated fundraising in both years and accounted for the overall fundraising growth in 2011 [SEE FIGURE 10.3].

Global life sciences public equity financings, which include IPOs, PIPEs, and follow-on offerings, totaled just $16 billion, an 8 percent increase over the $14.8 billion raised in 2010. Follow-on financings in China were largely responsible for the increase. [SEE FIGURE 10.5]. In the United States, public equity financings in 2011 totaled $5.7 billion, down 17.4 percent from the $6.9 billion raised in 2010. Fundraising slowed considerably in the second half of the year as markets swung wildly in the face of Europe's debt crisis, fighting raged in the United States Congress over the raising of the debt ceiling, **Standard and Poor's** downgraded U.S. credit, and lawmakers failed to reach agreement on how to reduce the budget deficit [SEE FIGURE 10.6]. The drop in the United States' share of global equity financings for the life sciences reflects the growing importance of the industry in other countries [SEE FIGURE 10.7].

# European Life Sciences VC Financings Reach $1.7B

## Debt crisis slams public life sciences companies

Innovative European privately held life sciences companies raised $1.7 billion in 150 venture and private capital rounds in 2011, 6 percent more than the $1.6 billion raised in 145 rounds in 2010 despite the debt crisis and stagnant economy. Average deal size was $11.1 million, just 2 percent above the $10.9 average deal size in 2010.

At the start of 2011 **Symphogen** completed the largest funding and the largest financing ever for a private European biotech company. The Danish biotech, which is developing antibody therapeutics to treat cancer, and infectious and autoimmune diseases, closed a $134 million (€100 million) placement of preferred stock to a group of investors led by **Novo A/S** with participation by **Essex Woodlands Fund VIII** and the **Danish Pension Fund PKA**, which joined as a new investor.

Symphogen's cancer pipeline includes its lead drug, Sym004, currently in an early-stage trial in patients with advanced solid tumors, as well as other clinical and preclinical compounds it intends to develop in-house or in partnerships. The company has partnerships with **Genentech** and Japanese pharma **Meiji Seika Kaisha**.

> European public financings, including debt, fell 50 percent in 2011 compared to 2010, with $5.2 billion raised, 93 percent of which came in the first half.

Sym004 is a recombinant IgG1 antibody product consisting of two antibodies against the epidermal growth factor receptor. It inhibits cancer cells by three separate and complimentary mechanisms of actions—ligand binding, activation and subsequent downstream signaling of the EGF receptor; and also induces rapid and efficient internalization and degradation of the EGF receptor causing immune-mediated killing of the cancer cells.

Companies based in the United Kingdom raised $446 million, slightly more than a quarter of the total, in 45 deals. T-cell vaccine developer **Circassia** raised $98 million in April in the second largest European financing in 2011. The money, which will be in two tranches over two years, will be used to fund late-stage development of its cat and ragweed allergy therapies, plus advance additional programs. Circassia has raised $159 million in four rounds since it was founded in 2006.

A growing biomedical sector in China contributed to the rise in total value of follow-on offerings while the European debt crisis cut access to capital for public companies there [*See Figure 10.8*]. A total of 93 percent of the $5.2 billion raised by public European life sciences companies occurred in the first half of the year [*See Sidebar: Europe*].

In the United States, the number of equity financings has held steady over the past two years, but there has been an upswing in the total value of both follow-on offerings and venture financings—capital raised by private companies [*See Figure 10.10, 10.11*].

## Risk aversion rules market for IPOs

After a flurry of IPO activity in February 2011, the fever for new issues died down. A total of 16 life sciences companies managed to go public in the United States during 2011, with 13 of the offerings completed before the market volatility in August. Together they raised $1.4 billion. That compares to 20 IPOs in 2010 that raised a total of slightly more than $1.4 billion. As a group, the life sciences IPOs of 2011 fell 27 percent from their initial offering prices as of the close of the year. Getting the deals done was not easy. Ten of these companies went public below their target price ranges and, as a group, these companies

Although Europe's mounting debt crisis during the second half of 2011 did not significantly dent the flow of venture dollars to private companies, it dealt a huge blow to public life sciences companies, battering their share price and making fundraising extremely difficult. Public financings, including debt, fell 50 percent in 2011 compared to 2010 with $5.2 billion raised. Activity was all but shut down in the second half of the year as 93 percent of the total capital was raised in the first half.

European life sciences companies raised $1.1 billion in private placements and rights offerings in 2011 compared to $1.8 billion in 2010, a drop of 40 percent. Initial public offerings were the one bright spot, as six companies went public to raise $391 million, an 87 percent increase over the $209 million raised by seven companies in 2010. In February, the 70-year-old Dutch orthopedic medical device company, **Tornier** raised $166.3 million on the **Nasdaq Global Select Market**. Tornier priced 8.75 million shares at $19 a share, the low end of its target range of $19 to $21. Of the other five IPOs, only one occurred after July.

At the end of the year, the U.K. government announced a new Life Sciences Strategy with initiatives promising $566 million (£360 million) in funding for life sciences biomedical research and startups. The initiatives include more than $200 million for research into stratified (personalized) medicines and research, and $285 million for a translational medicine fund that will advance innovative products toward commercialization. A portion of the money is slated to fund a collaboration with **AstraZeneca**, which is providing 22 compounds to academic researchers to be used to develop new treatments. ■

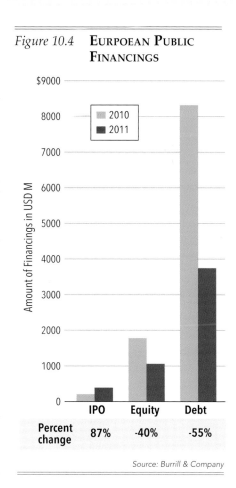

*Figure 10.4* **Eurpoean Public Financings**

Source: Burrill & Company

258

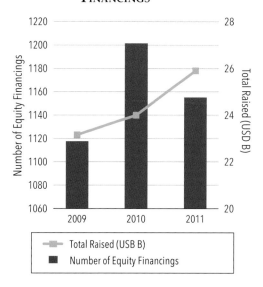

*Figure 10.5* **Total Global Equity Financings**

Source: Burrill & Company

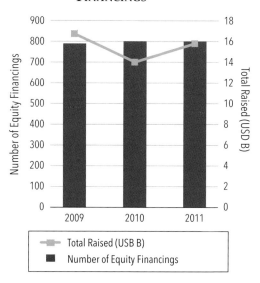

*Figure 10.6* **Total U.S Equity Financings**

Source: Burrill & Company

sold nearly 28 percent more shares than they had set out to sell while raising about 13 percent less than they had hoped [*See Figure 10.12*].

The specialty pharma **Sagent Pharmaceuticals**, which went public at the high end of its target range, was the biggest gainer as of December 30, 2011 closing up 31 percent at $21 per share. Medical device maker **Kips Bay Medical** had the steepest decline, falling 83 percent to finish the year at $1.34. Overall, the eight therapeutics companies fared better than most of the other sectors [*See Figure 10.13*].

The appetite for biotech IPOs has waned considerably since the bull market of 2000 when 63 U.S. biotechs went public and raised $5.4 billion. At that time, companies could go public with little more than a good idea and preclinical data. To go public today, companies must have revenues or have advanced their products to late-stage development with a market ready to accept them. It also helps to have a management team with a track record of success.

**Clovis Oncology**, a biopharmaceutical with two mid-stage candidates, successfully raised $139 million when it went public at the end of November 2011. It was the year's biggest IPO capital raise for a drug developer. The company's founders and management team had established a track record at **Pharmion**, selling it to **Celgene**

in 2008 for $2.9 billion.

Bruce Booth, a venture partner at **Atlas Ventures**, performed an analysis of U.S. therapeutics, diagnostics, and tools companies that went public in 2010 and 2011 and found that companies working on innovative new therapeutics have in general outperformed those with late-stage reformulated products. When he looked at companies' performance relative to additional paid-in capital, he

*Figure 10.7* **U.S. Equity Financings as a Percent of Global Equity Financings**

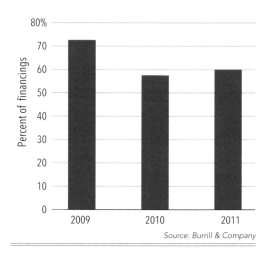

Source: Burrill & Company

found little correlation. He found that even top per-formers **Aveo Pharmaceuticals** and **Aegerion**—both of which went public in 2010—were barely returning twice their paid-in-capital. Despite some great performers post-IPO, the recent returns from acquisitions are more attractive to venture inves-tors, a sign of market disfavor that fuels itself by driving attractive private companies to consider providing exits to their investors through acquisi-tion rather than by going public.

## VC investments grow despite volatility

Global venture investment in life science companies grew 9.4 percent in 2011 to reach $9.9 billion. It accounted for more than 10 percent of total global financings for life sciences firms out-side of partnerships and acquisitions [*SEE FIGURE 10.14*]. Investment in privately-held U.S. firms reached $7.6 billion, a 9.2 percent increase over the $7 billion raised in 2011. In the past three years from 2009 through 2011, venture invest-ment has accounted for the lion's share of equity financings both globally [*SEE FIGURE 10.15*] and in the United States [*SEE FIGURE 10.16*].

Venture financings in 2010 and 2011 accounted for half of all equity financings in the United States, as public life sciences companies were hesitant to issue new shares at unfavorable

*Figure 10.9* **NUMBER OF GLOBAL EQUITY FINANCINGS BY TYPE 2009 TO 2011**

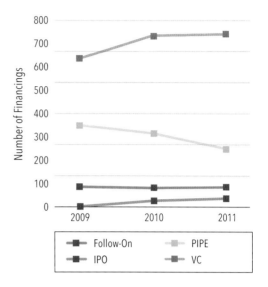

Source: Burrill & Company

valuations in the public markets.

In the United States, California continued to lead the nation in private capital financings with 176 companies raising almost $3 billion in 2011, accounting for one third of the total number of private companies that raised money in the year and 39 percent of the total dollars raised. The San Francisco-San Jose region continued to lead the nation in venture dollars at $1.9 billion in 2011, but raised 4.4 percent less than the $2 billion raised in 2010.

The Boston area was the biggest gainer in 2011 among the major life sciences hubs, with 125 companies in the area raising $1.7 billion during the year, a 22.6 percent increase over 2010. Companies based in the St. Paul and Min-neapolis areas, most of them medical device developers, raised $176 million in venture capi-tal in 2011 for the largest year-over-year increase in funding among United States life sciences hot spots, 85 percent.

Both San Diego and Seattle saw declines in venture capital funding. Seattle companies raised $110 million, a 58 percent drop over 2010. San Diego companies raised $705 million, a 23 percent decrease over the previous year. While a year-over-year change is not necessarily a trend, a comparison of regional financings between

*Figure 10.8* **TOTAL RAISED BY GLOBAL EQUITY FINANCINGS BY TYPE 2009 TO 2011**

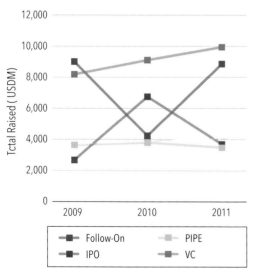

Source: Burrill & Company

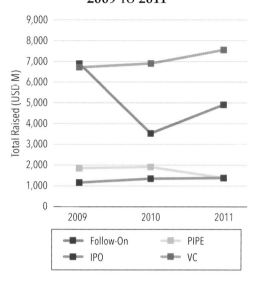

*Figure 10.10* **TOTAL U.S. EQUITY FINANCINGS BY TYPE 2009 TO 2011**

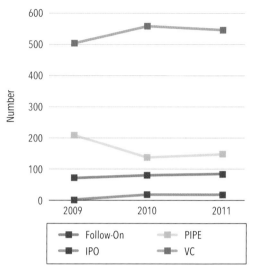

*Figure 10.11* **NUMBER OF U.S. EQUITY FINANCINGS BY TYPE 2009 TO 2011**

2008 and 2011 finds that while the amount of money flowing to companies based in the San Francisco-San Jose region has remained fairly constant, there have been increases in all areas except for Seattle. Companies based in the Seattle area raised $179 million in 2008, 38 percent more than what was raised in 2011. Venture financings for Seattle area companies peaked at $316 million in 2009 and have been declining since then.

Medical device and digital health startups were hot in 2011. Venture financing for medical device firms grew 37 percent in 2011 to $2.7 billion raised by 162 companies and accounted for 32 percent of total dollars raised. Digital health firms are a growing sweet spot for venture capitalists. Financings in the space grew 17 percent over the previous year with 41 companies raising $406 million.

Companies engaged in drug discovery and development continued to account for the majority of venture financings. In 2011, 180 such companies raised $2.7 billion, or 36 percent of the total venture capital. Industrial biotechs raised $823 million in 2011, slightly above the $808 million raised in 2010. Most of these companies are engaged in the development of bio-based fuels and chemicals. Average deal value for the 30 companies that got funding was $27.4 mil-

lion, well above the total life sciences average.

Tools and technology firms, which make products and offer services to life sciences industries, also saw a modest increase in funding with 77 companies raising $803 million in 2011, compared to $760 million raised in 2010. Diagnostics makers were the only companies that saw a decrease in venture financing, falling to $406 million in 2011 compared to $500 million in 2010, a 19 percent drop [*SEE FIGURE 10.17*].

Similar trends were seen in global financings, especially since the United States accounts for more than 76 percent of the total value of global venture financings [*SEE FIGURE 10.18*].

The number of deals in 2011 remained constant with 2010 at 587, which translated to a 15 percent increase in average deal size to $13.7 million, compared to $11.9 million in 2010. An analysis of average disclosed deal size by stage of investment from 2008 through 2011 shows an increase for seed and series A rounds, and a decrease in the size of all later stage financings [*SEE FIGURE 10.19*].

### Financing ideas

Early-stage companies have found raising capital increasingly difficult as many life sciences venture firms have shifted their focus to less risky investment of later stage deals. While

*Figure 10.12* **U.S. IPO Performance by Company in 2011**

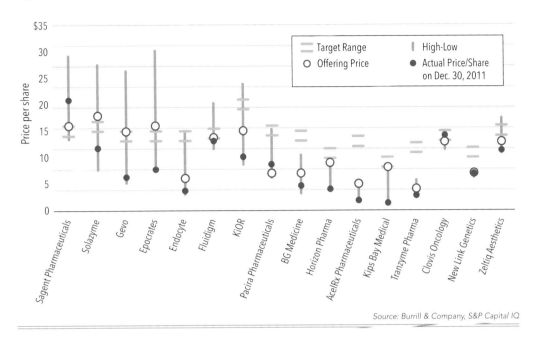

life sciences companies in the United States raised slightly more than $1 billion in early-stage venture financings in 2011, an analysis of those numbers reveals a great concentration of the funding going to just a handful of firms.

In 2011, 99 companies raised a little more than $1 billion in series A financings. But just 17 companies, 17 percent of the total number of companies closing first funding rounds, accounted for $532 million, or more than half of

the total raised. Their average deal size was $31.3 million. The average first funding round for the remaining 82 companies was only $6 million. This is partly due to early stage venture investors being more selective in the companies and technologies they fund. It is also reflective of a move by some firms to seed innovative companies with enough capital from the start to prove their technology works without having to interrupt development to raise more money. Besides

*Figure 10.13* **U.S. IPO Performance by Sector in 2011**

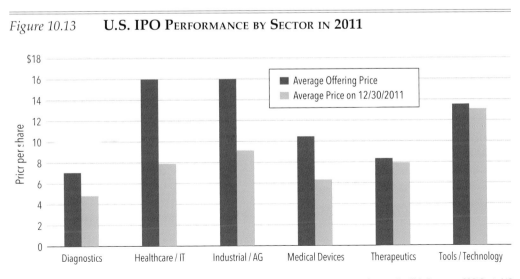

*Figure 10.14*   **GLOBAL LIFE SCIENCES FINANCINGS**

Source: Burrill & Company

a potential disruptive technology, these companies often have experienced management teams that have seen success in earlier ventures.

## Seeding to Proof

Third Rock Ventures launched two companies in 2011 with enough capital to see them through proof-of-concept. **Blueprint Medicine** was seeded with $40 million in a series A financing round in April led by Third Rock, which co-founded the company along with Nicholas Lydon, Brian Druker, Chris Varma, and David Armistead. Lydon and Druker were instrumental in the development of Gleevec, a targeted kinase inhibitor that was the first approved cancer drug in its class. It transformed chronic myeloid leukemia from a fatal cancer into a manageable disease for a subset of patients. Blueprint Medicine will use the proceeds from the financing to develop new cancer therapies using its proprietary compound library and technology platform that targets the driving molecular aberrations of cancer and emerging resistance mechanisms unique to certain cancer patients.

In October, Third Rock provided $35 million in series A funding to launch Sage Therapeutics to advance treatments for central nervous system disorders such as schizophrenia, depression, pain and traumatic brain injury, areas of high unmet need. Sage hopes to use its chemistry platform to develop novel allosteric receptor modulators that fine tune and balance the neuronal activity that is disrupted in these disorders.

## Venture reinvents itself

At life sciences gatherings in 2011, there was frequent debate about whether the venture capital model is broken. The industry has contracted, with the number of venture capitalists in the United States down almost 55 percent from the peak in 2000, according to the **National Venture Capital Association**. Venture capitalists have also had less money to put to work as the financial crisis put severe constraints on fundraising. Although venture capital fundraising increased in 2011 to $18 billion from the $14 billion raised in 2010, according to the NVCA, it still falls far short of the $28 billion disbursed by venture investors in 2011. These two trends have been going on since fundraising peaked at almost $100 billion in 2000 and venture investment in biotechnology startups reached a high of $5.4 billion in 2007 [*SEE FIGURE 10.20*].

The outlook appears dim when considering the challenges inherent in drug development and the difficulty of finding exits. However, innovative companies are still getting funded, says Bryan Roberts, venture partner at **Venrock**, and there are still some hot areas such as oncology and rare diseases. The trick is to ask the hard questions and take risk early when it's technical risk rather than clinical risk—an anti-specialty pharma in-licensing drug model, he says. "You want something at the end of the day that changes clinical care in a material way," says Roberts. He doesn't worry about the regulatory or reimbursement issues, because he believes they can be resolved if the technology can improve the standard of care and save lives.

In order to do this in challenging economic times, venture investors are exploring new models to fund biomedical innovation that lower their risks and raise the returns for their investors through a profitable exit either through an IPO or an acquisition.

Jonathan Norris, managing director at **SVB Capital**, analyzed six years of M&A in biotechnology between 2005 and 2010 showing only 60 out of more than 600 venture-backed companies companies saw exits of $100 million or greater

in upfront payouts. The highest pre-money valuations went to oncology firms, the lowest to cardiovascular drug developers [*See Sidebar Questioning*].

Once the traditional exit for venture capitalists when companies were still in the early stages of development, the IPO has instead become a financing event for companies in late-stage development or already earning revenues. Thinking of an exit at the outset, when a company is being created, is one of many approaches venture investors are taking to improve returns for their investors, according to Rod Ferguson, a managing director

## Questioning Assumptions about Biotech Investing

### Recent years' biotech exits come faster and smaller than device exits

There's a widespread belief that investors in biotech have to wait longer than investors in medical devices to reach an exit and that there are bigger rewards for doing so, but a May 2011 study from **Silicon Valley Bank** suggests the current environment is turning such presumptions on their head.

The bank looked at private merger or acquisition transactions of venture-backed companies in the United States since 2005. In all, the study examined 60 biotech and 58 medical device companies. It included M&A activity in excess of $50 million for device companies and $100 million for biotech companies.

The study found biotech companies overall have quicker exits and lower multiples versus medical device companies, which tend to have longer exits and higher multiples. The research also revealed that biotech companies that received series A venture capital investments at the preclinical stage made up the majority of the biotech exits over the past six years.

"We feel like we are mythbusters," says Jonathan Norris, managing director with SVB Capital's Venture Capital Relationship Management team. "Our research shows that many of the basic assumptions upon which life science investors base their decisions do not hold true in the current market."

The study also found that over the last six years, when large biotech exits were compared with large device exits, the multiples on the device deals exceeded the biotech deals each year. Overall device exits came at an average multiple of 5.3X versus an average 4.1X multiple for biotech exits. In fact, the device group had three times the number of 7X to 10X multiples and more than double the number of 10X multiple deals.

The report said that big exits typically come quickly in biotech with relatively few venture rounds. During the 2005-2010 period of the study, the average time from the close of a series A financing to exit was just under five years. The pace was accelerating in 2010 as that period dropped more than 18 months to less than four years.

While a return of the IPO market and the pipeline needs of Big Pharma are helping to improve liquidity for venture investors in biotech, the reality remains that the number of exits of at least $100 million represents a small portion of biotech investments. For each of these exits, the report notes, ten new companies received series A investments leaving a growing line of investments waiting for liquidity. Based on the ability to exit, the report says it will take some time to run through the backlog. ∎

*Figure 10.15*   PERCENT OF GLOBAL EQUITY FINANCINGS BY TYPE 2009 TO 2011

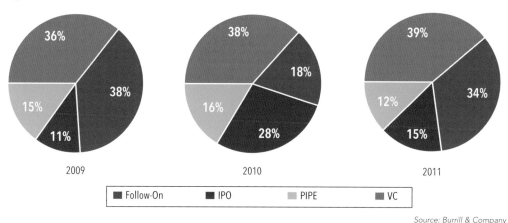

Source: Burrill & Company

at **Panorama Capital**. Unlike the early days of biotech, investors are less interested in building companies for the long haul. The days of another **Genentech**, **Vertex**, or **Biogen Idec** may be days of the past. This is due to many factors, not least of which is the increased risk aversion of investors that has made going public with early stage assets untenable [*SEE FIGURE 10.21*].

Although a flurry of IPOs in the first half of 2011 and a few promising acquisitions during the year provided welcome liquidity, pressure remains on venture investors to be creative in helping their companies forge licensing deals and option arrangements that could lead to an eventual takeout.

Good partners take away the need to take companies public, says Alison Kiley, a director at **Alta Partners**. She said that venture capital-

ists are getting better at being portfolio managers and asset managers and funding companies more smartly. Structured buyouts, the current structure of most private company acquisitions, are also becoming more favorable to venture investors, she says, because lawyers are getting better at formulating deal terms.

### Building in a potential exit

The practice of structuring deals so a potential exit is built-in to financings will likely gain traction going forward as a model for funding early-stage biotechs. Third Rock and Sanofi aren't the first venture-biopharmaceutical tie-up to explore the model. In November 2011, **Versant Ventures** teamed up with Celgene to fund the startup **Quanticel Pharmaceuticals** through a strategic collaboration that will provide the

*Figure 10.16*   PERCENT OF U.S. EQUITY FINANCINGS BY TYPE 2009 TO 2011

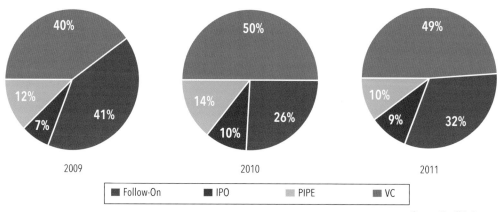

Source: Burrill & Company

# Reforms Would Help Emerging Growth Companies

## Legislation aimed at job creation while retaining investor protections

**A** bipartisan group of Senators in November 2011 unveiled legislation they say would make it easier for small and medium-sized companies to go public and raise capital through public markets. They say their package of reforms would spur job creation.

Senators Charles Schumer, D-New York, and Pat Toomey, R-Pennsylvania, say their bill would reduce the administrative and compliance hurdles that have become an obstacle to companies pursuing initial public offerings by phasing in many of the costliest obligations of being a public company while maintaining key investor protections. Senators Mark Warner, D-Virginia, and Mike Crapo, R-Idaho are co-sponsoring the legislation.

"The vast majority of job creation occurs after companies go public so it makes sense to make the IPO process easier for emerging firms, says Schumer. "This is a commonsense set of reforms that can bridge the partisan divide and have a real impact on job creation."

From 2001 to 2010 there were 478 IPOs of venture-backed companies. That compared to 1,975 IPOs of venture-backed companies from 1991 to 2000, according to the **National Venture Capital Association**. "Because 92 percent of all company job growth occurs after an initial public offering, the dearth of these IPOs is of national economic consequence," the organization said in a prepared statement to the **Senate Committee on Banking Housing and Urban Affairs**. "The opportunity to address this problem legislatively is one our country can no longer afford to forsake."

The *Schumer-Toomey* bill would establish a new category of issuers, called "emerging growth companies" that have less than $1 billion in annual revenues at the time they register with the **U.S. Securities and Exchange Commission** and less than $700 million in publicly-traded shares after their IPO.

Under the proposed law, these companies would have up to five years or until they reached the $1 billion in revenue or $700 million in publicly traded shares to reach full regulatory compliance with regulations phased in over that period. An estimated 11 to 13 percent of companies representing 3 percent of the market's total capitalization would qualify for this so-called "on ramp" status if these provisions were in effect today, the senators say.

Among the high-cost compliance issues that these companies would be exempted from is a section of *Sarbanes-Oxley* that requires public companies to pay an outside auditor to attest to a company's internal controls and procedures. The legislation was put into place following the **Enron** debacle. SEC studies have shown that compliance with that legislation costs companies more than $2 million per year. Companies with market capitalization of less than $75 million are already exempt. Under Schumer-Toomey, CEOs and chief financial officers would still be required to personally certify that the internal controls and procedures are adequate, exposing them to personal liability.

The proposals would update restrictions on communications to account for advances in modes of communication and the information available to investors. The bill would allow investors to have access to research reports about emerging growth companies prior to the IPO. It would also permit emerging growth companies to gauge preliminary interest in a potential offering by expanding the range of permissible pre-filing communications to institutional investors, and allow for filing a registration statement with the SEC on a confidential basis.

Additionally, the bill would exempt emerging growth companies from the requirement to hold a stockholder vote on executive compensation arrangements, including golden parachutes. "In this struggling economy, Congress should do everything it can to make it easier for small businesses to grow and create new jobs," says Toomey. "This legislation will make it easier for firms to go public and in turn, create many more jobs." ∎

*Figure 10.17*  **U.S. Venture Financings by Category 2009 to 2011**

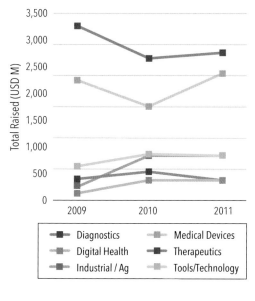

Source: Burrill & Company, S&P Capital IQ

*Figure 10.18*  **Global Venture Financings by Category 2009 to 2011**

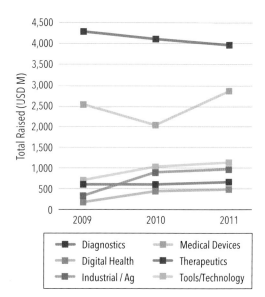

Source: Burrill & Company, S&P Capital IQ

startup with capital and the Big Biotech with an early option to acquire a potentially innovative platform for cancer drug discovery.

Celgene is committing $45 million to Quanticel during the first three years of their alliance and can extend the collaboration in exchange for additional funding. The biopharma is also taking an equity stake in the startup and has retained an exclusive option to acquire the company.

Quanticel's technology is based on the work of company founders and **Stanford University** professors Stephen Quake and Michael Clarke. The startup will use its proprietary platform to conduct single-cell genomic analysis of patient tumor samples and to identify predictive biomarkers for Celgene investigational drugs.

For Quanticel, Celgene's long-term financial commitment will allow it to build the R&D

*Figure 10.19*     **U.S. Venture Financings by Stage 2008 to 2011**

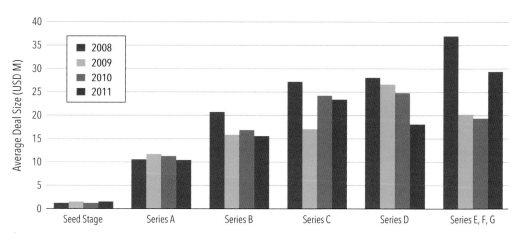

Source: Burrill & Company

*Figure 10.20*    **U.S. Biotechnology Venture Capital Financings**

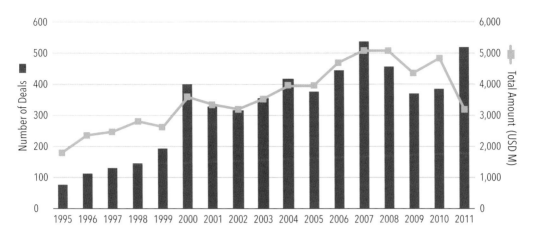

applications of its platform and also use it to generate its own drug candidates, which Celgene will eventually be able to develop if it buys the company. In the meantime, Celgene has early and exclusive access to Quanticel's R&D engine, a platform that it sees as capable of accelerating the pace of development for breakthrough cancer therapies.

For Versant, Quanticel's venture investor, the deal provides it with a strategic partner and a built-in exit strategy if successful. "Aligning our financing strategy to create a start-up that supports the needs of a pre-eminent global bio-pharmaceutical company such as Celgene," says

Bradley Bolzon, a managing director at Versant, "should build even greater value and liquidity than the traditional biotech venture approach."

### Financing molecules

In another of the models, venture investors are creating startups that in-license assets from pharmaceutical companies, develop them to proof-of-concept, and then sell them back to the pharmaceutical. This is a central idea behind the Velocity Pharmaceutical Development Model at venture firm **CMEA**. Karl Handelsman, a managing director at CMEA, says his firm looks to in-license molecules shelved by a pharmaceuti-

*Figure 10.21*    **Public Markets No Longer Favorable for IPOs**

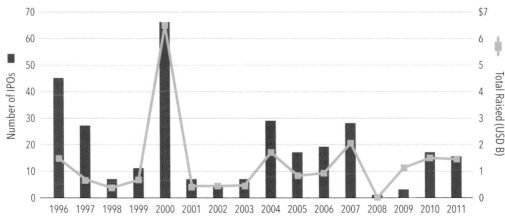

FINANCE

10

cal company because they don't fit with current development strategies. Specifically, CMEA looks for molecules that can be developed to proof-of-concept in two to three years for $10 million to $15 million per compound, he says.

CMEA creates a company to develop the molecule with the hope of eventually selling it back to the pharmaceutical company. It is still a gamble, says Handelsman, as the odds are that two-thirds of molecules will fail before they reach proof-of-concept. But at least the bet on each molecule is small, and the payout for the ones that succeed will likely more than cover the cost of the ones that fail.

**Inception Sciences** takes a similar approach. After **Bristol-Myers Squibb** bought San Diego-based **Amira Pharmaceuticals** in July 2011 for its fibrosis program, Peppi Prasit, Amira's co-founder and chief scientific officer teamed up with Versant Ventures to found Inception. The idea was to set up a holding company that would serve to spin out drug development programs as

# BARDA Awards $1.9 Billion in Contracts in 2011

## Radiation countermeasures and biomedical threats top agency's list

The **U.S. Department of Health and Human Services' Biomedical Advanced Research and Development Authority** awarded $1.3 billion in contracts to biomedical companies developing therapies to counter radiation exposure, influenza, and bioterror threats. The total value of the contracts, if milestones are met and options are exercised, will exceed $1.9 billion over two to five years.

The awards are part of BARDA's efforts in national preparedness and response as the nation marked the tenth anniversary of the 9/11 attacks. Pandemic threats, such as influenza, are also of immediate concern as global trade and travel continues to rise.

Programs developing antivirals and antitoxins against bioterror threats such as smallpox and anthrax received the largest portion of BARDA awards in 2011, valued at $753 million over the life

**Robin Robinson**

*Director,*

*U.S. Department of*

*Health and Human*

*Services' Biomedical*

*Advanced Research*

*and Development*

*Authority (BARDA)*

of the contracts. Flu preparedness was also a top priority, with $662 million in contracts awarded during March and April including $55 million to **BioCryst Pharmaceuticals** to fund completion of the late-stage development of its neuraminidase inhibitor, intraveous peramivir; and up to $179 million over five years to **Novavax** and up to $196 million to **VaxInnate** for the development of their seasonal and pandemic recombinant influenza vaccines. Australian biotech **Biota** will get $231 million in a five-year milestone-based contract designed to provide U.S.-based manufacturing and clinical data to support a new drug application in the U.S. for laninamivir, a long-acting neuraminidase inhibitor being developed to both treat and prevent influenza.

BARDA also awarded $503 million to biomedical firms to support development of drugs to treat injuries associated with acute exposure to radiation. Acute radiation exposure, such as from a nuclear fallout, can lead to injuries to multiple organs, hemorrhaging, infection, and suppression of the immune system's ability to fight organisms that cause infection. The companies receiving the awards are developing drugs to treat bone marrow, gastrointestinal, lung, and skin injury caused by radiation, injuries for which there are currently no treatments available. They stand to benefit from a dual purpose use for their investigational compounds.

"These contracts support development of products that have the potential to address urgent public health requirements for radiation medical countermeasures while also meeting other unmet medical needs," says BARDA Director Robin Robinson. "For example, they may find day-to-day use in treating the side effects of cancer radiation treatment and chemotherapy. These advanced development contracts demonstrate what can be achieved by repurposing drugs with commercial

separate companies, making it easier for pharmaceutical acquirers to buy a specific program without having to also buy additional assets in which it wasn't interested.

Amira's investors had run into that problem when they sought to sell the company. They had several potential suitors, each interested in a different program, but none willing to buy the whole company. Eventually they spun out two of Amira's drug development programs into separate companies—Inception 1 and Inception 2.

Amira's lead program in fibrosis, along with a preclinical program, was sold to Bristol-Myers Squibb for $375 million upfront and the potential for another $150 million in milestone payments.

Another twist on the asset-financing model is the mirror portfolio, created by pharmaceutical **Eli Lilly** to access innovation being developed outside the company's walls. Through the mirror portfolio, virtual companies financed by independent investment funds acquire molecules. The virtual companies and their investors man-

*Figure 10.22*    **HHS BARDA CONTRACTS IN 2011**

| COMPANY | AWARD USD M | POTENTIAL VALUE USD M | LENGHTH IN YEARS | PROGRAM |
|---|---|---|---|---|
| Siga Technologies | 433.0 | 433.0 | 5 | Smallpox antiviral |
| Biota (Australia) | 231.0 | 231.0 | 5 | Influenza |
| VaxInnate | 118.0 | 196.7 | Option | Flu vaccines |
| Novavax | 97.0 | 179 | Option | Flu vaccines |
| GlaxoSmithKline (UK) | 94.0 | 94.0 | 4 | GSK'052 Antibiotic |
| Elusys Therapeutics | 68.9 | 68.9 | 5 | Anti-toxin for anthrax |
| Biocryst Pharmaceuticals | 55.0 | 55.0 | | Influenza |
| Bavarian Nordic (Denmark) | 54.0 | 54.0 | Extension | Smallpox vaccine |
| Chimerix | 24.8 | 81.1 | 3 | Antivirals, smallpox |
| Neumedicines | 17.0 | 273.0 | 5 | Radiation countermeasures |
| Cellerant Therapeutics | 16.7 | 16.7 | | Cell therapy for acute radiation syndrome |
| RxBio | 15.0 | 15.0 | 2 | Radiation countermeasures |
| RxBio | 15.0 | 24 | 2 | Radiation countermeasures |
| Vaxin | 14.7 | 21.7 | 2 | Anthrax vaccine |
| U.S Biotest | 14.0 | 14.0 | | Radiation countermeasures |
| Aeolus Pharmaceuticals | 10.4 | 118 | 5 | Radiation syndrome |
| Nanotherapeutics | 4.8 | 31.1 | 5 | Radiation countermeasures |
| Humanetics | 3.5 | 3.5 | 2 | Radiation countermeasures |
| Araim Pharmaceuticals | 3.1 | 3.1 | 3 | Radiation countermeasures |
| Avaxia Biologics | 2.9 | 2.9 | | GI/radiation exposure |
| Rapid Micro Biosystems | 2.1 | 2.1 | 3 | Microbial detection |
| Apogee Biotechnology | 2.0 | 2.0 | | GI/radiation exposure |
| **TOTAL** | **1,296.9** | **1,919.8** | | |

*Source: Burrill & Company*

potential to meet public health emergency requirements, and we would like to encourage other pharmaceutical companies and their collaborators to follow this approach."

California-based **Neumedicines** and **Cellerant** Therapeutics, Tennessee-based **RxBio**, New York based **Araim Pharmaceuticals**, and Florida-based **Nanotherapeutics** received contracts at the end of September to help support the development of their products, which target the effects of damaging radiation. ∎

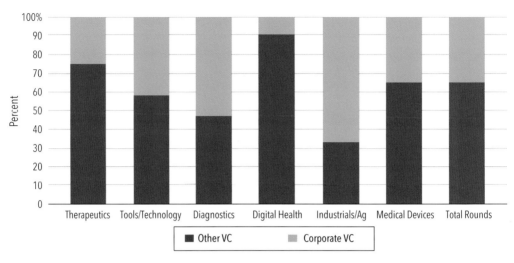

Figure 10.23    PERCENT OF GLOBAL VENTURE FINANCINGS WITH CORPORATE
                PARTICIPATION BY CATEGORY IN 2011

Source: Burrill & Company

age the financing and determine the scope, manner of execution and particular organization that will conduct preclinical to clinical proof-of-concept development, at which point they are offered for sale to drugmakers such as Lilly.

For the pharmaceutical company, the mirror portfolio provides a way to share risk and support the development of new medicines. "Another benefit of the mirror portfolio is that it provides access to capital, capacity, capability, and deep disease expertise that can be focused on developing molecules generated in research institutions or biotechnology companies, with the potential for rights to successful molecules to be purchased by Lilly," says Robert Armstrong, vice president of global external research and development at Lilly.

Lilly has committed to invest up to 20 percent of the capital in the investment funds that participate in its mirror portfolios, for a total commitment of up to $150 million. Lilly can out-license molecules to the funds, and will have first-purchase rights to the molecules, as well as preferential rights to evaluate and acquire a limited number of externally sourced compounds, all at fair market value.

One of the independent venture capital firms participating in the mirror portfolio acquired two molecules in February 2011, a preclinical molecule developed by researchers at a major academic institution that is being studied as a

potential treatment for congestive heart failure and a molecule from Lilly being studied for its potential in bone healing and cancer. Atlas Ventures is exploring a similar model through its new **Atlas Venture Development Corporation**, set up in early 2011.

## Pharma gets into the act

Pharmaceutical companies seeking to expand their pipelines with external sources of innovation are looking for new ways to access promising technologies. Long averse to investing in early-stage companies, Big Pharma has begun taking a pro-active approach in helping get innovative companies off the ground.

Pharmaceutical companies are teaming up with venture firms to seek out a broad range of investing opportunities where the two can benefit from each other's expertise while lowering the risk of an eventual exit for the venture firm. Such an approach can be particularly useful for pharmaceutical firms that don't have a corporate venture arm.

Atlas Venture teamed up with **Shire Human Genetic Therapies** in December 2011 to look at investment opportunities in early-stage, rare disease therapeutics. The partnership of the venture capital firm and the biologics division of the pharmaceutical Shire aims to leverage the venture firm's managerial expertise with the Dublin-based biopharma's R&D knowledge and capabilities in rare diseases to identify strategic investments for early-stage venture creation around rare genetic diseases, currently a hot target for drug development.

Researchers at Shire Human Genetic Therapies will work closely with Atlas venture partners in the multi-year collaborative effort. "The partnership with Shire is truly synergistic and leverages our individual strengths to create and fund new startups around high-potential medical science early in the R&D cycle," says Atlas Venture's Booth.

In a blog post, Booth says the partners will focus on diseases that extend well beyond what is currently in Shire's pipeline. Shire will do the wet diligence, test promising discovery and preclinical candidates in the lab, while Atlas will work on the diligence and structuring of new opportunities.

"The possibility for creating option-like structures for these deals is a key part of this alliance, and we anticipate setting them up as part of our initial investment where the structure makes sense," writes Booth. "In these deals, Shire will have the right to acquire and integrate the company/asset into its R&D pipeline at a pre-defined valuation upon reaching an agreed set of milestones. This secures access to these innovations for Shire, while mitigating the downstream liquidity risk for the team and investors."

Atlas isn't the only firm looking to fill the funding gap for early-stage therapeutics com panies at a time when many traditional VCs are limiting their exposure in life sciences or moving out of the sector altogether. **Access BridgeGap Ventures**, was set up in December 2011 to fund early-stage therapeutics startups and also create new companies around disruptive technologies including technology still in academic labs. The

> Venture investors are creating startups that in-license assets from pharmaceutical companies, develop them to proof-of-concept, and then sell them back to the pharmaceutical.

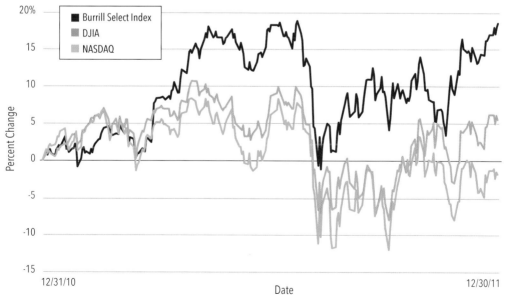

*Figure 10.24* **BURRILL BIOTECH SELECT INDEX PERFORMANCE IN 2011**

*Source: Burrill & Company*

new venture group is backed by **Access Industries**, a privately held, U.S.-based international industrial group.

Daniel Behr and Ben Bronstein, both well-known serial entrepreneurs and technology developers, are leading the venture firm. Funding activities will focus on scientists, entrepreneurs, and companies that are developing novel therapeutic approaches and platforms. Access BridgeGap expects to fund three to five companies per year and to deploy $75 million over the first few years.

Such early-stage funding tends to be one of the riskiest investments, but it can also lead to greater financial rewards. "Commercially promising innovations being developed in research institutions and in young startups are often deemed too early for partnering by industry or for investment by traditional venture capital," says Bronstein. "Our focus is to translate early-stage science into commercially relevant products and companies."

> Long averse to investing in early-stage companies, Big Pharma has begun taking a pro-active approach in helping get innovative companies off the ground.

## Corporate venture fills funding void

Corporate venture investing in life sciences has risen steadily over the last few years and accounted for about 20 percent of investment dollars in 2011. [*See Figure 10.23*]. With many traditional venture capitalists moving their focus to later-stage deals, corporate venture investing in early-stage rounds has helped lend credence to the startup's technology and raise the potential for downstream partnering opportunities. Venture investors willing to play in this area find corporate venture investors welcome partners because of their deep pockets, R&D and market insights, and their potential to become partners or acquirers of the companies they fund.

While traditional venture capitalists and their limited partners are demanding faster exits, corporate venture capitalists are in it as much for early access to innovation as for

*Figure 10.25* **Burrill Biotech Large-, Mid- and Small-Cap Performance in 2011**

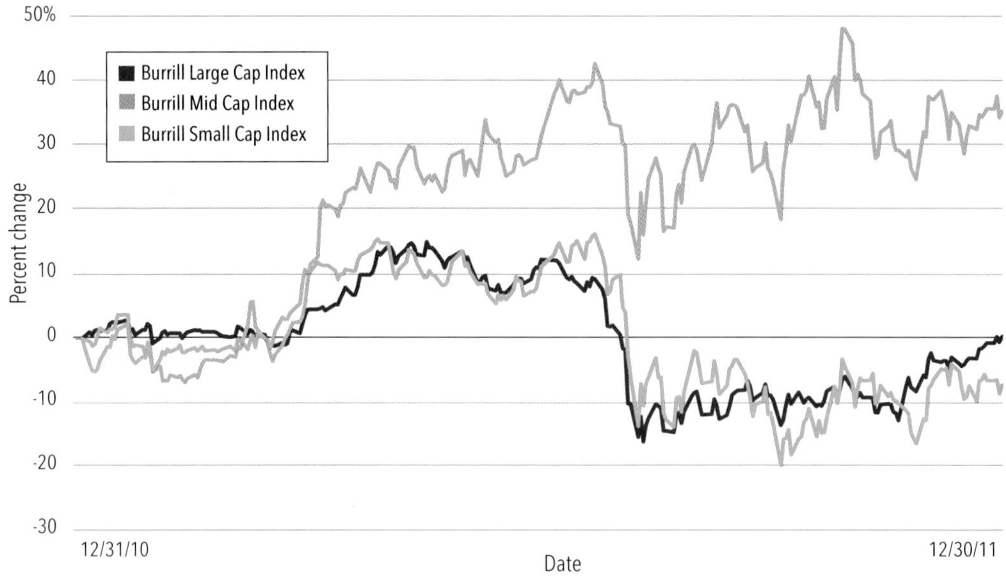

Source: Burrill & Company

*Figure 10.26* **INDICES PERFORMANCE FIRST AND SECOND HALF OF 2011**

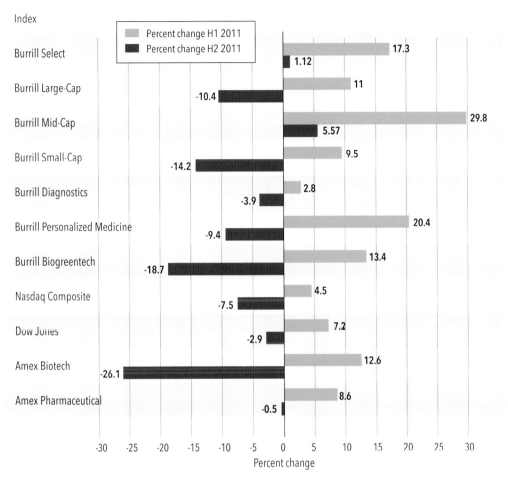

Index

Legend:
- Percent change H1 2011
- Percent change H2 2011

| Index | H1 2011 | H2 2011 |
|---|---|---|
| Burrill Select | 17.3 | 1.12 |
| Burrill Large-Cap | 11 | -10.4 |
| Burrill Mid-Cap | 29.8 | 5.57 |
| Burrill Small-Cap | 9.5 | -14.2 |
| Burrill Diagnostics | 2.8 | -3.9 |
| Burrill Personalized Medicine | 20.4 | -9.4 |
| Burrill Biogreentech | 13.4 | -18.7 |
| Nasdaq Composite | 4.5 | -7.5 |
| Dow Jones | 7.2 | -2.9 |
| Amex Biotech | 12.6 | -26.1 |
| Amex Pharmaceutical | 8.6 | -0.5 |

Percent change

*Source: Burrill & Company*

a direct financial return on investment. This is especially true at a time when many large pharmaceutical companies are cutting back on their internal R&D in favor of seeking innovation outside their own walls.

In September **Merck**, one of the few Big Pharmas to resist establishing a corporate venture arm, said it was setting up the **Merck Research Venture Fund** with $250 million that would be used in partnership with traditional venture firms to gain a window on innovative early-stage biopharma companies. The new fund followed the establishment of its **Global Health Innovation Fund**, set up in March 2011 with $250 million to invest in healthcare services and information technology, areas where Merck may see itself growing in the future.

In November, **AstraZeneca** committed an additional $100 million to its **MedImmune Ventures** group, bringing the unit's total funds under management to $400 million, an effort to expand its investing activity globally and broaden it across more therapeutic areas. Med-Immune plans to use the extra funding to continue to make investments in biotech startups as well as medical and healthcare technology outfits.

The company's support of corporate venture capital suggests that it is proving itself valuable in maintaining the health of the early-stage ecosystem that the life sciences industry relies on for future innovation. "We believe that in the current financial environment, there is a growing role for corporate venture capital funds such as MedImmune Ventures," says Ron Laufer, senior managing director for MedImmune Ventures.

**GlaxoSmithKline**, another Big Pharma,

FINANCE

10

274

*Figure 10.27*   **Burrill Biotech Select Index Performance 2007 to 2011**

*Source: Burrill & Company*

set up a $50 million fund to invest in Canadian life sciences companies ready to enter the clinic. The fund's main mission is financial rather than strategic, says GSK. It will look to invest in companies that are a strategic fit, but investments will not include a major stake or product rights. The fund will be managed by **SR One**, GSK's global venture arm, which has invested more than $600 million since its founding in 1985, according to *BioCentury*.

## Venture firms scale back on life sciences

At the same time as corporate venture was expanding its presence in financing privately-held biotechs, the sector saw an increasing number of investors exit the life sciences space or announce plans to curtail their activity. In October **Prospect Ventures** said it would not raise a fourth healthcare fund and would return committed capital to limited partners. One month later, the life science practices at **Morgenthaler** and **Advanced Technology Ventures** said they were breaking off from their IT counterparts to form a new firm. Meanwhile, **Scale Venture Partners**, a major investor in life sciences for the past 16 years,

said it would exit the life sciences, citing regulatory unpredictability and growing costs as major reasons for its decision.

While some firms are exiting the life sciences, other venture investors continue to raise funds to finance biomedical companies. More than 165 venture funds that invest in healthcare were raising new funds at the start of 2012, according to Atlas Venture, with a combined target of $22 billion. Approximately half of them are pureplay healthcare funds.

A survey from the NVCA, published in October, found that nearly 40 percent of life sciences venture capitalist firms planned to invest less in the sector during the next three years. That reflects both frustration with regulatory barriers and the weak market for initial public offerings that have made it difficult for venture investors to cash out of their investments.

The **Biotechnology Industry Organization** has attempted to address some of the issues facing small biotechs and their investors in its policy agenda unveiled at its annual meeting in June 2011 in Washington, D.C. BIO is pushing Congress to provide tax incentives for investing in biomedical innovation, which

Figure 10.28 **Burrill Biotech Large-, Mid-, and Small Cap Performance 2007 to 2011**

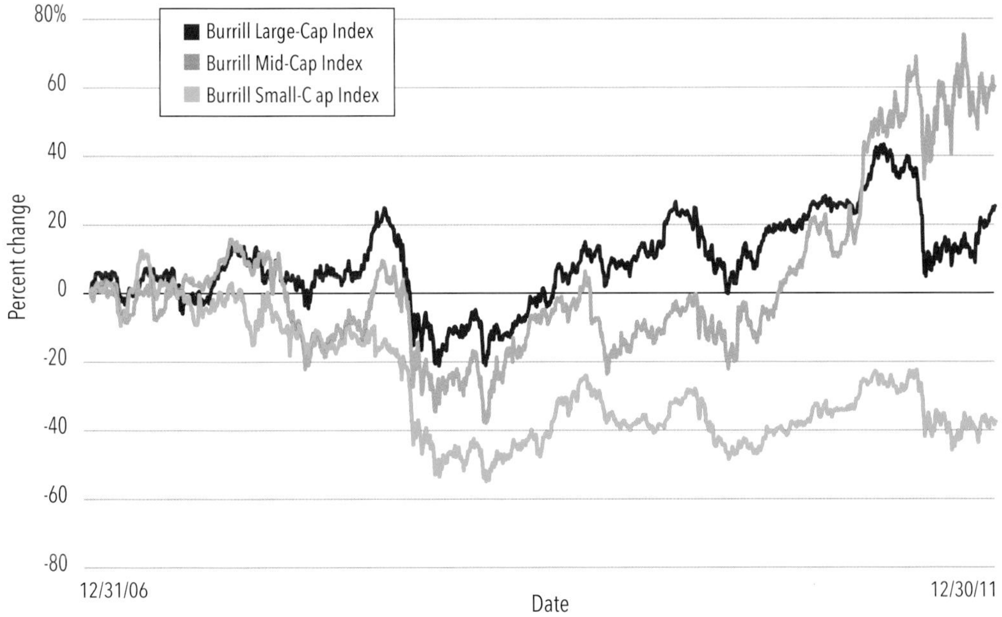

Source: Burrill & Company

historically does not fall under incentives provided for other high-risk endeavors such as energy exploration and high-tech startups. These incentives include a tax credit for angel investment, improved capital gains treatment for small businesses, matching grants to double private investments in startups, and removal of tax codes that penalize venture-backed companies for having institutional private backers.

In January 2012, changes were made to the funding requirements for grants under the Small Business Investment Research program of the NIH to include eligibility for companies majority-backed by venture capital. The requirements for becoming a public company may also be eased if a bill introduced in the U.S. Senate at the end of November 2011 becomes law. It eases requirements for small firms and gives them up to five years or until they reach $1 billion in revenue or $700 million in publicly traded shares to reach full regulatory compliance [*See Sidebar Reforms*].

Some companies have chosen to forego the IPO route to becoming a publicly traded company by filing a Form 10 with the SEC to register their private shares as common stock. Unlike the traditional route where bankers market an offering to potential investors, it is up to management to excite investors to buy their shares and get analysts to cover their stock. Companies that pursued this route include **Puma Biotechnology**, **Coronado Biosciences**, and **Radius Health**. All three have ties to **Cougar Biotechnology**, which followed the same route and was acquired by **Johnson & Johnson** for $1 billion in 2009.

> While traditional venture capitalists are demanding faster exits, corporate venture capitalists are in it as much for early access to innovation as for a direct financial return on investment.

*Figure 10.29*    U.S. Biotech Financings 2007 to 2011

Includes therapeutics, diagnostics, tools/technology, industrial/ag
Does not include digital health, healthcare IT, medical devices; Big Pharma debt raises

| | 2007 | 2008 | 2009 | 2010 | 2011 |
|---|---|---|---|---|---|
| **PUBLIC** | | | | | |
| IPO | 2,041 | 6 | 1,217 | 1,199 | 1,292 |
| PIPE | 1,618 | 1,174 | 1,713 | 1,802 | 1,389 |
| Follow-on | 6,311 | 2,081 | 6,297 | 3,234 | 4,895 |
| Debt | 6,749 | 5,273 | 11,201 | 17,846 | 29,239 |
| Other | 611 | 2,580 | 693 | 2,146 | 5,315 |
| **PRIVATE** | | | | | |
| VC | 4,236 | 5,050 | 4,383 | 4,831 | 4,823 |
| **TOTAL FINANCINGS** | **21,566** | **16,164** | **25,504** | **31,058** | **46,953** |
| **PARTNERING** | | | | | |
| | 17,268 | 19,782 | 33,913 | 34,001 | 22,888 |
| **TOTAL** | **38,834** | **35,946** | **59,417** | **65,059** | **69,841** |

*Source: Burrill & Company*

## Life after Pharma drops development

Big Pharma has restructured and reevaluated its R&D programs over the past two years, which has resulted in many biotechs seeing partnering deals cancelled and assets returned [*See Chapter 9*]. This is not always a bad thing. Both **Rigel Pharmaceuticals** and **Portola Pharmaceuticals** had programs cancelled by their Big Pharma partners in 2011 and took the opportunity to raise money.

Rigel, a clinical-stage drug developer of

*Figure 10.30*    Public Biotech Company Performance 2001 to 2011

| | 2001 | 2002 | 2003 | 2004 | 2005 | 2006 | 2007 | 2008 | 2009 | 2010 | 2011 | 2011 PERCENT CHANGE |
|---|---|---|---|---|---|---|---|---|---|---|---|---|
| **SALES/REVENUE (USD B)** | | | | | | | | | | | | |
| | 39.0 | 42.7 | 47.40 | 59.50 | 71.5 | 82.6 | 89.6 | 99.5 | 91.6 | 91.4 | 94.6 | 3.5 |
| **R&D EXPENSES (USD B)** | | | | | | | | | | | | |
| | 12.3 | 13.5 | 14.3 | 16.8 | 18.5 | 21.7 | 23 | 23.7 | 19.3 | 19.5 | 19.1 | -2.1 |
| **NET INCOME (LOSS) (USD B)** | | | | | | | | | | | | |
| | -4.7 | -11.6 | -4.1 | -4.4 | -4.1 | -3.2 | -0.6 | 3.7 | 4.3 | 7.5 | 9.75 | 30.0 |
| **CASH & EQUIVALENTS (USD B)** | | | | | | | | | | | | |
| | 45.3 | 41.9 | 41.6 | 45.5 | 47.7 | 51.4 | 71.2 | 75.6 | 74.7 | 112.1 | 50.3 | -55.1 |
| **MARKET CAPITALIZATION (USD B)** | | | | | | | | | | | | |
| | 383 | 224 | 344 | 400 | 490 | 492 | 454 | 404 | 346 | 372 | 337 | -9.4 |
| **NUMBER OF PUBLIC COMPANIES** | | | | | | | | | | | | |
| | 356 | 329 | 315 | 356 | 363 | 360 | 373 | 356 | 318 | 298 | 286 | -4.0 |

*Source: Burrill & Company, S&P Capital IQ*

*Figure 10.31* **CAPITAL RAISED BY U.S. BIOTECHS**

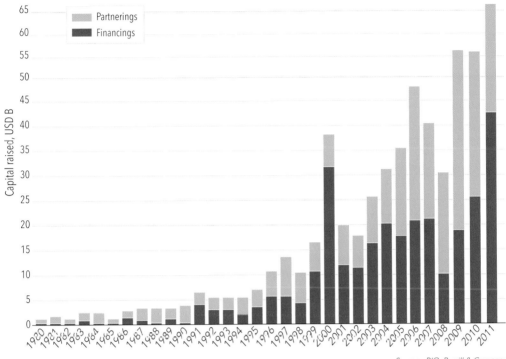

Source: BIO, Burrill & Company

small-molecule drugs for the treatment of inflammatory diseases, autoimmune conditions, and muscle disorders, raised $130 million in a follow-on offering to continue advancing its pipeline, including an asthma drug carried through an early-stage trial by Pfizer before it dumped its stake in the program during a portfolio review in May 2011. The drug is Rigel's inhaled Syk inhibitor for allergic asthma, a chronic inflammatory disorder of the lungs and respiratory passages caused in response to an allergen or pathogen.

Although Pfizer's decision left Rigel without a partner on R343, it also gave the company the opportunity to move ahead with a compound ready for mid-stage testing. "It is rare in our business," said Rigel CEO James Gower on the day Pfizer announced its decision, "that one has the opportunity to develop an asset [that] is both promising and on which the research and development has been as well done as the package that **Pfizer** is transferring to us."

Portola Pharmaceuticals raised $89 million in November 2011 to advance development of betrixaban, its late-stage anticoagulant

program that was returned to the biotech by Merck. Merck had paid $50 million upfront in 2009 to partner with Portola, but dropped the program in March 2011 after an internal review. **Temasek**, an investment firm based in Singapore, and **Eastern Capital Limited** joined Portola's existing investors in the financing.

Portola will use the capital to independently complete a pivotal late-stage betrixaban trial and develop a companion diagnostic that identifies patients most likely to experience side effects from the drug. "As a companion agent to betrixaban, our Factor Xa inhibitor antidote is a one-of-a-kind product that has the potential to significantly advance the field of anticoagulation," says Portola CEO William Lis.

### Looking ahead

The volatility that characterized the financial markets in the second half of 2011 is likely to continue. Europe's sovereign debt crisis will take years to work through and with 2012 being an election year in the United States, the divide between Democrats and Republicans is not likely to be bridged any time soon. Global events will also continue to exert greater force on market activity and the ability to raise capital when needed. But as the industry grows outside the United States, Europe, and Japan, so do funding opportunities.

Life sciences will continue to attract new ideas and people dedicated to improving lives around the world. The industry will also continue to raise a substantial amount of capital, although much of it will still go to fund large, well-established companies. Smart companies will raise money when they can and take advantage of financing opportunities that might be on more attractive terms in foreign markets hungry to tap innovation.

Private investment will come from many sources including venture, corporate, angel, and private equity. Investors will favor companies that create disruptive innovations over those that offer only incremental improvement

> As the industry grows outside the United States, Europe, and Japan, so do funding opportunities.

to existing products. Venture investors will be smarter and more creative in how they pick and structure investments, ensuring that the companies they fund have a good chance to prove themselves and that their limited partners profit. But policymakers concerned about the role innovation plays in driving the economy will need to address impediments to financing that can dissuade investors from backing promising technologies of tomorrow. ∎

*Figure 10.32*    **INDUSTRY SEGMENTED BY MARKET CAP**

Includes all publicly traded biotech, pharma, and tools and diagnostics companies on U.S. listed exchages

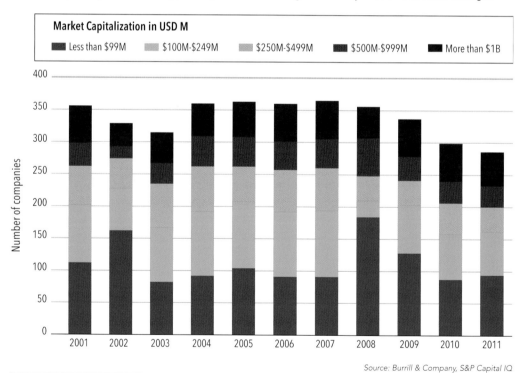

Source: Burrill & Company, S&P Capital IQ

*Figure 10.33* **U.S. PUBLIC COMPANY RECONCILIATION**

| | |
|---|---|
| **TOTAL PUBLIC COMPANIES AS OF 12/31/06** | **360** |
| 2007 IPOs | 28 |
| 2007 M&As | -9 |
| 2007 New or reinstated filings | 0 |
| 2007 Delisted and/or traded on bulletin board | -7 |
| 2007 Companies added based on biotech focus | 1 |
| 2007 Change in biotech focus | 0 |
| **TOTAL PUBLIC COMPANIES AS OF 12/31/07** | **373** |
| 2008 IPOs | 1 |
| 2010 M&As | -28 |
| 2008 New or reinstated filings | 31 |
| 2008 Delisted and/or traded on bulletin board | -22 |
| 2008 Companies added based on biotech focus | 0 |
| 2008 Change in biotech focus | 1 |
| **TOTAL PUBLIC COMPANIES AS OF 12/30/08** | **356** |
| 2009 IPOs | 3 |
| 2009 M&As | -8 |
| 2009 New or reinstated filings | 1 |
| 2009 Delisted and/or traded on bulletin board | -42 |
| 2009 Companies added based on biotech focus | 0 |
| 2009 Change in biotech focus | 0 |
| **TOTAL PUBLIC COMPANIES AS OF 12/31/09** | **318** |
| 2010 IPOs | 17 |
| 2010 M&As | -8 |
| 2010 New or reinstated filings | 1 |
| 2010 Delisted and/or traded on bulletin board | -30 |
| 2010 Companies added based on biotech focus | 0 |
| 2010 Change in biotech focus | 0 |
| **TOTAL PUBLIC COMPANIES AS OF 12/31/10** | **298** |
| 2011 IPOs | 16 |
| 2011 M&As | -21 |
| 2011 New or reinstated filings | 0 |
| 2011 Delisted and/or traded on bulletin board | -7 |
| 2011 Companies added based on biotech focus | 0 |
| 2011 Change in biotech focus | 0 |
| **TOTAL PUBLIC COMPANIES AS OF 12/30/11** | **286** |

Include all publically traded biotech, pharma, and tools and diagnostics companies on U.S. listed exchanges.

*Source: Burrill & Company*

FINANCE

10

280

*Figure 10.34*    **Biggest Market Movers in 2011 by Share Price (USD)**

Includes life sciences stocks with closing price of $1 or more on December 31, 2010

| COMPANY | TICKER | CLOSING PRICE 12/31/2010 | CLOSING PRICE 12/30/2011 | PERCENT CHANGE |
|---|---|---|---|---|
| **ADVANCERS** | | | | |
| Pharmasset | VRUS | 21.78 | 128.20 | 488.6 |
| Inhibitex | INHX | 2.6 | 10.94 | 320.8 |
| Adolor | ADLR | 1.21 | 4.77 | 294.2 |
| Icagen | ICGN | 1.77 | 5.99 | 238.4 |
| Medivation | MDVN | 15.17 | 46.11 | 204.0 |
| Questcor Pharmaceuticals | QCOR | 14.73 | 41.58 | 182.3 |
| Pharmacyclics | PCYC | 6.08 | 14.82 | 143.8 |
| Ariad Pharmaceuticals | ARIA | 5.1 | 12.25 | 140.2 |
| Elan Corporation | ELN | 5.73 | 13.74 | 139.8 |
| Curis | CRIS | 1.98 | 4.68 | 136.4 |
| Oncothyreon | ONTY | 3.26 | 7.58 | 132.5 |
| Vical | VICL | 2.02 | 4.41 | 118.3 |
| Spectrum Pharmaceuticals | SPPI | 6.87 | 14.63 | 113.0 |
| Cyanotech | CYAN | 3.38 | 6.95 | 105.6 |
| Taro Pharmaceutical Industries | TARO.F | 14.49 | 29.5 | 103.6 |
| Jazz Pharmaceuticals | JAZZ | 19.68 | 38.63 | 96.3 |
| Trius Therapeutics | TSRX | 3.71 | 7.15 | 92.7 |
| Cubist Pharmaceuticals | CBST | 21.40 | 39.62 | 85.1 |
| Achillion Pharmaceuticals | ACHN | 4.15 | 7.62 | 83.6 |
| Akorn | AKRX | 6.07 | 11.12 | 83.2 |
| **DECLINERS** | | | | |
| La Jolla Pharmaceutical | LJPC | 2.6 | 0.0027 | -99.9 |
| Genta | GNTA | 1.475 | 0.0026 | -99.8 |
| Radient Pharmaceuticals | RXPC | 1.01 | 0.0031 | -99.7 |
| Jiangbo Pharmaceuticals | JGBO | 5.72 | 0.13 | -97.7 |
| Neurologix | NRGX | 1 | 0.037 | -96.3 |
| Rosetta Genomics | ROSG | 3.76 | 0.18 | -95.2 |
| Marina Biotech | MRNA | 15.49 | 0.8912 | -94.2 |
| StemCells | STEM | 10.8 | 0.824 | -92.4 |
| Diamyd Medical AB | DMYD.Y | 18.57 | 1.43 | -92.3 |
| Emisphere Technologies | EMIS | 2.41 | 0.215 | -91.1 |
| Poniard Pharmaceuticals | PARD | 20.80 | 2.13 | -89.8 |
| Alimera Sciences | ALIM | 10.38 | 1.25 | -88.0 |
| Aoxing Pharmaceutical | AXN | 2.79 | 0.339 | -87.8 |
| NeurogesX | NGSX | 6.36 | 0.8214 | -87.1 |
| WaferGen Biosystems | WGBS | 1.22 | 0.16 | -86.9 |
| ULURU | ULU | 1.65 | 0.2208 | -86.6 |
| Lotus Pharmaceuticals | LTUS | 2.59 | 0.35 | -86.5 |
| China Pediatric Pharmaceuticals | CPDU | 4.35 | 0.6 | -86.2 |
| Somaxon Pharmaceuticals | SOMX | 3.15 | 0.45 | -85.7 |
| Soligenix | SNGX | 3.80 | 0.554 | -85.4 |

*Source: Burrill & Company, S&P Capital IQ*

*Figure 10.35*    **BIGGEST MARKET MOVERS IN 2011 BY MARKET CAPITALIZATION**

Includes life sciences stocks with closing price of $1 or more on December 31, 2010

| COMPANY | TICKER | MARKET CAP 12/31/2011 (USD B) | CHANGE IN MARKET CAP (USD B) |
|---|---|---|---|
| **ADVANCERS** | | | |
| Pfizer | PFE | 166.35 | 26.1 |
| Roche Holdings | SWX:ROG | 136.21 | 18.1 |
| Bristol-Myers Squibb | BMY | 59.72 | 14.4 |
| Sanofi | ENXTPA:SAN | 76.31 | 13.9 |
| Biogen Idec | BIIB | 26.72 | 10.8 |
| Johnson & Johnson | JNJ | 179.1 | 9.2 |
| GlaxoSmithKline | GSK | 72.89 | 8.5 |
| Pharmasset | VRUS | 9.7 | 8.2 |
| Eli Lilly | LLY | 48.12 | 7.7 |
| Valeant Pharmaceuticals | TSX:VRX | 14.68 | 6.2 |
| Alexion Pharmaceuticals | ALXN | 13.24 | 6.0 |
| Allergan | AGN | 2.68 | 0.6 |
| Elan Corporation | ELN | 8.09 | 4.7 |
| Shire | LSE:SHP | 12.65 | 4.2 |
| Novartis | SWX:NOVN | 129.88 | 4.1 |
| Merck | MRK | 114.91 | 3.9 |
| Perrigo | PRGO | 9.07 | 3.2 |
| Regeneron Pharmaceuticals | REGN | 5.13 | 2.2 |
| Celgene | CELG | 30.01 | 2.2 |
| Questcor Pharmaceuticals | QCOR | 2.59 | 1.7 |
| **DECLINERS** | | | |
| Teva Pharmaceutical Industries | TEVA | 35.72 | -11.1 |
| Thermo Fisher Scientific | TMO | 17.01 | -5.0 |
| Bayer AG | DB:BAYN | 40.69 | -4.8 |
| Hospira | HSP | 5 | -4.3 |
| Illumina | ILMN | 3.7 | -4.2 |
| China Pharmaceutical Group | SEHK:1093 | 2.62 | -4.1 |
| Dendreon | DNDN | 1.13 | -3.9 |
| Life Technologies Corporation | LIFE | 6.93 | -3.4 |
| Human Genome Sciences | HGSI | 1.47 | -3.0 |
| AstraZeneca | AZN | 38.45 | -2.7 |
| Warner Chilcott | WCRX | 3.84 | -1.9 |
| Qiagen | QGEN | 3.23 | -1.3 |
| InterMune | ITMN | 0.83 | -1.2 |
| Alere | ALR | 1.99 | -1.1 |
| Forest Laboratories | FRX | 8.08 | -1.1 |
| Amgen | AMGN | 50.93 | -0.9 |
| United Therapeutics | UTHR | 2.76 | -0.8 |
| PerkinElmer | PKI | 2.26 | -0.8 |
| Charles River Laboratories | CRL | 1.35 | -0.7 |
| Pacific Biosciences | PACB | 0.15 | -0.7 |

*Source: Burrill & Company, S&P Capital IQ*

FINANCE

10

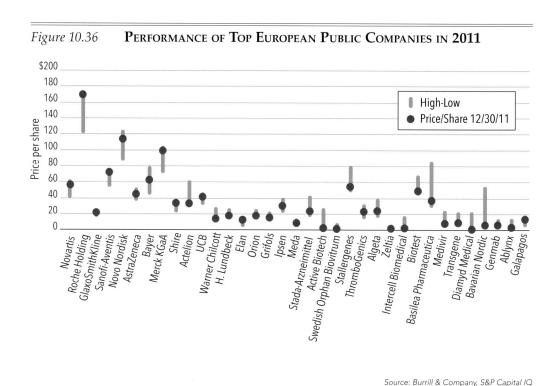

Figure 10.36    PERFORMANCE OF TOP EUROPEAN PUBLIC COMPANIES IN 2011

Source: Burrill & Company, S&P Capital IQ

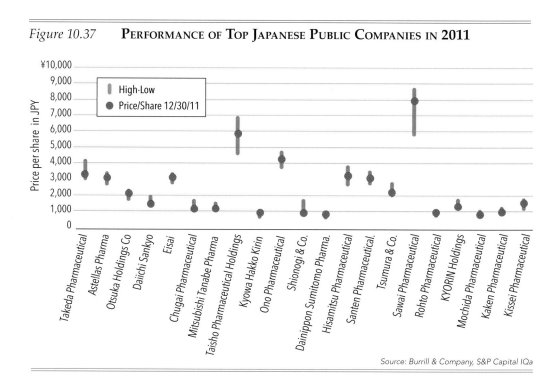

Figure 10.37    PERFORMANCE OF TOP JAPANESE PUBLIC COMPANIES IN 2011

Source: Burrill & Company, S&P Capital IQa

*Figure 10.38*     **PERFORMANCE OF TOP AUSTRALIAN PUBLIC COMPANIES IN 2011**

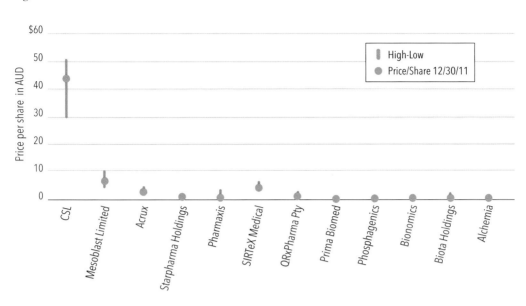

Source: Burrill & Company, S&P Capital IQ

*Figure 10.39*     **PERFORMANCE OF TOP CANADIAN PUBLIC COMPANIES IN 2011**

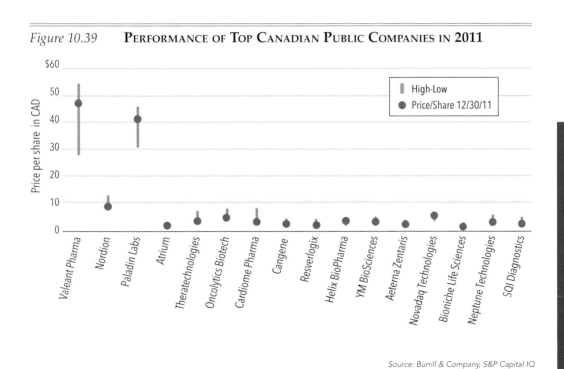

Source: Burrill & Company, S&P Capital IQ

FINANCE

10

## Figure 10.40  TOP U.S. PUBLIC LIFE SCIENCES COMPANIES

2011 Total Revenue and Net Income are extrapolated figures

| COMPANY | TICKER | MARKET CAP 12/30/11 USD M) | TOTAL REVENUE 2011 (USD M) | 2011 PERCENT CHANGE | NET INCOME 2011 (USD M) | 2011 PERCENT CHANGE |
|---|---|---|---|---|---|---|
| **PHARMACEUTICAL** | | | | | | |
| Johnson & Johnson | JNJ | 179,089.1 | 65,030.0 | 5.1 | 9,672.0 | -21.1 |
| Pfizer | PFE | 166,346.0 | 67,425.0 | 0.5 | 10,009.0 | 21.2 |
| Merck | MRK | 114,906.6 | 48,047.0 | 4.5 | 6,272.0 | 628.5 |
| Abbott Laboratories | ABT | 87,594.9 | 38,851.3 | 10.5 | 4,728.4 | 2.2 |
| Bristol-Myers Squibb | BMY | 59,715.3 | 21,244.0 | 9.0 | 3,709.0 | 19.6 |
| Eli Lilly | LLY | 48,116.6 | 24,286.5 | 5.2 | 4,347.7 | -14.2 |
| Allergan | AGN | 26,763.5 | 5,419.1 | 10.2 | 934.5 | 1556.1 |
| Mylan | MYL | 9,152.9 | 6,129.8 | 12.5 | 536.8 | 55.5 |
| Perrigo | PRGO | 9,067.6 | 2,959.7 | 17.6 | 344.9 | 25.1 |
| Forest Laboratories | FRX | 8,084.0 | 4,647.6 | 7.9 | 1,108.9 | 48.5 |
| Watson Pharmaceuticals | WPI | 7,672.7 | 4,584.4 | 28.5 | 260.9 | 41.5 |
| Hospira | HSP | 5,002.1 | 4,057.1 | 3.6 | -9.4 | -102.6 |
| Endo Pharmaceuticals | ENDP | 4,034.4 | 2,730.1 | 59.1 | 187.6 | -27.6 |
| Salix Pharmaceuticals | SLXP | 2,829.6 | 540.5 | 60.4 | 87.4 | 423.0 |
| Questcor Pharmaceuticals | QCOR | 2,594.1 | 218.2 | 89.5 | 79.6 | 126.9 |
| **BIOTECHNOLOGY** | | | | | | |
| Amgen | AMGN | 50,932.1 | 15,582.0 | 3.5 | 3,683.0 | -20.4 |
| Gilead Sciences | GILD | 30,744.1 | 8,385.4 | 5.5 | 2,803.6 | -3.4 |
| Celgene | CELG | 30,009.7 | 4,842.1 | 33.5 | 1,318.2 | 49.7 |
| Biogen Idec | BIIB | 26,733.0 | 5,037.6 | 6.8 | 1,234.4 | 22.8 |
| Alexion Pharmaceuticals | ALXN | 13,238.0 | 783.4 | 44.8 | 175.3 | 80.7 |
| Vertex Pharmaceuticals Incorporated | VRTX | 6,926.5 | 1,410.6 | 883.9 | 29.6 | 103.9 |
| Regeneron Pharmaceuticals, | REGN | 5,131.5 | 445.8 | -2.9 | -221.8 | -112.3 |
| BioMarin Pharmaceutical | BMRN | 3,926.7 | 441.4 | 17.3 | -53.8 | -126.2 |
| Onyx Pharmaceuticals | ONXX | 2,796.4 | 447.2 | 37.8 | 76.1 | 189.7 |
| United Therapeutics Corporation | UTHR | 2,756.3 | 743.2 | 25.3 | 217.9 | 105.7 |
| Cubist Pharmaceuticals | CBST | 2,439.4 | 754.0 | 18.5 | 33.0 | -65.0 |
| Cepheid | CPHD | 2,204.2 | 277.6 | 30.6 | 2.6 | 144.4 |
| Seattle Genetics | SGEN | 1,922.4 | 94.8 | -11.8 | -152.0 | -129.4 |
| Incyte | INCY | 1,895.9 | 94.5 | -44.4 | -186.5 | -485.8 |
| Ariad Pharmaceuticals | ARIA | 1,890.4 | 25.3 | -85.9 | -123.6 | -245.0 |

*Continued on next page*

*Figure 10.40* **Top U.S. Public Life Sciences Companies** *(continued)*

| COMPANY | TICKER | MARKET CAP 12/30/11 (USD M) | TOTAL REVENUE 2011 (USD M) | 2011 PERCENT CHANGE | NET INCOME 2011 (USD M) | 2011 PERCENT CHANGE |
|---|---|---|---|---|---|---|
| **TOOLS AND TECHNOLOGY** | | | | | | |
| Thermo Fisher Scientific | TMO | 17,011.3 | 11,725.9 | 10.9 | 1,329.9 | 28.4 |
| Agilent Technologies | A | 12,160.0 | 6,731.0 | 48.7 | 1,049.0 | 6656.3 |
| Life Technologies | LIFE | 6,934.0 | 3,775.7 | 5.2 | 378.5 | 0.1 |
| Waters Corp. | WAT | 6,635.4 | 1,851.2 | 12.6 | 433.0 | 13.4 |
| Mettler-Toledo International | MTD | 4,665.3 | 2,309.3 | 17.3 | 269.5 | 16.1 |
| Illumina | ILMN | 3,701.5 | 1,055.5 | 58.4 | 86.6 | 19.8 |
| Covance | CVD | 2,777.9 | 2,095.9 | 8.8 | 132.2 | 93.7 |
| Bio-Rad Laboratories | BIO | 2,697.0 | 2,073.5 | 7.6 | 178.2 | -3.9 |
| Techne | TECH | 2,525.7 | 306.6 | 12.4 | 112.7 | 1.4 |
| PerkinElmer | PKI | 2,261.7 | 1,921.3 | 23.9 | 7.7 | -90.7 |
| Bruker | BRKR | 2,059.8 | 1,651.7 | 26.6 | 92.3 | -3.2 |
| Charles River Laboratories | CRL | 1,351.2 | 1,142.6 | 0.8 | 109.6 | 132.5 |
| PAREXEL International | PRXL | 1,227.1 | 1,259.0 | 6.2 | 36.7 | 39.2 |
| Luminex | LMNX | 894.5 | 184.3 | 30.2 | 14.5 | 176.7 |
| Sequenom | SQNM | 442.1 | 55.9 | 17.8 | -74.2 | 38.6 |
| **MEDICAL DEVICE** | | | | | | |
| Medtronic | MDT | 40,366.8 | 16,479.0 | 6.7 | 3,402.0 | 51.3 |
| Baxter International | BAX | 27,900.1 | 13,893.0 | 8.2 | 2,224.0 | 56.6 |
| Synthes | SYST | 20,010.8 | 3,973.8 | 7.8 | 966.8 | 6.5 |
| Stryker | SYK | 19,022.7 | 8,307.0 | 13.5 | 1,345.0 | 5.7 |
| Becton Dickinson and Company | BDX | 15,960.5 | 7,874.5 | 7.2 | 1,218.0 | -7.5 |
| St. Jude Medical | STJ | 10,941.3 | 5,611.7 | 19.9 | 825.8 | 6.2 |
| Zimmer Holdings | ZMH | 9,571.6 | 4,451.8 | 5.5 | 760.8 | 27.5 |
| Edwards Lifesciences | EW | 8,065.1 | 1,678.6 | 16.0 | 236.7 | 8.6 |
| Boston Scientific | BSX | 7,911.2 | 7,622.0 | -2.4 | 441.0 | 141.4 |
| Varian Medical Systems | VAR | 7,556.6 | 2,642.2 | 10.3 | 392.7 | 3.8 |
| CR Bard | BCR | 7,334.4 | 2,896.4 | 6.5 | 328.0 | -35.6 |
| CareFusion | CFN | 5,707.5 | 3,590.0 | 3.6 | 292.0 | 86.0 |
| Hologic | HOLX | 4,607.2 | 1,829.5 | 7.6 | 167.0 | 314.2 |
| IDEXX Laboratories | IDXX | 4,321.2 | 1,218.7 | 10.4 | 161.8 | 14.5 |
| ResMed | RMD | 3,736.1 | 1,302.7 | 12.5 | 225.2 | 3.7 |

FINANCE

10

*Continued on next page*

*Figure 10.40* **Top U.S. Public Life Sciences Companies** *(continued)*

| COMPANY | TICKER | MARKET CAP 12/30/11 (USD M) | TOTAL REVENUE 2011 (USD M) | 2011 PERCENT CHANGE | NET INCOME 2011 (USD M) | 2011 PERCENT CHANGE |
|---|---|---|---|---|---|---|
| **U.S. INDUSTRIAL BIOTECHNOLOGY** | | | | | | |
| Archer Daniels Midland | ADM | 19,104.3 | 88,155.0 | 28.5 | 1,499.0 | -22.9 |
| KiOR | KIOR | 1,039.0 | 0.0 | N/A | -58.8 | -28.0 |
| Solazyme | SZYM | 710.8 | 39.0 | 2.6 | -53.9 | -231.1 |
| Amyris | AMRS | 525.7 | 147.0 | 83.0 | -178.9 | -118.5 |
| Rentech | RTK | 295.0 | 180.1 | 23.7 | -64.3 | -99.6 |
| Parabel Inc | PALG | 267.3 | 0.0 | N/A | -36.6 | 3.7 |
| Codexis | CDXS | 190.5 | 123.9 | 15.6 | -16.6 | -93.8 |
| Gevo | GEVO | 162.9 | 64.5 | 293.7 | -48.2 | -20.2 |
| Metabolix | MBLX | 155.2 | 1.4 | 218.1 | -38.8 | 0.0 |
| Senesco Technologies | SNT | 21.0 | 0.2 | N/A | -6.7 | 54.4 |
| 22nd Century Group | XXII | 11.7 | 1.1 | 2015.0 | -2.7 | -86.2 |
| Viral Genetics | VRAL | 3.0 | 0.0 | -100.0 | -6.7 | 7.2 |
| Consolidated Biofuels | CSBF | 0.2 | 0.0 | N/A | -0.6 | 0.0 |
| Kiwa Bio-Tech Products | KWBT | 0.1 | 0.0 | -100.0 | -1.9 | 16.1 |

*Source: Burrill & Company, S&P Capital IQ*

*Figure 10.41* **Top Global Public Pharma and Biotech Companies**

2011 Total Revenue and Net Income are extrapolated figures

| COMPANY | TICKER | MARKET CAP 12/30/11 (USD M) | TOTAL REVENUE 2011 (USD M) | 2011 PERCENT CHANGE | NET INCOME 2011 (USD M) | 2011 PERCENT CHANGE |
|---|---|---|---|---|---|---|
| **EUROPE** | | | | | | |
| Roche Holding | RHHBY | 145,731.0 | 59,375.0 | 15.2 | 9,113.0 | -7.0 |
| Novartis | NVS | 138,958.2 | 47,194.8 | -10.3 | 9,995.7 | 7.8 |
| GlaxoSmithKline | GSK | 113,455.6 | 42,629.0 | -3.8 | 8,189.0 | 221.0 |
| Sanofi-Aventis | SNY | 99,138.8 | 45,544.7 | 6.0 | 7,395.9 | 0.9 |
| Novo Nordisk | NOVO B | 64,108.2 | 11,595.7 | 6.1 | 2,988.2 | 15.3 |
| AstraZeneca | AZN | 59,844.5 | 33,591.0 | 1.0 | 9,983.0 | 24.0 |
| Bayer | BAYN | 52,855.9 | 47,454.4 | 0.9 | 3,208.8 | 83.9 |
| Merck KGaA | MRK | 21,776.2 | 13,711.6 | 10.1 | 710.4 | -16.2 |
| Shire | SHP | 19,683.0 | 4,263.4 | 22.8 | 865.0 | 47.1 |
| Orion | ORNBV | 8,094.9 | 1,921.5 | -6.9 | -156.5 | -137.4 |
| UCB | UCB | 7,564.6 | 4,723.0 | 9.5 | 220.7 | 59.8 |
| Grifols | GRF | 4,601.8 | 2,728.1 | -8.3 | 171.1 | 0.1 |
| Actelion | ATLN | 4,074.2 | 2,797.6 | 5.3 | 398.8 | -10.1 |
| Warner Chilcott | WCRX | 3,844.8 | 1,246.0 | 6.5 | 560.5 | 272.6 |
| Elan | ELN | 3,702.2 | 1,192.5 | 4.6 | 272.2 | 9.9 |
| Diamyd Medical | DIAM B | 38.6 | 190.0 | 3.7 | -23.1 | -493.7 |

*Continued on next page*

287

*Figure 10.41*   **TOP GLOBAL PUBLIC PHARMA AND BIOTECH COMPANIES** *(continued)*

| COMPANY | TICKER | MARKET CAP 12/30/11 (USD M) | TOTAL REVENUE 2011 (USD M) | 2011 PERCENT CHANGE | NET INCOME 2011 (USD M) | 2011 PERCENT CHANGE |
|---|---|---|---|---|---|---|
| **CANADA** | | | | | | |
| Valeant Pharma | VRX | 14436 | 2464.0 | 108.5 | 160.0 | 177.0 |
| Nordion | NDN | 524.6 | 274.0 | 33.1 | 16.8 | 106.0 |
| Paladin Labs | PLB | 829.5 | 139.2 | 8.1 | 50.2 | 39.2 |
| Atrium | ATRIUM | 41.1 | 4.6 | -2.4 | 17.1 | 581.8 |
| Theratechnologies | TH | 167.0 | 14.7 | -52.7 | -17.7 | -303.8 |
| Cardiome Pharma | COM | 161.2 | 1.5 | -97.8 | -29.3 | -1345.7 |
| Cangene | CNJ | 130.0 | 148.1 | -32.8 | 0.6 | -98.5 |
| Helix BioPharma | HBP | 125.6 | 4.5 | 19.1 | -11.0 | 20.2 |
| YM BioSciences | YM | 191.7 | 1.1 | -41.6 | -15.0 | -15.5 |
| Aeterna Zentaris | AEZ | 159.9 | 33.4 | 20.6 | -20.9 | 15.4 |
| Novadaq Technologies | NDQ | 161.2 | 15.3 | 10.2 | -10.2 | 32.3 |
| **JAPAN** | | | | | | |
| Takeda Pharmaceutical | 4502 | 34,678.6 | 19,052.0 | 8.9% | 3131.7 | -19.9% |
| Astellas Pharma | 4503 | 18,788.1 | 12,783.1 | 10.8% | 1052.0 | 7.6% |
| Otsuka Holdings | 4578 | 15,689.5 | 14,733.1 | 8.2% | 879.4 | 48.1% |
| Daiichi Sankyo | 4568 | 13,961.1 | 11,901.6 | -0.9% | 1014.0 | -89.7% |
| Eisai | 4523 | 11,796.5 | 8,576.2 | -14.4% | 663.0 | -3.5% |
| Chugai Pharmaceutical | 4519 | 8,975.6 | 4,854.6 | 3.8% | 510.7 | -10.3% |
| Mitsubishi Tanabe Pharma | 4508 | 8,881.9 | 5,273.3 | 5.9% | 454.6 | -1.8% |
| Taisho Pharmaceutical | 4581 | 6,392.0 | 3,536.5 | 9.0% | 365.5 | 5.0% |
| Kyowa Hakko Kirin | 4151 | 6,928.5 | 4,467.4 | -12.4% | 273.6 | 21.7% |
| Ono Pharmaceutical | 4528 | 5,953.4 | 1,903.2 | 17.6% | 274.8 | 8.3% |
| **AUSTRALIA** | | | | | | |
| CSL | CSL | 17061.2 | 4,292.6 | -1.4% | 947.6 | 1.3% |
| Mesoblast Limited | MSB | 1979.2 | -65.7 | -4614.8% | -46.6 | -155.2% |
| Acrux | ACR | 490.2 | 5.0 | -96.6% | 5.5 | -94.8% |
| Starpharma Holdings | SPL | 328.2 | 2.5 | -49.3% | -9.4 | -17.1% |
| Pharmaxis | PXS | 326.4 | 1.2 | 42.0% | -42.9 | 9.1% |
| SIRTeX Medical | SRX | 256.3 | 73.1 | 6.3% | 14.0 | 32.6% |
| QRxPharma Pty | QRX | 223.5 | 0.4 | -60.6% | -21.3 | 16.4% |
| Prima Biomed | PRR | 172.3 | 3.6 | 260.3% | -21.5 | -130.4% |
| Phosphagenics | POH | 208.5 | 2.7 | -44.2% | 1.1 | 109.8% |
| Bionomics | BNO | 208.7 | 3.9 | -16.5% | -8.3 | 4.7% |

*Source: Burrill & Company, S&P Capital IQ*

FINANCE

10

288

# THOUGHTS ON INNOVATION

It is easy to look at the financial pressures governments and other payers face today in contending with the rising costs of healthcare and see cost-cutting measures as an obvious, if not easy, approach. But healthcare systems are not the only place that pressures are being felt. Growing populations and rising standards of living are increasing demand for food and fuel as well. The question is, can austerity be a friend to innovation? By treating financial resources as finite, will we turn away from investing in innovation, or will society and investors become more thoughtful about how they deploy the investments they make? Rather than stifling innovation, the new austerity can help guide us to make the right investments in healthcare, energy, and agriculture by prioritizing technologies that can lead not only to solutions, but cost-effective ones. It can help prioritize investments into innovations that do not just provide improvements that are incremental, but disruptive. What we can't afford today is timidity in thought and action.

# MAKING AUSTERITY A FRIEND TO INNOVATION

On July 8, 2011 the space shuttle Atlantis raced toward the heavens at 17,000 miles per hour with its final payload, a Russian research module for the International Space Station. The 12-day mission brought to a close 30 years of NASA's space shuttle flights. In an obituary on the space shuttle program, *The Economist* called the program "a waste of time," saying "The flights are expensive (at the height of its Apollo-era pomp, **NASA** was sucking in around 4.4 percent of total government spending) and dangerous, and the benefits are hard to measure." Roger Handberg, a professor of Political Science at the **University of Central Florida**, writing in the online publication *The Space Review*, summed the end of the space shuttle program simply. "The national mantra now," he said, "is deficit reduction."

The space program has stood as a reflection of a boundless belief in innovation and man's ability—with enough money, creativity, and gumption— to harness science to break the bounds of nature. The danger before us is that in the face of austerity we grow timid in our ambitions at a time when our investment in harnessing the power of biology has brought us to the cusp of a new era of radical technologies that stand to reshape not just the way we diagnose and treat disease, but feed and fuel the world.

It is easy to look at the financial pressures governments and other payers face today in contending with the rising costs of healthcare and see cost cutting measures as an obvious, if not easy, approach. This includes shifting a greater share of the cost of healthcare to the individuals who consume the products and services, imposing price controls, and rationing care. Though such approaches may provide immediate results, they are not in the best interests of populations around the world and will perpetuate disease, economic malaise, and the divide between those who can afford healthcare and those who cannot. It is a solution void of vision, imagination, and compassion.

Our world faces significant challenges today that outstrip the ability of a single company, a single industry, or a single country to address. The world's population is growing. In 2011, the world surpassed the milestone of 7 billion people living on the planet. In addition, as emerging economies give rise to increased prosperity within their borders, consumption is growing. There is a new hunger for fuel, food, and healthcare around the world. With this prosperity, the burden on healthcare systems is growing. People are living longer, but the incidence of chronic diseases is also rising and this is becoming a worldwide problem.

In fact, non-communicable diseases such as heart disease, cancer, chronic respiratory diseases, and diabetes now account for 63 percent of deaths worldwide. But if the human toll hasn't been enough to convince policymakers about the importance of investing to combat the rise of these diseases, a 2011 report from the **World Economic Forum** and the **Harvard School of Public Health** seeks to make an economic case, saying it will cost more than $30 trillion over the next 20 years. This is no longer a problem of just advanced economies. The report notes that 80 percent of deaths from non-communicable diseases now occur in low- and middle-income countries with half of those deaths occurring in people who are in the prime of their productive lives. The authors say the lives that are being lost are "also endangering industry competitiveness across borders." Beyond the cost of these diseases are the economic tolls they will take on economies in terms of lost output. The researchers say cancer, cardiovascular disease, chronic respiratory diseases, diabetes, and mental health problems combined over the next 20 years will cost nations a total of $47 trillion.

But healthcare systems are not the only place that pressures are being felt. Demand for energy is expected to grow by 36 percent by 2035 as the world population is expected to increase 25 percent in the next 20 years. Growing populations and rising standards of living in emerging markets will lead that demand, with countries such as China expected to see energy consumption increase by 75 percent during that same period. The problem is not only that the supply of fossil fuels is finite, but also the consequences associated with their consumption, such as global warming, environmental degradation, and pollution will only worsen.

Then there's the question of how we will feed 9 billion people by 2050. Already we've seen spikes in food prices trigger political unrest in the Middle East, food exporters restrict sales of certain products

In the new austerity, innovation is needed
not just in the products we produce, but in the
way we fund ideas, conduct R&D, regulate our
industries, and deliver care.

outside their borders, and countries such as China buy agricultural land in Africa. As *The Economist* noted in a special report on the global food situation, "over the next 40 years farmers will find it harder to produce enough for everyone because of constraints on land, water, and fertilizers. There is limited opportunity for expansion onto virgin land, less water for crops as fast-growing cities consume more, and a diminishing return from fertilizer use."

All of these pressures come at a time of not only financial austerity, but intellectual austerity as well. Are we, as cultural historian Neal Gabler wrote in an opinion piece in *The New York Times* in August 2011, living in a post-idea world? "If our ideas seem smaller nowadays, it's not because we are dumber than our forebears but because we just don't care as much about ideas as they did," Gabler wrote. "In effect, we are living in an increasingly post-idea world — a world in which big, thought-provoking ideas that can't instantly be monetized are of so little intrinsic value that fewer people are generating them and fewer outlets are disseminating them, the Internet notwithstanding. Bold ideas are almost passé." Gabler argues that "rationality, science, evidence, logical argument and debate have lost the battle in many sectors, and perhaps even in society generally, to superstition, faith, opinion and orthodoxy."

In an age of austerity, luxuries will be viewed as dispensable. Who needs a Mercedes when a Hyundai, or for that matter, the bus, will get you to the same place just as fast. But let's be clear, big ideas and big visions are not a luxury; they are a necessity for finding solutions to the problems we face today.

The question is, can austerity be a friend to innovation? By treating financial resources as finite will we turn away from investing in innovation, or will society and investors become more thoughtful about how they deploy the investments they make?

THOUGHTS ON INNOVATION

Rather than stifling innovation, the new austerity can help guide us to make the right investments in healthcare, energy, and agriculture by prioritizing technologies that can lead not only to solutions, but cost-effective solutions. It can help prioritize investments into innovations that do not just provide improvements that are incremental, but disruptive.

In the new austerity, innovation is needed not just in the products we produce, but in the way we fund ideas, conduct R&D, regulate our industries, and deliver care. The challenge will be to leverage resources, operate with capital efficiency, and deliver value. Already there are many examples of new models rising to spread risk, share the cost of pre-competitive research, and fund the development of new therapies without funding the creation of new infrastructure that is duplicative and excessive.

Innovation is needed not only in the products we produce, but also in all aspects of how we fund, develop, manufacture, and distribute them. Creativity is essential throughout the ecosystem of innovation—not only from inventors and entrepreneurs, but also from investors, regulators, payers, and healthcare providers. We need to harness technology to improve access and delivery of healthcare. We need to tap into the massive amounts of data being collected in healthcare systems to hear what it tells us about the best way to treat and prevent disease. And we need to find new ways to reduce the cost and speed the development of new therapies that can bend the cost curve on healthcare.

There will be pressures on governments to cut spending, even when it has the potential to produce significant returns on investment. Consider the **Human Genome Project**, an effort that's been likened to the biological sciences moon shot. Though derided by critics for the lack of new medications the project has yielded, the scientific and economic payoffs have been enormous. A May 2011 **Battelle Technology Partnership Practice** analysis that examined the economic impact of the Human Genome Project found in the ten years since the U.S. government made its $3.8 billion investment, the research has paid dividends not only in the genomic revolutions' influence in healthcare, but in fields including renewable energy development, industrial

New models are rising to spread risk, share the cost of pre-competitive research, and fund the development of new therapies

biotechnology, agricultural biosciences, and others. The report found that between 1988 and 2010, the sequencing of the human genome and associated research and industry activity directly and indirectly generated $796 billion in economic output in the United States, $244 billion in personal income for Americans, and 3.8 million job years of employment.  In fact, in 2010 alone, Battelle found the genomics-enabled industry generated $3.7 billion in federal taxes and $2.3 billion in U.S. state and local taxes, essentially returning in one year nearly the entire investment made by the government over 14 years.

The end of the space shuttle program is not the end of space exploration. For now, NASA will let its astronauts hitch rides to the **International Space Station** while it plans for a new era of deep space exploration to take Americans where no man has gone before. In the same way, we will continue to drive biology to take us where we have not gone before. We need to think of new and less costly ways to fund our explorations of biology, but from time to time will have to fund ambitious projects. What we can't afford today is timidity in thought and action. While we need to be thoughtful about the investments we make as a society and cognizant of the choices before us, there is a role that government investment has played and must continue to play in funding biomedical research. It is in the interest of governments around the world to do so. Those that fail to adequately fund such research will do so at their own peril. In this century of biology, it is an imperative not only for the health of their populations, but for their global competitiveness, economic strength, and our collective wellbeing. ■

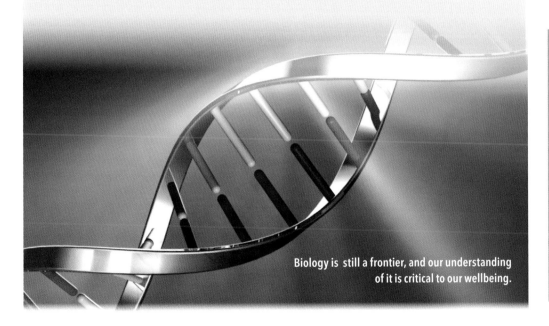

Biology is still a frontier, and our understanding
of it is critical to our wellbeing.

THOUGHTS ON INNOVATION

# ABOUT
# BURRILL & COMPANY

Founded in 1994, Burrill & Company
is a diversified global financial services firm
focused on the life sciences industry.

With $1.5 billion in assets under management, the firm's
businesses include venture capital/private equity, merchant
banking, and media. By leveraging the scientific and business
networks of its team, Burrill & Company has established
unrivaled access and visibility in the life sciences industry.
This unique combination of resources and capabilities enables
the company to provide life sciences companies with capital,
transactional support, management expertise, insight, market
intelligence, and analysis through its investments, conferences,
and publications. Headquartered in San Francisco, the company
oversees a global network of offices throughout the United
States, Latin America, Europe, and Asia.

VENTURE CAPITAL

INTERNATIONAL
INVESTING

PRIVATE EQUITY

MERCHANT
BANKING

MEDIA

EVENTS AND
CONFERENCES

# Overview

Burrill & Company, a diversified financial services firm, is focused exclusively on companies involved in biotechnology, pharmaceuticals, medical devices, diagnostics, human healthcare and related medical technologies, digital health, innovative healthcare delivery, nutraceuticals and wellness, agricultural biotechnology, and biogreentech. Burrill & Company has created a unique and highly effective platform for generating deal flow, assessing the scientific, commercial and investment viability of potential transactions, executing transactions, and creating value in portfolio companies.

Our capital base has been provided by more than 30 leading industrial companies, plus a larger group of financial institutions. Our global investment strategy gives us access to best-in-class life sciences deals, foreign capital, and public markets.

## Global Financing and Advisory Capabilities

**VENTURE CAPITAL**

- $1.5 billion under management
- More than 100 investments
- More than 50 board seats
- Healthcare & BioGreenTech

BURRILL & COMPANY

**MEDIA**

- Industry-leading conferences
- Books
- Publications
- Custom Reports
- Social Media News Network

**MERCHANT BANKING**

- **Strategic Advisory**
  Divestments/spinouts
  Strategic partnerships
  Project financings

- **Principal Investing**
  Growth capital

- **Public and private financings**
  Private placements/PIPES
  IPO/FO Underwriting
  Sales and trading
  Equity research

# Venture Capital

Burrill & Company invests exclusively in life science-based companies with breakthrough technologies and transformative business models to meet the world's need for better healthcare, food, and energy.

While generally investing in the United States, the team has invested worldwide and is active in Europe, China, Taiwan, India, the Middle East, North Africa, Australia/New Zealand, Russia, Scandinavia, and Latin America, especially Brazil. The worldwide growth of opportunities reflect the global importance of biotechnology, and we actively search for opportunities to invest in non-domestic markets to arbitrage technology, people, and innovation. We have only just begun to capture the value of the DNA age and the power of biotechnology to address global needs to heal, fuel, and feed the world.

## Unique Benefits

| VISION AND EXPERTISE | ACTIVE INVESTMENT MANAGEMENT |
|---|---|
| • Our global investment strategy gives us access to best-in-class life sciences deals, market efficiencies, global capital, and public markets<br><br>• We have more than 200 years of combined experience in the biotechnology industry as researchers, operating officers, and investment professionals | • Implement disciplined portfolio management practices<br><br>• Effect management team enhancements<br><br>• Create/rationalize pipeline – aggressive in-licensing & out-licensing<br><br>• Pursue add-on acquisitions and synergistic consolidations |

## The Burrill Family of Funds

The Burrill family of venture capital and private equity funds, with more than $1.5 billion under management includes:

- Burrill Capital Fund IV
- Burrill Life Sciences Capital Fund III
- Burrill Life Sciences Capital Fund II
- Burrill Life Sciences Capital Fund I
  - Burrill Agbio Capital Fund
  - Burrill Biotechnology Capital Fund
- Malaysia Life Sciences Capital Fund I&II
- Burrill Brazil Fund
- Burrill Canada Fund
- Burrill China Fund
- Burrill Digital Health Fund
- Burrill India Fund

# OUR PORTFOLIO COMPANIES

We partner with talented entrepreneurs with the vision to grow exciting life science opportunities world-wide. Our portfolio covers the following landscape:

## MEDICAL TECHNOLOGY AND DIAGNOSTICS

### AliveCor

AliveCor is a mobile health company developing innovative wireless biosensors and cardiac monitors that work with a variety of mobile platforms, including iPhones, iPads and Android devices.

### ACUSPHERE

Acusphere, Inc. is a specialty pharmaceutical company that develops new drugs and improved formulations of existing drugs using its proprietary porous microsphere technology. We are focused on developing proprietary drugs that can offer benefits such as improved safety and efficacy, increased patient compliance, greater ease of use, expanded indications or reduced cost.

Adlyfe develops screening and diagnostic products based upon its misfolded-protein detection (MPD) platform. The company is developing its MPD Platform technology to produce simple, highly sensitive, low-cost and rapid-action test kits for the blood screening, human diagnostics and animal testing markets.

### BIOMIMETIC THERAPEUTICS

BioMimetic Therapeutics specializes in the development and commercialization of clinically proven products to promote the healing of musculoskeletal injuries and diseases, including therapies for orthopedic and sports medicine applications.

DiaDexus is a biotechnology company focused on the discovery, development and commercialization of novel diagnostic and therapeutic products with high clinical value. The company's PLAC test, an approved and marketed product, is a blood test that measures serum concentration of lipoprotein-associated phospholipase A2 (Lp-PLA2). An elevated level of Lp-PLA2 is a significant risk factor for both coronary artery disease and ischemic stroke.

Flexible Stenting Solutions is a privately held medical device company focused on the development and commercialization of flexible stents built on a proprietary design platform.

HyperMed uses Medical Hyperspectral Imaging (HSI), an advanced form of spectroscopy, that provides a two-dimensional tissue oxygenation map to analyze tissue for medical applications.

### NOVADAQ

Novadaq Technologies develops and markets real-time fluorescence imaging technologies for use in the operating room. The company's primary core technology platform, SPY Imaging, provides clinically relevant, anatomic and physiologic images during surgical procedures.

## Medical Technology and Diagnostics *(continued)*

Primera BioSystems is developing a proprietary gene expression analysis system, "STAR" (Scalable Transcription Analysis Routine), that combines real-time PCR and DNA microarray technologies into a single system.

Spectral Image, Inc. is a privately held, early-stage medical device company focused on the development of imaging technology for biomedical use.

XDx is a molecular diagnostics company focused on the discovery, development and commercialization of non-invasive gene expression testing in the areas of transplant medicine and autoimmunity.

# Therapeutics and Wellness

Alexza Pharmaceuticals is a rapidly emerging pharmaceutical company focused on the research, development and commercialization of novel proprietary products for the acute treatment of central nervous system conditions

Attune produces and markets an innovative all natural probiotic formulated for the healthy living market. The current line of products includes a number of formulations, including a granola bar and a chocolate mint bar.

Ceptaris Therapeutics is a privately held, specialty pharmaceutical company developing a proprietary formulation of mechlorethamine gel for the treatment of early stage (stages I-IIA) mycosis fungoides, a type of Cutaneous T-Cell Lymphoma.

ADMA Biologics is a clinical stage biotechnology company focused on the development and commercialization of human plasma and plasma-derived therapeutics.

Catalyst Biosciences is developing the next generation of biopharmaceuticals, harnessing the catalytic power of proteases – naturally occurring protein-degrading enzymes that regulate a wide variety of biological processes – to degrade proteins that promote disease.

Corazonas offers snacks formulated using ingredients that are scientifically proven to help maintain heart health. The first offering in the Corazonas platform is heart-healthy tortilla chips, formulated using whole oats and plant sterols, with no trans fats, reduced sodium and virtually no saturated fat.

*(continued on next page)* »

# OUR PORTFOLIO COMPANIES

THERAPEUTICS AND WELLNESS *(continued)*

Corcept Therapeutics is dedicated to the development of treatments for the severe diseases caused by excess or irregular cortisol levels. The company's most advanced programs are for the treatment of Cushing's Syndrome and for psychotic depression.

Endocyte is a biopharmaceutical company developing targeted therapies for the treatment of cancer and other serious diseases. We use our proprietary technology to create novel small-molecule drug conjugates or SMDCs, and companion imaging diagnostics.

Ferrokin BioSciences is developing a safe and effective iron chelator for the treatment of iron-overload in patients with transfusion-dependent hereditary and acquired refractory anemias. Iron overload is the inevitable complication of chronic transfusion therapy for a variety of refractory anemias.

## evolva

Evolva Nutrition is building a pipeline of products with potential utility in consumer health, nutrition and the food chain.

Lentigen is a diversified biologics company focused on the development and commercialization of breakthrough treatments for human disease. Lentiviral vectors (LV), the company's technology platform, are recognized as the most efficient method for delivery of genetic sequence information into cells to reprogram their function.

Light Sciences (now LSO) was founded in 1994 to develop a commercially viable light-activated drug product to treat patients with solid tumor cancers.

Logical Therapeutics is a development stage biotechnology company, with clinical and pre-clinical stage medicines to treat diseases that are associated with poorly controlled or excessive inflammation. Inflammation is a key component of the body's response to injury or infection.

MabVax is a clinical-stage biopharmaceutical company focused on the commercialization of proprietary anti-cancer immunotherapies resulting from two integrated and successful technology platforms.

**NEUROTECH**

Neurotech, Inc. is a biotechnology company dedicated to the development of sight-saving therapeutics for chronic retinal diseases.

Neos Therapeutics is a privately owned drug delivery and full service contract manufacturing company serving prescription pharmaceutical and consumer healthcare markets.

Nora Therapeutics is an early stage specialty biopharmaceuticals company focusing on commercializing therapeutics to address issues in reproductive health.

 **ODYSSEY THERA**

Odyssey Thera is pioneering a pathway-based approach to drug discovery. The company has created a comprehensive strategy for cellular systems biology and drug discovery, and is utilizing this capability both for the benefit of its pharmaceutical partners and to identify small molecules that block key cancer pathways

OncoGeneX

OncoGenex Pharmaceuticals is a biopharmaceutical company committed to the development and commercialization of new cancer therapies that address treatment resistance in cancer patients.

SENTINEXT
therapeutics

Sentinext Therapeutics has been established to develop safe and efficacious vaccines and therapeutics for tropical infectious diseases.

 SCYNEXIS®

SCYNEXIS is a chemistry-focused drug discovery and development company. SCYNEXS' goal, from concept to clinic, is to deliver effective and innovative drug pipeline solutions to our pharmaceutical partners.

tlc

Taiwan Liposome Company (TLC) is a biopharmaceutical company focused on the research, development and commercialization of innovative pharmaceutical products based on its proprietary drug delivery technologies.

 TMune THERAPEUTICS

TMune Therapeutics is a venture stage biotechnology company focused on the development of T cell therapies for the treatment of cancer and infectious disease.

*(continued on next page)* »

ABOUT BURRILL & COMPANY

# OUR PORTFOLIO COMPANIES

## SPECIALTY PHARMACEUTICAL AND SERVICES

Cerca Insights is dedicated to helping our customers discover the next generation of CNS drugs. We are focused on delivering world-class behavioral pharmacology from our brand new lab in Penang, Malaysia.

NewBridge Pharmaceuticals is a specialty therapeutics and devices company positioned to become the leading provider of innovative healthcare products to the Middle East, North Africa and Turkey (MENA & Turkey).

Waterstone Pharmaceuticals, Inc. is an Indiana-based company with its main manufacturing operations in China. It aspires to be a leading developer and manufacturer of active pharmaceutical ingredients and finished pharmaceutical products. Waterstone's business focus is to take advantage of the high-quality and lost-cost value proposition and to capture the rapidly growing China pharmaceutical market opportunity.

Wellpartner is a nationally recognized provider of pharmacy distribution solutions for health plans, Medicaid programs, and safety-net providers nationwide. Dedicated to lowering the cost of medications using home delivery and Contract Pharmacy services, Wellpartner offers innovative solutions that improve pharmacy care for individuals.

## BIOGREENTECH

Akermin is developing new technology to significantly reduce the cost to separate and capture carbon dioxide from a variety of industrial processes. Akermin's technology uses an enzyme, Carbonic Anhydrase, to accelerate absorption of carbon dioxide.

Chromatin is developing plant mini-chromosome technology that will enable entire chromosomes to be designed and incorporated into plant cells. The mini-chromosomes will allow introduction of new genes, stacks of genes and whole metabolic pathways without disrupting the plant's own genome.

### Cobalt Technologies

Cobalt Technologies is developing novel technologies for the production of commercial renewable biobutanol, a drop-in replacement for petroleum-derived products, and a valuable industrial chemical used in paints, coatings, bio-based plastics, and a platform for the production of military-grade jet fuel.

## BioGreenTech *(continued)*

Codexis is creating sustainable chemicals, clean fuels, pharmaceutical processes, and renewable ingredients that make the industry more efficient, productive and profitable.

Gevo is a leading renewable chemicals and advanced biofuels company. We are developing biobased alternatives to petroleum-based products using a combination of synthetic biology and chemistry.

Glori Energy's mission is to sustainably and efficiently recover billions of barrels of oil trapped in reservoirs using existing oil wells. Glori partners with oil producers to significantly increase their oil production through the deployment of its AERO™ (Activated Environment for Recovery of Oil) System.

Virdia has developed a proprietary technology to make an old, industrially proven process converting lignocellulosic biomass to fermentable sugars economically very attractive. It is these fermentable sugars which are considered the gateway to advanced biofuels (biobutanols, biodiesel, jet fuel etc) and biochemicals (bioplastics etc). Virdia utilizes hydrochloric acid to break down and hydrolyze lignocellulosic biomass, with complete recycle of the acid.

## LanzaTech

LanzaTech was founded in early 2005 with a vision to be a dominant technology provider in the industrial bio-commodities arena. Our goal was simple: to develop and commercialize proprietary technologies for the production of low-carbon fuels that do not compromise food or land resources.

Mascoma is a renewable fuels company that has developed innovative technology for the low-cost conversion of abundant biomass to renewable fuels and chemicals.

### Segetis™

Segetis develops proprietary biologically based monomers that can be used as substitutes for petrochemicals as plasticizers, solvents, and polyols.

ABOUT BURRILL & COMPANY

306

# Merchant Banking

We advise companies on public or private financings and cross-border transactions, including M&A, strategic partnerships, spin-outs, and strategic development.

Our team has extensive experience and a comprehensive network to help life sciences companies identify and access companies strategic to building their businesses.

## Life Sciences-dedicated merchant banking

Our service lines include:

| STRATEGIC ADVISORY | CAPITAL MARKETS | SALES & TRADING |
|---|---|---|
| • Mergers & Acquisitions<br><br>• Divestitures/ new company spin-outs<br><br>• Strategic partnering<br><br>• Project financing | • Market insight<br><br>• Public offerings and private placements of equity and equity-linked securities | • Institutional Agency Execution, relationships with buyside trading desks<br><br>• Corporate buybacks (10b-18)<br><br>• Non-Deal Road Shows |

### Sectors

- Biotechnology
- Pharmaceutical
- BioGreenTech
- Tools, Diagnostics, and Devices
- Medical Devices
- Drug Discovery and Enabling Technologies
- Drug Delivery
- Healthcare Delivery
- Lab Services

### Combined strengths

- Global reach
- Boutique focus
- Highly experienced team
- Deep industry intelligence and contacts

### Selected clients

# International

Burrill & Company has a multicultural, multilingual team with extensive international business experience spanning the globe. Given that diseases know no borders, science/technology, intellectual property protection, and capital are ubiquitous worldwide. With instantaneous communications and a highly mobile workforce, globalization is a requirement, not an option. Burrill & Company is the leader in arbitraging value and integrating the most efficient life sciences resources worldwide.

### Venture Capital and Private Equity

Burrill & Company is actively seeking venture capital, growth capital, and private equity investment opportunities globally.

### Media

We organize global conferences focused on Greater China, Latin America, Europe, India, the United States, and topically relevant issues.

### Merchant Banking

We advise companies on public or private financings and cross-border transactions, including M&A, strategic partnerships, spin-outs, and strategic development.

# Media

Burrill's Media Group provides insight, intelligence, and information on life sciences that are unmatched in the industry. It is the creator of the Burrill Annual Biotech Report, now in its 26th year of publication. As the creator, sponsor, and facilitator of more than a dozen leading industry conferences globally and publisher of a wide range of bio-intelligence reports, the Burrill Media Group has developed a unique and highly effective platform for the industry's top executives, investors, scientists and consultants to find and make outstanding life sciences investments.

## Burrill Annual Report on the Life Sciences Industry

Provides readers with a clear perspective on the biotechnology industry, as well as detailed analysis and insight regarding how the industry performed in the year. Available in print and digitally.

## Weekly: The Burrill Weekly Brief

The Burrill Weekly Brief is a once-a-week email with a snapshot of the past week's news and events of significance for life sciences thought leaders and executives. The Brief has links to current stories on the website, including a weekly podcast on a newsworthy topic.

## Monthly: The Burrill Report

Provides actionable market intelligence on the latest global developments and trends in the life sciences industry. Includes Venture and Public Financings, Grants, Partnering and Licensing Deals, Mergers and Acquisitions, FDA New Product Approvals, PDUFA dates, and more.

## Daily: Burrillreport.com

Burrillreport.com is Burrill Media Group's web portal, with the most important podcasts, news, and numbers of the life sciences industry. It contains links to the reports and data produced by the team.

## Burrill Events

The Burrill Media Group hosts and sponsors more than a dozen major annual industry events, enabling Burrill & Company to remain on the cutting edge of the industry. By providing insight through our high quality keynotes, panel discussions, and presentations, our events are widely attended by key decision-makers and industry thought leaders. With strong ties to the life science and investment community, Burrill & Company provides a unique forum to build strategic relationships and address industry issues.

## Burrill Family of Life Sciences Indices:

Burrill publishes indices charting the biotech industry stock market performance on a monthly and quarterly basis.

- Burrill Biotech Select Index
- Burrill Large-Cap Biotech Index
- Burrill Mid-Cap Biotech Index
- Burrill Small-Cap Biotech Index
- Burrill Personalized Medicine Index
- Burrill Diagnostics Index
- Burrill BioPharma Index
- Burrill BioGreenTech Index
- Burrill Canada Index
- Burrill India Index

# G. Steven Burrill,

## Founder and Chief Executive Officer

G. Steven Burrill has been involved in the growth and prosperity of the biotechnology industry for more than 45 years. An early pioneer, Mr. Burrill is one of the original architects of the industry and one of its most avid and sustained developers.

Mr. Burrill currently serves on the boards of directors of AliveCor (Chairman), Catalyst Biosciences, Depomed (NASDAQ: DEPO), NewBridge, Novadaq (NASDAQ: NDQ), Targacept (NASDAQ: TRGT), and XDx. Previously he served as Chairman of the boards of BioImagene, Abunda Nutrition, and Pharmasset. Prior to founding Burrill & Company in 1994, he spent 28 years with Ernst & Young, directing and coordinating the firm's services to clients in the biotechnology, life sciences, high technology, and manufacturing industries worldwide.

In 1995 Mr. Burrill received BIO's "service award" for his global biotechnology leadership. In 2002 he was recognized as a biotech investment visionary by the prestigious Scientific American magazine (The Scientific American 50), and was also honored that year at the American Liver Foundation's Annual "Salute to Excellence" Gala, which honors the best and the brightest from the Bay Area's medical, biotech and biopharmaceutical industries. In 2008 he received the BayBio Pantheon DiNA lifetime achievement award for his worldwide biotech leadership; and in the same year he received the Alan Cranston Living Legend Award for his central role in advancing biomedical research globally. In 2011 he received a lifetime achievement award at Scrip Intelligence's annual Scrip Award ceremony in London; also in 2011 he received the Breath of Life Award from the Northern California Chapter of the Cystic Fibrosis Foundation to honor him for his contributions to the life sciences industry throughout his career.

In addition to his work with leading life science companies, Mr. Burrill is a founder and currently serves as Chairman of the board of the National Science and Technology Medals Foundation (NSTMF). Additionally, he serves as Chairman of the San Francisco Mayor's Biotech Advisory Committee (MAYBAC). Mr. Burrill chaired the National Research Council study on linkages in biotechnology between Japan and the United States and was also involved with the U.S.-Japan Science and Technology Agreement Study of Technology Transfer Mechanisms between the U.S. and Japan. Other not-for-profit activities include serving on the boards of directors of the Life Science Foundation (Chairman); the World Council for Ethical Standards (Chairman); the Vilas County (Wisconsin) Economic Development Corporation (Chairman); the National Health Museum (Vice Chairman); the Bay Area Science Infrastructure Consortium; BayBio (Emeritus); California Healthcare Institute (Emeritus); The Exploratorium (Emeritus); The Kellogg Center for Biotechnology; the MIT Center for Biomedical Innovation; BIO Ventures for Global Health (BVGH); The Gladstone Foundation; the Harvard Medical School Genetics Advisory Council; and the NIH Scientific Management Review Board.

He serves on the editorial boards of Scientific American, the Journal of Commercial Biotechnology, and Life Science Leader and also serves on the advisory boards of the Center for Policy on Emerging Technologies (C-PET) and BioAg Gateway, City of Madison. He is an advisor to the University of Illinois Institute for Genomic Biology, the University of Wisconsin College of Agricultural and Life Sciences, the University of Minnesota College of Biological Sciences, Duke University, University of California, Davis, and is an adjunct professor at University of California, San Francisco. He also serves on the advisory boards for the Department of Biology at San Francisco State University and the Biotechnology Master's Program in the Department of Biology at the University of San Francisco. He serves on the BioNJ Diagnostics & Personalized Medicine Committee. ■

# BURRILL & COMPANY

## LIFE SCIENCES VENTURE CAPITAL

### G. STEVEN BURRILL
*Chief Executive Officer*
*steve@b-c.com*

G. Steven Burrill has been involved in the growth and prosperity of the biotechnology industry for over 45 years. An early pioneer, Mr. Burrill is one of the original architects of the industry and one of its most avid and sustained developers. He currently serves as Chairman of AliveCor and sits on the boards of Catalyst Biosciences, Depomed (NASDAQ: DEPO), NewBridge, Novadaq (NASDAQ: NDQ), Targacept (NASDAQ: TRGT) and XDx. Previously he served as Chairman of the Boards of BioImagene, Evolva Nutrition, and Pharmasset. Prior to founding Burrill & Company in 1994, he spent 28 years with Ernst & Young, directing and coordinating the firm's services to clients in the biotechnology, life sciences, high technology, and manufacturing industries worldwide.

### DAVID WETHERELL
*Managing Partner*
*dwetherell@b-c.com*

David Wetherell has spent more than 20 years as a CEO in high-tech, as well as 17 years in venture capital, the last seven of which have been dedicated to biotech and life sciences. From 1986 to 2006, he served as both CEO and, later, chairman of CMGI, where he helped build the company from $3 million in annual revenues to more than $1 billion and started the first venture capital firm focused on the Internet, @Ventures. When CMGI, now ModusLink, turned its direction away from the Internet to cleantech venture investing and supply chain management, Mr. Wetherell turned his attention to the life sciences industry. In 2005, he started GBP Capital, a venture capital company

focused exclusively on leading edge life sciences. He has received numerous awards, including Ernst & Young's New England Entrepreneur of the Year in 2000 and recognition as one of Money Magazine's Top 25 investors. He obtained his B.A. in Mathematics from Ohio Wesleyan University and an honorary doctorate from Bryant University. He currently serves as chairman of Lentigen and sits on the boards of numerous other companies, including HyperMed, Flexible Stenting Solutions, TMune Therapeutics and Quintess.

### VICTOR A. HEBERT
*Managing Director,*
*Chief Administrative Officer,*
*and Chief Legal Officer*
*vhebert@b-c.com*

Victor Hebert joined the company in October 2008 after having been its principal outside counsel at Heller Ehrman LLP since the founding of Burrill & Company. Mr. Hebert is a business lawyer with extensive experience in mergers and acquisitions, corporate finance, corporate governance, fund formation and venture capital.

During his legal career, Mr. Hebert performed services for Heller Ehrman and clients in numerous industries, including biotechnology, healthcare, financial services, aluminum, steel, telecommunications, semiconductor equipment and services, analytical instruments, computer software and hardware, forest products, solid waste disposal, and food and beverages.

Mr. Hebert has a long history of serving on the boards of or as an officer of numerous public and private corporations and non-profit organizations. At Heller Ehrman, Mr. Hebert served as chairman of the management committee from 1981-1993 and as co-chairman from 1987-1993.

Mr. Hebert is a member of the State Bar of California and a member of the American Bar Association and Bar Association of San Francisco. Mr. Hebert holds undergraduate and law degrees from the University of California, Berkeley.

VENTURE CAPITAL *(continued)*

BRYANT E. FONG
*Managing Director*
*Co-Head of Venture Group*
bryant@b-c.com

DOUGLAS LIND
*Managing Director*
dlind@b-c.com

Bryant Fong joined Burrill & Company in 1998 and has more than 15 years of experience in the biotechnology industry. Prior to joining Burrill & Company, Mr. Fong held positions as a biochemist and molecular biologist with two early stage biotechnology companies located in the San Francisco Bay Area. His first position involved working with eukaryotic recombinant expression systems and was part of the first research group to publish on the expression of a four-gene system in S. cerevisiae in the production of recombinant human collagen. Later, Mr. Fong was hired as the first employee of a genomics company to help develop and validate its high-throughput functional genomics platform. Mr. Fong's aggregate research experiences include recombinant protein expression in yeast, development of linear artificial chromosomes for pathway engineering/heterologous gene transfer in yeast, and catalytic RNA technology. Mr. Fong currently serves on the boards of directors of a number of private companies including Neurotech Pharmaceuticals, Nora Therapeutics, Odyssey Thera, Alinea Pharmaceuticals, Ferrokin Biosciences, NEOS Therapeutics, Logical Therapeutics, and Yaupon Pharmaceuticals (observer).

Mr. Fong earned his bachelors degree with honors in Molecular and Cell Biology-Biochemistry from the University of California, Berkeley.

Douglas Lind joined Burrill & Company as a Managing Director in the company's venture group in January 2012. Previously he served as Managing Director at GBP Capital, a Greenwich, Connecticut-based healthcare venture firm. He has more than 20 years of experience in the life sciences industry, ranging from the practice of clinical medicine to work as a top tier Wall Street equity research analyst and venture capitalist. Throughout his career he has focused on identifying promising disruptive technologies and visionary leadership that offer high value solutions to pressing medical needs.

He served as senior biotechnology equity research analyst at Morgan Stanley from 1997 through 2002 and at PaineWebber from 1995 to 1997. His coverage of large and small capitalization biotechnology companies included Amgen, Biogen, Celera (acquired by Quest Diagnostics), Centocor (acquired by Johnson & Johnson), Chiron (acquired by Novartis), IDEC Pharmaceuticals (acquired by Biogen), ImClone (acquired by Bristol-Myers Squibb), MedImmune (acquired by AstraZeneca), Agouron (acquired by Warner Lambert), Axys Pharmaceuticals (acquired by Celera) and Millenium Pharmaceuticals (acquired by Takeda Pharmaceuticals).

Dr. Lind is a graduate of the University of Iowa College of Medicine. He served as an attending physician at St. Elizabeth's Hospital in Boston, a major teaching affiliate of Tufts University School of Medicine, where he completed residency training in internal medicine. He currently serves on the board of directors of Lentigen, MabVax, TMune, HyperMed Imaging, and Spectral Image.

ABOUT BURRILL & COMPANY

# THE BURRILL TEAM

### ROGER E. WYSE
*Managing Director,*
*Biogreentech, ASEAN*
roger@b-c.com

Roger Wyse joined Burrill & Company in 1998 and has led the development of its agriculture, nutraceuticals, health and wellness, and biogreentech-related activities in venture capital investing, and merchant banking.

Dr. Wyse is an internationally recognized scientist and was a dean at two major research universities. He served for five years as Dean of the College of Agricultural and Life Sciences at the University of Wisconsin-Madison. From 1986 to 1992 he served as Dean of Research at Rutgers University. Throughout his administrative career Dr. Wyse has been known for his vision and leadership in developing national policies and funding for life sciences research. Dr. Wyse chairs or serves on the boards of six private companies: Attune, Brand Accelerator (Chair), Chakra Biotech (Chair), Corazonas (Chair), Efficas, and Segetis. He is Co-Chairman of the Malaysian Life Sciences Capital Fund; and is a member of the International Advisory Panel for Biotechnology for the Prime Minister of Malaysia. He was founder and Chairman of the Alliance for Animal Genome Research. He is also on the board of the industry group BIO and on the executive committee of BIO's Industrial and Environmental section. In research, Dr. Wyse earned international recognition for his basic studies in plant biochemistry.

He has published more than 150 scientific papers. In recognition of his research accomplishments he received the Arthur Flemming Award in 1982 as the Outstanding Young Scientist in the U.S. Federal Service. He was elected a Fellow of both the Crop Science Society of America and The American Society of Agronomy. And in 2008, he was elected as a Fellow of The American Association for the Advancement of Science. He has also served as a consultant to numerous Fortune 500 companies.

### GREG B. YOUNG
*Managing Director,*
*Biogreentech, ASEAN*
greg@b-c.com

Greg Young joined Burrill & Company in 2000 and has been primarily involved in sourcing, evaluating and investing in new business opportunities as part of the firm's venture activities. His focus areas of investment cover green technologies and businesses addressing energy, climate and sustainability markets. He also acts as an investment manager for the Malaysian Life Sciences Capital Fund (MLSCF), a venture fund co-managed by Burrill & Company.

Greg currently serves on the board of Virdia and is a board observer on the boards of Akermin and GloriOil. Greg was instrumental in sourcing and consummation of Burrill & Company and MLSCF's investment in Gevo. Previously, Greg worked as a molecular biologist focused on protein expression at an early-stage biotech company located in San Diego. Greg received his B.S. in Biochemistry and Cell Biology from the University of California, San Diego and an M.S. in Biotechnology and Business from Northwestern University.

### ANN F. HANHAM
*Managing Director, Canada*
ann@b-c.com

Ann Hanham joined Burrill & Company in February, 2000, and has utilized her background in clinical and regulatory affairs to lead deals in diagnostic, device and therapeutic opportunities. Prior to joining Burrill & Company, Ann was a co-founder and Vice President of Clinical & Regulatory Affairs at InterMune Pharmaceuticals, and prior to that, the Senior Director for Oncology Product Development at Otsuka Pharmaceuticals and the Medical Director for Celtrix Pharmaceuticals. She has also worked for Becton Dickinson in both regulatory and clinical affairs in their monoclonal antibody program, and as a regulatory toxicologist with the Health Protection Branch of Health and Welfare Canada. Dr. Hanham holds a Ph.D. from the University of British Columbia, an M.Sc. from Simon Fraser University, and a B.Sc. from the University of Toronto. She was also Board Certified in Toxicology in 1986. She is currently the CEO of Adlyfe, and a member of the Board of Directors of Adlyfe, Aerovance, Cardiokine (observer), Endocyte, Logical Therapeutics (observer), SCYNEXIS, Taiwan Liposome Company, and Waterstone. Ann is also a charter member of the C100, a group dedicated to assisting Canadian entrepreneurs.

**MARTIN GODBOUT**
*Managing Director, Canada*
mgodbout@b-c.com

Martin Godbout will join Burrill & Company upon the first closing of the Burrill Canada Fund. Martin was previously the President and Chief Executive Officer of Genome Canada, and was formerly the Senior Vice President of BioCapital and President and General Manager of Société Innovatech Québec. He was a member of the Board of the "Conseil de la science et de la technologies du Québec" and has been an advisory member of several Canadian biopharmaceutical venture firms such as SGF Santé and Royal Bank Ventures Inc. He was also a Board Member of the Société Innovatech du Grand Montréal.

In 2005, Dr. Godbout was named Officer of the Order of Canada. He was also awarded the Grand Prix de Recherche from the Québec Foundation for Mental Disorders for his previous work on Alzheimer's disease in 1991, as well as the "Prix Summa" in 1994 from the Faculty of Sciences and Engineering of the Université

Laval. In 1994, he also founded BioContact Québec which has become one of the most important biopharmaceutical symposiums in North America.

Martin holds a B.Sc. in Biochemistry and a Ph.D. in Physiology and Molecular Endocrinology from Université Laval, followed by a postdoctoral training in Neuromolecular Biology at The Scripps Research Institute, in San Diego. He is presently board chairman of MethylGene, Genome Quebec, BioContact, and AmorChem (Advisory Committee), and a director of Acasti Pharma, AngioChem, Asmacure, BioQuebec, Fonds de la Recherche en Sante du Quebec (FRSQ), Montreal InVivo, and Ataxie de Charlevoix Fondation.

**MICHAEL KEYOUNG**
*Managing Director, Pan Asia*
mkeyoung@b-c.com

Michael Keyoung has more than 15 years of healthcare and life sciences experience through his role as scientist, surgeon, consultant and investor. At Burrill & Company, Dr. Keyoung manages Burrill's Pan-Asia Equity Fund, oversees Burrill's U.S. and European public portfolio companies and leads our Pan-Asia transaction business as well as our global arbitrage efforts across multiple countries in Asia. Previously, Dr. Keyoung was a co-founder of a life sciences healthcare investment partnership in New York. Dr. Keyoung also served as an advisor and consultant to leading life sciences venture capital firms, medical devices, pharma, and biotechnology companies. Previously, Dr. Keyoung was a Howard Hughes Medical Institute fellow and received his clinical surgical training at University of California, San Francisco and biomedical fellowship at Memorial Sloan Kettering Institute and Rockefeller University in New York. Dr. Keyoung performed preclinical drug discovery research for

# The Burrill Team

## Venture Capital (continued)

Aventis (now Sanofi-Aventis) and Merck while at Cornell and participated in cutting-edge translational clinical trials at leading academic centers. As a National Institute of Health-Medical Scientist Training Program scholarship recipient, Dr. Keyoung received both his Medical Doctorate and Doctor of Philosophy degrees in Neuroscience and Neurology from Cornell University Weill Medical College and Memorial Sloan Kettering Cancer Center. Dr. Keyoung has over 35 articles, book chapters, and presentations in publications such as Nature Biotechnology and Nature Medicine.

Dr. Keyoung has served on the Board of Directors at New York County Medical Society and Board of Overseers at the Cornell University-Weill Medical College in New York and currently serves on the boards of private biopharma companies and organizations in the U.S. and in Asia.

### Vincent Xiang
*Managing Director, China*
*wvxiang@b-c.com*

Vincent Xiang joins Burrill from Franklin Templeton Investments, where he served as vice president and portfolio manager/analyst, investing in global life sciences companies at all stages since 2004. Previously, Mr. Xiang was Vice President of Business Development at Genyous, a biotech startup based in China and the United States. He worked as Director of Venture Investment at Acacia Research, and as an associate at BioAdvance, a healthcare VC fund. He was an Irvington Fellow at Skirball Center and licensed his patented technology to Millennium Pharmaceutical for royalty payments.

Vincent began his career at Shanghai Biological Product Corporation in China. He has focused on the life sciences industry for 20 years. Mr. Xiang received his Ph.D. in molecular biology in four years with honors from SUNY at

Stony Brook. He obtained his MBA from the Wharton School. He graduated from Fudan University in China with a bachelor's degree in immunology and microbiology. He is a founding member of BayHelix Group, a network of Chinese executives who strive to bridge business and life sciences, and the East and the West.

### João Paulo V. Poiares Baptista
*Managing Director, Brazil*
*jbaptista@b-c.com*

João Paulo Baptista manages Burrill & Company's Latin America operations. He graduated in Economy at Universidade de Coimbra, Portugal. He began his career as analyst for the Department of Economy Industry Services (SE) in Macau, which operated as the economic authority of the Territory. In 1986, after leaving public service as Sector Chief, he joined the consulting firm Asiatec Consultadoria. In 1987 he joined Pacific Infotech Corp (PIC), an investment group with focus on technology-based companies, to serve as an analyst in Los Angeles, USA. Between 1990 and 1992, as General Director of PIC in Europe, he expanded its business in Europe, from their headquarters in Lisbon, Portugal. In 1992, he developed extensive consulting activities for new businesses in the sectors of IT and telecommunications. In 1999 he founded Mercatto Venture Partners Ltda (MVP), one of the pioneers in venture capital activities in Brazil. He actively participated on the development of Projeto Inovar from FINEP (Brazilian Ministry of Science and Technology), taking responsibility for the Venture Fórum Brazil. Also under the auspices of Inovar, he created and developed the first forums in partnership with BOVESPA. In a consultant role to Bovespa, João Paulo performed strategic analysis, and enabled positioning and preparation of companies for investor presentations under the development directives

## VENTURE CAPITAL *(continued)*

of the program Bovespa Mais. João Paulo was also one of the founders of former ABCR – Brazilian Association of Venture Capital, now ABVCap.

Prior to joining Burrill & Company, he served as a Director of Rio Bravo Venture Partners, created by the merger of MVP with the Venture Capital division of Rio Bravo Investimentos. He has served as the President of the Investment Committee of MVP Tech Fund since the beginning of its operations. João Paulo serves as a board member of seven leading technology-based companies in Brazil.

### MARIETTA WU
*Managing Director, Taiwan*
*mwu@b-c.com*

Prior to joining Burrill, Marietta Wu held professional positions with Edwards Lifesciences and Eli Lilly & Company. She was Director of Strategy at Edwards, responsible for the strategic planning in the biologics program. At Eli Lilly & Company Oncology and Integrated Biology, Dr. Wu oversaw finance, business development, pipeline valuation, organizational restructure and outsourcing strategy. She also worked at Eli Lilly's M&A Group and with Oncology Discovery Research. Dr. Wu founded BioHorizon, a consultancy focused on value creation in the life sciences industry across the Pacific Rim. She advised a number of biotech startups and venture capital firms.

Dr. Wu's scientific expertise centers on basic and clinical research in oncology and neuroscience. She was selected by Nobel Laureate Dr. Marshall Nirenberg as an IRTA Fellow at the National Institutes of Health. Dr. Wu received her M.D. from Shanghai Second Medical University, a Ph.D. in Medical Sciences from Medical College of Ohio, and an MBA from the University of Michigan Business School.

### DIRK LAMMERTS
*Managing Director,*
*Digital Health*
*dlammerts@b-c.com*

Dirk Lammerts has more than 20 years of professional experience in healthcare, life sciences, and high-tech industries. Dr. Lammerts has a combined medical and computer science background. He holds an M.D. from Dusseldorf University Medical School and trained in neurology at the University of Cologne Medical Center. He also received board certification in Medical Computer Science by the German Medical Association. Early in his career, Dr. Lammerts developed computer-based training programs for neurological patients suffering from memory and cognitive deficits.

Dr. Lammerts worked as a senior engagement manager for McKinsey & Company advising clients across a broad spectrum of industries in the U.S., Europe, and Asia-Pacific. He also held positions as Vice President Molecular Diagnostics at Affymetrix and as Vice President Marketing and Corporate Development at XDx, building businesses in molecular diagnostics and personalized medicine.

Throughout his career, Dr. Lammerts has been driving technology convergence through innovative use of computer technologies and online, mobile, and interactive media in medicine, based on the premise that these technologies are providing a platform to fundamentally improve access to and quality of healthcare worldwide.

# THE BURRILL TEAM

**SVEN ROHMANN**
*Managing Director,*
*Digital Health*
srohmann@b-c.com

**TANIA FERNANDEZ**
*Director, India*
tfernandez@b-c.com

Sven Rohmann has a scientific and academic background in clinical medicine and basic research. He spent 10 years at Merck Serono, which provided him with a strong foothold in the pharmaceutical industry. His career exposed him to pre-clinical, clinical development as well as marketing, business, and corporate development. During his tenure at Merck he was involved in the successful licensing of Erbitux from ImClone and the establishment of Merck Oncology. Dr. Rohmann joined Burrill & Company in 2010.

Prior to joining Burrill & Company, Dr. Rohmann worked as Venture Capital Fund Manager for Novartis Pharma AG, and as Managing Partner at Nextech Venture. In addition, Dr. Rohmann served as CEO of two European biotech startups and gained board experience at three SME's in Germany.

Dr. Rohmann has a unique blend of scientific, pharma, biotech, and venture knowledge; an extensive network of contacts among health care providers as well as academic and government research administrators; a thorough knowledge of European research and regulatory policies; and significant experience in global as well as European partnering.

Dr. Rohmann received his M.D. from the University of Mainz, Germany, and his Ph.D. from the Erasmus University, Rotterdam, Netherlands.

Tania Fernandez has more than 15 years of experience in the fields of oncology and molecular biology. She secured her doctorate at the Cancer Research Institute, India, having been awarded the Indo-U.S. scholarship from the National Institutes of Health. She won the Young Scientist Award and the most outstanding doctoral thesis award at Bombay University. She previously gained operational experience at Hoechst Pharmaceuticals, Mumbai, India.

After completing her doctorate, Dr. Fernandez specialized in the fields of protein chemistry, protein delivery systems, and genetic engineering at the College of Medicine, Texas A&M University. In 1999, she joined the National Cancer Institute at the National Institutes of Health as a post-doctoral associate and was appointed staff scientist in 2000.

Her work at the NIH resulted in two awards for excellence in biomedical research, and her research has been published in top scientific journals. She has been an invited speaker at national and international conferences. She completed courses in biotech startups for Scientists and Technology Transfer while at the NIH. She is an active member of the National Institutes of Health Bioscience Business Interest group, the NIH Stem Cell Group, the Women in Bio group (San Francisco chapter), and the Women's Technology Cluster (now Astia) where she assists with mentoring biotech companies and evaluating them.

Dr. Fernandez is also actively involved with sourcing and evaluating United States-India cross-border and pureplay Indian life sciences investment opportunities in venture capital and merchant banking. Her areas of focus include

## VENTURE CAPITAL *(continued)*

healthcare and healthcare delivery.

She sits on the board of Adlyfe, was board observer on BioImagene (exited via a sale to Roche), and is on the editorial advisory board of Express Pharma, Mumbai, India. She has authored several articles on the evolving life sciences landscape in India.

### THOMAS GERLACH
*Director, Brazil*
*tgerlach@b-c.com*

Thomas Gerlach joined Burrill & Company in 2012 after nearly 20 years in the pharmaceutical industry in different positions within multinational companies where he was involved in drug development, brand management. From 2002 to 2010 he served as general manager of Actelion Pharmaceuticals do Brasil, the Brazilian subsidiary of Actelion. There he laid the foundation for the company's Latin American operations. He originally joined Actelion as a project manager in Switzerland in 2000. Prior to that, Mr. Gerlach held positions with Novartis, Knoll AG, and BASF Pharma.

He has been a visiting scholar at Michigan State University where he worked on research projects in the field of retinoids. He holds a Ph.D. from the departments of biology and pathobiochemistry from the University of Mainz, Germany, a degree in chemistry (Staatsexamen) from the University of Mainz, Germany, and a masters in biology from the University of Mainz. He is fluent in German, English, Portuguese, and has some understanding of Spanish.

### IGOR KRASILNIKOV
*Director, Russia*
*ikrasilnikov@b-c.com*

Igor Krasilnikov has authored more than 100 publications, mainly in the fields of virology and production of pharmaceuticals. He is an international advisor to the World Health Organization in the field of vaccine development. Prior to joining Burrill & Company, he served as top manager in several private companies dedicated to vaccine and therapeutics development. Most recently, he was Chief of the Research and Development for Microgen, a state-owned Russian company with a leading position in the field of immunobiological products. Dr. Krasilnikov has also held positions in Russia's Medical Technological Holding, MPBP Production Company, Ecomed, and Combiotech.

Between 1975 and 1989, Dr. Krasilnikov was head of laboratory at the Ministry of Healthcare Institute of Immunology where he successfully developed the technologies for subunit influenza vaccine and polysaccharide vaccine against salmonellosis. In 1984 he received an award from the Council of Ministers of the Soviet Union for the development and implementation of the vaccine against the tick-borne encephalitis. He is a vice president and member of the board of the Russian Biotechnology Society. Dr. Krasilnikov earned an undergraduate degree in biophysics from the Lenidgradsky Polytechnical Institute, a Ph.D. in virology, Institute of Poliomyelitis and Viral Encephalitis at the Russian Academy of Medical Sciences, and a Dr.Sc. in biotechnology from the D. Mendeleev University of Chemical Technology of Russia, 1999, Thesis, Doctor of Science.

## Venture Capital *(continued)*

### Joshua Zelig
*Director, BCF IV*
*jzelig@b-c.com*

Joshua Zelig joined Burrill & Company as a Director in the Venture Group in 2011. Prior to joining the company, Mr. Zelig was an Associate Partner at GBP Capital, a Greenwich, Connecticut-based healthcare venture firm. In that capacity he was responsible for sourcing, evaluating, and executing investment transactions and new business opportunities. Additionally, Mr. Zelig managed the firm's intellectual property portfolios, oversaw the company's operations, and worked closely with portfolio companies in setting and delivering on strategic objectives.

Previously, Mr. Zelig was an equity research associate at Morgan Stanley where he covered biotech and consumer stocks. He later worked in real estate management, acquisition, and due diligence capacities on behalf of a number of large private real estate companies as well as public REITs.

Mr. Zelig is a graduate of Yeshiva University, Sy Syms School of Business, where he received a B.S. in Finance. He is currently a member of the board of directors of Flexible Stenting Solutions.

### Sergey Axenovich
*Senior Associate*
*saxenovich@b-c.com*

Sergey Axenovich originally joined Burrill Merchant Banking in 2007. Before joining Burrill & Company, Sergey managed the cancer drug discovery program and associated corporate collaborations at PPD. He began his research career at Genome Therapeutics. Subsequently, he received his MBA from the University of California, Berkeley Haas School of Business. Sergey

has a Ph.D. in Molecular Genetics from the University of Illinois, Chicago and an undergraduate degree in Molecular Biology from Moscow University.

### Marcus Albernaz
*Associate, Brazil*
*malbernaz@b-c.com*

Based in Rio de Janeiro, Brazil, Marcus Albernaz is focusing on Brazilian operations, contributing to the establishment and oversight of projected financial models per sector, market analysis, competitive intelligence as well as overall strategic partnerships and analysis of deal flow.

Mr. Albernaz gained four years of experience with investment and financial market analysis prior to joining Burrill & Company. His previous professional activities were at Banco UBS Pactual and Rio Bravo Investimentos. At Rio Bravo Investimentos, he served as a member of an analyst team covering venture capital investments, with direct and active participation in strategic, commercial and administrative decisions. At UBS Pactual he was responsible for structuring transactions involving futures as well as options and currency arbitrage. Marcus is an economist and graduated from PUC-Rio in 2005.

### Yuko Amizaki
*Business Analyst*
*yamizaki@b-c.com*

Yuko Amizaki joined Burrill & Company as Business Analyst in 2011. Ms. Amizaki provides support for decisionmaking associated with biogreentech and the Malaysian Life Sciences Capital Fund investments, and more generally in the life sciences. Ms. Amizaki recently graduated from MIT Sloan School of Management

## VENTURE CAPITAL *(continued)*

with an MBA. She worked in corporate planning at Regimmune, a drug development biotech in Mountain View, California. Previously, she was a consultant at Booz and Company in Tokyo, Japan. She holds a M.S. in biology and bachelor of agriculture in applied life sciences.

**VERONICA DESCOTTE**
*Associate*
*vdescotte@b-c.com*

Veronica Descotte was born and raised in Buenos Aires, Argentina. Trained as a scientist, she joined Burrill & Company in 2008 to focus on Latin America, where she has been leading fund-raising activities as well as establishing strategic partnerships with the healthcare and pharmaceutical communities. In addition to Latin America, Ms. Descotte is also responsible for overseeing deal flow analysis as well as being involved with several of our portfolio companies in the diagnostic, therapeutics, personalized medicine and pharmacy benefit management spaces. She is an observer on several boards, including WellPartner.

**CHEN YEE LIAW**
*Business Analyst*
*cliaw@b-c.com*

Chen Yee Liaw joined Burrill & Company in June of 2011 as Business Analyst, and has been working with the Malaysian Life Sciences Capital Fund (MLSCF) since 2009. She is instrumental in evaluating biotechnology companies in the cleantech sectors, where she helps develop insights and investment strategy for the Malaysian fund through market, technical, competitive and financial analyses. Concurrently, Chen Yee serves as Business Analyst at Abunda Nutrition, a portfolio company of MLSCF. At Abunda, she is actively involved in business and corporate development activities, where she helps to identify potential molecules for pipeline expansion, develop insights to guide manufacturing and commercialization strategies, as well as perform financial modelling. Prior to Burrill and MLSCF, Ms. Liaw interned at Deloitte Consulting, in strategy & operations. She also did research at Caltech, elucidating the molecular basis of early T-cell development defects that may impact autoimmunity in a type 1 diabetes mouse model. She holds a B.S. (Honors) in Biology and Business Economics from the California Institute of Technology, and was recipient of the Upper Class Merit Award.

**DEREK WONG**
*Analyst, Digital Health*
*dwong@b-c.com*

Derek Wong joined Burrill & Company in 2011 as an Analyst in the Digital Health Practice. He was instrumental in the Series A investment in AliveCor, the iPhone & Android ECG company. Prior to Burrill & Company, he taught physics at the University of San Francisco. He was a member of the QB3 New Venture Consulting Group at the California Institute of Quantitative Biology (QB3) and assisted spin-outs from the University of California in commercializing their technologies. Mr. Wong participated in the Management of Technology Program at U.C. Berkeley's Haas School of Business where he worked on various projects including electric vehicle deployment and computer user interface redesign for young children. Trained as an engineer and a scientist, Mr. Wong has co-authored several research articles published in top-tier scientific journals including Cell and Physical Review Letters. Derek holds a Ph.D. in Bioengineering from the University of California, Berkeley and San Francisco, a B.S.E. from the University of Pennsylvania, and a B.S. from Haverford College.

# THE BURRILL TEAM

VENTURE CAPITAL *(continued)*

### GARRETT VYGANTAS, M.D.
*Entrepreneur-In-Residence*
gvygantas@b-c.com

### SIMON WADDINGTON
*Entrepreneur-in-Residence*
swaddington@b-c.com

Garrett Vygantas founded the Burrill portfolio company NewBridge Pharmaceuticals late 2007 shortly after joining Burrill & Company's Venture Group as a Director. He is now an Entrepreneur-In-Residence. Dr. Vygantas has raised nearly $17 million in Series A and B financing rounds for New-Bridge at increases in valuation. He in-licensed the company's first oncology, gastrointestinal, and metabolic disease therapeutics and recruited key senior management. In 2010, Dr. Vygantas was appointed Vice President of Strategy & Business Development for NewBridge. In that role, he is responsible for identifying, evaluating, negotiating, and executing business development opportunities, and leading corporate planning and fundraising activities.

Before joining Burrill & Company, Dr. Vygantas was at Genentech (now Roche) where he was involved in the commercialization and launch of Lucentis for the treatment of wet age-related macular degeneration ($4 billion sales in 2011). In the past, he served on Cowen Group's Healthcare Investment Banking Group and at EntreMed in business development.

Dr. Vygantas was a board observer on the Burrill portfolio companies: Nora Therapeutics, Proteo-Genix, and Ikano Therapeutics. He is a co-instructor at the University of California, San Francisco's Center for Bioentrepreneurship's "Idea to IPO" curriculum and has advised in the formation of numerous start-up biotech and medical technology companies. Dr. Vygantas completed his Transitional Residency at the University of Pennsylvania and holds M.D. and MBA degrees from Georgetown University, as well as a B.S. in Biochemistry from Boston College. He is a Kauffman Fellow with the Center for Venture Education.

Simon Waddington serves as Entrepreneur-in-Residence where he is involved in building startup companies across the spectrum of the life sciences. He serves as CEO of Evolva Nutrition Inc., which is developing next generation nutritional ingredients.

Previously, he spent more than a decade as a venture capitalist. He was a Managing Partner at PolyTechnos Venture-Partners based in Munich, Germany where he led and supported investments in numerous life sciences and materials-related companies across Europe, Israel, and the United States. Prior to that, he started and ran Monsanto's European corporate venturing activities from Brussels, Belgium, and was Product Development Manager in the UK for Zeneca's biopolymers business, which pioneered the fermentation-based production of biodegradable polymers from renewable feedstocks. He also served as a Senior Research Scientist for ICI specializing in surface and interface science; his work on the development and advancement of surface analysis methods led to a long-standing interest in nanoscience and he was a co-founder of the European NanoBusiness Association and served on its Advisory Board.

He holds a Ph.D. in physics and an MBA from Harvard Business School (HBS). He is a former board member of the German HBS Alumni Association and currently serves as an International Alumni Ambassador for Liverpool University.

# BURRILL & COMPANY

## VENTURE PARTNERS

**STEPHEN M. SAMMUT**
*Venture Partner*
sammut@b-c.com

Stephen M. Sammut is a venture partner focused on special projects for the firm (Latin America, the Middle East, Japan and emerging markets). During his career he has been involved in the creation of nearly forty biotechnology, Internet, and information technology companies. His experience includes Vice President of S.R. One (the venture fund of GlaxoSmithKline), Vice President of Corporate Development at Teleflex Incorporated, Managing Director of Technology Transfer at the University of Pennsylvania, and Founder and CEO of one of the first and largest transplant organ banks in the United States. He is on numerous Boards of Directors and Advisory Boards, including Mitsubishi International Corporation, Combinent BioMedical Systems, Gentis, and Dynamis Therapeutics. In addition, he is on the boards of the Cornell University Research Foundation, the Massachusetts General Hospital Technology Transfer Committee, and the American Type Culture Collection. Mr. Sammut holds an academic appointment as Senior Fellow in Entrepreneurship and Health Care Systems at the Wharton School of the University of Pennsylvania, where he teaches courses on venture capital, private equity in emerging markets, intellectual property strategy, biotech entrepreneurship, and private sector participation in global health. He is also an advisor to the joint MBA/Masters in Biotechnology Program.

He holds graduate and undergraduate degrees in biological sciences and humanities from Villanova University, attended Hahnemann Medical College for two years, and holds an MBA from the Wharton School of theUniversity of Pennsylvania.

**PAUL FREIMAN**
*Venture Partner, Brazil*
pfreiman@b-c.com

With more than forty years of experience in founding and management of biotechnology and healthcare companies, Paul Freiman, former CEO of Syntex, led the company through its acquisition by Roche Holdings in a $5.3 billion transaction. He has been chairman of the Pharmaceutical Manufacturers of America Association (PhRMA) and has also chaired a number of key PhRMA committees both domestic and international. He served as CEO of a biotech firm based in California. He serves on three biotechnology boards as well as that of a major Japanese company.

Currently domiciled in Rio de Janeiro, Mr. Freiman has extensive experience in Latin America, having also served as Burrill & Company's Vice President Latin America.

**KONSTANTIN SKRYABIN**
*Venture Partner*
kskryabin@b-c.com

Konstantin Skryabin is a leading figure in Russia's biotechnology industry. He earned his Ph.D. in Molecular Biology at Lomonosov Moscow State University, where he is now Head of the Department of Biotechnology. He is Director and founder of the Russian Academy of Sciences' Center for Bioengineering. In addition to serving in leadership roles with several international biotechnology organizations, he has consulted for many pharmaceutical and biotech companies in Russia. Together with Bioprocess Holding and other partners, he founded Bioprocess Capital Partners LLC, which managed the first Russian venture capital fund focused on life sciences.

Through his pioneering research, Professor

# The Burrill Team

Skryabin established genomic sequencing in Russia, developed systems for the production of a variety of biologically active compounds, and enhanced the elucidation of biosafety and ethical issues posed by genetic engineering. He has published more than 450 scientific papers and is assigned 59 patents and inventions.

Professor K. Skryabin is a full member of the Russian Academy of Sciences and the Russian Academy of Agricultural Sciences. He is also a member of the Council of the President of the Russian Federation on Science, Technologies and Education and Chairman of the Russian Academy of Sciences' Scientific Council on Biotechnology. Among his many distinctions, he has been recognized in the Order for Service to the Motherland in Russia.

### Dag Dvergsten
*Venture Partner, Scandinavia*
*ddvergsten@b-c.com*

Dag Dvergsten is the president and sole owner of Dag Dvergsten AS. Prior to establishing the company in 1994, Mr. Dvergsten held several positions in Fred Olsen & Co., a Norwegian shipping conglomerate. Mr. Dvergsten has through Dag Dvergsten AS initiated and developed several industrial projects within the areas of energy/resources, marine sectors, life science, and technology.

Dvergsten has served and is currently serving on several corporate and civic organisation boards. Mr. Dvergsten holds a Master of Science in Business degree from the Norwegian School of Economics and Business Administration (NHH).

### Tee Wee Lee
*Venture partner*
*twlee@b-c.com*

Tee Wee Lee is a venture partner heading up Burrill & Company's Singapore office. He has more than 25 years of experience working with both the public and private sectors, helping companies and governments manage complexity, logistics, and security. Mr. Tee Wee has held senior roles with Rare Medium and Andersen Consulting and has also helped develop China's education market, through his work in the Singapore Institute of Management, Cynefin Centre, and the Asia Pacific Learning and Knowledge Management Council. He was Managing Director of one of the largest electrical contractors in Southeast Asia and has also built and managed hotels in Singapore, Malaysia, and China. He has a master's degree in electrical engineering from the University of Waterloo and is an alumnus of IMD Switzerland. While at the Ministry of Foreign Affairs, he represented Singapore at the 50th United Nations General Assembly on the International Economics Committee and was an active participant in APEC and WTO. He was Centre Director of the Beijing Office of the Singapore Economic Development Board, where he worked to promote collaboration between China and Singapore in the biotech industry.

## International Venture Capital Group

| | | | |
|---|---|---|---|
| **Burrill ASEAN** | G. Steven Burrill | *CEO* | *steve@b-c.com* |
| | Roger Wyse | *Managing Director, Biogreentech, ASEAN* | *dwetherell@b-c.com* |
| | Greg Young | *Managing Director, Biogreentech, ASEAN* | *greg@b-c.com* |
| **Burrill Pan-Asia** | G. Steven Burrill | *CEO* | *steve@b-c.com* |
| | David Wetherell | *Managing Partner* | *dwetherell@b-c.com* |
| | Michael Keyoung | *Managing Director, Pan Asia* | *mkeyoung@b-c.com* |
| **Burrill Brazil** | G. Steven Burrill | *CEO* | *steve@b-c.com* |
| | João Paulo V. Poiares Baptista | *Managing Director, Brazil* | *jbaptista@b-c.com* |
| | Paul Freiman | *Venture Partner, Brazil* | *pfreiman@b-c.com* |
| | Thomas Gerlach | *Director, Brazil* | *tgerlach@b-c.com* |
| | Marcus Albernaz | *Associate, Brazil* | *malbernaz@b-c.com* |
| **Burrill Europe** | G. Steven Burrill | *CEO* | *steve@b-c.com* |
| | Sven Rohmann | *Managing Director, Europe* | *srohmann@b-c.com* |
| | Dag Dvergsten | *Venture Partner, Scandinavia* | *ddvergsten@b-c.com* |
| **Burrill India** | G. Steven Burrill | *CEO* | *steve@b-c.com* |
| | Tania Fernandez | *Director, India* | *tfernandez@b-c.com* |
| **Burrill Malaysia** | G. Steven Burrill | *CEO* | *steve@b-c.com* |
| | Roger Wyse | *Managing Director* | *roger@b-c.com* |
| | Greg Young | *Managing Director* | *greg@b-c.com* |
| **Burrill Russia** | G. Steven Burrill | *CEO* | *steve@b-c.com* |
| | Igor Krasilnikov | *Director, Russia* | *ikrasilnikov@b-c.com* |
| | Sergey Axenovich | *Senior Associate* | *saxenovich@b-c.com* |
| **Burrill Canada** | G. Steven Burrill | *CEO* | *steve@b-c.com* |
| | Ann Hanham | *Managing Director, Canada* | *ann@b-c.com* |
| | Martin Godbout | *Managing Director, Canada* | *mgodbout@b-c.com* |
| **Burrill Digital Health** | G. Steven Burrill | *CEO* | *steve@b-c.com* |
| | David Wetherell | *Managing Partner* | *dwetherell@b-c.com* |
| | Dirk Lammerts | *Managing Director, Digital Health* | *dlammerts@b-c.com* |
| | Sven Rohmann | *Managing Director, Digital Health* | *srohmann@b-c.com* |
| **Burrill Taiwan** | G. Steven Burrill | *CEO* | *steve@b-c.com* |
| | Marietta Wu | *Managing Director, Taiwan* | *mwu@b-c.com* |
| **Burrill China** | G. Steven Burrill | *CEO* | *steve@b-c.com* |
| | David Wetherell | *Managing Partner* | *dwetherell@b-c.com* |
| | Michael Keyoung | *Managing Director, Pan Asia* | *mkeyoung@b-c.com* |
| | Vincent Xiang | *Managing Director, China* | *wvxiang@b-c.com* |
| | Wenyong Wang | *Managing Director, Merchant Banking* | *wwang@b-c.com* |

# The Burrill Team

## Advisory Boards

### Burrill Advisory Board

Frederick Frank
*Vice Chairman, Peter J. Solomon Company*

Jeffrey B. Kindler
*former Chairman & CEO, Pfizer*

Dr. George Poste
*Chief Scientist, Complex Adaptive Systems Initiative, Arizona State University; Regent's Professor and Del E. Webb Distinguished Professor of Biology, Arizona State University*

Franklyn Prendergast, MD, PhD
*Director, Center for Individualized Medicine, The Mayo Clinic*

Prof. Konstantin G. Skryabin
*Head of the Department of Biology at Lomonosov Moscow State University and the institution's Chair of Biotechnology; Member of the Presidential Council (Russian Federation) for Science, Technology and Education*

### Scientific Advisory Board

Boro Dropulic
*Founder, President, and Chief Scientific Officer, Lentigen*

Prof. Konstantin G. Skryabin
*Head of the Department of Biology at Lomonosov Moscow State University and the institution's Chair of Biotechnology; Member of the Presidential Council (Russian Federation) for Science, Technology and Education*

Inder Vermer
*Professor, Irwin and Joan Jacobs Chair in Exemplary Life Science Laboratory of Genetics, Salk Institute for Biological Sciences*

# BURRILL & COMPANY

## A LIFE SCIENCES MERCHANT BANK

**STEPHEN HURLY**
*CEO, Burrill Merchant Banking and Head of Investment Banking*
shurly@b-c.com

Stephen Hurly joined Burrill Merchant Banking as its CEO and head of investment banking in June 2011. He brings an expertise in assisting public and private firms with strategic transactions, difficult financings, product licensing, joint ventures and restructurings. He has experience at both bulge bracket firms as well as specialized boutiques. Through extensive industry relationships and global transaction experience in China, Japan, Australia, the European Union and North America, Mr. Hurly and his team provide tailored solutions and insight to assist clients in reaching their strategic goals.

Mr. Hurly was previously with Boenning & Scattergood, as a Managing Director and Global Head of the firm's Health Care Investment Banking Practice. Prior to that appointment, Mr. Hurly was the Managing Director and Head of the Life Sciences Group at Janney Montgomery Scott. His earlier investment banking experience was with Hambrecht & Quist in San Francisco, where he closed over 30 public and private financings as well as M&A transactions, eventually becoming a member of the executive offices.

Mr. Hurly is an expert in strategic transactions and associated capital raising, and has completed over 100 deals with an aggregate value over $10 billion and over $400 million in capital. He has an MBA from the University of Chicago and a B.S. in Engineering from Swarthmore College.

**MIKE CARPENTER**
*Managing Director and Head of Institutional Trading*
mcarpenter@b-c.com

Mike Carpenter has more than 20 years of institutional sales and trading experience in both domestic and international equity markets. He started his career at Morgan Stanley, where he became an executive director in the institutional equity division. He spent 19 years at the firm trading for institutional clients primarily based on the West Coast. During his time there he was also responsible for developing new client relationships in U.S. equity sales in London, Paris, Geneva, and Frankfurt. He also served as a member of the firm's MBA recruitment team at Stanford and UCLA.

During his career, Mr. Carpenter also worked as an institutional buy side trader at Dodge and Cox. In 2004, he became a partner at Pacific Growth Equities in San Francisco, where he provided research and trading coverage of emerging growth companies in healthcare and technology. Most recently, he served as managing director and head of the San Francisco office of Summer Street Research Partners, a healthcare focused investment bank. Mr. Carpenter holds a B.A. from the University of California, Santa Cruz.

**DAVID C. PARKE**
*Managing Director*
dparke@b-c.com

David Parke joined Burrill & Company in June 2011 as a Managing Director of Burrill Merchant Banking. Mr. Parke specializes in public offerings, private placements, fairness opinions, and mergers and acquisitions for emerging-growth companies. His experience delivers a strong background in capital markets with an

## MERCHANT BANKING *(continued)*

in-depth understanding of the issues particular to life sciences and healthcare companies.

Mr. Parke joined Burrill & Company from Boenning & Scattergood. Prior to that, he was with Mufson Howe Hunter & Company for three years, where he was instrumental in launching and developing the firm's emerging growth practice. He was previously with the corporate finance department of Investec and its predecessor, Pennsylvania Merchant Group. Mr. Parke has managed or participated in 40 public offerings and private placements, raising more than $1 billion for emerging growth clients. In addition, he has managed mergers and acquisitions assignments ranging from $5 million to $500 million. Prior to joining Investec in 1992, he was in the corporate finance departments of Wheat First Butcher & Singer, now Wachovia Securities, and Legg Mason.

He has been a director of Petroleum Development Corporation, a publicly-traded natural gas exploration and production company, since 2003. He chairs the board's Finance and Planning Committee, and is a member of its Compensation and Audit Committees.

Mr. Parke received his MBA with Honors from The Wharton School of the University of Pennsylvania, and graduated summa cum laude and Phi Beta Kappa from Lehigh University with a B.S. in Finance.

### WENYONG WANG
*Managing Director*
*wwang@b-c.com*

Wenyong Wang joined Burrill & Company in 2011 and has more than 18 years experience in the healthcare industry. Prior to joining Burrill Merchant Banking, Dr. Wang was a senior executive member of Boenning & Scattergood Global Healthcare investment banking practice, where he initiated and led merger & acquisition, licensing & partnering, capital raising, fairness opinions,

as well as other financial and scientific advisory activities in public and private life sciences companies. He had managed over 25 public offerings and private placements, as well as M&A assignments ranging from $5 million to $500 million, in an aggregated value of over two billion dollars. Dr. Wang's prior investment banking experience was with Janney Montgomery Scott in Philadelphia as a vice president. With Janney, Dr. Wang and his team provided investment banking services to public and private healthcare clients throughout Asian Pacific, Europe and North America. Prior to Janney, Dr. Wang worked on drug research and development at GlaxoSmithKline for more than six years. At GSK, he oversaw two drug candidates selected to clinical trials. Previously, Dr. Wang conducted independent research at the University of Pennsylvania and in Beijing, China.

Dr. Wang received his Ph.D. in Organic Chemistry from the University of Pennsylvania, his BS from Shandong University, and his MBA from Penn State.

### LINDA MOLNAR
*Managing Director*
*lmolnar@b-c.com*

Linda Molnar has advised early-stage life sciences companies in the structuring and management of corporate development and financing opportunities in order to maximize capital efficiency by utilizing non-dilutive funding. Previously she served as a consultant at the National Cancer Institute, where she was instrumental in the launch and implementation of the Program in Cancer Nanotechnology. Dr. Molnar has a breadth of experience in collaborations and partnerships between academic institutions, large companies, and biotechnology startups for the successful translation of fundamental research into products and businesses.

She received her Ph.D. in Materials Science

## MERCHANT BANKING *(continued)*

and Engineering from the Massachusetts Institute of Technology and her B.S. in Chemistry with Honors from the University of Pittsburgh. She also completed the Wharton Management Program.

### PETER M. FRY
*Managing Director*
pfry@b-c.com

Peter Fry joined Burrill & Company in 2010 as Managing Director and Head of Alternative Equities to build out the firm's principal investment directly into public Life Sciences companies. Mr. Fry has been providing investment, investment banking, and advisory services to emerging growth companies for more than 18 years and has specific expertise in the placement of private/public equity, debt and convertible securities as well as committed equity lines of credit. Prior to joining Burrill & Company, Mr. Fry spent seven years as the Senior Investment Officer of Kingsbridge Capital where he played an integral role in numerous Healthcare investments (PIPEs, Registered Directs, Follow-Ons) while executing almost $2 billion in more than 35 Committed Equity Financing Facilities (CEFFs).

Prior to joining Kingsbridge, Mr. Fry spent 11 years in investment banking. He was a Director of Investment Banking and Head of Private Placements for Investec, a global, full-service financial services firm and had held similar senior banking positions while directing the private placement efforts at RBC/Tucker Anthony Sutro and Gruntal & Co. Mr. Fry has worked in both corporate finance and institutional sales capacities for most of his career and has also spent time on the buy-side with FBS Management, a dollar-neutral investment fund, and First Capital Strategists, an independent securities lender and overlay manager. Mr. Fry is a graduate of Bucknell University with a Bachelor of Arts in Economics.

### DARREN N. STREILER
*Principal*
dstreiler@b-c.com

Darren Streiler joined Burrill & Company in 2011 and works as a Principal in the Merchant Banking Group serving the agricultural and industrial biotechnology sectors. Mr. Streiler has 13 years experience in the investment industry including over nine years spent with fundamentally driven buy-side funds and three years on the sell-side. Most recently, Mr. Streiler was a Vice President with HighMark Capital Management, a division of The Bank of Tokyo-Mitsubishi UFJ, where he managed the energy, industrials, and materials sectors. Prior to this position, Mr. Streiler was an analyst at SAC Capital Advisors where he co-managed a $100 million healthcare hedge fund. Prior to SAC, he was an analyst at Amerindo Investment Advisors. Mr. Streiler began his career in equity research at Citigroup.

Mr. Streiler received a B.S. in Finance from Boston College and a MBA from the University of California, Berkeley.

### JASON ZHANG
*Equity Research Analyst*
jzhang@b-c.com

Jason Zhang joined Burrill & Company as an Equity Research Analyst in the Company's Merchant Banking Group in 2012. Based on the East Coast, he covers the biotech and biopharmaceutical sector, in which he has extensive experience. Most recently, Mr. Zhang has been a research analyst covering the biotech/biopharmaceutical sector for BMO Capital Markets, Prudential Equity Group, Independent Research Group and Stephens. Mr. Zhang has earned many awards for his equity research and stock recommenda-

## MERCHANT BANKING *(continued)*

tions, including No. 3 Stock Picker in the Biotechnology Industry in the 2009 Financial Times StarMine Analyst Awards, No. 5 in Biotechnology in the 2009 Wall Street Journal "Best On The Street" stock analysts competition and No. 5 (139% return) in the 2007 Zacks Top Ten Analysts Survey (across all industries).

He received his Ph.D. in Cell, Molecular & Neurosciences/Botanic Sciences from the University of Hawaii, an MBA from Indiana University's Kelly School of Business, an M.S. from China Agricultural University and a B.A. from Huazhong (Central China) Agricultural University. He conducted research in the field of signal transduction as a postdoctoral fellow at Indiana University's School of Medicine and Oncology and as a postdoctoral scientist at Eli Lilly and Company.

**NEIL LITTMAN**
*Senior Associate*
nlittman@b-c.com

Neil Littman joined Burrill & Company's Merchant Banking Group in 2009. Previously, Mr. Littman worked in the Healthcare Investment Banking group at Thomas Weisel Partners where he focused on public and private financings as well as strategic advisory assignments. Prior to Thomas Weisel Partners, Mr. Littman worked in the Healthcare Investment Banking group at Deutsche Bank Securities.

Mr. Littman received an M.S. in Biotechnology from The Johns Hopkins University in 2003, and a B.A. in Molecular, Cellular and Development Biology from the University of Colorado, Boulder in 2002.

**NEAL FISCHER**
*Senior Associate*
nfischer@b-c.com

Neal Fischer joined Burrill & Company's Merchant Banking Group in 2011 as senior associate. Previously, Mr. Fischer worked at BNY Mellon for a subsidiary focusing on portfolio performance analytics for numerous financial institutions and broker/dealers. Prior to BNY Mellon, Mr. Fischer worked in the Healthcare Investment Banking group at Janney Montgomery Scott, where he focused on capital raising, M&A, and strategic advisory.

Mr. Fischer is a Master of Finance candidate at Pennsylvania State University, and graduated Cum Laude from Dickinson College with a B.A. in International Business & Management and East Asian Studies. He also completed certificate programs at Peking University and Beijing Language & Culture University in China.

**MAURICE ENDERLE**
*Associate*
menderle@b-c.com

Maurice Enderle joined Burrill & Company's Merchant Banking Group in 2010.

Previously, Mr. Enderle worked in the Healthcare Investment Banking group at Thomas Weisel Partners where he focused on public and private financings as well as strategic advisory assignments.

Mr. Enderle received his B.A. in Finance from the McCombs School of Business at The University of Texas, Austin.

## MERCHANT BANKING *(continued)*

### JOHN MCLAUGHLIN
*Sales Trader*
*jmclaughlin@b-c.com*

### JASON TRIPP
*Chief Compliance Officer*
*jtripp@b-c.com*

John McLaughlin joined Burrill & Company in 2011 and works as a sales trader in the Merchant Banking Group. Mr. McLaughlin has more than 20 years of experience in both the domestic and international equity markets. He began his career at Cantor Fitzgerald in New York and then moved on to Furman Selz, also in New York, where he became a senior vice president in the equity trading division. Mr McLaughlin worked at Bank of America securities in San Francisco until 2003. He spent the eight years prior to joining Burrill & Company at BTIG in San Francisco as a senior vice president. There he developed a business servicing small- to medium-sized hedge funds. During his career, Mr. McLaughlin has traded a variety of products including equity options, futures, bonds and, currency transactions.

He holds a B.A. in History from Boston College.

Jason Tripp joined the Burrill Merchant Banking Team in 2007 and has over a decade's experience in FINRA/SEC regulation. Prior to joining Burrill, Mr. Tripp performed statistical analysis for IBP, served as an Examiner at the NASD, worked for the broker dealer division of Golden West Financial, and designed Anti Money Laundering Compliance programs for Bay Area Broker Dealers and Investment Advisors.

Mr. Tripp holds degrees in Accounting and Political Science from the University of Arizona.

ABOUT BURRILL & COMPANY

# BURRILL & COMPANY

## MEDIA & EVENTS

### DANIEL S. LEVINE
*Managing Director*
*dlevine@b-c.com*

Prior to joining Burrill & Company in 2007, Daniel Levine worked as special projects editor for the San Francisco Business Times where he won numerous awards for his coverage of the biotechnology industry. His work has appeared in the New York Times, The Industry Standard and theStreet.com as well as other national publications. He is the author of Disgruntled: The Darker Side of the World of Work, (Berkley/Boulevard Books). Before he became a journalist, Mr. Levine served as a Vice President and General Principal with Herbert Young Securities in Great Neck, New York. He holds a B.A. in English from Vassar College and a Masters in Journalism from the University of California, Berkeley.

### JENNIFER GREGOIRE
*Director, Events*
*jgregoire@b-c.com*

Jennifer Gregoire joined the Burrill & Company Events Team in July of 2009. Her focus is on individual event management, venue selection, marketing and client retention for Burrill & Company's collection of conferences, meetings and special events. Prior to joining Burrill & Company, she served as a Convention and Event Manager for two major San Francisco area hotels, Marriott & Hyatt International. Ms. Gregoire also worked for Pebble Beach Company where she participated in management of the AT&T Pebble Beach Pro-Am Golf Tournament. Ms. Gregoire earned a B.A. from California Polytechnic State University in San Luis Obispo in Recreation Administration with a Concentration in Special Events.

### NICOLE BOICE
*Director, Business Development*
*nboice@b-c.com*

Nicole Boice joined Burrill & Company in April 2005. As Director of Business Development, she is responsible for generating revenue for all activities related to Burrill's growing events portfolio, and advertising and sponsorship development for newsletters and other media. Nicole has over 20 years in sales and marketing – specializing in new product launches, business development and in building out integrated marketing and custom publishing in media. She has worked with world-class organizations spanning pharma, high tech and media.

### MARIE DAGHLIAN
*Managing Editor*
*mdaghlian@b-c.com*

Marie Daghlian joined Burrill & Company in July 2010 as Associate Editor of publications. Prior to that she worked for the company on a contract basis, helping to launch The Burrill Report in 2009 and contributing to it on a monthly basis, as well as working on the company's annual state-of-the-industry report for the past six years. Ms. Daghlian started her career in the fashion industry as an owner, designer, and manufacturer of women's apparel for 28 years. She attended the University of Pennsylvania and holds a B.A. in Communication Studies from Sonoma State University.

## MEDIA & EVENTS (*continued*)

**MICHAEL FITZHUGH**
*Associate Editor*
mfitzhugh@b-c.com

Michael Fitzhugh joined Burrill & Company in April 2011 as Associate Editor after contributing to Burrill Media publications for two years as a freelance writer and editor. Prior to that Mr. Fitzhugh covered biotechnology for American City Business Journals. He received his Masters in Journalism from the University of California Berkeley Graduate School of Journalism and holds a B.A. from the University of Michigan, Ann Arbor.

**BRYAN PLESCIA**
*Director, Business Development*
bplescia@b-c.com

Bryan Plescia joined Burrill & Company in February 2012 as the Director of Business Development in the company's Media Group. He is responsible for securing advertising and sponsorship opportunities for the growing number of special events, conferences, publications and other media needs.

Prior to joining Burrill & Company, Mr. Plescia worked with a number of media outlets including Newsweek and CBS Television where he was able to plan and develop marketing strategies to increase revenue for the brands. Mr. Plescia's most recent position was for a technology publishing group in the Bay Area where he was successful in launching the magazine, Maximum Tech, and brokered deals for such conferences as ComicCon and CES.

**VINAY SINGH**
*Researcher and Staff Writer*
vsingh@b-c.com

Vinay Singh joined Burrill & Company in 2011 as an intern and became a researcher and staff writer in the media group at the start of 2012. Prior to joining Burrill & Company, Mr. Singh worked at the University of California, San Francisco Hospital in the emergency room and in the childcare services All-Star room with pediatric cancer patients as a volunteer. Mr. Singh also served as a summer intern as a research associate at Exclixis in the new drug discovery group focusing on high-throughput compound screening.

He is a graduate of Lehigh University with a B.S. in Biology/pre-medicine.

**ANN MEANS**
*Registration Manager*
ameans@b-c.com

Ann Means joined Burrill & Company in April 2003 as part of the events team. She is focused on ensuring a positive experience for our conference attendees and assisting them with any help needed from registration through departure. Prior to joining Burrill & Company, Ms. Means worked at The Boston Consulting Group for seven years. She earned a B.A. from the California State Univeristy, Sacramento in Business Administration with a concentration in Marketing.

# The Burrill Team

## Administration

**Victor A. Hebert**
*Managing Director*
*Chief Administrative Officer*
*and Chief Legal Officer*

**Helena Sen**
*CFO*

**Aubree Wermelinger**
*Human Resources*
*Manager*

**Jean Yang**
*Accounting Manager*

**Sarah Thompson**
*Executive Assistant*
*to the CEO*

**Monique Tjong**
*Staff Accountant*

**Mary Patterson**
*Executive Assistant*
*to Victor Hebert*

**Susan Panell**
*Receptionist*

**Mary Lopes**
*Executive Assistant*

**Mike San Pedro**
*Facilities Coordinator*

**Leilani Santiago**
*Executive Assistant, Merchant*
*Banking*